Norfolk Record Society
Volume LXVI for 2002

William Windham's Green Book

1673–1688

Edited by
Elizabeth Griffiths

Norfolk Record Society
Volume LXVI
2002

First published in 2002
by the Norfolk Record Society

ISBN 0 9538298 4 7

Typeset by Carnegie Publishing Ltd
Chatsworth Road, Lancaster LA1 4SL

Printed and bound by Cambridge University Press

Contents

To the Memory of
ROBERT WYNDHAM KETTON-CREMER
1906–1969
Historian
and Squire of Felbrigg

Acknowledgements

The Norfolk Record Society gratefully acknowledges the support given to this publication by the National Trust. Permission to publish the Green Book, held by the Norfolk Record Office on behalf of the National Trust, was given by the County Archivist, Dr John Alban. Philip Judge did the drawings. The editor wishes to thank Dr Joan Thirsk for advice and encouragement.

Introduction

The Green Book: Origins, Layout and Content [1]

In June 1673 young William Windham, recently married and preparing to settle permanently on his estate at Felbrigg, noted his intention to record:

> 'A particular of the yearly value of my manors, lands & tenements in Norfolk, Suffolke & Essex. And what farme rents, Quite Rents, Annuityes, Rent chages and other incumbrances are upon & issuing out of my estate & how they have been paid this last half yeare, & also what money is owing to me by Mortgages, Bonds & arrears or rent. With an account what moneys I have received out of the rents & profit of my estate what I have allowed for taxes, repaires & other incident charges from Our Lady to Mich 1673' [2]

His first attempt, based on the bailiff's accounts of the 1650s and 1660s, was not a success: the layout and accounting system did not yield the information required.[3] However, by October 1673, when he started afresh in a large paper book with green vellum covers, he had learned double entry keeping which transformed the enterprise into a comprehensive record of estate management. Windham probably acquired these commercial skills from his father-in-law, Sir Joseph Ashe, a merchant from Twickenham. Besides a dowry of £10,000, his daughter brought to the marriage in 1669 a keen eye for business.[4] Throughout her adult life she invested enthusiastically in stocks and shares, keeping a precise record of transactions and profits in her personal diary. She also undertook responsibility for the family and household, maintaining a parallel set of domestic and kitchen accounts.[5] On William's early death in 1689 she supervised estate business, making entries in the new Green Book, until their eldest son Ashe assumed control in 1694. The Windhams were a genuine working partnership and the Green Book was at the heart of a system they devised to manage their family, household, estate and business affairs.

The Green Book appears to be a unique document. Certainly no other comparable work has been published or found for the seventeenth century. The nearest would be Henry Best's Farming and Memorandum Books, 1617–1645 and Robert Loder's Farm Accounts, 1610–1620, but the Green Book is no mere account.[6] The explicit motives behind its creation offer an extraordinary insight into the mentality of a young Norfolk landowner as he embarked on family responsibilities and the management of his estate. He planned for the long term, designing the Green Book as a guide for his son. The tone is conversational, reminiscent of the dialogue format used by classical authors in similar manuals, with asides warning the son against certain courses of action.[7] It had the desired effect on Windham's successors. In the eighteenth century Felbrigg became a byword for the excellence of its tree planting and the organisation of its farms; it was commended by Nathaniel Kent and William Marshall as an example for others to follow. Indeed, Kent may have used the Green Book for inspiration as his own instructions for tree planting bear a marked resemblance to Windham's careful descriptions set out in the 1670s. Without doubt, the influence of the Green Book extended well beyond Felbrigg.[8]

As a record of the management of a medium-sized estate in North-East Norfolk in the second half of the seventeenth century, the Green Book comprehensively challenges the traditional assumption that agricultural improvement in the county was pioneered by the Cokes, Walpoles and Townshends on their large West Norfolk estates in the eighteenth century. It supports the alternative view, advanced by Marshall and Kent in the 1780s, that East Norfolk was the true area of agricultural innovation and that much had been achieved by the 1680s.[9]

A great deal of thought went into the layout of the Green Book. When Windham took possession in 1673 the affairs of the estate were in disarray and he determined to reverse the decline. He gathered together historic material – old accounts and leases – and devised a system which gave him easy access to all relevant records while keeping a current account of the estate. In his new estate book he numbered every page and used a cross-referencing system which allowed the user to move easily from the Particular of the Estate at the front (his page nos. 1–15) to the individual accounts (16–337) and then to the leases (478–564) entered at the back. Pages 338–477 remain blank. In this way he was able to quickly build up a profile of each holding. In the centre pages (172–176) he outlined his policy for the park, describing tree planting schemes, plans for his deer and fish and the areas to be cultivated. He also included summaries of accounts (216–220), details of moneys on loan (178–179), family affairs and legal cases (512–527). The numbering system allowed further cross-referencing into subsidiary notebooks which record sales of timber, livestock (200–212) and corn providing a wealth of information on prices at that time. Throughout the book he modified his procedures, explaining his actions in the margins. In 1688 he started a new Green Book with a simplified format; he abandoned the particular of every farm in favour of an alphabetical list of tenants in effect a prototype of the eighteenth century 'Tenants' Ledger', thus reflecting his changing approach to estate management. These notebooks and accounts, with the Green Book as the centrepiece, show how Windham developed, through trial and error, a modern system of estate management.

The period 1673–1689 covered by the Green Book is of particular significance. For landowners these were years of unrelenting economic adversity when they had to devise new strategies to make farming pay. Between 1664 and 1689, as corn prices continued to fall, they had to deal with bankruptcies, un-let farms and

outstanding debts on a regular basis (see Fig. 1, p. 5). Windham tried new contracts
with his tenants, including share farming. 'Letting to halves', as it was known, was
an unusual practice in England, and in fact no other evidence has been found of
a landowner operating such an arrangement on a systematic basis. The difficulties
Windham encountered may explain the rarity of the practice, and why he resorted
to simpler methods by the late 1680s, placing his trust in large tenants rather than
risking capital in partnership with small operators. In this way the Green Book
offers an insight into the developing relationship between landlord and tenant, and
may help to explain why in England that relationship became so sharply defined.
However, we need to be careful. In a national context, Windham's energy and
enthusiasm for experimentation may have been untypical as no other document of
this nature has come to light. Nevertheless, the Green Book stands as a working
document, a tool of management, designed to facilitate improvement; it also offers
a contemporary assessment of the relative success of different courses of action.
Above all, it shows a landowner responding pro-actively, intellectualising his approach, and applying commercial solutions to the management of his estate. He
was not indifferent, inflexible or bound by tradition, as some historians have
portrayed landowners of this period.[10]

Methodology

In editing the Green Book for publication every effort has been made to retain the
spirit and experimental nature of the original manuscript. As far as possible, it has
been confined to standardising Windham's entries, but some compromises, particularly on the layout of the accounts, have been necessary. In this introduction,
the numbers in round brackets and bold type refer to the relevant pages of the
Green Book. The accounts, as devised by Windham, followed a rudimentary double
entry system with Debit and Credit placed on opposing pages. In the margin and
in the text he included further references to leases, accounts and notebooks. Centred
at the foot of the text he invariably included a reference to the next account. As
the Credit side included much more detail he inserted horizontal lines to guide
himself through the account, leaving the Debit side with blank sections. In some
cases he departed from the double entry system and simply listed the payments of
rent. He also experimented with different types of numbering in the cash columns,
and different abbreviations for the dates. In the editing these idiosyncrasies have
been removed, and no attempt made to replicate the lopsided double entry
arrangement. In this edited version, for each tenant, Credit *follows* Debit. The title
of each account starts with the page number and the name of the tenant, followed
by the page references to the relevant leases and accounts grouped together. Where
they occur in the body of the account, these numbers are retained to ease the
reader through Windham's cross-referencing system. All dates have been stand-
ardised, and the use of capitals and punctuation modernised, but Windham's
spelling has been retained. For the leases, entered at the back of the book, references

to the relevant account and to additional leases were placed in the left hand margin
and at the foot of the entry; these have been grouped at the head of each account
in bold type face. Apart from some consolidation, the summaries, detail of park
management and tree planting, and notes on family finance remain as Windham
wrote them.

The Felbrigg Estate: Structure and Topography [11]

The Felbrigg Estate is situated in north east Norfolk, about two miles inland from
the coast, on the south-facing slope of the Cromer-Holt Ridge running down to
a tributary of the River Bure.[12] To the north of the estate are broad stretches of
undulating heathland, which generations of owners have planted with trees to
protect the house and park from the biting North Sea winds (see Map 2). South
of Felbrigg Hall the parkland descends gradually to fertile meadow land, which
extends into the tiny parishes of Sustead and Metton. Light soils dominate to the
west in the parishes of Aylmerton and Gresham and into East Beckham beyond.
To the east of the hall lies Felbrigg church and the site of the earlier Felbrigg
village where open fields survived into the seventeenth century. With its highly
valuable meadow land, enclosed pastures, easily worked arable land and scope for
improvement on the light sandy soils, the estate offered its owners much opportunity
for commercial exploitation. In the thirteenth and fourteenth centuries, at an
estimated 400 acres, the demesne at Felbrigg was one of the largest and most
productive in Norfolk; by 1616 this area extended to 732 acres, with just 94 acres
in Felbrigg field awaiting enclosure.[13]

The success of the Felbrigg estate owed much to geography, but stability of
ownership was a key factor, allowing the expansion of demesne lands to continue
unimpeded. The estate has experienced only three changes of ownership since the
Norman Conquest and each transfer was accomplished with little disruption. The
medieval owners retained possession until 1450 when John Wymondham famously
secured the estate by dubious means.[14] His descendants remained at Felbrigg until
1863 when the estate was sold to a Norwich feedstuffs merchant, John Ketton. The
suddenness of the sale allowed Ketton to purchase the core of the estate around
Felbrigg, with the hall and all its contents and so it remained very much a
'Wyndham' house. His daughter married Thomas Wyndham Cremer of Beeston
and their son inherited the estate in 1924, returning Felbrigg to the Wyndhams.
Their grandson, the historian R. W. Ketton-Cremer, left the estate to the National
Trust in 1968.[15]

The Felbrigg Estate which appears in the Green Book was built up over several
generations; by 1673 there were properties in east and central Norfolk, Suffolk and
Essex (see Map 1). Parts of the estate were treated differently and clearly enjoyed
a different status, which helps to explain the policies pursued in individual cases.
The estate that John Wymondham secured in 1450 lay in the Felbrigg area with
offlying portions in Banningham, Tuttington, Colby and Ingworth, which lie on

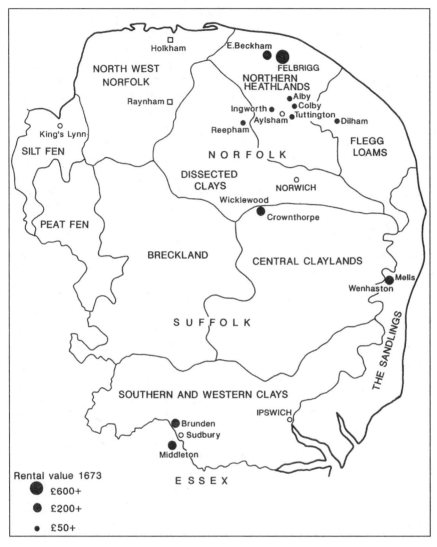

Map 1. The distribution of the Felbrigg Estate in 1673 with approximate rental values. Landscape regions of East Anglia from T. Williamson and S. Wade-Martins, *Roots of Change: Farming and the Landscape in East Anglia* (1999).

the fertile loamy soils to the east of Aylsham. He had earlier established himself in the Wymondham area by purchasing a few hundred acres at Wicklewood and Crownthorpe.[16] As part of the Howard connection the family advanced, but in the early sixteenth century they suffered a severe setback when Sir John Wyndham supported Edmund de la Pole's claim to the throne, resulting in his attainder and the loss of estates. The attainder was reversed in 1512, but it served as a warning to a family who henceforth avoided court life and concentrated their efforts in Norfolk. Edmund Wyndham added to the estate by purchasing land in Metton and Sustead from the Pastons and Dammes.[17] He acquired Beeston Priory at the Dissolution and in the 1530s bought the estate of the Ingloos family at Dilham.[18] At some stage, the family also acquired property at Thurlton and Toft Monks on the marshes between Loddon and Great Yarmouth. The purchaser may have been Sir John Wyndham who secured the reversion of the Felbrigg estate from his uncle Roger in 1599.

Sir John, descended from Edmund's younger brother, had married an heiress from Somerset and established a new branch of the family. He used his Felbrigg inheritance to endow his four younger sons, Thomas, George, Hugh and Wadham. He left Thomas the estate at Felbrigg with its offlying lands in the Tuttington area. George he settled at Beeston, the branch of the family which eventually inherited the estate in 1924, while Hugh and Wadham enjoyed the rents from Thurlton, Dilham and the estate at Wicklewood and Crownthorpe.[19] Henceforth, Thomas distinguished himself from his cousins by changing the spelling of Wyndham to Windham.

Thomas Windham was the founder of the modern Felbrigg Estate. He came into his inheritance in 1616 and swiftly consolidated the existing holdings at Felbrigg, Tuttington and Dilham.[20] In 1628 he and his father purchased the East Beckham Estate and in the 1640s, following a second marriage, his new father-in-law assisted in the acquisition of similarly sized estates in Suffolk and Essex, and a farm at Reepham.[21] Between 1616 and 1654 Thomas increased the rental of the estate from £562 to £2400.[22] From the frequent references in the Green Book it is clear that William Windham modelled himself on his example.

Thomas Windham died in 1654 and left his estate divided between the eldest son from his first marriage, John, and his widow Elizabeth Mede with her six young children. This second family enjoyed the £1200 annual income from the estates at Beckham, and in Suffolk and Essex.[23] John produced no heirs and on his death in 1665 the estate passed to his much younger half-brother William. Neither John nor William added to the estate, indeed no more acquisitions were made until Ashe Windham revived the policy in the 1700s.[24]

The Estate in 1673

By 1673 William had recovered much of the property assigned to his mother and John Windham's widow, Frances. In 1669 he bought out the latter's interest for £4500; in the same year he paid his mother £2000 'for debts incurred in my minorilye' and left her to enjoy the estate at East Beckham, with her new husband Richard Chamberlaine, until her death in 1679. Thomas Windham had also set aside a cash portion of £4000 for William's younger brother John and provision for dowries of £1500 for his two sisters. The details of these arrangements caused

Map 2. The Felbrigg Estate map of 1830.

much rancour and occupy many pages in the Green Book. The estate in 1673 was worth £2114 a year, but in the adverse economic climate of the 1670s and 1680s farm rentals never reached this level (see Table 5, p. 41).

The analysis of the Felbrigg Estate (Tables 1–4, pp. 35–41) is based on Sir John Wyndham's Deed of Settlement of 1616, the accounts of his steward John Blinman from 1609 to 1615 and the Particulars contained in the Green Book.[25] These early documents highlight the improvements undertaken by Thomas Windham between 1616 and 1654, providing a firm base for William's reforms. Details of tenancies and rents are given in the Tables which allow comparisons of various portions of the estate between 1615 and 1673. The different typefaces on the tables reflect the relative position of holding and tenant in the two accounts. Blinman placed the holding with its acreage first, followed by the tenant's name, while William listed only the tenant's name in the Particulars, leaving details of the holding to the account and lease; he did not always include the acreage. The difference indicates a change of emphasis, signalling the growing importance of the relationship between landowner and tenant. Italics have been used to show the value of lands held in hand.

The Felbrigg Area

Unlike other parts of the estate, the approximate location of the lands in the Felbrigg area in 1673 can be pieced together (Map 3). Working backwards from the Estate Map of 1830 (Map 2), the extensive common lands from the Enclosure Awards (1822) and earlier roads from the Road Orders of 1777 and 1802 have been identified; these routes were realigned to accommodate the enlargement of the park and woods undertaken by William Windham III (1750–1810).[26] The approximate location of the seventeenth-century holdings have been plotted using the very detailed descriptions (with acreages and abuttals) contained in Blinman's Accounts and the Deed of Settlement. Purchase documents, leases and entries from the Green Book flesh out the picture (see Map 3). In the 1830s and 1840s W. H. Windham, imitating his friend and neighbour T. W. Coke of Holkham, embarked on a rebuilding programme, placing his initials on the gable of every farm building, and this has helped to identify certain farmsteads.

Map 3 and Table 1 show the development of tenancies in the Felbrigg area between 1615 and 1673. The Deed of Settlement only listed the demesne lands in the Felbrigg area, but Blinman's accounts are much more instructive. Significantly, he divided the estate into three elements. Firstly, the 'demeanes lands' totalling 715 acres; secondly, the 'fearme lands' 'late in possession by copie', worth a fraction of the demesne lands, but let on 'unfixed' rents, and thirdly, scores of copyhold tenants who paid fixed rents, averaging 2d. per acre, for hundreds of acres of land. These amounts, listed under Rents of Assize, remain the same in 1673. Between 1609 and 1615 Blinham raised the unfixed rents from an average of 1s. to 4s. per acre. The total of demesne and leasehold land amounted to 921 acres, excluding the large area of heathland and warren.

Purchase documents show that Thomas Windham acquired a further 257 acres in the Felbrigg area, mostly the small estates of yeomen; these have been reshaped into new farms by 1673. Thus Bartram and Deane's lands in Felbrigg and Metton and some of Thomas Blofield's in Gresham formed *Felbrigg-Gresham Farm* of 101 acres. *Wilson's Dairy* occupied more land in Gresham, probably 50 acres. Webster's lands in Roughton became *Felbrigg-Roughton Farm* of 69½ acres. In Aylmerton he made a *new farm of 63 acres* with the addition of the Aylmerton Closes, enclosed from heathland, and at Runton he formed a similar holding of 26 acres. The reduced rent for the Foldcourse in 1673 is shown clearly in Table 1 (pp. 35–8). By land purchase, raising rents, enclosure and rationalization the rental for the Felbrigg area doubled between 1616 and 1673. However a stubborn tail of tiny holdings, the old 'copieland', survived; they caused much trouble to William Windham as tenants disputed the nature of their rent.

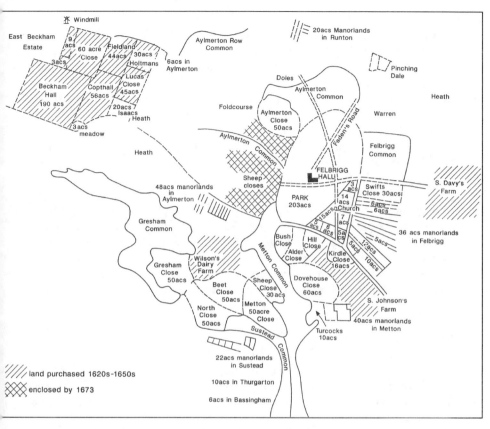

Map 3. The approximate location of the estate in the Felbrigg area, 1615–1673.

East Beckham did not return to the estate until 1679, nevertheless, William listed the property after Runton, a recognition of its importance and location within the Felbrigg area. The Beckham estate consisted of about 500 acres, compact and free of manorial complications, with scope to develop the heathland which lay to the north and west of the property. For an improving landowner it offered flexibility and opportunity. In the 1630s Thomas Windham reorganised the estate into six tenancies of varying sizes, leasing the principal holding, Beckham Hall with 190 acres, to a partnership of two tenants. However, between 1669 and 1672 further restructuring led to the creation of more evenly sized holdings, which suggests some difficulty and that the optimum size for a commercial farm on these very light soils was between 65 and 115 acres. In the restructuring, rents at Copthall and Beeston's were reduced by 1s. an acre, but they maintained the overall rental by letting the foldcourse as a separate tenancy, and later developing it as a farm – Heath Farm, underlining the potential and versatility of this kind of property.

Lands in East Norfolk

The most severe erosion of ownership had occurred in Tuttington, Colby, Ingworth and Banningham. The quality of the land and its proximity to markets, especially by the River Bure navigable at least as far as Coltishall, dictated that some attempt at recovery should be made. Blinman raised unfixed copyhold rents fivefold, and effected a similar increase in existing leasehold rents as terms expired in 1614 (see Table 2, p. 39). Thomas Windham tried to consolidate the fragmented holdings by purchasing yeomen estates in Tuttington and nearby Alby. But estimates of value proved over optimistic; between 1664 and 1673 rents were reduced by 13 *per cent.* In the accounts, (112–126) and leases (535, 538, 542, 548) William frequently complained of the tenants in this area.

The Dilham Estate situated in the fertile Broadland region did not pass to William in its entirety. In 1623 Sir John Wyndham had granted his youngest sons Hugh and Wadham a ninety-nine year lease of the property, and in 1635 they leased it back to Thomas Windham for £100. In 1639 and 1644 Thomas purchased two small estates in the area, Scriveners and Debneys, and it is this portion, belonging to Thomas outright, which passed to William and appears in the Green Book. These farms, which had been attached to other holdings, were re-formed and re-let when the arrangement with Hugh and Wadham ceased.

Lands in Central Norfolk

William owned two properties situated on the heavy clays of central Norfolk, Reepham Farm lying about fifteen miles south west of Felbrigg, and the estate at Wicklewood and Crownthorpe ten miles south west of Norwich (Table 3, p. 40). In 1623 Sir John Wyndham granted his fifth son Francis a ninety-nine year lease of the property, and he, like his brothers, had leased it to Thomas in 1639 for eighty years for £110. The farms also formed part of Elizabeth Windham's jointure, and they were returned with Reepham to William in 1668. When the twenty-one year lease expired in 1613, Blinham effected a three-and-a-half-fold increase in rents. Further improvements were achieved in the mid 1650s, before prices started to decline.

Lands outside Norfolk

Thomas Windham purchased estates in Suffolk and Essex to raise portions for younger children and to support his wife in her widowhood (Table 4, p. 41). Both formed part of Elizabeth Windham's jointure. She leased them to John Windham from 1662 and they returned to William in 1668.[27] The Suffolk Estate at Wenhaston and Mells, situated south east of Halesworth, was an attractive property, consisting of six holdings which included two mills and a brick kiln, with the remaining 242 acres divided between three good farms. The 'Essex' Estate, situated in fact partly in Suffolk north and west of Sudbury, consisted of two very large farms, Brunden Farm and Middleton Hall farmed by two brothers Robert and John Kingsberry (see Map 1). The organisation of the farms was simplicity itself, but Windham's dependence on two big tenants led to conflict, eviction and the difficulty of finding a suitable replacement. They show, once again, the type of property landowners favoured when they had the opportunity to make a purchase.

William Windham at Felbrigg 1673–1689

Plans and policies

From the outset William adopted a highly personal style of management, which affected every part and aspect of his estate. With the farms he clearly believed that with timely action and investment, rent levels could be maintained despite the fall in corn prices (see Table 5, p. 41; Fig. 1 and 2, pp. 31–32). He conceded a reduction to the new tenants of Tuttington Hall in 1673, as 'I was loathe to take the farme into my hands not then living in the countye' (544). But when Mr Forby of Reepham made similar demands, William terminated his lease and kept the farm in hand for four years. In 1674, 11 *per cent* of the estate including the park was in hand (206); by 1683 the figure had risen to 35 *per cent*, and it remained at over 30 *per cent* in 1687. The policy required intensive management and proved costly as large sums were lost supporting hard-pressed tenants, but in the long term his efforts paid dividends. He created a flexible, well organised and fully capitalised estate capable of responding effectively to changes in market conditions. Moreover, the experience of the 1650s and early 1660s had shown that lack of intervention cost even more, as farms entered a downward spiral of debt, dilapidation and low rents. This had occurred at Tuttington, where John Crome had 'brought an ill repute upon the farme that I could not let it to able men for more' (544).

William's pro-active approach to estate management reflected closely the advice of agricultural writers. In response to falling corn prices, William increased his range of activities placing his emphasis on livestock enterprises. He built dairies, leased out cows, improved neglected pastures, bought clover seed, bred herd replacements, and experimented with agreements which shared the risk between landlord and tenant. Samuel Hartlib had recommended just this kind of assistance.[28] Utilising the park and land in hand, and working with dealers and local butchers, he also fattened hundreds of bullocks for sale at nearby markets. However, William reserved his greatest efforts for the remodelling of his park and woodland. In this he closely followed informed opinion, led by John Evelyn, which strongly advocated the planting of timber, the enlargement of parks and the creation of reserves for deer and game. It was a policy actively supported by the government which passed a series of protective acts.[29] It made sense economically as well as aesthetically, as timber, venison and fish commanded high prices. William may well have been encouraged in his endeavours by the family physician, Sir Thomas Browne, re-nowned philosopher and naturalist and a close acquaintance of Hartlib and Evelyn, who had lived in Norwich since the 1630s.[30] Browne's essay, *The Garden of Cyrus* (1658) inspired John Evelyn to write his great work *Elysium Britannicum*, calling for the creation of an earthly paradise. This manuscript, never published, heralded more practical works. Evelyn's *Sylva, A Discourse of Forest Trees* (1664) clearly influenced William Windham's planting schemes. The care and effort he lavished on his young trees, deer and fish suggest a young man acting under guidance.

Park, woods and ponds

William's plans for the park, woods and ponds occupy a double page in the Green Book (172–173) and continue in his Memo Book – the first discarded estate book – relegated to recording details on specific plantings, pond maintenance, and the care of fish and deer.[31] The park was far from being a simple amenity area, William used it in several ways to support the various elements of his household economy. The park itself provided grazing for his 'sadle horses', for sheep and deer consumed by the family in great quantities, and a few dairy cows supplying milk, butter and cheese. He fed his cart horses in Church Close and kept the meadow for hay. He also cultivated areas in the park, experimenting and noting the success of different rotations. In 1673 the thirty acres behind the house 'were sowne with severall sorts of Corne'; in 1674 he sowed part of Church Close, and in 1677, he broke up twenty four acres of the Upper Parke, sowing it in a four year rotation with buckwheat, or somerley, wheat and meslin, barley and finally oats undersown with nonsuch. In 1679 he broke up the rest of Upper Park, which produced 'very good Winter Corne' the next year. He used the oats for his horses, buckwheat for poultry, wheat for bread, and barley for malting; in 1681 he built a new brewhouse.[32] The park did not supply all their needs. William and Katherine purchased corn, meat, butter and cheese from tenants, and paid various suppliers for fish, eggs and poultry, which Katherine records in her kitchen accounts.[33]

Woodland management interested William deeply. The entries in the Green Book and Memo Book show a man with a passion for trees, but his planting schemes were not purely decorative. He needed huge supplies of timber for a variety of purposes on the estate – for paling, fencing, building and repairs. Moreover, timber and topwood fetched a good price which he noted carefully (209–212). Long before he tackled estate management he was selling and planting trees: 'in 1670 & 1671 I had planted the Oaks in the bottome by the Deer-house' (209). In 1676 he established a tree nursery, buying in thousands of seedlings – oak, ash, birch, beech, crab; coombs of acorns, ash keys and haws; bushels of holly berries, maple, sycamore, beechmast and some chestnut. He approached this task most professionally, noting the origin of seed and seedlings. By 1679 these were ready for transplanting into areas enclosed for the purpose. From the 1680s, his planting schemes show more concern for design as he experimented with different species, planting Scotch firs along the Pond Walk and 'in the Cross Walks in the Nursery'. In 1683 he planted forty-nine trees, including walnuts, chestnuts, oaks and limes, to 'stand square 7 every way', imitating the pattern of the 'Quincunx', described by Browne in *The Garden of Cyrus*. In 1687 he 'inlarged the Wood from the 3rd Cross-Walk to the Wall', planting out the seedlings of 1676 which amounted to several thousand trees. This final entry gives some idea of the scale and complexity of William Windham's achievement between 1673 and his death in 1689.

The management of deer and fish received much attention. He kept records of the type, age and number of his deer, inserting tags into their ears to monitor progress. He built a deer house and yard to protect them in winter, and in 1679 he planned a new nursery 'for Cops-wood to shelter deer' (209–210). In the Memo Book he used the terms fawn, pricket, sorrel and soar, which refer to the different ages of the male fallow deer, but the reference to a hinde, knobler and brockets suggests that he was introducing some red deer into the herd.[34] These efforts, particularly the tagging of the castrated males – havers – and the keeping of 'paled' deer, indicate a serious interest in venison production. John Salman, the Felbrigg bailiff, recorded the purchase of six pots and 'hampers and holters' for venison. For similar reasons, William recorded details of his carp, noting when ponds were restocked, the numbers involved and the size and growth of the fish, which he measured from 'eye to tayle'. He moved carp from one pond to another to prevent overstocking, and tried to keep the same size fish in each location to ensure an even growth pattern. He enlarged existing ponds by removing gravel, and built extra ponds to accommodate the surplus. He was clearly fascinated by the mechanics of fish and deer production; no evidence survives of him selling these products on a commercial basis, but they supplied the household and made welcome gifts.

House and garden

Between 1675 and 1687 William added a new wing to the west side of the house, to the plans of William Samwell. In 1675 he 'felled all the Timber used about my new building at Felbrigg' (210), and in 1684 he 'ordered all the trees in the two Upper Closes to be digged up [and] used about my Building Anno 1685' (198). Although the Green Book does not include further mention of this enterprise, which must have absorbed much energy and time, Salman's accounts refer to the making of huge quantities of bricks and tiles, the purchase of lead and the employment of an army of skilled workmen including plumbers, tilers, carpenters, sawyers, painters, coopers and bricklayers, all supervised by a Mr Skerry between 1681 and 1683. Other buildings were being constructed at the same time, including the brewhouse, but the scale and quality suggests that most of the materials were destined for the west wing.[35]

When William inherited Felbrigg the house comprised only what is now the south front. Samwell planned three new wings to make a quadrangle, with service buildings neatly housed in an east wing, but much to his dismay William vetoed the idea in favour of the L shaped house with just two fronts, which survives today. His successors never satisfactorily resolved the jumble of service buildings to the east of the house. Only on the far side, walking away from the house, can Samwell's stylish west wing be appreciated. In this matter William's prudence in curtailing his architect's schemes is a matter of regret.

Various entries in the Green Book provide more detail of William's plans for landscaping the area around the house. In 1670 he felled an oak to enlarge the Parlour Garden (209); in 1678 he planted trees on the west side of the Flower

Garden (172); at other times he fenced in the Privy Walk and needed '2 Oaks to make my Coach Yard Gates' (210). Salman's accounts, and those kept by Samuel Smith, Joseph Elden and Edward Fairchilde in the 1680s, contain several references to gardening activities, including the payment of £8 a year to 'Daryell the Gardener', day wages for weeding, and the purchase of cherry trees, a grafting knife and seed – 'turnip sede, carret sede & sedge for the Gardener to sow'.[36]

Land in hand and letting to halves

Throughout the period William kept land in hand which he managed as an extension of his enterprise in the park. These areas included the Sheep Walk run by his shepherd Henry Bally (174–175) and the Dovehouse Close in Metton, (206) where he fattened his bullocks; from these animals Thomas Sexton, the butcher, ensured Katherine a regular supply of meat. William also kept a herd of sixteen cows at the Dairy Grounds in Gresham, which he leased to Michael Wilson (162) who supplied additional dairy products for the household. In his 'Account of the Stock of Beasts upon my Grounds' William noted the date of purchase and price paid for each animal, their location on the estate and their disposal. From 1674, as farms failed, or under-performed, he drew them into this operation, notably at Reepham, Crownthorpe and Keeble's farm in Suffolk. In 1680, as the business grew in complexity, he diverted these accounts to the Memo (Quarto) Book. The entries show that Salman co-ordinated the entire operation, using the grounds at Felbrigg as a clearing house for stock received from farms and for newly purchased beasts awaiting their destination. In this way William created a profitable business, building up a team of professionals skilled at farming and dealing in stock; this enabled him to experiment with different policies. His first attempt at a new strategy, fully recorded in the Green Book, was the management of Reepham Farm.

By the time he took Reepham Farm in hand in 1673 he had already invested heavily in the property. In 1668 he agreed 'to build a bakehouse and dairy with as much expediency as may be' so he had little sympathy when Mr Forby fell behind with his rent.[37] From 1673 Thomas Sexton worked the farm alongside his fattening and butchering enterprise at Sustead and Metton and in conjunction with Wilson's dairy. Salman supervised the operation, but despite his efforts William calculated in the bi-annual accounts that the farm in hand made a loss in 1675 and 1677 (164–165). His expectation that the sales of corn, beef and sheep would pay a rent and cover the costs of production proved optimistic. The problem was that his costs, including parish rates, tithes, purchase of stock, Sexton's wages and husbandry charges, were more or less fixed while corn prices declined. Moreover, Sexton's accounts required the closest scrutiny by Salman, which was time-consuming. To reduce the level of management, William entered into a sharefarming agreement with Sexton: 'the trouble in looking after this farme made me let it to halves' (166, 167). The rarity of this arrangement necessitates some explanation of the procedures and their subsequent modifications.

In the agreement for Reepham Farm, Windham leased Sexton a dairy herd of ten cows at 45s. a head (552). On the arable side William provided the land, Sexton the labour, and in return each received half of the corn crop. William calculated that the income from the cows and his half of the corn would equal the old rent of £52 a year (166). However, for three years Sexton failed to pay the full rent for the dairy, while William's return on the arable declined with the falling price of corn. He noted at the end of each year the amount 'Lost for want of a Tennant' (167). Nevertheless he did not abandon the idea, which suggests that other reasons may have contributed to the failure of the scheme. First, the agreement itself was poorly drafted with no clear division of responsibility, which allowed Sexton to submit every kind of demand. Secondly, it made no provision for independent assessors to ensure that William received a genuine 'half'. Thirdly, William may well have taken advantage of the clause which allowed him to 'lay on what stock I please for my own benifit', thereby reducing the pasture available for the cows. Fourthly, Sexton had no interest in the well-being of the dairy herd as William took responsibility for all replacements. Finally, far from reducing the management burden, the arrangement required even closer scrutiny as so much depended on the honesty of the 'operator'.

To correct these shortcomings, William engaged Edmund Britiffe to draw up future agreements, which were copied in their entirety into the Green Book. The first of these, for 'hiring a Dairie of Cows' and 'plowing ground to halfes' in Felbrigg Park, he arranged with John Masters in 1678. His motive was 'to have the conveniencye of a Dairie near me, & bee free from the trouble of plowman'. Masters cultivated areas directed by William, while his wife ran the dairy. The scheme lasted until 1681 when 'Master's wife died, which made him not fit for imployment' (564). However, his successor Thomas Cussens continued until 1693, leasing the dairy and 'sowing to halfes' 67½ acres in the Park with wheat, meslin, barley, buck, peas, vetches, turnips and clover.[38]

Less successful was the agreement with John Fincham for Selfe's Felbrigg-Roughton Farm (536). William made no charge for the land and buildings, laid on a small dairy herd and gave Fincham a loan to set up his farming operation. However, the arrangement collapsed in 1681 when Fincham 'left too poor to continue' (537). Thus William sacrificed a return on fixed capital, lost all his working capital, and finally had to buy in Fincham's stock, corn and chattels to clear his debts.[39] This debacle, combined with Sexton's rising debts at Reepham Farm, may well have persuaded William to lease both farms at reduced rents in 1681.[40] In the same year, when Felbrigg-Gresham Farm failed (18, 541, 553), he chose to take it in hand; although he received less from the sale of stock and corn than the farm rent, he at least retained control over the farming operation, and did not lose his working capital. In 1687 he leased the farm to John Tomson of Gresham at a reduced rent (230, 483).

From 1681 William only used letting to halves agreements as a last resort. In 1682 when his tenant William Parke died at Alby, 'for fear I should not git a Tennant for the rest of Parke's farm, I agreed with Dan Shepherd to live in the house rent free'. William also laid on a small dairy herd of four cows and let the ground to halves. He retained the right to terminate the agreement at three months' notice, but in the event Shepherd stayed for three years and tried to dissuade the new tenant from entering the farm. William was forced to offer the new man more inducements to take the lease 'to avoid a sute' (509, 505, 492). At Scrivener's Farm, Dilham, which in 1681 he 'could not let ... without great abatement', he agreed with John Applebye 'to sow Mack's farme to halfs'. He renewed the agreement annually until Applebye took a lease, at a reduced rent, in 1683 (509, 530, 276).

The relative success of Applebye's agreement may have led to the annual renegotiation of terms; there is also the possibility that letting to halves was established practice in the Dilham area. The earliest example on the Felbrigg Estate was at Dilham Hall Farm in 1662, when, unable to find a replacement, John Windham broke up the holding and let several closes to halves for one year. This was the way the arrangement was more commonly used between peasants to overcome periods of sickness or widowhood; typically a neighbour would step in and sow the land to halves.[41] In 1610, for example, Robert Loder, when he entered his estates, 'put forth to halves', part of his 'mother's joynture'. An agreement from the Westwick Estate, a few miles from Dilham, shows John Berney in 1698 letting to halves the farm occupied by Widow Westhorp for one year to John Ollyet yeoman of Worstead.[42] These parishes lie close together in the fertile and intensively cultivated Broadland region where small landowners still predominated; in this type of area such a system of mutual support would have flourished. The likelihood is that Dilham was the source of the idea, and William, probably on Salman's recommendation, adopted and developed the practice as a solution to his growing management crisis in the late 1670s.

At an early stage William was attracted to the idea and its possibilities. In fact his first use of letting to halves was not as an alternative to direct farming, but to effect the improvement of neglected pasture, Rush Close, part of Wilson's dairy farm at Gresham (162, 190–191, 557). The agreement was for thirteen years. In the first seven years, Waterson, the tenant, was to break up the pasture, level, drain, plough, muck and cultivate it. The rotation included: 1. Buck or Summerley; 2. Wheat; 3. Barley; 4. Oats, to be followed by five years of Olland (fallow) – a true system of up and down husbandry.[43] To encourage Waterson, William accepted half the corn and paid the parish rates for the cultivated area, whereas he charged 18s. an acre for the remaining pasture. The arrangement ran its term, indicating that lettings to halves worked well within a limited application and a restricted time scale, but as an alternative to leasing farms for a negotiated rent for a term of years they were hazardous arrangements. Between 1690 and 1693 Katherine Windham, faced with mounting debts at Beckham Hall, revived the idea, but the agreement, the last at Felbrigg, cost her hundreds of pounds.[44]

The Windhams never let to halves beyond a fifteen mile radius of Felbrigg, attesting to its experimental nature. When farms failed on offlying properties, such as at Crownthorpe in 1676–1677, the responsibility for running the farm fell on the bailiff – a huge task when the outgoing widow left debts of £522. (146–147, 192–195, 538, 551). To reduce this sum Edmund Bale supervised the sale of corn, stock and chattels. The following year William Howard from Beckham worked the farm while Salman co-ordinated the sale and purchase of stock, but losses remained substantial, prompting William's warning to his son (194). Bailiffs were not always reliable or effective. In Suffolk, Henry Houseman's arrears accounted for much of the accumulated debt by 1682 (148–151, 224–227, 296–297). William resolved the situation by relieving Houseman of his farm, finding a new bailiff, Francis Robinson, combining some of the holdings, and reducing the rent. The experience with direct farming, letting to halves, and management by bailiffs underlined the importance of supporting tenants to the uttermost.

Leased farms

William's primary objective was to have farms leased to reliable tenants for terms of years. In written leases, summarized in the Green Book, he specified their obligation to look after the woods, buildings and infrastructure, to follow beneficial husbandry practices, and to pay their rents. In return he agreed to invest in new farm buildings, assist with repairs and ease their burden in times of difficulty. The latter often included generous treatment to widows or 'antient men'. In other words, he aimed for a stable framework in which improvement could be sustained despite the adverse economic climate. The idea of a mutually beneficial contract between landlord and tenant can be seen in the lease for Reepham Farm in 1668, where *The Landlord Covenants* were followed by *The Tennants Covenants*.[45] William's entries at the back of the Green Book merely note the essentials of the agreement, but he had a clear idea of the principle of mutual support and trust behind such contracts. When tenants reneged on the terms of their leases or behaved badly, he acted swiftly. In 1678 he did not allow John Kingsberry of Middleton Hall £10 'because he had been too long in the Wheelwright's companye' (156–159, 272–273). In 1682, the relationship reached a crisis over Kingsberry's mistreatment of young trees, 'I am sure noe Tennant will take less care of the Timber & young stands than Jo. Kingsberry have done', so he 'resolved to run the hazard of getting a new Tennant' (546, 496). But his hasty eviction proved disastrous as Kingsberry's successor, Jeremiah Prance, was 'not able' and finally failed in 1694 owing £555.[46]

William's allowances for repairs, taxation and abatements averaged 20 *per cent* of estate income between 1673 and 1687, compared to 10 *per cent* in the 1650s and early 1660s.[47] The most significant change was the increased expenditure on repairs. The full leases for Reepham Farm (1668) and Henry Grime's farm at Tuttington (1672) show that when William inherited the estate, buildings and structures had been allowed to deteriorate. In both years he put the houses 'into good, tenantable and sufficient repair', provided wood to mend fences and gates, and glazed the windows.[48] He allowed the tenants rough timber to maintain the property, and repeated this concession in the majority of his leases. On building work he stipulated the contribution of the tenant: they had to provide so many days works of a thatcher and dawber and often materials, but the time and the amount remained negotiable. Thus in 1683 at Scrivener's Farm, Dilham, the requirement for four days thatching was reduced to three (558, 530), and at Felbrigg-Gresham Farm in 1687 Tompson was relieved of all dawbing work. (541, 553, 483). The summaries in the Green Book do not, however, accurately reflect the scale of William's expenditure. He invested in new buildings and other improvements, such as ditching and marling, as and when required, and made special allowance for the upkeep of mills (547, 548). William tried to be constructive in his approach to rent reductions and abatements. Frequently incoming tenants paid a lower rent for the first few years of their term so they could establish themselves, but leaving the agreed rent intact. He often promised them new buildings, particularly on difficult farms like Crownthorpe, where in 1683 he agreed 'to make a new Plank threshing floor ... Repayr the Barne floor ... lay boards over the Calf House', shelve the cheese chamber, ditch the mowing meadow and 'give him £10' (494). From the early 1680s he accepted corn in payment of rent much more readily, a genuine concession as the price of corn continued to fall (see Fig. 1, pp. 32–3).

Beyond the requirement to leave the farm 'in a husbandlye manner' and 'in good heart', William rarely specified the farming practice to be followed, simply noting 'with other covenants how to use the ground', which clearly refer to more detailed leases. When counterparts of leases have survived they invariably restate, clarify or slightly modify husbandry clauses dating back to the 1620s and 1630s. Thus in 1632, Hubberds Close, Wicklewood was 'not be plowed any part which is not in Tillage, nor sowe any which is already plowed once more oftener than 3 yeres together, without somerlayinge the same'.[49] In 1678 the tenant 'shall not sowe more than 3 cropps of corne together and will somerlay and leave fallow every 4th year, as such grounds as are in Tillage; except such grounds as are new ploughed and then to somerlay the 5th year after 1st ploughing and every 4th year thereafter'.[50] Restrictions on overcropping and ploughing feature prominently. In Suffolk, Houseman was not to 'plow above 40 A[acres] in any one year, nor Oats 2 years togeather; in one piece' (495), and in 1678, Gresham Close was not to be ploughed 'in payne of forty shillings an Acre' (533). As a general rule, William did not attempt to introduce innovative farming practice through leases, especially on established holdings where he left the business of farming to the tenant. His main concern was that the ground should be used beneficially, mucked well – especially before winter corn – and left well ordered for the incoming tenant. Hence the requirements at Dilham to leave a third in wintercorn stubble, a third in summercorn stubble and a third olland, summerley or buck stubble and muck in the yards (558). From the 1680s, reflecting his concern for the condition of the soil, he started to include clauses on marling. In 1683 he agreed with William Tower of Beckham 'that the said Wm shall lay on 200 Loads of Marle yearly the first 6 years. I diging and filling the same' (531). The accounts show that the contract being completed (251, 329).

Farming practices

Although William rarely used leases to promote innovative husbandry, other evidence in the Green Book shows that tenants had been experimenting with new crops for some time and that he encouraged their adoption, particularly the use of clover. In 1672 he paid for forty-two pound of clover seed for Smith's farm at Dilham; in 1678, £1 5s for clover seed for Reepham Farm; and in 1679 he directed that the closes on Aylmerton heath should be sown with clover or left olland (*i.e. fallow*) 'Mr Windham finding seed' (**52, 166, 534**). In 1674 he had reduced the rent for the Sheep Closes at Aylmerton because 'the Clovergrass decayed'. By the 1670s one of the large closes in Metton was called the Clover-grass Close. Turnips were also introduced into the estate quite early and used extensively to feed beasts and cows. In 1676 he had '3 Beasts at Turnops', and in several accounts he made allowances for turnips, including £10 for Widow Scipper's 'turnups'; £5 10s to William Frost at Gresham for a 'Close of Turneps' at Gresham; and to Plummer of Debney's Farm, Dilham for his 'Turnups' (**201, 146, 267, 301**). The letting to halves agreement for the Park (1690–93) shows that turnips and clover were grown with grain crops, peas and vetches in what appears to be an informal rotation.[51] The use of clover and turnips was clearly well established by the 1670s, but not enforced as a matter of estate policy. In contrast, at Blickling, a neighbouring estate mainly on the northern heathlands, leases for light-soiled farms at Horsham St. Faith's and Swardeston directed the tenant to grow turnips from the mid 1660s, and included instructions as to their cultivation.[52] At Felbrigg, William preferred to leave these initiatives to the discretion of the tenant.

Manorial jurisdiction

William allotted several pages in the Green Book to manorial jurisdiction and clearly took these responsibilities seriously. His bailiffs collected the rents of assize, and held court 'diners' and 'supers' for the tenants, while William pursued claims over copyhold land and asserted his rights over timber and game.

Rents of Assize, the fixed rents payable on copyhold land, amounted to £141 11s. 11¾d a year in 1673 (**14**). Four bailiffs collected the rents: Robert Cooke for the Felbrigg, Beckham and Banningham area (**180–183,290–291**); Edmund Bale for Wicklewood and Crownthorpe (**170–171, 238–239**); John Perry for Toft Monks and Thurlton (**168–169, 234–237**); Henry Houseman for Suffolk (**149–151, 224–227, 296–297**); and the Kingsberry brothers in Essex, where the tiny sums formed part of their farm rents (**546**). For Bale and Houseman, manorial duties occupied only a fraction of their time. In 1682, reflecting the declining importance and mechanical nature of this role, William terminated Robert Cooke's employment at Felbrigg, saving himself £5 by arranging for the rents to be collected by his 'menial servant', Nevertheless, by collecting these seemingly trivial rents landowners asserted a legal right, which others might have challenged. For a similar purpose, William recorded rents, fines, and fees payable by him to other manors from which he held land (**14**).

The type of rent payable on parcels of copyhold land became the subject of several disputes in the 1670s and 1680s. The majority of copyhold rents on the estate were fixed, but some were unfixed, leaving the landowner the right to raise them. John Blinman had carried out a survey of copyhold land between 1609 and 1615, to distinguish the different types of rent and ascertain the scope for improvement. Much had been achieved and Thomas Windham continued to increase rents where possible and keep a watchful eye on any attempts at evasion. John Windham and the family lawyer, Dr Robert Peppar, had been less careful and allowed payments to lapse, leaving William with the burden of reasserting his rights. He faced several challenges either to his title or his claim that rents were unfixed and could be improved. The most persistent litigant was Clement Herne, whose family had successfully pursued similar claims in the Queen's Manor of Cawston.[53] By winning judgements in their favour they had secured outright possession of a substantial acreage, which lay close to their estate at nearby Haveringland. The case started in 1672 when the family refused to pay the rent of £3 14s. 0d., set by Thomas Windham in 1640, for nine acres one rood in Metton. William threatened the family with a Bill of Chancery, which had the desired effect, but when Widow Herne died in 1681 her son Clement reopened the issue by offering William the old copyhold rent of 9s. 3d. The case went to court, and the judges found in William's favour, but Herne did not pay any rent until 1685 and only after much pressure (90–91, 491, 532, 507).

Thomas Doughty of Hanworth gained much encouragement from Herne's case. In 1673 William restated his claim to charge Doughty rent for one acre two roods in Metton. Doughty paid the 16s. rent until 1681, but ceased when Herne's case came to court. William and Doughty were already in dispute over a right of way in Metton, which gave access to one of William's holdings. In the 1650s Thomas Windham had seized this parcel when the Doughtys failed to pay their copyhold rent. William settled the matter, with counsel's advice, by granting Doughty a ninety-five year lease, charging him a rent of £2 6s. a year, and Doughty agreed to allow William access to his holding, but neither party was satisfied (98, 559, 506).

Another dispute erupted in Metton, when the tenant refused to pay £3 13s. 4d. for eight acres in twelve pieces (554). The threat of legal action once more disciplined the tenant, but William needed to exercise constant vigilance. These cases all occurred in Metton, which suggests an element of copycat tactics amongst those tenants. William certainly thought so, and acted firmly to deter further challenges. In 1687 he went through his father's Audit Books noting the tenurial details and historic rent of several small holdings, equipping himself with crucial evidence if the need arose (481, 482).

William stipulated his rights over timber, game and access in leases for the larger properties, and a few of the summaries in the Green Book record such details, notably for Beckham foldcourse and Houseman's farm in Suffolk (480, 495). These clauses were no formality as John Kingsberry learned to his cost in 1682, when William evicted him for maltreating young trees (496). William also retained payments in kind, in addition to the money rents, with tenants on several manors contributing a hen, capon or pullet (509, 529, 540, 542, 555, 556, 558). The miller at Ingworth had to provide '60 Roasting Eles' and half his fish (478, 510, 548).

The Estate Community

A husband and wife team

On 9th June 1689 Katherine noted, 'this day my dear, dear husband left me, having made me hapy for 20 years'.[54] It was the final entry in her personal diary as she turned her attention to managing the estate and the family's financial affairs.[55] She was, however, no stranger to the task; her comments and initiatives, recorded in the new Green Book, indicate a long standing involvement with a complex and diverse business. She had acted as manager, producer and consumer, co-ordinating a range of activities. Entries in the Memo Book show her receiving deliveries of meat from Thomas Sexton, selling the hides and skins and paying wages to labourers engaged in work about the house and garden. Several accounts in the Green Book record her receiving rents, and from the 1680s, she supervised the Park Dairy (23, 41, 564). From the interlocking accounts kept by husband and wife we can see their procedures becoming steadily more proficient, with each learning from the other. From 1689 Katherine's domestic accounts, which were hitherto rather scrappy, resemble the layout of the Green Book, with a table of contents, numbered pages and double entry book-keeping. Together they created a management structure, organising their estate community to perform a variety of functions, adapting and modifying their roles over time.

The professionals

William employed a range of professionals to assist him in the management of his estate. The lowest layer of management consisted of a team of 'men on the ground', who received rents, made assessments for repairs, bought and sold stock and corn, and ran the farms in hand. The most influential of this group was John Salman who had supervised day to day business at Felbrigg since the late 1660s, a role which had brought him into conflict with Dr Robert Peppar, the family lawyer, nominally in charge of the estate from 1665 to 1671.[56] Peppar had complained bitterly of Salman's rudeness, but as Judge Hugh Wyndham pointed out the deficiencies invariably rested with the lawyer who had neither the time nor the practical skills to deal with either farming matters on the ground or to establish good working relationships with tenants.[57] Wyndham solved the situation at Dilham by employing a local man on an annual salary, and paying an attorney a fee to perform specialised services, such as holding the manorial court and auditing the annual account. William reorganised his management structure at Felbrigg along similar lines, dispensing with Peppar's costly services, engaging Salman as his principal man of business, and undertaking the overall supervision of the estate himself. Gradually, more names appear in the Green Book supporting Salman in various ways: Samuel Smith from 1679, Joseph Elden from 1682, John Barham and

Edward Fairchilde in 1686. They received rents and in turn paid the 'weekly bills' and kept the supplementary accounts; disbursements included paying labourers' wages, building repairs, fencing, ditching, and buying and selling sheep and cattle.[58] Salman kept his own accounts to which the Green Book refers (31, 35, 70, 71, 83, 115, 147, 201, 218).[59] Stephen Legge, who became the principal accountant after William Windham's death, made his first appearance as a witness to a lease in 1678 (534). Following Salman's retirement in 1688, he took responsibility for rent collection and negotiations with tenants and from 1694 he kept the main estate accounts and assumed the title of steward.[60]

On the off-lying properties, William relied on his bailiffs to look after his affairs, while Salman came over to receive rents and adjudicate on repairs and abatements. The bailiff, invariably, held one of the tenancies and bills for salary, repairs, fencing, ditching and manorial dues were set off against his rent. On occasion his duties were particularly onerous, as when Crownthorpe Farm failed in 1676, and William paid Edmund Bale £4 10s. for 'his trouble in looking after my farme' (146–147, 192–194). The Suffolk bailiff, Henry Houseman, had greater responsibilities, accounting for all the rents directly to William; this may well have contributed to the accumulation of debts and his failure in 1682 (148–151, 224–227, 296–297). On the Essex properties, the Kingsberry brothers paid their rents to William's financial managers in Norwich, Alderman Briggs or Mr Fowle, who either returned the money to London or sent it to Briggs in Norwich or even to William at Felbrigg. (152–159, 278–279, 308–309). Alderman Augustine Briggs played a central role in William's affairs, managing his financial business (514–515). He had served as Sheriff of Norwich (1660), Mayor (1670), Treasurer for Norfolk (1662) and MP for the City of Norwich in 1678, 1679 and 1681.[61] With his connections, he was well placed to receive payments, return sums of money to London for investment, and pay election expenses and any outstanding debts.[62] Mr Fowle, later Sir Thomas Fowle, performed a similar, but more limited role.

From time to time, William appointed outside professionals for specific purposes. When he pursued the legal claim against Clement Herne he instructed counsel, Sir Robert Baldock, to draw a bill in chancery and ordered his attorney, Palmer, to prefer a bill against Herne (90, 532, 507, 491). With his own legal training, William had no need to retain a lawyer to manage his affairs; he was quite able to direct the course to be followed. When he wanted advice on estate manage-ment, he consulted Edmund Britiffe of Baconsthorpe, who drew up the letting to halves agreements with John Masters and John Fincham and was retained as an intermediary in case of disputes.[63]

William directed his management structure to achieve an effective relationship with his tenants and the efficient management of his farms, particularly if they failed and the farms needed to be taken in hand. He placed his emphasis on the level of management that would directly influence these matters, employing practical professionals, such as Salman, on a permanent basis and engaging lawyers and consultants as and when required. This strategy served his purposes, namely to maintain rent levels by intervention and positive management, but it was only possible because of his enthusiasm and the day to day control he exercised over estate business. As soon as Katherine Windham withdrew from this degree of involvement in 1694, Stephen Legge quickly emerged as the full- time professional estate steward, with a very different approach. Without the freedom and authority to experiment with risky options, he played safe; estate management became a professional business designed to reduce risk, simplify procedures and secure a reliable income for the landowner (see Table 5, p. 41).[64]

The tenants

The farm tenants were a mixed group, socially and economically. A huge disparity existed between the Kingsberrys of Brunden and Middleton Hall who paid their rents in hundreds of pounds and dealt with William almost on equal terms, and those tenants who lived from hand to mouth and could not sign their names, like the share farmer Fincham 'too poor to continue' (537). John Johnson of Felbrigg owned his own farm, in addition to renting Felbrigg-Gresham Farm, and in 1677 he left to 'live in his owne' (18). Some tenants William addressed with respect, such as Mr. Harris of Roughton, but others he summarily dismissed, Crome of Tuttington Hall Farm as 'a lazy ignorant man' and Downing, the new tenant of Alby, as 'a sullen fellow' (505). Many families in the Felbrigg area, including the Abbs, Palls, Johnsons, Drakes, Powles and Lounds, had served the Windhams as tenants for generations and appear in Blinman's account of 1609 to 1615. William sometimes called on these men, whom he knew and trusted, to farm difficult holdings: William Frost and Richard Lowne (Lound) held the tenancy of Tuttington Hall Farm until 1680, when a local man, Richard Lilly accepted a seven year lease. William preferred local men, familiar with local conditions and practices. When Mr Harris of Roughton gave up his lease of the Sustead Closes in 1681 after only a year which had 'proved so very dry and bad', he noted he had 'lately come into Norffolk'. He offered this as an explanation for his action because 'he lost nothing' (80). For tenants with particular skills he was often forced to look further afield. Gorse the Warrener came from Haveringland and his successor Thomas Wegg from Banningham, both parishes ten miles or more from Felbrigg (544, 511). In 1684 William made the comment that the new tenant of Ingworth Mill, although from Aldborough, had been 'bred in Ingworth', clearly a point in his favour (510).

The specialist tenants, who included the limeburner, brickmaker, shepherd and butcher as well as the warreners and millers, possessed skills which set them apart from their neighbours and meant they could negotiate their own arrangements. At Felbrigg, the warren appears to have been very lucrative: in 1682 Gorse 'grew rich, married and would noe longer endure the hardship of a Warrener's Life' (270). The Sexton family were notably versatile. William the limeburner provided lime and marl (32, 540); his brother Thomas supplied butchered meat to the house and hired Reepham Farm to halves (74, 560, 164–167); while Robert leased Ingworth Mill, with comparative success, between 1673 and 1682 (126, 548). With the falling price of corn, coupled with the high cost of maintaining buildings and equipment, millers led a precarious existence; Ingworth Mill changed hands six times between 1673 and 1686 (126, 286, 548, 510, 478). In 1682 'William Greenacre brought me word his son was run away. And begged that I would release him', and in 1686 Sam Curril 'carried away his goods in the night'. To secure a tenant, William was forced to make substantial concessions; as he said 'Corne is so low and Millers doe scramble for grist by fetching and carrying (which was not formerly done) 'tis hard to get a Tennant' (478). At Wicklewood in 1677 he laid out £27 11s. 3d. in repairs for the new tenant (138), and for Beckham Mill in 1683 he agreed to lay two hundred loads of marl for the first six years of the lease (251, 531). In Suffolk a struggle for business between Thomas Arteshall of Lower Mill and Robert Keeble of Upper Mill led to disaster: 'Keeble desired to leave the Mill ... because Arteshall had got many of his customers' (508). At Brunden Mill Francis Reynolds went bankrupt in 1674, resulting in a loss of £200. To attract a new tenant William had to spend a further £195 on repairs; he noted 'By his account one may see how little Mills are worth' (161). In 1683, in some desperation, he leased the mill to Robert Kingsberry 'The Poverty and Knavery of Millers made me earnest to bring R. K. to the aforesd Agreement' (497).

Widows were another group who encountered difficulties, few surviving the season following their husband's death. Invariably, William made allowances and wrote off their debt 'more out of charity than reason' (300/301, 286, 293). However, there were exceptions and some women proved most capable. Widow Skipper continued for five years at Crownthorpe Farm before she was forced to a sale in 1676. The inventory shows a well stocked and fully equipped farm, growing a range of fodder crops including £10 worth of turnips (146–148). In one instance, the case of the Felbrigg Dairy in 1682, the death of the wife led William to terminate the agreement. (565). Compassion extended to the old and infirm; 'Ransome is soe old & his son lame they can't order the ground as it should bee therefore I advise him to leave farming & tould him I would forgive him £10 arrears' (274).

At all levels William enjoyed a close, if sometimes robust relationship with his tenants. On certain occasions he lost his temper which could lead to disastrous consequences, as with the eviction of John Kingsberry in 1682 (159, 496). He clearly found the Kingsberrys overmighty tenants, and was 'glad Jo. K goes out, for I have found inconvenience in having Brothers my Tennants'. Jeremiah Prance, the new tenant, proved equally troublesome, complaining about the state of the farm and the buildings left by John Kingsberry and the expense he faced.[65]

The task of dealing with the arrogant, the whiners, the knaves, the lazy, the ignorant and the 'ill husbands' played havoc with William's nerves. The saga with the millers, in particular, helps to explain his growing frustration. The close relationship which he conducted with his tenants was not easy, and probably inadvisable in the difficult economic circumstances. The situation called for a professional intermediary to stand between landlord and tenant.

The labourers

The Green Book is concerned principally with William's relationship with his tenantry. The labourers who did the felling, ditching, fencing, husbandry, marling and carrying appear mainly in the subsidiary accounts kept by Salman, Elden, Smith and Fairchilde who paid their wages and organised their work. But there is mention of Fox and Pye who cut the flags and several smaller tenants who ditched, thatched and carried in lieu of rent (496, 121, 299). Some outside craftsmen were employed, including Jo Harwold who did all the carpentry work in Essex. For the building of the brewhouse they engaged Mr Skerry and Mr Vidler who organised the craftsmen and labourers (see p. 13). In his weekly account Salman distinguished between daywork and those paid an annual wage. The former were paid 8d. and 10d. per day for a variety of menial jobs, such as gardening, looking after the ewes, and husbandry work.[66] Other tasks included greasing lambs, catching rats, spreading molehills, cleaning ponds, dragging for carp, carting hay, glazing windows, coopering and brewing. More skilled workers were retained with an annual wage: Bally the shepherd and the keeper in the park earned £10 a year, the cooper £8 10s., Daryell the gardener £8, the tiler £7 and the husbandmen £4 10s. Joseph Elden's account of 1683 includes a few more names, some of them familiar.[67] Fincham and Masters were paid for carrying, collecting and carting, Flaxman for pulling turnips, Pooly for mucking and Dix and his son for 'larth riving' (i.e. splitting laths). From Samuel Smith's account a cycle of seasonal tasks can be discerned. Winter jobs included threshing, stopping gaps, ditching, cutting drains, 'shulving' muck, brewing, cleaning the dovehouse, fetching hay, collecting coals, pulling turnips for the fat sheep, tying trees in the Park and killing cattle for Christmas. In the spring, they harrowed, ploughed, worked in the nursery, mowed the walks, felled alders, fed turnips to sheep, and then moved on to weeding in the garden and nursery, mowing, turning and making hay, washing and clipping sheep, turning water into the grazing ground, spreading earth for turnips and watering trees. Harvest was accompanied by mowing and cutting brakes, making faggots, hoeing turnips, cleaning the ponds, moving fish, ploughing and muck spreading. All through the year, they thatched roofs, and repaired buildings and fences as and when required.[68] In addition to the labourers employed on the estate, the Green Book refers to personal and household servants: Jon Francis my Butler, Mark my Groom. In her Personal Account Book 1669–89, Katherine kept a record of wages paid to indoor servants, including £3 a year to wet nurses.[69]

The estate community formed a pyramid with William and Katherine at the apex directing and keeping a tight rein on estate and household business. Closest to them and employed on a permanent basis, were the household servants, accountants and practical 'men on the ground' who ensured the smooth running of the estate. They provided the link with the tenants who leased the farms by written contract. Below this managerial level, were the labourers, indoor and outdoor, paid either wages or daily rates, who performed all kinds of menial tasks through the year. Like a modern landowner, William bought in specialist professional skills as and when required, but from the entries in the Green Book, his relationship with these individuals always appears more distant.[70] The estate generated a substantial economy and employed a huge number of individuals, who interacted with William and Katherine in different ways, but they all expected them to provide them with a livelihood and to protect them in their old age or widowhood.

Family Matters

Family, feuds and finance

In the Green Book, William included several accounts relating to family matters and his personal finances (514–527). The impression gained is that he wished to set out clearly his role in a number of family disputes, and show that in all cases he had acted honourably. The disputes dated back to the late 1660s when he was completing his education and Dr Robert Peppar administered the affairs of the family and managed the estate. William did not believe Peppar acted in his interests; his letters of 1671 show a growing distrust of his activities, as Peppar demanded extra remuneration and borrowed money on his behalf, 'which I have never heard of'.[71] William referred to this sum in rather sceptical terms in the Green Book, when he settled Peppar's Account (512). Peppar he dealt with quite easily, dismissing him in 1673, but his mother proved more difficult. Richard Chamberlaine her second husband handled her affairs (516, 517) and in 1669 he lent William £2000 to 'pay off debts contracted in my minoritye upon my account as my Mother pretended'. William paid her 7½ *per cent* interest on this sum until her death in 1679. His mother also tried to obtain £1000 from William for her younger son John Windham claiming that his father had promised it on his deathbed (518, 519). But statute law disallowed the alteration of the will 'by word of mouth'. John, in fact, died in 1676, and William inherited £1000 out of his portion of £4000 charged on the Manor of Worle in Somerset. He carefully noted his contribution of some £130 to John's medical and funeral expenses (518–519, 521).

His sister Elizabeth who had married Lord Maidstone without the approval of that family in 1669 was a further drain on William's resources. In addition to her portion he made further payments for her maintenance (520–523). In 1670 the young couple claimed that he had promised them £5000, enlisting Edward and Anne Browne, children of Sir Thomas Browne, to support their case.[72] The scheme came to nothing, but it shows the close connection between the Windhams and the family of Sir Thomas Browne (see pp. 11–12).[73] In 1676, William used the legacy from his younger brother to pay off the portion, but that did not prevent Lady Maidstone borrowing money after his death from Katherine Windham. He also reached an accommodation with Frances, the widow of his elder brother John, who had married John Thompson, the son of Maurice Thompson,[74] but intermediaries, including Sir Joseph Ashe, Dr John Collinges and Sir John Thompson, had to be called in to settle aspects of John Windham's personal estate claimed by William, notably his father's books (526, 527).

By the early 1680s William earned a useful income from his savings, including part of his wife's portion, which he lent at 5 *per cent* and 6 *per cent* interest. Borrowers, including the Pastons, Bacons and Earles, paid interest amounting in all to several thousand pounds (178, 179, 524, 525). Katherine invested £3000 in stocks and shares, saved from her pin money, while her father invested the remainder of her portion of £9500 for the benefit of their younger children. William and Katherine resolved their family problems and managed their finances with skill and determination, but not without alienating the less fortunate and astute members of the family.

The Wider Context

Farming in adversity

Emphasis has been placed on the uniqueness of the Green Book, which raises the possibility that Windham may have been untypical in his interest and commitment to estate management. However, his strategy reflected the recommendations of government, the Georgicall Committee of the Royal Society and agricultural writers of the day.[75] Diversification from corn into stock, schemes for planting trees, rearing fish, fattening venison, and developing a brewing outlet were the classic responses in this period of adversity. Historians often question whether landowners read the agricultural texts or paid much attention to the exhortations of agricultural writers. Certainly, if they had acted fully on the advice of Samuel Hartlib, Walter Blith and John Worlidge the concept of a seventeenth century 'agricultural revolution' would not be in doubt. But the relationship between culture and action was more complex; economic inducements, the movement of prices and individual circumstances all played their part. Windham's strategy was clearly affected by his commercial connections, but he was also exposed to the deeply cultural influence of his friend and mentor Sir Thomas Browne, long standing member of the Hartlib circle. Already a scholar of European repute, Browne maintained a wide correspondence with other 'men of genius', including John Evelyn and the naturalist and historian Sir William Dugdale, exchanging the latest ideas and information. Such a man, serving as physician to the Townshends, Hobarts, Bacons, Pastons, Le Stranges and Windhams, was well placed to influence at least two generations of Norfolk gentry. The cultural climate in Norfolk may not have been the deciding factor, but it was certainly favourable to innovation, and there clearly existed a network for the dissemination of these ideas.

Price movements

Price movements may be a more reliable determinant of landowner action.

The Green Book and subsidiary accounts include corn and stock prices for the 1670s and 80s and from these we can create some rudimentary graphs (see Figs. 1 and 2, pp. 32–34). Unfortunately, the earlier accounts of Thomas Blofield, the Felbrigg bailiff, and Dr Robert Peppar contain few prices for the 1650s and 1660s apart from 'rent barley' from 1655, so that a broader comparison of prices based on the Felbrigg material alone is difficult to formulate. However, by using Sir John Hobart's accounts for the neighbouring Blickling Estate, we can roughly trace the movement of prices between 1647 and 1707. A gap appears between 1649 and 1651, when no account for either estate survives; wheat prices are patchy before 1673, and deficient from 1699. The paucity of material from the late 1690s was due to the simplification of estate management policy and the curtailment of direct farming and interventionist policies on both estates. Prices for cows and fat bullocks disappear as interest shifted back to sheep and corn. The pattern identified at Felbrigg and Blickling compares closely to the cyclical trends outlined by Peter Bowden.[76]

Corn prices had been volatile since the early 1640s, but not until the early 1660s did they settle into a pattern of long term decline. By 1664 wheat prices at Felbrigg and Blickling had dropped from a peak in 1647 of 36s. a coomb to a new low of 16s. In the years that followed they showed no sign of recovery, falling to 9s. by 1683; a brief rally to 14s. was followed by a further collapse to 9s. between 1689–1691.[77] Oat prices experienced a similar fate, falling from 12s. per coomb in 1661 to 4s. 6d. in 1664, and dipping to 3s. 6d. and 4s. in the mid 1680s. Barley, sustained by the demand for malt, maintained its price more successfully. Prices ranged between 8s. 4d. and 12s. per coomb in 1661, edged lower in the late 1670s, but did not fall below 6s. per coomb until 1683. All corn prices staged a recovery between 1693 and 1699, only to retreat to very low levels by 1704.

Prices varied for each commodity at any one time. Seed corn, malting barley and oats, specifically for riding and coach horses, commanded the highest price in their range. Some prices were maintained artificially. John Talbott received 4s. for his oats in 1684, but Windham allowed him 9s. in 1685 (281). Sir John Hobart followed a similar policy at Blickling even devising Corn Agreements, guaranteeing prices, with tenants on struggling light soiled farms. Prices at Blickling tended to be at the higher end of the range; this might be explained by the proximity of many properties to the Norwich market and the amount purchased by Sir John to supply his households in London, Norwich and Blickling. Prices do not appear to reflect seasonality; in July 1687 at Felbrigg wheat prices ranged from 12s. to 16s., and oat prices from 4s. to 6s., which covered the full range of prices over the year.

Stock prices varied greatly, depending on the age, condition and quality of the animal. A cow in milk was worth double a dry or old one; heifers in calf were much more valuable than two year olds or barren heifers which were fattened for meat. Calves might be weaners or yearlings. Bullocks matured differently, were sold at different weights, and some breeds, such as Scotch runts, were particularly favoured. When bulls grew old and lazy they commanded little more than a mediocre bullock. Sheep prices include those for lambs, wether hoggs purchased and later sold fat, and old ewes, often called 'crones'. The price for horses showed the greatest variation from £1 to £16, depending on whether they were used for riding, pulling coaches and carts or ploughing; the cheapest were the old and lame destined for the knacker.

The graphs of corn and stock prices show that while the former fell steeply from the mid 1660s, the value of stock and animal products remained relatively consistent throughout the whole period, after a downward adjustment in the 1670s. An estimate of crop yields on the Blickling estate, carried out in 1682, shows the expected return from wheat at two coombs to the acre, meslin at three coombs, barley at four coombs and oats at five coombs. At Felbrigg in 1687 William 'judged' wheat at 3. 3 coombs to the acre, and barley and oats both at three coombs to the acre. Given the cost of cultivation and the likelihood of a fallow year, the return on corn compared unfavourably to the improvement possible on bullocks, with a stocking rate of one animal to the acre.[78] However, the high capital investment made bullock fattening and dairy farming a difficult option for tenants; few could effect the change without assistance from the landowner, which limited the scope for wholesale diversification from corn into cattle. The Windhams lost a great deal of money leasing out dairies, which may explain why they withdrew from milk production as soon as corn prices showed the first hint of recovery in the mid 1690s. Fat wethers and lambs offered a cheaper and more simple alternative, and landowners could avoid involvement in risky tenant-driven operations. Prices set the context for decision making, but landowners and tenants had to consider other factors too.

Government policy

Government policy could also influence landowners' decisions. Tudor governments, with their anti-Enclosure Acts, intervened in agriculture to halt the conversion of open field arable into enclosed pasture, to ensure supplies of corn and to protect employment.[79] Never easy to enforce and highly unpopular with landowners, James I relaxed the implementation of these laws and encouraged a more commercial approach to agricultural management. Landowners won applause for cultivating waste and derelict lands, whereas twenty years before such an approach would have courted suspicion and possibly legal action.[80]

Land reformers directed their attention particularly to the improvement of pastoral areas and the creation of a more diversified agriculture; milk, cheese and meat were highly profitable. At Felbrigg, in the 1620s, Thomas Windham developed a big bullock-fattening enterprise based on the enclosed pasture and meadow of the demesne; he operated the system through grazing agreements with local butchers, overcoming the problems of disposing of the stock at the right time and price. In his leases he included clauses which either prohibited ploughing in certain areas or permitted it only for a stipulated number of years. In other words he developed a carefully organised system of up and down husbandry. William Windham, following his father's example, was clearly receptive to ideas which involved diversification into stockfarming.

In the late 1640s agricultural improvement became a national crusade. The civil wars, the need to supply troops, the possibility of social upheaval and high prices for food provided the stimulus for the Commonwealth to formulate a constructive policy towards agriculture as part of their wider plans for economic renewal and social reform. Through their publications, the agricultural writers Samuel Hartlib and Walter Blith spearheaded the campaign.[81] Although few of their proposals reached the statute book, the debate attracted a wide audience amongst landowners and sowed the seed for future action. Moreover, the government had established a basis for developing policies and enacting laws. When corn prices slumped in 1653, after much deliberation restrictions were lifted on the export of corn to encourage landowners to maintain production. This decision taken in 1656 paved the way for further manipulation of regulations governing the trade in agricultural products to the benefit of English producers and consumers. Restrictions on the importation of Irish cattle to persuade English farmers to diversify into bullock fattening and dairy farming were under discussion. The government also came close to enacting a policy to promote the planting of trees and fruit, but high taxation and a reluctance to interfere in the business and the rights of landowners put a stop to many reforms.

With the recovery of corn prices in the late 1650s and early 1660s the incoming Restoration government resorted, at first, to traditional policies, prohibiting exports and acting against hoarders to ensure adequate food supplies. However, by 1663 the return of good harvests and the accompanying fall in prices brought renewed demands for the lowering of export controls; by 1670 these had been removed and imports suspended. At the same time they removed restrictions on the export of beer and encouraged distilling, greatly assisting Norfolk barley growers. Fearful of the continuing depression in prices, the impact on rent levels and the landowners' ability to pay increased taxation, the government in 1672 went further and introduced a system of bounties payable on corn exported. Bounties had a remarkable effect on production. Between 1660 and 1672 no British port exported more than two thousand quarters, but in 1674, in the first year of operation, twenty three thousand quarters passed through Kings Lynn alone. Bounties continued until 1681; the government renewed them in 1689, when prices fell sharply, and in 1693, when they imposed a new Land Tax. At Felbrigg William Windham eased the burden of taxation on his tenants by setting payments against their rent.

The Restoration government, like the Protectorate, preferred to regulate markets rather than direct landowners to particular courses of action. However, even this policy could prove controversial. In 1666 they encouraged diversification into stock breeding by prohibiting the importation of Irish cattle. However, not everyone benefited. Buyers of lean stock, like William Windham, saw the cost of beasts rise and profit margins narrow, as English and Scottish breeders could not meet the demand. Nevertheless, despite a temporary lifting of the ban between 1679 and 1681, the Cattle Act remained in force until 1759 to the benefit of graziers. From the mid 1670s calf prices appear more regularly in the accounts suggesting that William took the initiative and increasingly bred his own replacements, particularly for his new dairies. The government encouraged dairy farming by removing restrictions on exports of butter and cheese in 1670; they also took steps to improve the marketing of dairy produce by tackling the problem of adulteration and deficient weights. They did not compel landowners to breed animals and move into dairy farming, but provided inducements which made these options attractive.

In one area – sheep and wool – the government turned a deaf ear to the interests of landowners and farmers; the ban on wool exports imposed in 1614 remained until the mid-eighteenth century to protect the interests of the textile industry. At Felbrigg, despite the extensive area of heathland, wool features very little in the accounts. William noted the decline in the value of the foldcourse from £40 to £22, but the government would doubtless have argued that landowners in East Anglia were fully compensated by corn bounties. The government also actively encouraged the development of parkland, tree-planting and game reserves. This policy made sense economically as timber, venison and fish commanded high prices, but possibly of greater importance was the intrinsic appeal such schemes had for landowners. In response to John Evelyn's investigation on woodlands for the Royal Society, the government passed a series of laws in the 1660s designed to protect timber and encourage new planting. They also acted swiftly against poachers, even giving keepers the right to apprehend, and in 1670 they accepted the landowners' claim to reserve all the game on their estate. In this context, William Windham's enthusiasm for deer, fish and tree-planting can be fully understood. As far as possible the government, by their regulatory policies, tried to look after the interests of landowners; a close and mutually beneficial relationship which continued until the repeal of the Corn Laws in 1846. From the pages of the Green Book, William Windham emerges as a conscientious, thoughtful and enterprising landowner, responding in textbook fashion to the spirit of the times. He may not have been typical, but he certainly became a model for others to follow. The Green Book is testimony of his commitment to his family, Felbrigg and the estate community.

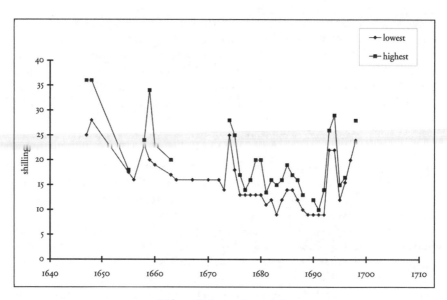

Wheat Prices, 1647–1698.
Note: no figures are available post-1698

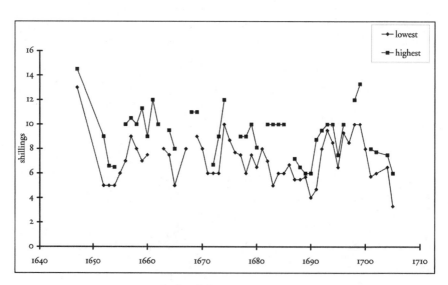

Barley Prices, 1647–1705.

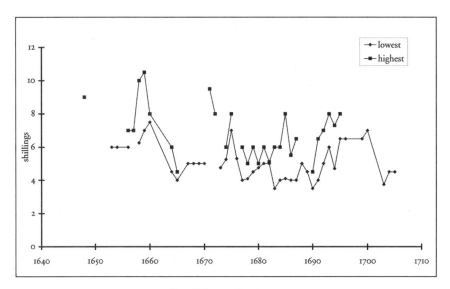

Oat Prices, 1647–1705.

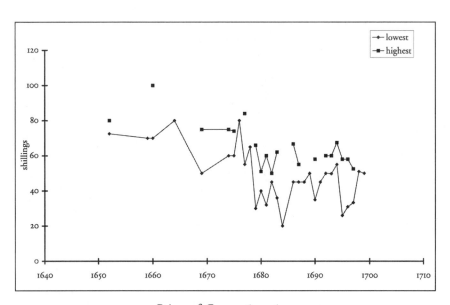

Prices of Cows, 1652–1699.

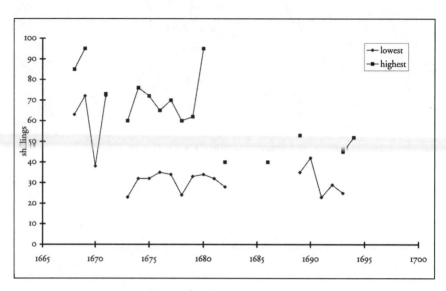

Prices of Bullocks, 1668–1694.

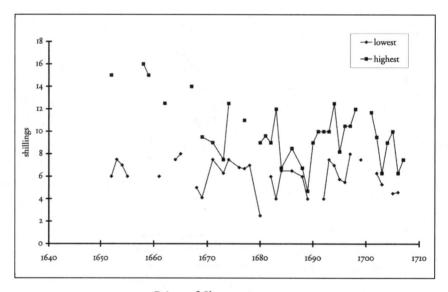

Prices of Sheep, 1652–1707.

Table 1: The Estate in the Felbrigg Area 1615–1673

Blinham's Account 1615	£	s	d	The Green Book 1673	£	s	d
Felbrigg Demesne Lands				**Felbrigg Manor**			
Felbrigg Hall and Park				**Felbrigg Park**	60	00	00
203 acres + 20 acres				**Church Close** 37 acres	16	00	00
1611/ 5 years T. Cutlacke	65	00	00	**Pond Meadow** 12 acres	07	00	00
Foldcourse				**Foldcourse**	25	00	00
1614/ 6 years K. Hobart	40	00	00				
Doles (average)	03	00	00	**Flaggs** (Doles)	10	00	00
				In Hand 1678 values	*118*	*00*	*00*
Warren	22	00	00	T. Gorse 1672/ 5 years	22	00	00
				Warren and Rabbits	09	00	00
Bush and Hill Close				T. Abbs 1670/ 11 years			
and Aldercarre 30 acres				Bush and Hill Close	11	00	00
1611/ 5 years R. Lound	12	00	00	J. Drake 1665/ 1 year			
Swifts Close 30 acres				Swifts Close	12	12	00
1611/ 1 year W. Coppin	09	00	00				
Kirdle Close 16 acres							
1611/ 5 years R. Jell	10	13	04				
Fieldground 74 acres in				J. Powle 1670/ 7 years			
13 parcels				28 acres field land	15	00	00
1611/ 5 years: 7 tenants	23	11	06	W. Sexton 1670/ 6 years			
				Lymekiln 12 acres	07	00	00
				R. Pall 1670/ 12 years			
'Manorlands' 'lands				Conyhill 17 + 21 acres	12	19	00
lately let by copie':				M. Gregory 4 acres	01	12	00
36 acres – 9 tenants	05	12	08	R. Hammond	00	01	04
	190	17	06		91	04	04
				J. Johnson 1673/ 4 years			
				Felbrigg-Gresham Farm			
				101 acres + Kirdle Close	48	10	00
				S. Davy 1665/ 10 years,			
				Felbrigg-Roughton Farm			
				69½ acres	44	00	00
					92	10	00
				House in Cromer	02	00	00
				Lady Windham	02	15	09
				House in Norwich	36	00	00
					40	15	09
Rents of Assize below				**Total Rents**	224	10	01
				In Hand	*118*	*00*	*00*

Aylmerton Demesne Lands
Aylmerton Close – 50 acres
1614/ 7 years – 7 tenants   14   15   00

1 acre pightle   00   10   00

Manorlands
40 acres) tenants   09   08   01
   24   13   02

Rents of Assize below

Aylmerton Manor
T. Richerson   30   00   00
1671/ 8 years – house, sheep closes + 63 acres
Sheep Close Park Gate   *10   00   00*
R. Abbs 14 acre close + 17 acres   09   01   00
J. Flis 1665/ 12 years   95   12   00
19 acres in E. Beckham
H. Bally shepherd   06   10   00
Hall Close 5 acres + 16 acres heath
Cosens and Bond   03   00   00
20 acres heath
W. Johnson 1 acre   00   08   00
N. Abbs   00   04   00
J. Lound 'about 2 acs'   00   14   00
Bessesson 1 acre 1 rood   00   08   00
E. Pall 2 roods   00   03   04
F. Flaxman 'little close'   00   10   00
Frost's Meer   02   00   00
M. Wilson – 1670   24   00   00
Dairy Farm – Gresham
Rent for 10–12 cows
Farm Rents   82   10   04
In Hand   *10   00   00*

Gresham Demesne Lands
40 ac. Close + 10 ac. Close
1599/ 21 years   08   00   00
1½ acre meadow   00   18   00
Sustead Demesne Lands
Beef Close 50 acres
North Close 50 acres
1611/ 5 years
Cubitt and Thompson   80   00   00

6 acres for 99 years   01   00   00
2 pightles 1½ acres   00   15   00
Manorlands

Sustead Manor
T. Cooke   40   00   00
Closes in Gresham

P. Abbs, Wm Frost   41   13   06
1671/ 3 years Hall yard, 2 Great Closes 60 acres
W. Ransome: 22   00   00
1656/ 12 years House + 37 acres,
T. Sexton, butcher 1673   36   00   00
Sustead Church Close
G. England 6 acres   01   15   00

J. Seckar house, 1ac 1r   01   10   00

22 acres – 8 tenants	04	16	02	J. **Colls** 8 acres 1 rood	05	00	00
Rents of Assize below				R. **Russell** 1667	11	13	00
				House + 17 acres			
				W. **Barnes** – Bunswood	06	00	00
				Earl of Yarmouth	00	02	08

Metton Demesne Lands				**Metton Manor**			
50 Acre Close 1611/ 5 years				**Dovehouse Close**	*40*	*00*	*00*
Cubitt and Thompson	20	00	00	**Hay of Long Meadow**	*07*	*00*	*00*
Dovehouse close 60 acres				N. **Abbs**	12	00	00
1615/ 1 year T. Cutlacke	20	00	00	Clovergrass Close			
1 acre pightle	00	10	00	R. **Foster** 12½ acres	06	00	00
3½ acres	01	03	04	M. **Miller** 5 + 1½ acres	02	06	00
				H. **Smith** 22 acres	11	00	00
Manorlands				**Parson Taylor** 3 acres	01	10	00
Sheep Close 30 acres				T. **Warner** 8 acres	03	13	04
Turcocks 10 acres				R. **Doughty** 1½ acres.	00	16	00
+ 40 acres – 5 holdings	10	10	09	J. **Woodrow** 1acre	00	05	00
Rents of Assize below				W. **Hirne** 9 acres 1 rood	03	14	00
				T **Sexton** 14 acres 1 rood	06	10	00
Total for Sustead				Farm Rents for Sustead,			
Metton, Gresham	127	13	03	Gresham, Metton	213	08	06
				In Hand	*47*	*00*	*00*

Runton Demesne Lands				**Runton Manor**			
Pinching Dale 18 acres				Barn + 26 acres			
				J. **Woodrow**	16	11	00
Manorlands				9 acres: 1671/ 21 years			
20 acres – 10 holdings	07	00	00	**Widow Feazer**	03	00	00
				P. **Abbs** 13½ acres	04	01	00
Rents of Assize below				W. **Dawson** 1ac. 1r.	00	08	00
				N. **Dawson** 1½ acres	00	07	06
				J. **Barker** 2 acres	00	12	00
				Parson Flint 1 rood	00	01	00
				Johnson and Elis 2 roods	00	00	04
				Farm Rents	25	00	10

Total Area:				**Total Farm Rents**	545	09	09
921 acres and heathland				*In Hand*	*175*	*00*	*00*
Total Leased	350	03	11	+ 257 acres purchased	720	09	09

Rents of Assize				**Rents of Assize**			
Felbrigg	09	14	05	Felbrigg	07	16	0½

76 tenants app. 600 acres								
Aylmerton:	10	00	07	Aylmerton		09	16	02
42 tenants app. 600 acres								
Runton:	05	15	07	Runton		05	17	0¼
53 tenants app. 350 acres								
Sustead:	04	19	08	Sustead		05	00	1½
27 tenants app. 300 acres								
Metton:				Metton		05	17	07
~~54 tenants app. 550 acres~~	~~11~~	~~17~~	~~11~~					
	36	08	04			34	06	11¼

The estate at East Beckham 1630–1673

Based on leases from the 1630s [82]				Green Book 1673			
	£	s	d		£	s	d
Beckham Hall + 190 acs				J. Lound	60	00	00
(9 closes 12–30 acres each)				1669/ 7 years			
1635/ 10 years				Beckham Hall 113 acres			
W. Howard, H. Spurgeon	100	00	00	W. Howard 1670/	32	00	00
				9 years 84½ acres +			
Copthall & Beestons				Copthall & Beestons			
100 acre: 56 acres – 7 closes				H. Johnson 1670/	30	00	00
44 acres – field land				9 years 90½ acres +			
1631/ 7 years W. Neale	40	00	00	Beeston house, barn			
Beckham Mill + 9acres	10	00	00	J. Tower 1668/ 7 yrs	32	00	00
1632/ 10 years E. Riches				Beckham Mill + 64 acres			
Holtman's Close 30 acres;				L. Moneyman	24	00	00
20 acres Isaacs Heath				1672/ 10 years			
6 acres Aylmerton				Lucas Close 48 acres			
1634/ 7 years				Holtman's Cl. 30 acres			
L. Moneyman	12	00	00	6 acres, doles 20 acres			
Lucas Close 45 acs				W. Howard 1671/	09	08	00
2 pightles 1636/ 8 years				9 years foldcourse			
L. Moneyman	08	00	00	J. Ellis	05	12	00
				shepherd's house			
60 Acre Close; 9ac 1r							
fieldland; 3ac pightle				R. Lound			
1636/ 9 years H. Johnson	25	05	00	Kistrell's Cl. 6 acres	02	00	00
Damme Meadow 3 acs	01	06	08	**Mr. Britiffe**	03	00	00
1636/ 7 years J. Neale				3 closes – 16 acres			
Total area: 478 acres 1 rood				Total area: 478 acres			
Farm Rent	196	11	08		198	00	00
				Rents of Assize	05	05	2½

Table 2: Lands in East Norfolk 1615–1673

Blinman's Account 1615	£	s	d	Green Book 1673	£	s	d
Tuttington Hall Close				**Frost and Lowne**	37	00	00
1½ acres meadow, ½ acre arable				1673/ 7 years			
1599/ 21 years J. Neave	03	00	00	Tuttington Hall,			
Hegge Peece				Hegge Peece			
1614/ T. Cutlacke	20	00	00	Crome's estate 28 acres			
(leased in 1591 for 21 years at £3 6s 8d per annum)				*(1654 J. Crome leased above holdings for £47 3s 8d per annum)*			
'old copieland' 23 acres				**Henry Grime**	17	00	00
1 rood in 'divers pieces'	06	00	00	1672/ 5 years			
6 acres – 3 holdings	01	06	00	Tuttington Farm			
				Searle – Sweepage	01	00	00
				R. Kilby – 2 roods	00	03	00
Colby Hall Close 12 acs				**J. Black** 1671/ 9 years	37	07	00
1614 R. Allen	05	18	00	Colby Hall Close 11 acres			
1591/21 years £1 6s 8d				Ingworth Hall Cl. 20 acres			
6acs Colby field				23½ acres fieldland, 9 acres			
1597/ 21 years R. Allen	00	08	00	**Sexton** 1671	30	00	00
'old copieland':				Ingworth Mill *1663 £34*			
36 acres – 8 holdings	09	10	08				
Ingworth Hall Close				**J. Richman** 1665/	05	00	00
+ 1 acre W. Neave	03	00	00	1 year, cottage + 6 acres			
Hatons Close J. Neave	03	16	00	**J. Allison** 1665/ 2 years	11	10	00
Mill – W. Neave junior.	10	00	00	27 acres 3 roods in Aylsham			
'old copieland'				**W. Parke** 1671/ 7 years	85	00	00
3 acres – 2 holdings	00	15	04	Alby house and grounds			
Banningham				120 acres			
3 acres marsh –	00	08	00	*(1654 let for £102)*			
A. Starling							
Farm Rents	64	02	08	*(1664 £257 3s 8d)*	224	00	00

Rents of Assize	£	s	d		£	s	d
Tuttington	10	04	01		10	03	04
27 tenants: 300/500 acs							
Colby	06	06	08		06	08	7½
26 tenants: 200/300 acs							
Ingworth	08	16	04		08	17	04
23 tenants: 250/400 acres							

Banningham	14	II	03		14	13	7½
25 tenants: 500/800 acres							
	39	18	05		40	12	II

The Estate at Dilham 1673

T. Macke	Scrivener's Farm 56 acres	1665	33	05	00
J. Winter	Debney's Farm 48½ acres	1665	32	00	00
T. Smith	part of Debney's 19 acres	1670/ 21 years	13	15	00
Hugh and Wadham Windham's widow Moiety of Dilham			02	00	00
			81	00	00

Table 3: Land in Central Norfolk (purchased in the 1640s)

	£	s	d
Reepham Farm (purchased in the 1640s)			
House, grounds + 190 acres 1668/ 5 years	52	00	00
Forby of Woodbastwick			

The estate at Wicklewood and Crownthorpe 1615–1673

Blinman's Account 1615				Green Book 1673			
	£	s	d		£	s	d
Hoods Close 60acs				E. Bale 1670/ 11 years	36	II	00
1614/ 7 years H. Meene	23	00	00	87 acre 2 rood in Wicklewood Crownthorpe			
Watermill				M. Norton			
1613/ 7 years R. Juby	20	00	00	1663/ 12 years Wicklewood Mill	26	13	04
Wicklewood Manor				F. Gould,			
+ 160 acres				1655/ 20 years	60	00	00
1615 – 10 tenancies	53	13	08	Wicklewood Manor			
(*Above holdings leased to T. Pettus*				F. Marshall 2 roods	00	03	04
1591 for 21 years at £28 per annum)							
				R. Kett	00	00	04
				Osborne	01	00	00
Crownthorpe Manor				J. Scipper	127	06	08
Windham's Close and				1655/ 16 years			
meadow 1599/ 21 years				Crownthorpe Farm			
J. Founteyne	55	00	00	approx. 220 acres			
	151	13	08		251	14	08
Rents of Assize							
Wicklewood				Bailiff – Edmund Bale			
37 tenants: app. 800 acres	17	07	00		15	05	09

Crownthorpe

15 tenants: app. 300 acres	07	15	00		08	16	07
	25	02	00		24	02	04
				Thurlton Assize Rents	14	18	02

Table 4: Land outside Norfolk (purchased in the 1640s)

Suffolk			£	s	d
H. Houseman	Manor of Mells + 170 acres				
	Bailiff: £3 for Rents of Assize	1654/ 7 years	83	00	00
R. Keeble	Messuage + 122 acres in Mells	1654	48	00	00
W. Peppar	Brickiln + 27 acres 1 rood in Mells	1675/ 7 years	17	10	00
H. Aldred	50 acs in Wenhaston	1676/ 3 years	30	00	00
T. Artesan	Lower Mill Wenhaston +2 ½ ac	1673/ 7 years	21	00	00
T. Keeble	Upper Mill Wenhaston + ½ acre	1673/ 11 years	18	00	00
Rents of Assize			15	05	10
			232	10	00
Essex					
R. Kingsberry	Brunden Farm + 456 acres	1670/ 15 years	180	00	00
F. Reynolds	Brunden Mill + 12 acres	1668/ 3 years	055	00	00
J. Kingsberry	Middleton Hall + 556 acres 2 rood and Rents of Assize	1668/ 7 years	194	08	00
			429	08	00

Table 5: Movement of rent on the Felbrigg Estate [83]

	1673	1681	1687	1695	1709	1717	percentage decline in rents 1673–1717
		William Windham			*Ashe Windham*		
Felbrigg	580	399	356	431	680	673	
In hand	*175*	*359*	*357*	*191*			
TOTAL	755	758	713	622	680	673	*11*
Tuttington	265	272	266	146	148	136	*25*
In hand				*60*			
Dilham	81	82	47		82	82	
In hand		*2*	*30*	*77*			
E. Beckham	E. W	204	181	112	254	275	*3*
In hand			*24*	*86*			
Reepham					41	41	*21*
In hand	*52*	*52*	*52*	*50*			
Wicklewood &							
Crownthorpe	301	301	301	241	245	245	*18*

Assize Rents							
In hand				*101*			
Suffolk	233	217		K. W	K. W	K. W	*13*
In hand			203				
Essex	429	412	412	K. W	K. W	K. W	*4*
Farm Rents	1889	1887	1523	928	1450	1453	
In hand/let to halves	227	413	705	566			
Total	2116	2300	2229	1494	1450	1453	*11*

Notes.

East Beckham formed part of E. Windham's jointure until 1679. The increased rental at Beckham from 1709 – and the sharply reduced rent for Tuttington – can be explained by the leasing of Alby Farm, worth £60 a year, to the tenant of Beckham Hall, and also by the purchase of Beckham Parsonage worth £13 a year.

The Assize Rents were listed under individual properties until 1695 when they were taken in hand.

The Suffolk and Essex estates formed part of K. Windham's jointure from 1689. No figures are available for these properties after 1695, and so the 11% decline in the total rental for the Felbrigg Estate excludes the Suffolk and Essex estates.

For a full discussion of the problems facing K. Windham between 1689 and 1694, and the less interventionist strategies employed by Ashe Windham from 1695, see E. M. Griffiths, 'Management' pp. 388–396, 462–482. Also p. 23 below.

In the text, L(ady) day is 25th March and Mich(aelmas) 29th September.

Abbreviations

AHEW   The Agrarian History of England and Wales
AHR   Agricultural History Review
BAHS   British Agricultural History Society
NRO   Norfolk Record Office
RHS   Royal Historical Society

Editorial Conventions

Insertions in the text are indicated thus * — * deletions thus < — >; and marginalia are brought into the text and indicated thus / — /. Editorial comments are between square brackets.

Notes

1. NRO, WKC 5/152, 400 x. See also E. M. Griffiths, 'The Management of Two East Norfolk Estates in the Seventeenth Century: Felbrigg and Blickling 1597–1717', University of East Anglia Ph.D. thesis, 1987.

2. NRO, WKC 5/151, 400 x 5.

3. NRO, WKC 5/442, 464 x 4.

4. NRO, WKC 6/12, 401 x 4. Sir Joseph Ashe provided an equally large portion for his daughter Mary Ashe who married Horatio, Viscount Townshend in 1673. Following Towshend's death in 1685 Windham acted as legal guardian to his son Charles, later 'Turnip' Townshend. With his widowed mother and her young family, Townshend was a frequent visitor to Felbrigg in the 1680s. Mary Ashe died in 1687. J. M. Rosenheim, *The Townshends of Raynham: Nobility in Transition in Restoration and Early Hanoverian England* (Connecticut, 1989) *passim*.

5. NRO, WKC 6/13–18, 401 x 5; for a history of the Windham family see R. W. Ketton-Cremer, *Felbrigg: the Story of a House* (Ipswich, 1962).

6. *The farming and memorandum books of Henry Best of Elmswell 1642*, ed. D. Woodward, Records of Social and Economic History, new series 8 (British Academy, Oxford, 1984). *Robert Loder's Farm Accounts*, ed. G. E. Fussell (RHS Camden 3rd series, liii, 1936).

7. When Crownthorpe Farm failed in 1677, he 'kept a strict account of it, that my son may see the inconveniency of having farms come into his own hands'. See account (**194**).

8. N. Kent, *Hints to Gentlemen of Landed Property* (1775); *General View of the Agriculture of Norfolk* (1796); W. Marshall, *Rural Economy of Norfolk* (1787) 2, pp. 356–371.

9. The most recent survey of Norfolk agriculture, S. Wade-Martins and T. Williamson, *Roots of Change, Farming and the Landscape in East Anglia c. 1700–1870* (BAHS, 1999) makes no reference to the Green Book. However, in their article, 'The Lease and East Anglian Agriculture 1660–1870' *AHR*, 46, part ii (1998), 127–141, they recognise the importance of the heathlands of north-east Norfolk as an area of innovation.

10. Windham's enterprise contrasts sharply with the examples cited by M. Davies, 'Country Gentry and Falling Rents 1660s and 1670s', *Midland History*, 4 (1978), 86–96, who 'responded with little flexibility to losses in rental income.' See also H. J. Habbakuk, 'Economic Functions of English Landowners in the Seventeenth and Eighteenth Centuries', *Explorations in Entrepreneurial History, Volume VI* (1953), p. 191.

11. *Roots of Change*, chapters 1 and 2.

12. *Ibid.* pp 13–16, 43–46 for Northern Heathlands specifically.

13. B. M. S. Campbell, 'Field Systems in Eastern Norfolk during the Middle Ages: A Study with Particular Reference to the Demographic and Agrarian Changes of the Fourteenth Century', Cambridge University Ph.D. thesis, 1975.

14. *The Paston Letters*, ed. N. Davies (Oxford, 1983), pp. 10–13, 227, 257.

15. Ketton-Cremer, *Felbrigg, passim*.

16. NRO, WKC 1/304, 392 x 6; 1/307, 392 x 6; 1/309, 392 x 6.

17. NRO, WKC 1/236, 392 x 2; 1/240, 392 x 2; 1/277, 392 x 4.

18. T. W. Swales, 'The Redistribution of Monastic Lands in Norfolk', *Norfolk Archaeology* XXXIV (1966), 23; NRO, WKC 1/100, 391 x 4; 1/101, 391 x 5.

19. NRO, WKC 3/16; 3/18, 399 x 4.

20. NRO, WKC 1/156, 391 x 8; 1/242, 392 x2; 1/172, 391 x 9; 1/153, 391 x 8; 1/260–3, 392 x 3; 1/290–292, 392 x 5; 1/8, 390 x 7; 1/116, 391 x 5; 1/115, 391 x 5.

21. NRO, WKC 1/47, 391 x 1; 3/17, 399 x 4; 1/354, 392 x 8; 1/342, 392 x 7; 1/183, 392 x 2.

22. NRO, WKC 5/420, 464 x; 5/442, 464 x 4.

23. NRO, WKC 5/442, 464 x 4.

24. Ashe Windham purchased the Palgraves' estate at Barningham and the Pastons' property at Gresham. Further consolidation created the compactness which appears on the Felbrigg Estate Map of 1830 in Felbrigg Hall. By 1854 the estate in the Felbrigg area extended to some 7000 acres with a further 600 acres at Alby, Ingworth, Colby and Tuttington. 1000 acres at Dilham and the Hanworth estate of 1500 acres were purchased from the Doughtys in 1845. In 1863, following the bankruptcy of 'Mad Windham', John Ketton purchased 3000 acres in Felbrigg, Aylmerton, Sustead and Metton. Windham's estranged wife secured the settled estates for her son Frederick Howe Windham and the rest was sold to a Norwich banker, Robert Harvey. Felbrigg continued to decline under the stewardship of the Kettons. By 1960 when it passed to the National Trust, the estate amounted to no more than 1700 acres – the great demesne at Felbrigg and a couple of farms at Metton. See NRO Felbrigg Catalogue for references.

25. NRO, WKC 3/14, 399 x 4; 5/419, 464 x.

26. Norfolk County Council Road Orders 1777 and 1802, NRO, Box No. 21; NRO, WKC 5/241, 464 x 3; 7/148, 404 x 8; NRO BR 90/52/12.

27. NRO,WKC 5/442, 464 x 4.

28. 'I only desire that industrious gentlemen would be pleased to encourage some expert workmen into the place where they live and let them land at a reasonable rate, and if they be poor and honest to lend them a little stock'. Sir Richard Weston's 'Legacie to his Sons', p. 10, printed in Samuel Hartlib, *His Legacie or An Enlargement of the Discourse of Husbandry Used in Brabant and Flanders* (2nd edn 1652).

29. J. Thirsk, 'Agricultural Policy: Debate and Legislation', in *AHEW vol. v, ii* (1985), 325–388.

30. Hartlib Papers: folio 7/27/ 25 A-B dated 4 July 1643, Sheffield University Library. G. Parry, 'John Evelyn as Hortulan Saint' in M. Leslie and T. Raylor (eds.), *Culture and Cultivation in Early Modern England* (Leicester, 1992), pp. 134–135. See also D. D. C. Chambers, *The Planters of the English Landscape Garden* (Yale, 1993), pp. 32–49.

31. NRO, WKC 5/151, 400 x 5.

32. NRO, WKC 5/151, 400 x 5.

33. NRO, WKC 6/15, 401 x 5.

34. E. P. Shirley, *Some Accounts of English Deer Parks* (1867), *passim*.

35. J. Maddison, *Felbrigg Hall* (National Trust, 1995), pp. 12–17, includes a section on W. Windham's rebuilding, including Samwell's plans with his terse comments following William's modifications. Also Ketton Cremer, *Felbrigg*, pp. 56–58.

36. NRO, WKC 5/154; 5/155; 5/157, 400 x 6. Sedge listed by J. Harvey, *Medieval Gardens* (1981), p. 163.

37. NRO, WKC 7/154, 404 x 8; 5/151, 400 x 5.

38. NRO, WKC 5/158, 400 x 6.

39. NRO, WKC 5/151, 400 x 5.

40. Thomas Harris of Roughton farmed Felbrigg-Roughton successfully until he surrendered the lease in 1690. (**26, 540; 260, 336, 509**); NRO, WKC 5/158, 400 x 6.

41. NRO, WKC 5/442, 464 x 4. For a fuller discussion see R. H. Hilton, 'Why was there so little champart rent in Medieval England?', *Journal of Peasant Studies,* 17 (1990), 510–519.

42. *Robert Loder's Farm Accounts*, Fussell, pp. 1–4, 19; NRO, Pet. 159, 97 x 2.

43. Up and down husbandry entailed the ploughing *up* of pasture for cultivation for a period of years, then laying it *down* to pasture once again. Adopted extensively by Thomas Windham in the 1620s; leases for East Beckham include detailed clauses specifying its use.

44. NRO, WKC 5/158, 400 x 6.

45. NRO, WKC 7/154, 404 x 8.

46. NRO, WKC 5/158, 400 x 6.

47. E. M. Griffiths, 'Management', pp. 349–350 for tables showing the performance of the estate 1673–88.

48. NRO, WKC 5/154, 404 x 8.

49. NRO, WKC 5/136, 400 x 5.

50. NRO, WKC 5/61, 400x 1.

51. NRO, WKC 5/158, 400 x 6.

52. NRO, NRS 21135, 74 x 2; NRS 11122, 25 E 5; NRS 16023, 31 F 10.

53. NRO, NRS 27218, 361 x 3; Also E. M. Griffiths, 'Management', pp. 153–155.

54. NRO, WKC 6/12, 401 x 4.

55. NRO, WKC 13–18, 401 x 5.

56. NRO, WKC 7/5, 404 x 1, in his correspondence with William, Peppar complains 'I have been silent under some other of Salmon's affronts of this nature and pray let me have nothing to do with him ... I am not so low a man to truckle under so rude and unmannerly a fellow'!

57. NRO, WKC 7/15, 404 x 1, correspondence between William and his uncle Hugh Wyndham regarding the management of the Dilham Estate, in which they shared an interest, see p. 130.

58. NRO, WKC 5/155, 400 x 6; 5/157, 400 x 6.

59. NRO, WKC 5/154, 400 x 6.

60. NRO, WKC 5/211, 400 x 6; 5/162–210, 400 x 6.

61. A. Moore with C. Crawley, *Family and Friends: A Regional Survey of British Portraiture* (HMSO, 1992), pp. 202–203.

62. Ketton-Cremer, *Felbrigg*, pp. 64–67, tells the story of the 1679 election when William Windham, with little enthusiasm, partnered Sir John Hobart at the polls.

63. Three generations of Britiffes appear in the records of several county families, including the Walpoles of Houghton, the Hobarts of Blickling and the Harbords of Gunton, as advisers on estate business and family affairs. Identified as yeomen in land transactions of the 1560s, they built up useful estates in the Cley, Hunworth, Baconsthorpe and Plumstead area. The first Edmund Britiffe advised Thomas Windham on his grazing agreements in the 1620s; his son drew up the sharefarming agreements for William Windham. Robert Britiffe served as Recorder of Kings Lynn, MP for Norwich and acted as Sir Robert Walpole's political agent. He was particularly skilful in the land and marriage market. Besides executing deals for Sir Robert, in the 1710s he arranged the marriage of his daughter to Sir John Hobart, and his nephew to Hester Harbord of Gunton, contributing to the revival of two important county families. See E. M. Griffiths, 'Management' pp. 505–508 for further references.

64. D. R. Hainsworth, *Stewards, Lords and People: The estate steward and his world in later*

Stuart England (Cambridge, 1992), pp. 251–264, discusses the inhibition of stewards and their reluctance to act on their own initiative in this period, when their role was still at a formative stage. The tendency was to err on the side of caution.

65. 'Sir this is to let you understand in whot condiscion John Kingsberry left Midlton Hall in, first ye Cotidge new dobed, The Planchers are all rotin & the groundseles. And there is another which lie by the woodside in the same condish but he stoped ye peples mouths from spaking ... the cotidges will cost at ye lest £4 to repaire and one of them I have given order to doe sum thing to all ready or eles I must a lost ye tenante ... The stie for hoges to lie in he pulled downe and carried away, meney gates are missinge sence you ware thare wich he must a made away he set his brother to draw all ye greatest part of the Eyrnes belonginge to the gates ... & carried them away staples hooks hinges cokes hawsps & such a things as never was done to no farm in England soe that I cannot lock 3 gates to the whole farme [S]old all the boardes etc for 40s & railes in the yard to fodder his cattle & great part of the brick kill is downe & sum say thare was benches & dressers in the marchant house if thare were he have carried them away. And meney of the fruit trees are carried away ...'. NRO, WKC 7/10, 404 x 1.

66. NRO, WKC 5/154, 400 x 6.

67. NRO, WKC 5/157, 400 x 6.

68. NRO, WKC 5/155, 400 x 6.

69. NRO, WKC 6/12, 401 x 4.

70. Hainsworth, pp. 251–264 notes the closeness of the relationship between landowner and steward, compared to the more distant relationship with the family lawyer. While the former was dependent on the family, the latter was a professional, often a gentleman, with other clients and independent interests.

71. NRO, WKC 7/5, 404 x 1.

72. Ketton-Cremer, *Felbrigg*, pp. 51–55.

73. Moore and Crawley, *Family and Friends*, p. 89; Ketton-Cremer, *Felbrigg*, pp. 44–6, 52, 62, 65, 67.

74. Ketton-Cremer, *Felbrigg*, p. 47.

75. The Georgicall Committee on the improvement of agriculture established by the Royal Society in 1664.

76. P. Bowden, 'Agricultural prices, wages, farm profits and rents', Section D. Annual Price Movements, *AHEW* vol. v, ii, 41–54, Figs. 13. 2–13. 10; see also 'Statistical Appendix', 828–884.

77. 2 coombs = 1 quarter; 4 quarters = 1 ton.

78. T. Windham's Cattle Accounts: NRO, WKC 5/420 x. See also *AHEW* vol. v, ii, 9–10, Bowden on yields per acre, and Fig. 3. 14, comparing the profitability of wheat against other commodities.

79. Thirsk, 'Agricultural Policy: Public Debate and Legislation', *AHEW* vol. v, ii, 298–386.

80. Sir Richard Weston in S. Hartlib, *His Legacie* (see note 28 above).

81. Hartlib, *His Legacie*.

82. NRO, WKC 5/30–45, 400 x 1.

83. E. M. Griffiths, 'Management', tables showing movement of rent 1673–1687, p. 343; 1695–1717, p. 481

Accounts

[Prefatory Notes]

Will Windham : 1672

➤ Noat: where I say, such a day payd Salman, or Salman received, 'tis to bee understood he chargeth himself in his account bearing that date to have receiv'd soe much of such a man since his former account.

Noat: The heads of all the leases I make (except in Worle) are enter'd in this booke.

Where the taxes are not mentioned in this booke, I pay'd the collectors and where I sett downe repayres, and doe not give the tennant credit for soe much, there I pay'd the money.

Memorandum: my father died March 1653

My brother John Windham died 30 September 1665

In Feb. and March 1665 the tenants in Norfolk; Suffolk and Essex did generally take leases of me for one year, as appeare in the booke of atturnments

My mother died July 1679

Observe: from this time I will not keep an account of the small farme rents by way of debt and credit, but will enter the monye I receive, as I have done Yarmouth's account, page 82, 10 Dec. 1685, because this booke may last longer.

Page

14th October 1673: A particular of my estate

from 30 Oct. 1676 profits of my reall and personal estate from 30 Oct.
1676 to 29 Nov. 1677   216
The yearly value of all my mannors < and profits of court >   14
Stock of cattle upon grounds in hand at Mich. 1673 to 5 Aug. 1675,
4 Feb. 1676, 5 Dec. 1677, Mich   200
Sale of topwood and underwood.   212
Timber used, or sould since 25 March 1672.   210
Rents of Assize goeing out of my freehold and coppyhold lands and tenements   500
What lands are in hand   206, 219, 499
Timber sould since my brother died *anno* 1665 to 25 March 1672   209
An account of moneys disposed of at interest   178
Trees and woods planted   179, 209

Page   9

		Felbrigg Manour *per annum*	£	s	d
172		The Parke			
174		The Sheepcourse			
176	498	Flaggs and Brakes on the heath			
172		Church close			
172		Pond Meadowe			
22	270	The Warren 300 coneis	022	00	00
20		Richard Pall	012	19	00
18	230	John Johnson	048	10	00
24		Drake John	012	12	00
26	200	Davye Stephen	044	00	00
28	318	Powle John	015	00	00
30		Maurice Gregory	001	12	00
32	282	Sextan William	007	00	00
83		Hammond Robert gent.	000	01	04
34		A house in Cromer	002	00	00
36		Lady Windham of Cromer	002	15	09
38		Abbs Thomas	011	00	00
40	261	A house in Norwich	036	00	00

Page		Aylemerton Manour *per annum*	£	s	d
46	284	Richerson Thomas	030	00	00
42	102	Abbs Richard	009	01	00
44		Abbs Nicholas	000	04	00
48		Bally Henry	006	10	00
50		Flaxman Francis	000	10	00
162		Wilson	036	00	00
84		William Frost < and Lowne, Richard >	002	00	00
58		Reave	000	08	00
56		Johnson William	000	08	00
62		Pall Edmund	000	03	04
60		Ellis John	005	12	00
54		Lownd John	000	14	00
52		Cosens and Bond	003	00	00

Page		Sustead Manour	£	s	d
64	266	Cooke Thomas	040	00	00
66		Seckar John	001	10	00
68		Ingland George	001	15	00
70	274	Ransome William 320	022	00	00
72		Barnes William	006	00	00
74	332	Sexton Thomas the butcher	036	00	00
76		Colls John	005	00	00
78	298	Russells Robert	011	13	00
80		Frost and Abbs	041	13	06
82		Lord Yarmouth for Whiting Ollands	000	02	08

Page		Metton Manour *per annum*	£	s	d
86		Doughty gent. of Hanworth	000	16	00
88		Warner Thomas	003	13	04
90		Herne Widdow	003	14	00
92	280	Smith Henry	011	00	00
85		Woodrowe	000	05	00
94		Taylor Parson	001	10	00
96	86	Miller Miles	002	06	00
44		Abbs Nicholas	012	00	00
98		Foster Robert	006	00	00
200		Dovehouse grounds			
74		Thomas Sextan for grounds < late > *in* Mariss's use	006	10	00

Runton Manour

100	334	Woodrowe John	016	11	00
102		Abbs Peter	004	01	00
104		Feazer Widdow	003	00	00
106		Dawson William	000	08	00
107		Dawson Nicholas	000	07	06
108		Barker John	000	12	00
109		Flint Parson of Runton	000	01	00
110		Johnson and Ellis	000	00	01

Beckham was my mothers jointure

244	326	Lowne John	060	00	00
246		Howard William and John	041	08	00
248		Johnson Henry	030	00	00
250	328	Tower James	032	00	00
252		Moneyman Lawrence	024	00	00
254		Elis John	005	12	00
256		Lowne Richard	002	00	00
258		Mr Britiffe	003	00	00
			198	00	00

Page   12

Banningham, Tuttington Ingworth and Colby	} Manours *per annum*		£	s	d
112	288	Frost and Lowne	037	00	00
114	324	Grime Henry	017	00	00
111		Kilby Richard	000	03	00
116		Searle	001	00	00
118	268	Parke William	085	00	00
120	314	Richman John	005	00	00
122		Allison John	011	01	00
124	262	Black John	037	07	00
126	286	Sextan	030	00	00
		Dilham			
128	276	Mack Thomas	033	05	00
130	300	Winter John	032	00	00
132	292	Smith Thomas	013	15	00
134		Hugh Windham and Wadham Windham's widdow	002	00	00

				£	s	d
164	294	**Repham, Wicklewood and Crownethorp Manours**				
136	184	Bale Edmund 238, 306		036	11	00
138	302	Norton		026	13	04
140		Marshall Francis		000	03	04
142	242	Gould Francis		060	00	00
144		Osborne		001	00	00
146	196	Skipper Widdow		127	06	08
141		Thomas Kett		000	00	04

Page   13

			£	s	d
		Mells Manour in Wenhaston in Suffolke	£	s	d
148	224	Howsman Henry	083	00	00
296		Keeble Robert	048	00	00
		Aldred Henry	030	00	00
		Arterson Thomas	021	00	00
		Nickolls Widdow	015	00	00
		Pepper William	000	10	00
		Aldred William	018	00	00

The said Peppar have Nicholl's farme and pay from Mich. 1675 £17 10s
per annum 002 00 00

217 00 00

			£	s	d
		Brunden Manour, Essex			
152	278	Kingsberry Robert 308	180	00	00
160	214	Reynolds Francis *stet* 55 ❯	053	00	00
		Midleton Manour, Essex			
156	272	Kingsberry Widdow 322	194	08	00
		The Manour of Worle, Somersett			
178		£4000 upon Mr Clement Paston's estate	240	00	00
178		£1247 in Alderman Backwell's hands at interest	074	16	04

14. The yearly value of the Rents of Assize belonging to these manours *scilicet:*

	£	s	d		£	s	d	£	s	d
Felbrigg	7	16	0½	Aylemerton	9	16	2			
Sustead	5	00	1½	Metton	5	17	7	028	09	11
Runton Hays				E. Beckham						
	5	17	6¼	Issaks	0	3	10¾			
E. Beckham Marriots					2	1	4½	008	02	9½
Banningham	14	13	7½	Tuttington	10	3	4			
Ingworth	8	17	4	Colby	6	18	7½	040	12	11

Robert Cooke is bayliffe for the afore said manours and have   077   05   7¼
£5 *per annum* for collecting the rents / *180, 290* /

Wicklewood	15	5	9	Crownethorp	8	16	7	024	02	04

Edmund Bale is bayliffe for these two manours and have
£2 per annum   / *170, 238* /

Toffts Overhall and Netherhall	21	10	2			
Thurlton Bainards	3	8	0½	024	18	2½

John Perry is the bayliffe for the two last manors.
And have £2 6s 8d yearly / *168, 234* /

Mells in Wenhaston in Suffolke	15	5	10	015	05	10
				141	11	11¾

Henry Howsman is bayliffe of this manour, and of my estate
in Suffolke. And have £3 *per annum* for his paines / *148* /

The Rents of Assize belonging to the manours of Brunden and Midleton are included in
Robert and John Kingsberrie's leases / *546* /

15. Arrears of rent due 14 October 1673

Cromes * **544/3** * John at (by bond) Mich. 1670		087	18	11
Willis Widdow, is dead **p. 548**, Mich. 1671		026	16	01
Pye Widdow, **p. 539**, Mich. 1671		002	00	00
Kason, Thomas **539**		007	16	00
Kaderin Widdow **539**, Mich. 1670		008	11	00
Betson **539**, Mich. 1670		029	16	02
Walker, Bret, executor	X	001	07	00
< Maries, Widdow >, Mich. 1671 / **186** /		003	10	00
Diboll, John is dead **539**, Mich. 1672		000	05	00
Knevet **539** / **188** /		000	10	00
< Wilson, Nicholas >, Mich. 1668 / **186** /	X			
< Springall, John payd > Mich. 1668 / **186** /	X	004	07	06
Flaxman, Dennis by bond **539**, Mich. 1668		004	14	02
< Blowfield, Thomas > Mich. 1673 / **198** /	X	013	00	00
< Forby, gent.> Mich. 1673 / **186** /	X	004	00	00
< Carryer, John by Bond > / **186** /	X	011	00	00
Doughty of Tuttington **539**, Mich. 1672		010	18	00
< Bessesson of Aylemerton > Mich. 1673 / **58** /	X	003	04	00
< Miles Miller > (as by page 97) at Mich. 1674 / **96** /	X	002	06	00
Fran Reynolls (p. 160) at Lday 1675		216	09	05
John Drake (p. 25) at Mich. 1674		014	18	02
Widdow Scipper (p. 146) at Mich. 1676		024	00	00
Sam Smith p. 97 at Mich. 1687		006	01	4½
Greenacre p. 286 at Mich. 1682		035	18	02
Curril (p. 286) at Mich. 1686		007	10	00
Riseborow (p. 34) at Mich. 1680		002	03	00
Smith (p. 92) Mich 1678		000	18	05
Colls (p. 77) *anno* 1681		005	12	06

Lowne (p. 257) 1686	001	15	10
Talbott 281 1687	014	15	05
Blofield *anno* 1684	011	19	3¾

18. Johnson's Debt (541, 230)

14 Oct. 1673	For Denis Flaxman by noate	008	08	05
	For rent ending at Mich. 1672	020	09	00
	A years rent at Mich. 1673	048	10	00
	A years rent at Mich. 1674	048	10	00
		125	17	05
20 Feb. 1674	In arrear for rent ending Mich. 1674	042	07	05
25 Mar. 1674	A years rent ending Lday 1675	024	05	00
	Half a years rent ending Mich. 1675	024	05	00
	Half a years rent ending Lday 1676	024	05	00
	Half a years rent ending Mich. 1676	024	05	00
		139	07	05
30 Oct. 1676	In arrear at Mich. 1676	042	07	05
	Halfe a years rent Lday 1677	024	05	00
	At Mich 1677	024	05	00
		090	17	05
29 Nov. 1677	In arrear at Mich 1677	027	07	05

Then his lease ended, and he left the farme to live in his owne
The next tennant's account (p. 230)

19. John Johnson's Credit (553, 230)

16 May 1674	Payd Salman in part for Flaxman's debt	005	00	00
	And for rent	018	02	01
	Allowed for tax and repaires	006	17	11
20 Feb. 1674	Payd Salman	048	12	00
	Allowed	004	12	00
		083	10	00
20 Feb 1674	Rest due to me	042	07	05
30 Nov. 1675	Payd Salman in full ending Mich 1674	042	07	05
	And	012	02	07
3 Oct. 1676	Payd Salman	042	10	00
	Rest in arrear by Salman's account	097	00	00
	but £41 18s 4d soe mistaken 9s 1d	042	07	05
		139	07	05
29 Nov. 1677	Salman chargeth himselfe with	063	10	00
	Respit him but £26 18s 4d			
	more due 9s 1d	027	07	05
		090	17	05

21 Mar. 1677	Receiv'd of Goodman Johnson	010	00	00
Allow'd him then the two first quarters by payment of the tax				
for building ships, for lands in my hands at Felbrigg		001	03	09½
	And for his owne farme	000	16	04
	For the muck which he left / *p. 553* /	006	00	00
	The carriage of the same to the Pit Close gate	001	00	00
	For carriage of several things for me	001	00	00
	A bushell of tarris for my use	000	05	06
	Naylor imployed about the farme	000	01	05
24 July 1678	Receiv'd of Johnson in full of all demands	006	10	00
Soe lost by Salman's mistake in his account dated 30 Oct				
1676 and I did give him 3½d		000	09	04½
	Vide p. 230	027	07	05

20. Rich Pall's Debt (508)

14 Oct. 1673	For rent ending at Mich. 1673	006	09	06
	A years rents at Mich. 1674	012	19	00
20 Feb. 1674	Clear	019	08	06
25 Mar. 1675	For halfe a years rent Lday 1675	006	09	06
	Half a year ending Mich. 1675	006	09	06
	Halfe a year rent ending Lday 1676	006	09	06
	At Mich. 1676	006	09	06
		025	18	00
	At Lday 1677	006	09	06
	At Mich. 1677	006	09	06

➤ Noat at Mich. 1677 Pall lett about 5 acres lying upon the heath at £1
5s *per annum*

		012	19	00
	Halfe a years rent at our Lday 1678	005	17	00
	At Mich. 1678	005	17	00
		011	14	00
	At Lday 1679	005	17	00
	At Mich. 1679	005	17	00
		011	14	00
31 Oct. 1679	Owe	005	17	00
	At Mich. 1680	011	14	00
	At Mich. 1681	011	14	00
Pall leave all but the 17 acres nere Cony Hill		029	05	00
	At Mich. 1682	005	19	00

Pall will not hold this ground because corne is so low there is nothing or very little got by plowing, besides Parson Taylor and he did differ about herbage

21. Richard Pall's Credit

4 May 1674	Payd John Salman	005	19	00
	And by tax	000	10	06
20 Feb. 1674	Payd Salman	012	08	06
	And in tax	000	10	06
		019	08	06
30 Nov. 1675	Payd Salman	010	09	06
30 Oct. 1676	Payd Salman	015	08	06
		025	18	00
29 Nov. 1677	Salman chargeth himselfe with	012	15	06
	Allowed 6 months tax	000	03	06
		012	19	00
10 Dec. 1678	Salman chargeth himselfe with	011	08	4½
	Allow'd 11 moneths tax	000	05	4½
	And the amonition rate	000	00	3½
		011	14	00
31 Oct. 1679	Salman chargeth himselfe with the two first payments of	005	14	01
the 18 months tax for disbanding the army		000	02	11
		005	17	00
	Rest	005	17	00
		011	14	00
1 Oct. 1680	Salman chargeth himselfe with 12 months	011	07	11½
	of the said 18 months tax and amonition	000	06	0½
10 Oct. 1681	Smith charge himselfe with	017	08	01
	6 months supply	000	02	11
		029	05	00
1 Oct. 1682	Salman account for	002	19	06
25 Nov. 1682	Pall's son payd me	002	19	06
		005	19	00

22. Thomas Gorse's Debt (544, 530, 270)

14 Oct. 1673	His halfe years rent ending Mich. 1673	011	00	00
	Halfe a years rent due 2 Feb. 1673	011	00	00
	And for 300 coneis	009	00	00
	Arears rent ending 2 Feb. 1674	022	00	00
	And for 300 coneis	009	00	00
	Half years rent ending Mich. 1675	011	00	00
	Half years rent ending 2 Feb. 1675	011	00	00
	And for 300 coneis	009	00	00
		093	00	00
20 May 1676	In arrear of rent due 2 Feb. 1676	006	12	00
	Halfe a years rent at Mich. 1676	011	00	00

And 2 Feb. 1676	011	00	00
And for 300 coneis	009	00	00
At Mich. 1677	011	00	00
And for 300 coneis 2 Feb 1677	009	00	00
At the 2 Feb. 1677	011	00	00
	068	12	00

7 Jan. 1677: I gave Gosse a discharge for 5 years rent under my hand and seal: and 'twas agreed he should have the warren 5 years more upon the same covenants in the old lease

1678 / *lease 330* /

Halfe a years rent Mich. 1678	011	00	00
And the 2 Feb. 1678	011	00	00
At Mich. 1679	011	00	00
	033	00	00
2 Feb. 1679	011	00	00
Mich. 1680	011	00	00
Page 270: owe £18	022	00	00

23. Thomas Gorse's Credit (270)

16 May 1674	Payd John Salman	020	00	00
20 Feb 1674	Payd Salman	005	00	00
And by a years interest of £30 which was layd in my hand				
25 March 1673 to secure the stock upon the warren more one years				
interest of the said £30 to 25 March 1675		001	06	00
30 Nov. 1675	Payd Salman	010	00	00
20 May 1676	Salman charged himselfe to have receiv'd of Gorse 31 Jan 1675	025	00	00
And he delivered in the 3 years to the 2 Feb. 1675 700 coneis		021	00	00
One years interest of the said £30 to 25 Mar. 1676		001	06	00
		086	08	00
20 May 1676	Rest due	006	12	00
		093	00	00
29 Nov. 1677	Salman chargeth himselfe with	010	00	00
Allow'd one years interest of the £30 ending 25 Mar. 1677		001	16	00
7 Jan. 1677	Receiv'd of Goss by the £30 which was layd downe to secure the stock	030	00	00
And for one years interest more of the said £30 though not due til 25 Mar. 1678		001	16	00
And he deliver'd since 20 May 1676: 800 rabits, at six score to the hundred		024	00	00
		067	12	00
Rest due to ballance which I forgave him		001	00	00
		068	12	00

	3 Jan. payd me	011	00	00
19 Mar. 1678	Payd my wiffe	006	00	00

And July 1679 accounted for two hundred and sixty rabits
from 2 Feb 1677

30 Dec 1679	payd me	016	00	00
		033	00	00
	And then more	004	00	00
➤ 1 Oct 1680	Rest	018	00	00
	Vide page 270	022	00	00

24. John Drake's Debt (539, 260, 228, 553)

14 Oct. 1673	In arrear for rent ending Mich. 1670	008	17	02
	And for 3 years rent ending Mich. 1673	037	16	00
	A years rent Mich. 1674	012	12	00
		059	05	02

Memorandum: John Drake did run away from his creditors *anno* 1674
and at Mich. 1674 I did take the ground into my hands, and did then

let his wife 1½ acres at 12s yearly, soe she owe Mich. 1675		000	12	00
	And at Mich. 1676	000	12	00
	And at Mich. 1677	000	12	00
	At Mich. 1678	000	12	00
		002	08	00
	A years rent at Mich. 1679	000	12	00
	A years rent at Mich. 1680	000	12	00
	At Mich. 1681	000	12	00
		001	16	00

At Mich. 1681 Mr Harris hired it.

	A years rent at Mich. 1682. *Vide* 260	000	12	00

/ *Memorandum: 29 Jan 1677: I let 18 acres of Swifts (p. 228, 553)* /

25. Drake's Credit (15)

16 May 1674	Payd Salman	009	10	00
A crop of corne seised and valued *anno* 1674		034	07	00
		044	07	00
	Page 15, rest due	014	18	02
		059	05	02

Goodye Drak's Credit (*quarto book* 32)

30 Nov. 1675	Payd John Salman	000	06	00
30 Oct. 1676	Payd Salman in full end Mich. 1676	000	06	00
29 Nov. 1677	Salman receiv'd in full Mich. 1677	000	12	00

	And <with>	000	06	00
10 Dec. 1678	Salman chargeth himselfe with	000	16	11
	And then in tax 17 months Mich. 1678	000	01	01
		002	08	00
31 Oct. 1679	Salman charge himselfe with	000	06	00
1 Oct. 1680	Salman chargeth himselfe with	000	11	02
	12 months tax	000	00	10
10 Oct. 1681	Salman account for	000	12	00
	And Smith for	000	05	08
	Tax	000	00	04
		001	16	00
30 Oct. 1682	Payd in his general account / *quarto book 32* /	000	12	00

26. Stephen Davye's Debt (540)

14 Oct 1673	In arrear for rent ending Mich. 1672	039	17	00
	A years rent Mich. 1673	044	00	00
	A years rent ending Mich. 1674	044	00	00
	Halfe a years rent at Lday 1675	022	00	00
	Halfe a years rent at Mich. 1675	022	00	00
		171	17	00

Richard Selfe's Debt (540)

	For halfe a years rent ending Lday 1676	018	10	00
	And at Michaelmas *anno* 1676	018	10	00
		037	00	00
30 Oct. 1676	In arrear at Mich. 1676	030	00	00
	Halfe a years rent at Lday 1677	019	00	00
	At Mich 1677	019	00	00
		068	00	00
29 Nov. 1677	In arrear at Mich. 1677	059	10	00
	At Lday 1678	019	00	00
	At Mich. 1678	019	00	00
	At Lday 1679	019	00	00
	At Mich. 1679	019	00	00

Memorandum: 24 July 1679: Roughton Pit was allmost dry, and then I tooke out 51 brace of good carp, and 16 brace the next day. Stored it 1680   135   10   00

27. Stephen Davye's Credit

1 Oct. 1673	Payd to me	008	08	10
	And in tax	001	11	02
16 May 1674	Payd Salman	014	08	10

	And in tax	001	11	02
8 Mar. 1674	Payd me	028	04	06
	And in bills of repayres	005	15	06
	And by abatement	008	00	00

9 Aug. 1675 Richard Bartram and Clement Davye did give me bond to pay me £64 3s 4d upon 25 Mar. 1676:

Receiv'd 15 May 1676		064	03	04
27 Sep. 1675	Robert Harmer did ingage to pay me £22			
	15s: 29 Sep. 1675, payd John Salman	022	15	00
	And in bills of repayres	001	08	00
	By abatement	004	00	00
9 Oct. 1675	Payd Salman for I did give Goody Davye an			
	acquittance in full for rent ending Mich. 1675	005	00	00
	Soe I did clearly forgive her more, besides	165	06	04
	£4 yearly abated as aforesaid	006	10	08
		171	17	00

Richard Selfe's Credit (260)

30 Oct. 1676	Payd Salman	007	00	00
➤	And by Salman's account he is in arrear	030	00	00
		037	00	00
29 Nov. 1677	Payd Salman	007	10	00
	And then allow'd for repayres	001	00	00
	Salman respit him	059	10	00
		068	10	00

30 Jan. 1677 Salman payd the carpenter for 3 days worke about this farme 8s 0d. 25 Nov. 1678 thatcher 5s

10 Dec. 1678	Salman account to me for				016	00	00
20 Dec. 1678	Payd me				010	00	00
	Allow'd the 17 months ship tax	£2	4s	3d			
	Amonition 1s 5d, repayres 2s:		3s	11d			
	Pidgeons		1s	10d	002	10	00
	/p. 260/				028	10	00
	Due at Mich. 1679				107	00	00
					135	10	00

28. John Powle's Debt (540, 541)

14 Oct. 1673	In arrear for rent ending Mich. 1673	014	10	01
	A years rent ending Mich. 1674	015	00	00
20 Feb. 1674	Clear	029	10	01
	Half a years rent ending Lday 1675	007	10	00
	Half a years at Mich. 1675	007	10	00

	Halfe a years rent due at Lday 1676	007	10	00
	And at Mich. 1676	007	10	00
		030	00	00
30 Oct. 1676	In arrear at Mich. 1675	015	00	00
	At Lday 1677	007	10	00
	At Mich. 1677	007	10	00
		030	00	00

Miles Grand's Debt (541)

	Halfe a years rent at Lday 1677	007	10	00
	At Mich. 1678	007	10	00
	At Lday 1678	007	10	00
	At Mich. 1679	007	10	00
Grand died, and I released his widow		030	00	00

Thomson's Debt (537, 318)

1 Feb. 1679	The ballance of Grand's account p. 29	016	18	00
	A years rent at Mich. 1680	013	10	00
	A years rent at Mich. 1681 / *p. 537/2* /	015	00	00
		045	08	00
10 Oct. 1681	Owe	015	00	00
	At Mich. 1682	015	00	00
	At Mich. 1683	015	00	00
		045	00	00
21 Oct. 1683	Owe me	022	15	00
	Half a years rent at Lday 1684	007	10	00
	And at Mich. 1684	007	10	00
		037	15	00
	A years rent at Mich. 1685	015	00	00
	Half a years rent Lady 1686	007	10	00
I shall owe my land lord at Mich. next £32 10s, thirty two		060	05	00

pounds ten shillings. Witness my hand *Martin Thomson* 21 Sep 1686 p. 318

29. John Powle's Credit

16 May 1674	Payd Salman	013	15	07
	And in tax	000	14	06
20 Feb. 1674	Payd Salman	006	18	04
	And in tax and bills	008	01	08
		029	10	01
30 Nov. 1675	Payd by bill of worke done	006	14	10
30 Oct. 1676	Payd Salman	008	05	02

015	00	00

Rest due by Salman's account.	015	00	00
	030	00	00
29 Nov. 1677 Salman chargeth himselfe with	029	12	09
And then allow'd 6 months tax ending Mich. 1677	000	07	03
	030	00	00

Grand's Credit

31 Oct. 1679 Payd by Salman's booke	011	14	03
The last 11 months of the 17 months Ship Tax	000	13	03
The first 12 months of the 18 months tax for disbanding the army and other uses	000	14	06
	013	02	00
Martin Thomson did give me his bond for repayres 16s 10s	016	18	00
	030	00	00

Thomson's Credit

1 Oct. 1680 Salman chargeth himselfe with	011	08	00
1 Oct. 1681 Salman charge himselfe with	019	00	00
	030	08	00
Rest	015	00	00
	045	08	00
1 Oct. 1682 Salman account for	007	10	00
21 Oct. 1683 Salman account for'	013	15	00
Allow'd him for carrying furs to the kill	001	00	00
Repayres £1 18s od	022	05	00
Due to me	022	15	00
	045	00	00
25 Oct. 1684 Salman account for	007	10	00
And Elden account for	005	00	00
A cow and calf in May 1684	002	15	00
17 Oct. 1685 Elden account for	012	10	00
12 Mar. 1685 Elden account for	006	11	00
A comb of seed wheat	000	19	00
21 Sep. 1686 Mr Windham allow'd me a cart which was	035	00	00
Selfe's valued £3; for soe much wages due to my brother			
anno 1680. Soe I owe	025	00	00
	060	05	00

30. Gregory Morrice's Debt (539)

14 Oct. 1673	A years rent ending Mich. 1673	001	12	00
	A years rent ending Mich. 1674	001	12	00
20 Feb. 1674	Clear	003	04	00
	Halfe a years rent ending Lday 1675	000	16	00
	And at Mich. 1675	000	16	00
	Halfe a years rent due Lday 1676	000	16	00
	And at Mich. 1676	000	16	00
	At Lday 1677	000	16	00
	At Mich. 1677	000	16	00
		004	16	00
29 Nov. 1677	In arrear at Mich. 1677	001	12	00
	At Lday 1678	000	16	00
	At Mich. 1678	000	16	00
		003	04	00
10 Dec. 1678	In arrear at Mich. 1678	001	12	00
	At Mich. 1679	001	12	00
	At Mich. 1680	001	12	00

31 Aug. 1680 Morrice say he is antient and desire to leave   004 16 00
the ground at Mich.

Kason's Debt

	A years rent at Mich. 1681	001	12	00
	At Mich. 1682	001	12	00
	At Mich. 1683	001	12	00
	Half a years rent at Lady 1684	000	16	00
	At St. Michael 1684	000	16	00
		006	08	00
	A years rent at Mich. 1685	001	12	00
	Halfe a years rent at Lady 1686	000	16	00
		008	16	00
	At Lady 1687	000	16	00
	At Mich. 1687	000	16	00
		011	04	00

31. Gregory Morrice's Credit

6 May 1674	Payd Salman	001	09	00
	And in tax in full for rent ending Mich. 1673	000	03	00
20 Feb. 1674	Payd Salman	001	10	06
	And in tax in full for rent ending Mich. 1674	000	01	06
		003	04	00

30 Nov. 1675	Payd Salman in full Mich. 1675	001	12	00
29 Nov. 1677	Salman chargeth himself with	001	12	00
	And respit him	001	12	00
		004	16	00
10 Dec. 1678	Salman account for	001	10	09
	And for taxes 9 months	000	01	03
	And respit him at Mich. 1678	001	12	00
		003	04	00
31 Oct. 1679	Paid by Salman's booke	001	10	7½

For the last 8 months of the ship tax, and the first 3 months
of the 18 months tax for disbanding the army 1678

		000	01	4½
1 Oct. 1680	Salman chargeth himselfe with	001	10	06
	12 months tax	000	01	06
23 Nov. 1680	Payd Smith	001	12	00
		004	16	00

Kason's Credit

10 Oct. 1681	Salman account for 1681	001	12	00
1 Oct. 1682	Salman account for Mich. 1682	001	12	00
21 Oct. 1683	Salman account for 1683	001	12	00
12 Dec. 1685	Elden account for 1684	001	12	00
26 Sep. 1687	Allow'd for carpenter's worke ⎤ years 1685,	002	12	09
6 Feb	Allow'd Kason for worke ⎦ 1686, 1687	002	03	03
March		011	04	00

32. William Sextan's Debt (540)

14 Oct. 1673	In arrear at Mich. 1673	003	10	00
	A years rent ending Mich. 1674	007	00	00
20 Feb. 1674	Clear	010	10	00
	Halfe a years rent ending Lday 1675	003	10	00
	And at Mich. 1675	003	10	00
	Halfe a years rent ending Lday 1676	003	10	00
	And at Mich. 1676	003	10	00
		014	00	00

Gregorye's Debt (232, 74, 535/2,540, 92, 282)

For Sextan's farme, and about 5 or 6 acres of land late in widdow
Marie's use Lday 1677

		005	00	00
	At Mich. 1677	005	00	00

And for halfe a years rent of the 5 or 6 acres of ground late in Marie's
use ending Mich 1676 / *page 232* /

		001	10	00
		011	10	00

29 Nov. 1677	In arrear at Mich. 1677	005	00	00
	At Lday 1678	005	00	00
And for 7a. 3r. more of Marie's land in Metton		001	15	00
	At Mich. 1678	006	15	00
Maries his £6 10s / *p. 74, 535/2* / and William Sexton's £7 page 540 make				
Gregorye's rent £13 10s *per annum*		018	10	00
	In arrear	006	10	00
	At Mich. 1679	013	10	00
	At Mich. 1680 / *Talbots p. 92 have £6 10s* /	007	00	00
		027	00	00
1 Oct. 1680	Owe	005	17	04
	At Mich. 1681	007	00	00
	At Mich. 1682	007	00	00
		019	17	04

33. William Sextan's Credit

6 May 1674	Payd Salman	003	05	02
	And in tax in full for rent ending Mich. 1673	000	04	10
20 Feb. 1674	Payd Salman	006	10	04
	And in tax in full for rent ending Mich. 1674	000	09	08
		010	10	00
30 Nov. 1675	Payd Salman full Lday 1675	003	10	00
30 Oct. 1676	Payd Salman Mich. 1675	003	10	00
	And in full of rent ending Lday 1676	003	10	00
29 Nov. 1677	Payd Salman in full Mich. 1676	003	10	00
		014	00	00

Gregorye's Credit (*quarto book* 30, 282)

29 Nov. 1677	Salman chargeth himselfe with	006	10	00
	And respit him	005	00	00
		011	10	00
10 Dec. 1678	Salman account for	005	14	03
	For 19 chalder and a halfe for lyme at 6s	005	17	00
	For 2 loads of marle	000	00	06
	For the 17 moneths tax	000	08	01
	Amonition rate	000	00	02
		012	00	00
	Salman respit him	006	10	00
		018	10	00
31 Oct. 1679	Salman charge himselfe with	005	10	00
	And with	003	00	00
	For 8 chalders and ¼ of lyme	002	09	06

1 Oct. 1680	Salman account for	003	00	00
	Payd Smith in Sep. 1680	003	00	00
The 18 months army tax and 6 months supply		000	09	08
	Lyme £3 12s, marle 1s 6d	003	13	06
		021	02	08
1 Oct. 1680	Rest	005	17	04
		027	00	00
1 Oct. 1681	Salman account for	003	10	00
1 Oct. 1682	Salman account for	002	00	00

Allow'd for 56 chalder and ¾ of lyme from Mich. 1680 to
8 Aug 1682   £17 0s 6d / *quarto book 30* /
which Salman payd him in part   6   0   0 soe   011 00 06

016 10 06

1 Oct. 1682   Rest   003 06 10

34. Riseborow's Debt (15)

He came into the house a little before our Lday 1674
And was to pay rent at Mich. 1674   001 06 00
And afterwards 40s *per annum*

	Halfe a years rent Lday 1675	001	00	00
	Half a yeare Mich. 1675	001	00	00
	A years rent ending at Mich. 1676	002	00	00
		005	06	00
30 Oct. 1676	In arrear for rent at Mich. 1676	002	06	00
	At Lday 1677	001	00	00
	At Mich. 1677	001	00	00
		004	06	00
29 Nov. 1677	In arrear at Mich. 1677	003	10	00
	At Lday 1678	001	00	00
	At Mich. 1678	001	00	00
		005	10	00
10 Dec. 1678	In arrear	004	11	00
	At Mich 1679	002	00	00
	At Mich. 1680	002	00	00

Riseborow would not continue at £2 *per annum*   008 11 00
1 Oct. 1680   Owe   004 03 00

The ballance of the account *anno* 1677. This house with
about half the towne was burnt downe   002 03 00
➤ Note: the 3s on t'other side was not receiv'd of this
Riseborow. *Vide* page 15   000 03 00

35. Riseborow's Credit

20 Feb. 1674	Payd Salman	001	00	00
30 Nov. 1675	Payd Salman in full Mich 1674	000	06	00
	And	000	06	00
30 Oct. 1676	Payd Salman	001	00	00
	And then allowed in repayres	000	08	00
		003	00	00
	And by Salman's account rest in arrear	002	06	00
		005	06	00
29 Nov. 1677	Payd Salman by his account	000	16	00
	Rest due by the said account	003	10	00
		004	06	00
10 Dec. 1678	Salman account for	000	19	00
	Rest due by his account	004	11	00
		005	10	00
31 Oct. 1679	Salman account for	001	19	00
21 July	Payd Smith	000	10	00
1 Oct.	Salman account for	001	06	00
	Paid Smith	000	13	00
		004	08	00
1 Oct. 1680	Rest	004	03	00
		008	11	00
10 Oct. 1681	Payd Smith in Feb. last	000	10	00
1 Oct. 1682	Salman account for	000	10	00
25 Oct. 1684	Salman account for	000	10	00
	And Elden account for	000	10	00
		002	00	00
	Rest due	002	03	00
		004	03	00
5 July 1687	Fairchilde account for *vide* t'other side	000	03	00

36. Lady Windham's Debt (543)

14 Oct. 1673	Halfe a yeare ending Mich 1673	001	07	10½
	A years rent at Mich 1674	002	15	09
	Halfe a yeare Lday 1675	001	07	10½
	Half a yeare Mich. 1675	001	07	10½
	Halfe a years rent at Lday 1676	001	07	10½
	And at Mich. 1676	001	07	10½
30 Oct. 1676	Ladye Windham owe me as above	009	15	1½
	And at Lday 1677	001	07	10½
	At Mich. 1677	001	07	10½
	At Lday 1678	001	07	10½

At Mich. 1678	oo1	07	10½
At Mich. 1679	oo2	15	09
	o18	o2	o4½
At Mich. 1680	oo2	15	09
	o20	18	o1½

1 Oct. 1680	Owe	o11	o4	o5½
	At Mich. 1681	oo2	15	09
	At Mich. 1682	oo2	15	09
		o16	15	11
1 Oct. 1682	Rest	oo2	15	09
	At Mich. 1683	oo2	15	09

A years farme rent 15s od, and a years rent reserved out of
Thurlton £2 both due at St. Michael 1684

	oo2	15	09
	oo8	07	o5
At Mich. 1685	oo2	15	09
At Mich. 1686	oo2	15	09
At Mich. 1687	oo2	15	09

37. Lady Windham's Credit

29 Nov. 1677	Salman chargeth himselfe with	oo9	13	o8

For which he gave my Lady Windham an acquittance in full
for rent ending at Mich 1676, which is 1s 5d ½ less then she
did then owe 1 Oct. 1680. Rest

		o11	o4	5½
		o20	18	1½
15 Oct. 1681	Payd me	oo4	10	o6
	Allow'd for 100 deals £6 15s od			
	1100 bricks 14s 8d	oo7	09	o8
17 Mar. 1681	My cosen Windham payd	oo2	oo	oo
		o14	oo	oo
1 Oct. 1682	Rest	oo2	15	9½
		o16	15	11½
22 Nov. 1682	My cosen Francis Wyndham payd me	oo2	15	9½
23 Oct. 1684	He payd me £5 3s and discounted 8s 6d upon			

account of disbursements at London for my wife.

		oo5	11	o6
		oo8	07	3½
May 1686	Cosen Wyndham payd for pictures	oo2	10	o6
9 Oct .	Payd me in full	oo3	o1	oo
10 Nov. 1687	Payd me	oo2	15	o8

38. Thomas Abbs his Debt (552)

14 Oct. 1673	Thomas and William Abbs at Mich. 1673	o12	oo	oo
	A years rent < from Abbs > Mich. 1674	o11	oo	oo

20 Feb. 1674	Clear	023	00	00
	Halfe a years rent at Lday 1675	005	10	00
	and at Mich. 1675	005	10	00
	Halfe a years rent at Lday 1676	005	10	00
	And at Mich. 1676	005	10	00
		022	00	00
	At Lday 1677	005	10	00
	At Mich. 1677	005	10	00
		011	00	00
	At Lday 1678	005	10	00
	At Mich. 1678	005	10	00
		011	00	00
	At Lday 1679	005	10	00
	At Mich. 1679	005	10	00
	At Mich. 1680	011	00	00
		022	00	00
1 Oct. 1680	Owe	005	10	00
	At Mich. 1681	011	00	00
	Abbs leave the ground	016	10	00

William Sextan's Debt (537, 283)

	Half a years rent at Midsummer 1683	003	15	00
	Half a year at Christmas 1683	003	15	00
	A years rent at Christmas 1684	007	10	00
		015	00	00
	At Christmas 1685	007	10	00
Note: Sextan is the lymeburner's partner page 283				
	At Midsummer 1686	003	15	00
		026	05	00
	A years rent at Midsummer 1687	007	10	00
	Half a years rent at Christmas 1687	003	15	00
6 Feb. 1687 I owe Mr Windham eleven pounds five		011	05	00

shillings for rent as abovesaid.
Made before me *John Francis* William Sextan's marke *M*

39. Thomas Abbs's Credit

16 May 1674	Salman receiv'd of Will and Thomas Abbs	008	07	10
	And in tax	000	12	02
20 Feb. 1674	Salman receiv'd of Thomas Abbs	010	05	08
	And in tax	000	14	04
	And of William Abbs	003	00	00
		023	00	00

30 Nov. 1675	Payd Salman in full Mich. 1675	011	00	00
15 May 1676	Payd to me in full Lday 1676	005	10	00
30 Oct. 1676	Payd Salman in full Mich. 1676	005	10	00
		022	00	00
29 Nov. 1677	Salman chargeth himselfe with	010	16	05
	Allow'd 6 months tax	000	03	07
		011	00	00
10 Dec. 1678	Salman account for	010	13	01
	For the last 11 months tax	000	06	6½
	The amonition rate	000	00	4½
		011	00	00
28 Apr. 1679	Paid my footman	005	00	00
1 Oct. 1680	Salman account for	010	18	11
	18 months tax 10s 9d. Amonition 4d	000	11	01
		016	10	00
	Rest	005	10	00
		022	00	00
10 Oct. 1681	Salman account for	005	10	00
	And Smith for	005	10	00
11 Oct. 1681	Payd Smith	005	10	00
Anno 1682 and 1683 ditching the Bush Close £6 4s 8d, Hill Close £4 10s.		016	10	00

William Sextan's Credit

21 Oct. 1683	Joseph Elden account for	003	15	00
25 Oct. 1684	Elden account for	007	10	00
12 Mar. 1685	Elden account for	003	15	00
		015	00	00
27 Nov. 1686	Allow'd William Sextan for lyme 1685 as by account dated 20 Aug 1685	007	10	00
	Lyme delivered since 1 Mar. 1685	003	15	00
		026	05	00
28 Feb. 1687	William Sextan payd me	004	14	00
10 Mar. 1687	Payd me	001	08	00
	12 days thatching at my farmes	001	08	00

40. Mrs Bendish's Debt (510, 264)

14 Oct. 1673	In arrear of rent ending Mich. 1673	018	00	00
	A years rent ending Mich. 1674	036	00	00
		054	00	00
20 Feb. 1674	Due at Mich. 1674	004	00	00
	And at Lday 1675	018	00	00

	At Mich. 1675	018	00	00
	Halfe a years rent at Lday 1676	018	00	00
	And at Mich. 1676	018	00	00
		076	00	00
30 Oct. 1676	In arrear at Mich. 1676	009	00	00
	At Lday 1677	018	00	00
	At Mich. 1677	018	00	00
		045	00	00

Noat: 7s of the 14s 10d. allow d Nov. 1677 was for 7 years
rents due to the City Mich 1676: 6s. 6d the first quarterly
payment of tax, is 4d for the Militia Tax.

29 Nov. 1677	Arrear Mich. 1677	009	00	00
	At Lday 1677	018	00	00
	At Mich. 1678	018	00	00
		045	00	00
10 Dec. 1678	In arrear	011	00	00
	At Lday 1679	018	00	00
	At Mich. 1679	018	00	00
		047	00	00
31 Oct. 1679	Owe	018	00	00

41. Mrs Bendish her Credit (265)

16 May 1674	Payd John Salman	015	00	00
	And in tax	002	12	00
20 Feb. 1674	Payd Salman	031	14	02
	And in tax	000	05	10
		050	00	00
	Rest due to me	004	00	00
30 Nov. 1675	Payd Salman in full Mich. 1675	004	00	00
	More payd	024	00	00
	And in tax and repayres	001	06	00
30 Oct. 1676	Payd Salman	035	00	06
	Allowed then in repayres	002	13	06
		067	00	00
	Salman respit her in his account.	009	00	00
		076	00	00
29 Nov. 1677	Salman chargeth himselfe with	035	05	02
	And then allow'd a bill of	000	14	10
	Salman respit Bendish / page 40 vide /	009	00	00
		045	00	00
2 Aug. 1678	Bendish sent me by my grome	008	00	00
10 Dec. 1678	Salman account for	025	12	06

	For the 2nd quarterly payment of the tax	000	06	06
	A years rent due to the City at Mich 1677	000	01	00
19 June 1678	I paid Mundey the mason £2 5s 8d for repayring the house in 1677	034	00	00
	Rest due	011	00	00
		045	00	00
26 Aug 1679	Payd my wife	017	02	08
	6 moneths tax	000	13	00
	Repaires and amonition	000	04	04
31 Oct. 1679	Salman charge himselfe with	000	14	08
Allow'd the last 5 months of the Ship Tax and 6 months of the Armye Tax		001	03	10
To my souldier for serving 4 times in his owne arms and amonition		000	08	06
The 3 and 4 quarterly payments of the the 18 months tax for disbanding of the armye		000	13	00
	Payd my wife as *per* noat 20 Jan. 1678.	005	00	00
		029	00	00
	Rest	018	00	00
		047	00	00

42. Richard Abbs's Debt (505, 102)

14 Oct. 1673	In arrear Richard and William Abbs Mich. 1673	005	10	00
	Richard in arrear at Mich. 1673	003	11	00
	Richard's years rent at Mich. 1674	009	01	00
		018	02	00
20 Feb. 1674	Rest due to me	004	11	00
25 Mar. 1675	Halfe a years rent ending Lday 1675	004	10	06
	Half a yeare ending Mich. 1675	004	10	06
	Halfe a years rent at Lday 1676	004	10	06
	And at Mich. 1676	004	10	06
		022	13	00
30 Oct. 1676	Rest due half years rent end Mich. 1676	004	10	06
	At Lday 1677	004	10	06
	At Mich. 1677	004	10	06
		013	11	06
29 Nov. 1677	In arrear at Mich. 1677	004	10	06
	At Lday 1678	004	10	06
	At Mich. 1678	004	10	06
		013	11	06
10 Dec. 1678	In arrear	004	10	06
	At Lday 1679	004	10	06

	At Mich. 1679	004 10 06
		022 12 06
1 Oct. 1680	Owe	004 10 06
	At Mich. 1681	009 01 00

1681 Richard Abbs went away from his creditors.

9 Aug Peter Abbs of Runton promised to pay me at Christmas if his brother did not. From Mich 1680 Peter Abbs hire this ground / *p. 102* /

43. Richard Abb's his Credit

16 May 1674	Salman receiv'd of Richard and William	005	01	06
	And in tax in full of their arrear	000	08	06
	And of Richard in full of his arrear	003	11	00
20 Feb. 1674	Salman receiv'd of Richard Abbs	004	01	06
	And in tax	000	08	06
		013	11	00
20 Feb. 1674	At Mich. 1674	004	11	00
30 Nov. 1675	Payd Salman	004	02	00
	And in tax full Mich. 1674	000	09	00
	And more in money Lday 1675	004	10	06
30 Oct. 1676	Payd Salman in full Lday 1676	009	01	00
		018	02	06
	Rest due to me	004	10	06
		022	13	00
29 Nov. 1677	Salman chargeth himselfe with'	009	01	00
	And respit him	004	10	06
		013	11	06
10 Dec. 1678	Salman account for	008	12	1½
	For the 1st 4 payments of the tax	000	08	06
	Amonition rate	000	00	4½
		009	01	00
	Rest due	004	10	06
		013	11	06
31 Oct. 1679	Salman charge himselfe with	008	13	03
	The 5 last months of the Ship Tax	000	03	06
	The 1st 6 months of the tax for the armye	000	04	03
1 Oct. 1680	Salman account for	004	06	03
	6 months tax	000	04	04
	Payd Smith	004	05	10½
	6 mths tax 4s 3d. Amonition 4d½	000	04	7½
		018	02	00
1 Oct. 1680	Rest	004	10	06
		022	12	06

10 Oct 1681	Salman account for	004	06	03
	6 months supply for the armye	000	04	03
21 Dec	Peter Abbs payd Salman	009	01	00
		013	11	06

44. Nicholas Abbs's Debt (541, 45)

14 Oct. 1673	In arrear at Mich. 1673	006	04	00
	A years rent Mich. 1674	012	04	00
	Halfe a years rent ending Lday 1675	006	02	00
	And at Mich. 1675	006	02	00
	Half a years rent at Lday 1676	006	02	00
	And at Mich. 1676	006	02	00
		042	16	00
30 Oct. 1676	In arrear at Mich. 1676	006	04	00
	At Lday 1677	006	02	00
	At Mich. 1677	006	02	00
		018	08	00
29 Nov. 1677	In arrear at Mich. 1677	006	04	00
	At Lday 1678	006	02	00
	At Mich. 1678	006	02	00
		018	08	00
10 Dec. 1678	In arrear	006	04	00
At Mich. 1678	Abbs left the Clovergrass close in Metton and the Pitles			
	At Mich. 1679 / 541 /	000	04	00
	At Mich. 1680	000	04	00
	At Mich. 1681	000	04	00
	At Mich. 1682	000	04	00
	At Mich. 1683	000	04	00
	/ Vide p. 45 /	001	00	00
July 1687	Nick Abbs's widdow payd Fairchilde for			
	3 years rent ending Mich 1686	000	12	00

45. Nicholas Abbs's Credit

16 May 1674	Payd John Salman	006	04	00
20 Feb. 1674	Payd Salman in full of rent Mich 1674	012	04	00
30 Nov. 1675	Payd Salman	006	00	00
30 Oct. 1676	Payd Salman	012	04	00
		036	12	00
	Rest	006	04	00
		042	16	00
29 Nov. 1677	Salman chargeth himselfe with	012	04	00
	Respit him	006	04	00

		018	08	00
10 Dec. 1678	Salman account for	012	04	00
	Respit him	006	04	00
		018	08	00
31 Oct. 1679	Salman account for	006	04	00
1 Oct. 1680	Salman account for	000	04	00
10 Oct 1681	Salman account for	000	04	00
1 Oct. 1682	Salman account for 1681	000	04	00
21 Oct. 1683	Salman account for 1682	000	04	00
25 Oct 84	Salman account for 1683	000	04	00

➤ Observe: from this time I'll keep N. Abbs's account on the other side
only as I doe Yarmouth's p. 82   001   00   00

46. Thomas Richerson's Debt (542)

14 Oct. 1673	In arrear for rent ending Mich. 1673	017	00	00
	A years rent ending Mich. 1674	030	00	00
	Halfe a years rent ending Lday 1675	015	00	00
	And half a years rent at Mich. 1675	015	00	00
	Halfe a years rent at Lday 1676	015	00	00
	And at Mich. 1676	015	00	00
		107	00	00
30 Oct. 1676	In arrear at Mich. 1676	015	00	00
	At Lday 1677	015	00	00
	At Mich. 1677	015	00	00
		045	00	00
29 Nov. 1677	In arrear at Mich. 1677	015	00	00
	At Lday 1678	015	00	00
	At Mich. 1678	015	00	00
		045	00	00
10 Dec. 1678	In arrear	015	00	00
	At Lday 1679	015	00	00
	At Mich. 1679	015	00	00
		045	00	00

Jo. Yaxely is Tenant (542, 284)

31 Oct. 1679	Owe	023	00	00
	At Mich. 1680	030	00	00
	At Mich. 1681	030	00	00

Yaxley died and 15 March 1681 Mr Maris gave me his bond
to pay the rent due at Mich 1682 being £64 19s 9d   083   00   00

10 Oct. 1681	Owe		045	00	00
	At Mich. 1682		030	00	00
			075	00	00

47. Thomas Richerson's Credit (285)

16 May 1674	Payd John Salman		015	13	03
	And in taxes in full for rent due Mich. 1673		001	06	09
20 Feb. 1674	Payd Salman		027	06	04
	And in tax in full for rent due Mich. 1674		002	13	08
30 Nov. 1675	Payd Salman in full due Lday 1675		015	00	00
30 Oct. 1676	Salman receiv'd a years rent Lday 1676		030	00	00
			092	00	00
	Rest		015	00	00
			107	00	00
29 Nov. 1677	Salman accounted for		030	00	00
	And respit him		015	00	00
			045	00	00
10 Dec. 1678	Salman account for		028	10	2½
	For 12 months tax		001	07	00
	Amonition rate		000	01	3½
	Worke about a new pump		000	01	06
I paid this summer 9s 2d for the pump and setting it up			030	00	00
	Rest		015	00	00
			045	00	00
31 Oct. 1679	Salman account for		014	19	06
	For 25 comb of oats		005	12	06
	The 5 last months of the ship tax		000	11	03
The 1st quarterly payment of the 18 months tax for					
disbanding the army			000	06	09
	A court diner at Mich. 1678		000	10	00
	Repayres 8s 3d		022	00	00
	Rest		023	00	00
			045	00	00
9 Aug. 1680	Paid me		008	02	06
	2, 3, 4, 5 payments of the 18 months tax		001	07	00
	Three court diners ending Lday 1680		001	10	00
	Mending the pump		000	04	06
1 Oct. 1680	Salman account for Mich. 1679		011	16	00
10 Oct. 1681	Salman account for		015	00	00
			038	00	00
	Rest		045	00	00
			083	00	00

1 Oct. 1682	Salman account for			007	16	06
Allow'd Yaxly the last payment of the 18 months tax		6s	9d			
and the 6 months tax		13s	6d	001	00	03
	Two court diners			001	02	00
	Bringing some things from Norwich			000	01	06
				010	00	03

48. Henry Bally his Debt (534/3, 543/4)

14 Oct. 1673	In arrear of rent ending Mich. 1673	003	05	00
	A years rent ending Mich 1674	006	10	00
	A years rent ending Mich 1675	006	10	00
Noat ➤ The said £16 5s, and a years rent end Mich. 1676 is		022	15	00
30 Oct. 1676	In arrear at Mich. 1676	003	05	00
	At Lday 1677	003	05	00
	At Mich. 1677	003	05	00
		009	15	00
29 Nov. 1677	In arrear at Mich. 1677	003	05	00
	At Lday 1678	003	05	00
	At Mich. 1678	003	05	00
		009	15	00
10 Dec. 1678	In arrear	006	10	00
	At Lday 1679	003	05	00
	At Mich. 1679	003	05	00
And for 5 years of Marget's then due / 534/5 /		000	05	00
	At Mich. 1680	006	11	00
	At Mich. 1681	006	11	00
	At Mich. 1682	006	11	00
		032	18	00
	Half a years rent ending Lday 1683	003	05	06
		036	03	06
	Half a years rent at Mich. 1683	003	05	06
	At Lady 1684	003	05	06
	And at Mich. 1684	003	05	06
	At Mich 1685	006	11	00
	Half a years rent Lady 1686	003	05	06
I owe my Land Lord thirteen pounds two shillings for 2 years		019	13	00

rent at Our Lady last. Witness my hand 24 Sep. 1686
Henry Balley. Signed before *Edward Hagerchild*

29 Sep 1686	He owe me	016	07	06
29 Sep 1687	A years rent	006	11	00

49. Henry Bally's Credit

16 May 1674	Payd John Salman	002	19	00
	And in tax in full ending Mich. 1673	000	06	00
20 Feb. 1674	Payd Salman	005	18	00
	And in tax in full ending Mich. 1674	000	12	00
30 Nov. 1675	Payd Salman	003	05	00
30 Oct. 1676	Payd Salman	006	10	00
		019	10	00
	Rest due	003	05	00
		022	15	00
8 Jan. 1676	Payd to me	003	05	00
29 Nov. 1677	Payd Salman	003	05	00
	Rest due	003	05	00
		009	15	00
2 Feb 1677	Bally payd me	003	01	09
And the two first payments of the tax 3s and to the Militia				
Tax 3d		000	03	03
		003	05	00
10 Dec. 1678	Rest due	006	10	00
		009	15	00
31 Oct. 1679	Salman account to me for	006	08	06
	The last 11 months of the Ship Tax	000	05	06
17 Jan. 1679	Payd me	006	06	06
	9 months of the 18 months Armye Tax	000	04	06
24 Dec. 1680	Payd me	006	06	06
	9 mths tax *stet* 1680	000	04	06
1 Oct. 1682	Salman account for 1681	006	11	00
21 Oct. 1683	Salman account for	009	16	06
		036	03	06
25 Oct. 1684	Salman account for	003	05	06
17 Oct. 1685	Elden account for	003	05	06
24 Sep. 1686	Rest	006	11	00
		013	02	00
		019	13	00
14 Dec 1686	Payd me	003	05	06

50. Francis Flaxman's Debt (556)

14 Oct. 1673	In arrear for rent ending Mich. 1673	000	10	00
	A years rent ending Mich. 1674	000	10	00
	Halfe a yeare ending Lday 1675	000	05	00
	Half a yeare ending Mich. 1675	000	05	00
	Half a yeare at Lday 1676	000	05	00

	At Mich. 1676	000	05	00
		002	00	00
30 Oct. 1676	In arrear at Mich. 1676	000	10	00
	At Lday 1677	000	05	00
	At Mich. 1677	000	05	00
	Flaxman died	001	00	00

Cosens's Debt (38)

	A year rent at Mich. 1678	000	10	00
	At Mich. 1679	000	10	00
	At Mich. 1680	000	10	00
	At Mich. 1681	000	10	00
	At Mich. 1682	000	10	00
	At Christmas 1682 / 38 /	000	02	06

51. Flaxman's Credit

16 May 1674	Payd John Salman	000	09	01
	And in tax in full ending Mich. 1673	000	00	11
30 Nov. 1675	Payd Salman	000	09	06
	And in tax full of Mich. 1674	000	00	06
30 Oct. 1676	Payd Salman Mich. 1675	000	10	00
		001	10	00
	Rest due	000	10	00
		002	00	00
29 Nov. 1677	Salman chargeth himselfe with	000	19	08
	Allow'd 6 months tax ending Mich. 1677	000	00	04
		001	00	00

Cosen's Credit

10 Dec. 1678	Salman account for	000	09	06
	In taxes	000	09	06
		000	10	00
1 Oct. 1680	Salman account for	000	09	06
	12 months tax	000	00	06
10 Oct. 1681	Smith account for 1680	000	10	00
27 Nov. 1686	William Sextan payd me for the year ending			
	Mich 1681 by lyme	000	10	00
And he did satisfie me that I had the close in my hands from				
Mich. 1681		000	12	06
		002	02	06

52. Cosens and Bond's Debt (510)

14 Oct. 1673	In arrear for rent ending Mic. 1673	003	17	06
	A years rent ending Mich. 1674	003	17	00
		006	17	06

Noat: the £3 17s 6d for the close conteyning 6 acres next the
parke gate leading to Aylemerton church; and the reson why
the rent fell to £3 was the clovergrass decay'd. From Mich 1674
in hand, t'other *3* Closes, in all about 20 acres. Let 1682 p. 510

53. Cosens and Bond's Credit

16 May 1674	Payd Salman	003	17	06
20 Feb 1674	Payd Salman in full Mich 1674	003	00	00
The ditch which went cross one of the Sheep Closes was		006	17	06

throwne downe 1681. Nov. 1681 repayring the bank against the Heath
cost £1 16s 6d

54. John Lowne's Debt (539)

14 Oct. 1673	A years rent ending Mich. 1673	000	14	00
	A years rent ending Mich. 1674	000	14	00
	A years rent ending Mich. 1675	000	14	00
	Half a years rent at Lday 1676	000	07	00
	And at Mich. 1676	000	07	00
		002	16	00
30 Oct. 1676	In arrear at Mich. 1676	000	14	00
	At Lday 1677	000	07	00
	At Mich. 1677	000	07	00
		001	08	00

James Jeks's Debt

	At Mich. 1678	000	14	00
	At Mich. 1679	000	14	00
	At Mich. 1680	000	14	00
	At Mich. 1681	000	14	00
	At Mich. 1682	000	14	00
	At Mich. 1683	000	14	00
	At Mich. 1684	000	14	00
	At Mich. 1685	000	14	00
		004	10	00
19 Apr. 1686	Mr Powle of Northreps payd the ballance for a years rent ending at Mich. 1685	000	14	00
5 July 1687	Fairchilde account for 1686	000	14	00

55. John Lowne's Credit

16 May and	Payd Salman 12s 8d and 13s 4d	001	000	06
20 Feb 1674	And in tax full ending Mich. 1674	000	02	00
30 Nov. 1675	Payd Salman in full Mich. 1675	000	14	00
		002	02	00
	Due 30 Oct. 1676 by Salman's account:	000	14	00
		002	16	00
29 Nov. 1677	Salman chargeth himself with	001	07	08
	Allow'd 6 months ending Mich. 1677	000	00	04
		001	08	00

Jeck's Credit (54)

10 Dec. 1678	Salman account for	000	13	05
	For 11 months tax and amonition rate 1678	000	00	07
		000	14	00
31 Oct. 1680	Salman account for	000	13	04
	12 months tax 1679	000	00	08
1 Oct. 1682	Salman account for 1680 and 1681	001	08	00
21 Oct. 1683	Salman account for 1682	000	14	00
25 Oct. 1684	Salman account for 1683	000	14	00
17 Oct. 1685	Elden account for 1684	000	14	00
	Payd p. 54	004	04	00
	Due to me	000	14	00

Observe: I'll keep account of this rent as it is payd on the other side.
Note: Lowne and Jeks were Powle's tenants, and soe is Compling who
payd Fairchilde the 14s   004   18   00

56. William Johnson's Debt (538)

14 Oct. 1673	A years rent ending Mich. 1673	000	08	00
	A years rent ending Mich. 1674	000	08	00
	A years rent ending Mich. 1675	000	07	00
	A years rent ending Mich. 1676	000	07	00
	At Mich. 1677	000	07	00
		001	17	00
	A years rent at Mich. 1678	000	07	00
	At Mich. 1679	000	07	00
	At Mich. 1680	000	07	00
	At Mich. 1681	000	07	00
	At Mich. 1682	000	07	00
		001	15	00

	At Mich. 1683	000	07	00
	A years rent at Mich. 1684	000	07	00
	At Mich. 1685	000	07	00
		001	01	00
May 1685	Widow Johnson payd Elden	000	07	00
5 July 1687	Fairchilde account for 3 years rent ending at Mich. 1686	001	01	00

57. William Johnson's Credit (56)

16 May and	Payd Salman 7s and 7s is	000	14	00
20 Feb. 1674	And by abatement in full ending Mich. 1674	000	02	00
30 Nov. 1675	Payd Salman in full ending Mich. 1675	000	07	00
30 Oct. 1676	Payd Salman ending Mich. 1676	000	07	00
29 Nov. 1677	Payd Salman Mich. 1677	000	07	00
		001	17	00
10 Dec. 1678	Salman account for 1678	000	07	00
10 Oct 81	Salman account for 1680	000	14	00
1 Oct 82	Salman account for 1682	000	14	00
From this time *vide* p. 56 when payd		001	15	00

58. Bessesson's and Reave's Debt (556, 15)

Memorandum: I charge the 8 years rent ending Mich. 1673 upon

Bessesson's (*vide* p. 15)	003	04	00
A years rent ending Mich. 1674	000	08	00
A years rent ending Mich. 1675	000	08	00
A years rent at Mich. 1676	000	08	00
At Mich. 1677	000	08	00
	004	16	00
At Mich. 1678	000	08	00
At Mich. 1679	000	08	00
At Mich. 1680	000	08	00
At Mich. 1681	000	08	00
At Mich. 1682	000	08	00
At Mich. 1683	000	08	00
At Mich. 1684	000	08	00
At Mich. 1685	000	08	00
	003	04	00

59. Bessesson's and Reave's Credit (58)

29 Nov. 1677	Salman chargeth himselfe with the	004	16	00
31 Oct. 1679	Salman account for 1678: 1679	000	16	00
10 Oct. 1681	Salman account for 1680	000	08	00

1 Oct. 1682	Salman account for 1681	000	08	00
21 Oct. 1683	Salman account for 1682	000	08	00
25 Oct. 1684	Salman account for 1683	000	08	00
		002	08	00
	Rest due	000	16	00
From this time *vide* p. 58 when payd		003	04	00

60. John Elis his Debt (528)

14 Oct. 1673	His halfe years rent ending Mich. 1673	002	16	00
	A years rent ending Mich. 1674	005	12	00
		008	08	00

Henry Johnson's Debt (556, 248)

	A years rent at Mich. 1675	005	12	00
	Halfe a years rent at Lday 1676	002	16	00
	And at Mich. 1676	002	16	00
		011	04	00
30 Oct. 1676	In arrear at Mich. 1676	002	16	00
	At Lday 1677	002	16	00
	At Mich. 1677	002	16	00
		008	08	00
29 Nov. 1677	In arrear at Mich. 1677	002	16	00
	At Lday 1678 / *lease p. 556* /	003	00	00
	At Mich. 1678	003	00	00
		008	16	00
10 Dec. 1678	In arrear	003	00	00
	At Mich. 1679	006	00	00
	At Mich. 1680	006	00	00
	Mich 1681 *Vide* p. 248	015	00	00

61. John Elis his Credit

16 May 1674	Payd Salman	002	10	08
	And in tax Mich. 1673	000	05	04
20 Feb. 1674	Payd Salman	005	01	04
	And in tax in full ending Mich. 1674	000	10	08
		008	08	00

Henry Johnson's Credit

30 Nov. 1675	Payd Salman	002	16	00
30 Oct. 1676	Payd Salman	005	12	00
		008	08	00
	Rest due	002	16	00
		011	04	00
29 Nov. 1677	Salman chargeth himselfe with	005	12	00
	And respit him	002	16	00
		008	08	00
10 Dec. 1678	Salman account for	005	10	05
	12 months tax 5s 4d, amonition 3d	000	05	07
		005	16	00
	Rest due	003	00	00
		008	16	00
31 Oct. 1679	Salman charge himselfe with	005	12	02
The last 5 months of the ship tax 2s 2d, 6 months of the				
18 months tax for disbanding 2s 8d		000	04	10
15 Jan. 1679	Payd me	002	17	04
	3, 4 payments of the armye tax 1679	000	02	08
	29 Nov and 22 March 80. Payd me	005	14	05
	12 months tax 5s 4d, amonition 3d	000	05	07
		015	00	00

62. Edmund Pall's Debt (482, 63)

14 Oct. 1673	A years rent ending Mich. 1673	000	03	04
	A years rent ending Mich. 1674	000	03	04
	A years rent ending Mich. 1675	000	03	04
	At Mich. 1676	000	03	04
	At Mich. 1677	000	03	04
		000	16	08
	At Mich. 1678	000	03	04
	At Mich. 1679	000	03	04
	At Mich. 1680	000	03	04
	At Mich. 1681	000	03	04
	At Mich. 1682	000	03	04
	At Mich. 1683	000	03	04
From this time *vide* p. 63 how this 3s 4d a year is payd me.		001	00	00

63. Edmund Palls Credit (482)

16 May 1674	Salman receiv'd Mich. 1673	000	03	04
20 Feb. 1674	Salman receiv'd in full ending Mich. 1674	000	03	04
30 Nov. 1675	Payd Salman in full Mich. 1675	000	03	04
30 Oct. 1676	Payd Salman Mich. 1676	000	03	04
29 Nov. 1677	Payd Salman Mich. 1677	000	03	04
		000	16	08
10 Dec. 1678	Salman account for 1678	000	03	04
31 Oct. 1679	Salman account for 1679	000	03	04
10 Oct. 1681	Salman account for 1680	000	03	04
1 Oct. 1682	Salman account for 1681	000	03	04
21 Oct. 1683	Salman account for 1682	000	03	04
25 Oct. 1684	Salman account for 1683	000	03	04
		001	00	00

17 Oct. 1685   Elden account for 3s 4d received of Waterson,
who hire Pall's estate in Aylmerton for rent *anno* 1684   000 03 04
12 Dec.   Elden account for rent *anno* 1685   000 03 04
9 Jan. 1686   Waterson payd Fairchilde 1686   000 03 04
29 Jan. 1687   He payd me 1687   000 03 04

64. Thomas Cooke's Debt (560, 533)

14 Oct. 1673	A years rent ending Mich. 1673	040	00	00
	A years rent ending Mich. 1674	040	00	00
		080	00	00
20 Feb. 1674	In arrear for rent ending Mich. 1674	020	00	00
	Halfe a years rent ending Lday 1675	020	00	00
	And at Mich. 1675	020	00	00
	Half a years rent at Lday 1676	020	00	00
	At Mich. 1676	020	00	00
		100	00	00
30 Oct. 1676	In arrear at Mich. 1676	020	00	00
	At Lday 1677	020	00	00
	At Mich. 1677	020	00	00
➤ Cooke is to have £2 abated next year		060	00	00
29 Nov. 1677	In arrear at Mich. 1677	022	00	00
	At our Lday 1678	019	00	00
	At Mich. 1678	019	00	00

Cooke woud not continue at £38 unless I would let his term end at
Christmas, paying nothing for that quarter   060 00 00
4 Nov. 1678 Frost hired this ground at £40 p. 533
10 Dec. 1678   In arrear   019 00 00

Frost's Debt (533, 266)

	A years rent at Mich. 1679	040	00	00
	At Mich. 1680	040	00	00
		080	00	00
1 Oct. 1680	Rest due	020	00	00

65. Thomas Cookes Credit

16 May 1674	Payd Salman	017	01	00
20 Feb. 1674	Payd Salman	018	05	02
	And in tax in full Mich. 1673	004	13	10
	And then paid Salman	014	17	6½
	And in tax	005	02	5½
		060	00	00
20 Feb. 1674	Due at Mich. 1674	020	00	00
30 Nov. 1675	Payd Salman in full Mich. 1674	020	00	00
	And at Lday 1675	020	00	00
30 Oct. 1676	Payd Salman	040	00	00
		080	00	00
	Rest due by Salman's account	020	00	00
		100	00	00
29 Nov. 1677	Salman chargeth himselfe with	038	00	00
	And respit Cooke	022	00	00
		060	00	00
25 Sep. 1678	Cooke payd me £17 16s 1d½.			
	Disbursd for me 8s	018	04	1½
	Allow'd the 2 last payments of ship mony	000	13	1½
	And the weekes pay by the militia act	000	01	09
	And to Parson Harley a years rent of a peice			
	of Gleab ending Mich. next	000	01	00
10 Dec. 1678	Salman account for	019	14	01
	12 months tax £1 11s 4d, amonition 1s 7d	001	12	11
	Parson Harley's rent at Mich. 1677	000	01	00
	Cooke disbursed 2d tax of my land in Sexton's			
	use, *scilicet* Church close and meadow	000	12	00
This year the long water ditch was new ditcht, it cost 10s		041	00	00
and the wood upon it. Rest due		019	00	00
		060	00	00
28 Dec. 1678	Mr Cooke payd me	019	00	00

Frost's Credit (267)

31 Oct. 1679	Salman charge himselfe with	018	14	04
	6 months of the 18 months for the armye	000	15	08
	Dreyning Frost's part	000	10	00
30 June 1680	Payd me	005	00	00
1 Oct.	Salman account for	027	10	04
	Allow'd for straw £5 6s,			
	disbuns'd for me 5s 9d	005	11	09
12 months tax £1 11s 4d, amonition 1s 7d, repayrs 5s		001	17	08
	Vide p. 267	060	00	00

66. John Seckar's Debt (535)

14 Oct. 1673	A years rent ending Mich. 1673	001	10	00
	A years rent ending Mich. 1674	001	10	00
	A years rent ending Mich. 1675	001	10	00
	At Mich. 1676	001	10	00
	At Lday 1677	000	15	00
	At Mich. 1677	000	15	00
		007	10	00
	At Mich. 1678	001	10	00
	At Mich. 1679	001	10	00
	At Mich. 1680	001	10	00
	At Mich. 1681	001	10	00
	At Mich. 1682	001	10	00
	At Mich. 1683	001	10	00
	A years rent at Mich. 1684	001	10	00
		010	10	00
	A years rent at Mich. 1685	001	10	00

67. John Seckar's Credit (66)

16 May 1674	Payd Salman in full ending Mich. 1673	001	10	00
20 Feb. 1674	Payd Salman in full ending Mich. 1674	001	10	00
30 Nov. 1675	Payd Salman in full ending Mich. 1675	001	10	00
30 Oct. 1676	Payd Salman in full at Mich. 1676	001	10	00
29 Nov. 1677	Payd Salman £1 9s 4d, and 6 months tax 8d	001	10	00
		007	10	00
14 Oct. 1678	Payd me £1 9s 2d, and in tax 10d	001	10	00
31 Oct. 1679	Salman account for 1679	001	10	00
10 Oct. 1681	Smith account for £1 9s 2d, and tax 10d	001	10	00
1 Oct. 1682	Salman account for 1681	001	10	00
13 [Oct]	Payd me 1682	001	10	00

21 Oct. 1683	Salman account for 1683	001	10	00
25 Oct. 1684	Elden account for 1684	001	10	00
		010	10	00
17 Oct. 1685	Elden account for 1685	001	10	00
	From this time *vide* p. 66 when payd			

68. George Ingland's Debt (545)

14 Oct. 1673	A years rent ending Mich 1673	001	15	00
	A years rent ending Mich. 1674	001	15	00
	A years rent Mich. 1675	001	15	00
	Halfe a years rent at Lday 1676	000	17	06
	At Mich. 1676	000	17	06
		007	00	00
	At Lday 1677	000	17	06
	At Mich. 1677	000	17	06
	At Mich. 1678	001	15	00
	At Mich. 1679	001	15	00
	At Mich. 1680	001	15	00
	At Mich. 1681	001	15	00
	At Mich 1682	001	15	00
Noat: The rent fowles are delivered yearly into the house		010	10	00
Mich. 1683	A years rent of the ground	001	15	00
	And at Mich. 1684	001	15	00
	At Mich. 1685	001	15	00
		005	15	00
5 July 1687	Fairchilde account for Lady 168 <6>7	002	12	06

69. George Ingland's Credit (68)

16 May 1674	Payd Salman	001	12	00
	And in tax in full ending Mich. 1673	000	03	00
30 Nov. 1675	Payd Salman	001	12	00
	And then allowed full Mich. 1674	000	03	00
	More in money full Mich. 1675	001	15	00
30 Oct. 1676	Payd Salman Mich. 1675	001	15	00
		007	00	00
10 Dec. 1678	Salman account for 1677	001	15	00
31 Oct. 1679	Then Salman account for	001	12	04
	The last 11 months of the Ship Tax	000	02	06
	Amonition 1678	000	00	02
1 Oct. 1680	Salman account for	001	12	04
	12 months tax 1679	000	02	08
10 Oct. 1681	Smith account for 1680	001	15	00

1 Oct. 1682	Salman account for 1681	001	15	00
21 Oct. 1683	Salman account for £1 14s 10d, allow'd amonition 2d 1682	001	15	00
		010	10	00
25 Oct. 1684	Salman account for 1683	001	15	00
17 Oct. 1685	Elden account for 1684	001	15	00
12 Dec.	Elden account for 1685	001	15	00
From this time *vide* p. 68 when payd		005	05	00

70. William Ransome's Debt (555, 274)

14 Oct. 1673	In arrear for rent ending Mich. 1671	008	05	00
	And a years rent ending Mich. 1672	022	00	00
	And a years rent ending Mich. 1673	022	00	00
	A years rent ending Mich. 1674	022	00	00
	Halfe a years rent ending L-day 1675	011	00	00
	Half a years ending Mich. 1675	011	00	00
	Halfe a year rent Lday 1676	011	00	00
	And at Mich. 1676	011	00	00
		118	05	00
30 Oct. 1676	In arrear at Mich. 1676	068	02	02
	At Lday 1677	011	00	00
	At Mich. 1677	011	00	00
Noat: Salman in his account 20 Feb 1674 page 2 debtor		090	02	02

Ransome at Mich 1673: £39 11s 10d, which is 17s more than
he did then owe.

29 Nov. 1677	In arrear at Mich. 1677	060	00	06
	At Lday 1678	011	00	00
	At Mich. 1678	011	00	00
		082	00	06
10 Dec. 1678	Arrear	061	10	02
	At Mich. 1679	022	00	00
	At Mich. 1680	022	00	00
		105	10	02
1 Oct. 1680	Owe	060	16	08
	At Mich. 1681	022	00	00
	Vide p. 274	082	16	08

71. William Ransome's Credit (275)

16 May 1674	Payd Salman	005	10	00
	And in a bill of worke in full Mich. 1671	002	15	00
	More in money	005	05	02
30 Nov. 1675	Payd John Salman	010	07	00
30 Oct. 1676	Payd Salman	026	05	08

➤ By Salman's account he is arrear at Mich. 1676:		050	02	10
£68 19s 2d. But the b*a*llance is		068	02	02
		118	05	00
29 Nov. 1677	Salman chargeth himselfe with	025	19	02
Allow'd him for 6 days thatching and finding materialls at 6s 4d *per* day		002	00	00
	And for 1 day of a mason and his man	000	02	06
	For carrying brick 8 days to Felbrigg	001	16	00
	For bringing 1 lode of hurdles Felbrigg	000	04	00
		030	01	08
	Salman respit him £60 17s 6d,	060	17	06
	soe the aforesd mistake remaine	090	02	02
10 Dec. 1678	Salman account for	014	10	00
The 5 quarterly and 2 months payments of the tax for building 30 ships of war.		001	16	10
	Amonition	000	01	00
	Carriage of several things for me	002	16	00
	Thatching and finding materials 3 days	001	00	00
For the 1st quarterly payment of the 18 months tax for disbanding the armye.		000	06	06
	Salman payd the carpenter in Nov. 8s 1d	020	10	04
	Rest	061	10	02
31 Oct. 1679	Salman chargeth himselfe with	015	10	00
22 June 1680	Payd in monye and corne	004	12	00
1 Oct.	Salman account for	019	00	00
	Allow'd for pegs	002	02	09
	Last 15 months of the said 18 months tax	001	11	03
	Amonition	000	01	00
	Repayres	000	16	00
	Carting for me	001	00	06
	Repayres £2 12s 4d	044	13	06
	Rest	060	16	08
	Vide p. 275	105	10	02

72. William Barne's Debt (560, 15)

Memorandum: I charge Thomas Blowfeild with the rent ending Mich 1673
vide p. 15

	A years rent ending Mich. 1674	006	00	00
	A years rent ending Mich. 1675	006	00	00
	A halfe years rent Lday 1676	003	00	00
	At Mich. 1676	003	00	00
		018	00	00
30 Oct. 1676	In arrear	003	00	00
	At Lday 1677	003	00	00

	At Mich. 1677	003	00	00
		009	00	00
29 Nov. 1677	In arrear at Mich. 1677	003	00	00
	At Lday 1678	003	00	00
	At Mich. 1678	003	00	00
	Barnes left my ground, because I left his shop	009	00	00

73. William Barne's Credit

20 Feb. 1674	Payd Salman	005	15	00
	And in tax in full for rent ending Mich. 1674	000	05	00
30 Nov. 1675	Payd Salman	003	00	00
30 Oct. 1676	Salman receiv'd of him	006	00	00
		015	00	00
	Rest due	003	00	00
		018	00	00
29 Nov. 1677	Salman chargeth himselfe with	006	00	00
	And respit him	003	00	00
		009	00	00
10 Dec. 1678	Salman account for	002	17	06
	Tax 6 months	000	02	06
31 Oct. 1679	Salman account for	003	16	7½
	The last 11 months of the Ship Tax	000	03	4½
15 Aug. 1680	Payd by bill of iron worke for coach wheels done 1678	002	00	00
		009	00	00

74. Thomas Sexton's Debt (560, 32, 535/2, 332)

14 Oct. 1673	Thomas Luffe the butcher was in arrear for			
	rent ending Mich. 1673	018	00	00
	A years rent ending Mich. 1674	036	00	00
	A years rent Mich. 1675	036	00	00
A years rent (for grounds late in widow Maries's use)				
ending Mich. 1675 / p. 32 535/2 /		006	10	00
	A years rent of Sustead ground Mich. 1676	036	00	00
		132	10	00
30 Oct. 1676	In arrear at Mich. 1676	018	00	00
	At Lday 1677	018	00	00
	At Mich. 1677	018	00	00
		054	00	00
	At Lday 1678	018	00	00
	At Mich. 1678	018	00	00
		036	00	00
	At Mich. 1679	036	00	00

At Mich. 1680	036	00	00

3 Dec. 1680 accounted with Mr Windham, and there rest clear due to
him ten pounds nine shillings for rent at Mich last past *Thomas Sexten*

	072	00	00
Owe as above	010	09	00
At Mich. 1681	036	00	00
At Mich. 1682	036	00	00
At Mich. 1683	036	00	00
	118	09	00
A years rent at Mich. 1684	036	00	00
At Mich. 1685	036	00	00
Half a years rent at Lady 1686	018	00	00
At Mich. 1686	018	00	00
	108	00	00
A years rent at Mich. 1687	036	00	00

16 Jan. 1687 I accounted with Mr Windham and acknowledge to owe
him seventeen pounds six shillings.

	144	00	00
Witness my hand *Thomas Sexten. Vide* p. 332	017	06	00

75. Thomas Sexton's Credit (333, *quarto book* pp. 22, 23, 63; 106)

16 May 1674	Salman receiv'd of Thomas Luffe	015	04	06
	And in tax in full of rent at Mich. 1673	002	15	06
20 Feb. 1674	Salman receiv'd of Thomas. Sexton in full of			
	his rent ending Mich. 1674	036	00	00
30 Nov. 1675	Payd Salman in full Lday 1675	018	00	00
	And in full for Maries's at Mich. 1675	006	10	00
30 Oct. 1676	Payd Salman Lday 1676	036	00	00
		114	10	00
	Rest due	018	00	00
		132	10	00
29 Nov. 1677	Salman chargeth himselfe with	054	00	00
10 Dec. 1678	Salman account for	036	00	00
31 Oct. 1679	Salman charge himselfe with	030	18	07
17 Aug. 1680	Payd me	018	00	00
1 Oct. 1680	Salman account for	009	07	08
	Allow'd for the 18 months to the armye	002	15	06
	The first payment of the 6 months tax	000	09	03
		061	11	00
	Rest due	010	09	00
		072	00	00
23 Jan 1681	Payd by his general account, *quarto* book p. 23	006	09	00
6 June 1683	Payd by his account, / *quarto book p. 22* /	094	00	00

Whereas by Sexten's general account *quarto* book p. 23 I did
owe £30 14s 10d in June 1683. Oct 1683 I doe here give

him credit for ditching in the long meadow 1682, £3 1s 6d

			018	00	00
			118	09	00

21 Oct. 1686	Payd as appear in his general account *quarto* book p. 63		027	19	10
5 July 1687	Fairchilde account for		013	00	00
16 Jan. 1687	I must give Sexton credit for		085	14	02
Because the farme rent is included in his general account by			126	14	00
which he owe me *quarto* p. 106			017	06	00
			144	00	00

76. John Colls his Debt (538)

14 Oct. 1673	In arrear for rent ending Mich. 1672		002	10	00
	And a years rent ending Mich. 1673		005	00	00
	A years rent ending Mich. 1674		005	00	00
	A years rent Mich. 1675		005	00	00
	Half a years rent at our Lday 1676		002	10	00
	At Mich. 1676		002	10	00
			022	10	00
30 Oct. 1676	In arrear at Mich. 1676		002	10	00
	At Lday 1677		002	10	00
	At Mich. 1677		002	10	00
			007	10	00
	At Lday 1678		002	10	00
	At Mich. 1678		002	10	00
	At Mich. 1679		005	00	00
	At Mich. 1680		005	00	00
	At Mich. 1681		005	00	00
	At Mich. 1682		005	00	00

Mem: Colls died in winter 1681, and Peter Wilson held the ground till Mich. 1682.

			025	00	00

Then Black of Thurgarton hired it at £5 *per annum*

1 Oct. 1682	Colls owe me		010	12	06
Mich. 1684	For two years rent of the land late in Colls use at £5 yearly		010	00	00
	At Mich. 1685		005	00	00
	Half a years rent at Lday 1686		002	10	00
	At Mich. 1686		002	10	00
	A years rent at Mich. 1687		005	00	00
			035	12	06

77. John Colls his Credit (15)

20 Feb 1674	Payd Salman in full at Mich. 1673		007	10	00
30 Nov. 1675	Payd Salman		004	04	00

		£	s	d
	And then allow'd in full Mich. 1674	000	16	00
	More payd to Salman	002	13	04
30 Oct. 1676	Payd Salman	004	16	08
		020	00	00
	Rest due	002	10	00
		022	10	00
29 Nov. 1677	Salman chargeth himselfe with	007	10	00
10 Dec. 1678	Salman account for	002	03	04
	17 months tax	000	06	08
31 Oct. 1679	Salman account for 1678	002	10	00
17 July 1680	Payd me	004	15	08
	18 months tax to disband the armye	000	08	00
	Amonition	000	00	04
1 Oct. 1680	Salman account for	002	06	00
1 Oct. 1682	Salman account for	001	17	06
		014	07	06
	Colls owe me	010	12	06
		025	00	00
25 Oct. 1684	Elden charge himself with £5 receiv'd of Mr Peter Wilson upon account of this rent Apr. 1684.	005	00	00
24 Nov.	Black payd me	010	00	00
12 Oct. 1685	Black payd me	005	00	00
12 Oct. 1686	Black payd me	005	00	00
26 Dec. 1687	Black payd me	004	19	00
	Allow'd him the poor rate for Bunswood	000	00	04
	And amonition for his farme	000	00	08
		030	00	00
Observe: The ballance was due at Colls death and therefore I place it page 15		005	12	06
		035	12	06

78. Robert Russells his Debt (560, 298)

		£	s	d
14 Oct. 1673	In arrear for rent ending Mich. 1671	004	13	00
	And a years rent ending Mich. 1672	011	13	00
	And a years rent ending Mich. 1673	011	13	00
	A years rent ending Mich. 1674	011	13	00
		039	12	00
20 Feb 1674	In arrear at Mich. 1674	023	08	04
	halfe a years rent ending Lday 1675	005	16	06
	Half a years rent Mich. 1675	005	16	06
	Half a years rent due at Lday 1676	005	16	06
	At Mich. 1676	005	16	06
		046	14	04

30 Oct. 1676	In arrear Mich. 1676	032	09	00
	At Lday 1677	005	16	06
	At Mich. 1677	005	16	06
		004	02	00
29 Nov. 1677	In arrear at Mich. 1677	032	12	00
	At Lday 1678	005	16	06
	At Mich. 1678	005	16	06
		044	05	00
10 Dec. 1678	Owe	028	17	05
	At Mich. 1679	011	13	00
	At Mich. 1680	011	13	00
	At Mich 1681	011	13	00
	At Mich. 1682	011	13	00
		075	09	05

79. Robert Russells his Credit (299)

16 May 1674	Payd Salman	003	00	00
20 Feb 1674	Payd Salman	006	00	00
	And by bills	007	03	08
		016	03	08
20 Feb 1674	Rest due at Mich. 1674	023	08	04
		039	12	00
30 Nov. 1675	Payd Salman	009	00	00
30 Oct. 1676	Payd Salman	005	05	04

➤ Rest by Salman's account dated 30 Nov. 1676, but £31 16s soe
mistaken 13s, by reason he charged him but £11 for his years rent ending   014 05 04
Mich 1674, when his rent was £11 13s so due at Mich. 1676   032 09 00

| | | 046 | 14 | 04 |
| 29 Nov. 1677 | Salman chargeth himselfe with | 011 | 10 | 00 |

Salman respit him in his account £31 19s soe the aforesaid
mistake of 13s stil remained, and he owe at Mich. 1677   032 12 00

| | | 044 | 02 | 00 |
| 27 Nov. 1678 | Payd me | 001 | 10 | 00 |

And then allow'd the 17 months tax for building ships ending 24 Aug
1678: 16s 2d. To the amonition rate 7d. To the 1st quarterly payment of
the tax for disbanding the army 2s 10d   000 19 07

	For thatching the houses	003	12	00
10 Dec. 1678	Salman account for	009	06	00
		015	07	07
	Rest due	028	17	05
		044	05	00
28 July 1679	Payd me	003	00	00

31 Oct. 1679	Salman charge himselfe with	005	00	00
1 Oct. 1680	Salman account for	002	18	00
10 Oct. 1681	< Salma > Smith account for	004	15	00
1 Oct. 1682	Smith account for	003	00	00
21 Oct. 1683	Salman account for a horss	004	00	00
	Elden account for	002	05	00

Thatching 10s, dawbing 9s 2d, underpining 5s 6d ... 001 04 08

Anno 1682   Working at Barber's, late in Parke's use ... 000 10 00

Payd Smith for my use 23 Nov. 1682 ... 001 10 00

Mem: Nov. 1682. Russels made over his goods and chattels to me for
security of the arrears / p. 299 / ... 028 02 08

80. Frost and Abbs his Debt (541, 64)

14 Oct. 1673	In arrear for rent ending Mich. 1673	021	03	06
	A years rent ending Mich. 1674	041	13	06
	A years rent Mich. 1675	041	13	06
	Half a years rent at Lday 1676	020	16	09
	At Mich. 1676	020	16	09
		146	04	00
30 Oct. 1676	In arrear at Mich. 1676	021	03	06
	At Lday 1677	020	16	09
	At Mich. 1677	020	16	09

➤ Frost is to have £1 abated next year ... 062 17 00

29 No: 1677	In arrear at Mich. 1677	021	03	06
	At Lday 1678	019	16	09
	At Mich. 1678	020	16	09

Frost left the ground and hired Cooke's p. 64 ... 061 17 00

10 Dec. 1678   Arrear at Mich. 1678 ... 020 15 00

Harris

At Midsummer and Christmas 1681 ... 040 00 00

1681 proved so very dry and bad a year, Mr Harris (who is lately come into
Norfolk) was not willing to hold it at £40 though he confess'd, he lost nothing.

81. Frost and Abbs his Credit (84)

16 May 1674	Payd John Salman	016	18	11
	More paid him	000	13	06
	And in tax in full ending Mich. 1673	003	11	01
20 Feb 1674	Payd Salman	038	05	00
	And in tax in full ending Mich. 1674	003	08	06
30 Nov. 1675	Payd Salman	020	10	00
30 Oct. 1676	Payd Salman	041	02	06

	Allow'd then for thatching Old Hall	000	11	00
		125	00	06
30 Oct. 1676	Rest due	021	03	06
29 Nov. 1677	Salman chargeth himselfe with	041	13	06
	And respit Frost	021	03	06
		062	17	00
10 Dec. 1678	Salman account for	038	14	07
	12 months tax at 11s 5d for 3 months	000	03	08
	Amonition	000	02	03
	6 months tax of the land in Gresham p. 84	000	01	00
		041	03	06
	Rest due	019	13	06
		061	17	00
31 Oct. 1679	Salman charge himselfe with	019	14	06
	The last 5 months of the Ship Tax	000	19	00
		020	13	06

Harris

3 Jan. 1681	Payd in his general account quarto book p. 25	040	00	00

82. Lord Yarmouth's Account (511)

16 May 1674	Salman receiv'd in full ending Mich. 1673	000	02	08
20 Feb. 1674	Salman recd in full ending Mich. 1674	000	02	08
30 Nov. 1675	Salman receiv'd in full ending Mich. 1675	000	02	08
30 Oct. 1676	Payd Salman in full Mich. 1676	000	02	08
	Clear	000	10	00
29 Nov. 1677	Payd Salman Mich. 1677	000	02	08
10 Dec. 1678	Salman account for in full Mich. 1678	000	02	08
1 Oct. 1680	Salman account for 1679	000	02	08
20 Nov. 1680	Mr Hurton payd me for 1680	000	02	08
1 Oct. 1682	Smith account for 1681	000	02	08
21 Oct. 1683	Salman account for 1682	000	02	08
25 Oct. 1684	Salman account for 1683	000	02	08
24 Nov.	Mr Hurton, Yarmouth's Steward payd	000	02	08
10 Nov. 1685	Hurton payd me for Mich. 1685	000	02	08
29 Nov. 1686	Hurton payd Fairchilde Mich. 1686	000	02	08
24 Oct. 1687	Hurton payd Stephen Legge Mich. 1687	000	02	08

83. Mr Hammond's Account (482)

16 May 1674	Salman receiv'd in full ending Mich. 1673	000	01	04
30 Oct. 1676	Mr Hammond payd Salman in full for two			

	years ending Mich. 1675	000	02	08
	In arrear by Salman's account dated 30 Oct.	000	04	00
	1676: one years rent	000	01	04
		000	05	04
29 Nov. 1677	Payd Salman in full Mich. 1676	000	01	04
10 Dec. 1678	Salman account in full of Mich. rent 1677	000	01	04
21 Dec. 1678	Foster payd me Mich. rent 1678	000	01	04
1 Oct. 1680	Salman account for 1679	000	01	04
1 Oct. 1682	Salman account for 1680 and 1681	000	02	08

84. William Frost's Account (505)

16 May 1674	Payd Salman in full of his years rent ending Mich. 1673	002	00	00
20 Feb. 1674	Payd Salman in full ending Mich. 1674	002	00	00
30 Nov. 1675	Payd Salman in full ending Mich. 1675	002	00	00
30 Oct. 1676	Payd Salman Mich. 1676	002	00	00
29 Nov. 1677	Payd Salman Mich. 1677	002	00	00
10 Dec. 1678	S. account for his rent ending Mich. 1678	002	00	00
1 Oct. 1680	Salman account for Mich. 1679	002	00	00
10 Oct. 1681	Smith account for Mich. 1680	002	00	00
1 Oct. 1682	Salman account for Mich. 1681	002	00	00
21 Oct. 1683	Salman account for Mich 1682 and 1683	002	00	00
25 Oct. 1684	Elden account for Mich. 1684	002	00	00
17 Oct. 1685	Elden account for 1685	002	00	00
13 Oct. 1686	Frost payd me for Mich. 1686	002	00	00
6 Oct. 1687	Frost sent me by John Barham Mich. 1687	002	00	00

85. Woodrow's Account (558)

16 May and 20 Feb. 1674	Salman receiv'd in full of two years rent ending Mich. 1673	000	10	00
30 Oct. 1676	Payd Salman in full Mich. 1675	000	05	00
29 Nov. 1677	Payd Salman in full Mich. 1676	000	05	00
10 Dec. 1678	S. account for his rent ending Mich. 1677	000	05	00
1 Oct. 1680	Salman account for Mich. 1679	000	10	00
1 Oct. 1682	Salman account for 1680 and 1681	000	10	00
5 July 1687	Fairchilde account for 5 years end 1686	001	05	00

86. Mr Doughtye's Debt (559, 506)

14 Oct. 1673	In arrear for < nine > *eight* years rent ending Mich. 1673	006	08	00
	A years rent ending Mich. 1674	000	16	00
	A years rent ending Mich. 1675	000	16	00
	A years rent ending Mich. 1676	000	16	00

30 Oct. 1676	In arrear as abovesaid	008	16	00
	At Mich. 1677	000	16	00
	At Mich. 1678	000	16	00
	At Mich. 1679	000	16	00
		011	04	00
	A years rent at Mich. 1681 / *p. 559* /	002	06	00
	At Mich. 1682	002	06	00
	At Mich. 1683	002	06	00
	At Mich. 1684	002	06	00
	Vide page 506	009	04	00
	A years rent at Mich 1685	002	06	00
	At Mich. 1686	002	06	00
	At Mich. 1687	002	06	00
		016	02	00

87.

1679 Upon discourse with Sir Robert Baldock, I concluded 'twas a folly to aime at recovering this rent for the Doughtye's have payd noe farme rent since 1638. And then Thomas Doughtye denyed in Chancery the having any farme ground. Sir John Windham replyed he woud prove it. I have seen some rough interrogations and a warrant dated Sep. 1640 to summon witnesses. What more was done I don't knowe. But I beleive Doughtye have 1a. 2r. of land belonging to me as antient demeanes of Metton manor for *for 1a. 2r* from 1622 to 1638 inclusive; 9s a year have constantly been payd from 1638 to 1644; 9s charged and respited *anno* 1644, the Baylye don't charge himself with the 9s for he say, page 21, the lord receive the rest of the farme rents, 1651, 1652, 1653.16s a year charged upon the landholders of Thomas Doughtye and respite: 1655, 1656. Charged by my brother's balye as in 1653 but respited, and respited all my brother's time.

9 Nov. 1685	Mr Doughtye brought me	011	10	00
12 Jan. 1686	Mr Doughtye payd me	002	06	00
13 Jan. 1687	Payd me	002	06	00
Observe: From this *vide* p. 86 when payd		016	02	00

88. Thomas Warner's Debt (554)

14 Oct. 1673	A years rent ending Mich. 1673	003	13	04
	A years rent ending Mich. 1674	003	13	04
	A years rent Mich. 1675	003	13	04
	Half a years rent at Lday 1676	001	16	08
	At Mich. 1676	001	16	08
		014	13	04
	At Lday 1677	001	16	08
	At Mich. 1677	001	16	08
		003	13	04
	At Lday 1678	001	16	08

At Mich. 1678	001	16	08
At Mich. 1679	003	13	04
At Mich. 1680	003	13	04
At Mich. 1681	003	13	04
At Mich. 1682	003	13	04
At Mich. 1683	003	13	04
	022	00	00
A years rent at Mich. 1684	003	13	04
A years rent at Mich. 1685	003	13	04
At Mich. 1686	003	13	04
At Mich. 1687	003	13	04

89. Thomas Warner's Credit

16 May 1674	Payd Salman	003	07	00
	And in tax	000	06	00
20 Feb. 1674	Payd Salman	003	07	00
	And in tax	000	06	00
30 Nov. 1675	Payd Salman	003	13	00
	And 4d yearly abated is in full Mich. 1675	000	01	00
30 Oct. 1676	Salman receiv'd	003	13	00
	And abated 4d, which is in full Mich. 1676	000	00	04
		014	13	04
29 Nov. 1677	Salman chargeth himselfe with	003	13	00
	And abated	000	00	04
		003	13	04
10 Dec. 1678	Salman account for	003	08	04
	17 months tax and amonition rate	000	05	00
31 Oct. 1679	Salman account for	003	09	10
12 months of the 18 months tax for the armye		000	03	06
10 Oct. 1681	Smith account for	003	09	10
	12 months tax 1680	000	03	06
1 Oct. 1682	Salman account for 1681	003	13	04
21 Oct. 1683	Salman account for 1682 and 1683	007	06	08
		022	00	00
25 Oct. 1684	Elden account for 1684	003	13	04
17 Oct. 1685	Elden account for 1685	003	13	04
5 July 1687	Fairchild account for 1686	003	13	04

90. Widdow Herne's Debt (532)

14 Oct. 1673	By bond dated 4 June 1673 payable 15 Oct. 1673	028	18	00

Memorandum: £5 of the £28 18s od was towards my charges of suit, which I did commence against her and her son Clement for non payment of the rent, and t'other £23 18s od was in full of rent ending Mich 1672.

	Two years rent ending Mich. 1674	007	08	00
	A years rent Mich 1675	003	14	0
	Half a years rent at Lday 1676	001	17	0
	At Mich. 1676	001	17	0
		043	14	0
30 Oct. 1676	In arrear by Salman's account at Mich. 1676	003	14	00
	At Lday 1677	001	17	00
	At Mich. 1677	001	17	00
		007	08	00
29 Nov. 1677	In arrear at Mich. 1677	003	14	00
	At Lday 1678	001	17	00
	At Mich. 1678	001	17	00
	At Mich. 1679	003	14	00
	At Mich. 1680	003	14	00
	At Mich. 1681	003	14	00

Noat: John Herne was the Widow Herne's executor and John Talbot her tenant

018	10	00

Clement Herne (532, 507)

	A years rent of 9a. 1r. of antient demeasn in Metton Mich. 1682	003	14	00
	Two years rent ending Mich. 1684 / p. 507 /	007	08	00
	A years rent at Mich. 1685	003	14	00
	At Mich. 1686	003	14	00
	At Mich. 1687	003	14	00
		022	04	00

91. Herne's Credit (92, 90)

16 May 1674	Payd Salman in full Mich. 1672	028	18	06
20 Feb. 1674	Payd Salman	006	17	06
	And in tax in full ending Mich. 1674	000	10	06
30 Nov. 1675	Payd Salman in full Mich. 1675	003	14	00
		040	00	00
30 Oct. 1676	In arrear by Salman's account	003	14	00
		043	14	00
29 Nov. 1677	Salman chargeth himselfe with	003	14	00

	And respit him	003	14	00
		007	08	00
10 Dec. 1678	Salman account for rent ending Mich. 1677	003	14	00
1 Oct. 1680	Salman account for	007	00	01½
	Tax 1679	000	07	10½
5 Oct. 1682	Mr John Talbott pay me p. 92	007	04	06
	Taxes	000	03	06
		018	10	00

/ *Vide* p. 90 /. *Memorandum:* Mr John Herne order'd me to pay Mr Windham two
years rent ending Michaelmas 1681 for nine acres and one *rood* of ground in Metton.
Witness my hand this 5 Oct. 1682. The rent being three pounds fourteene shillings a
yeare I pay [Note as to rent in Talbott's hand]
Sam Smyth John Talbott

Clement Herne

12 Dec. 1685	Mr Clement Herne brought me	014	16	00

92. Henry Smith's Debt (554, 96)

14 Oct. 1673	In arrear for rent ending Mich. 1671	005	00	00
	And two years rent ending Mich. 1673	022	00	00
	A years rent ending Mich. 1674	011	00	00
		038	00	00
20 Feb. 1674	In arrear at Mich. 1674	022	05	00
	At Lday 1675	005	10	00
	At Mich. 1675	005	10	00
	Halfe a years rent at our Lday 1676	005	10	00
	At Mich. 1676	005	10	00
		044	05	00
30 Oct. 1676	In arrear by Salman's account at Mich. 1676	029	15	02
	At Lday 1677	005	10	00
	At Mich. 1677	005	10	00
		040	15	02
29 Nov. 1677	In arrear at Michaelmas 1677	015	12	05
	At Lday 1678	005	10	00
	At Mich 1678	005	10	00

Smith left the ground and then Talbot had of it 14 acres at £7   026   12   05
< p. 266 > And Sam Smith 8 acres at £4 *per annum* / *p. 96* /

Talbot's (32, 98, 90, 280)

	A years rent of the 14 acres at Mich. 1679	007	00	00
	A years rent at Mich. 1680 / *p. 32* /	013	10	00
	And for Fosters / *p. 98* /	006	00	00

A years rent at Mich. 1681	019	10	00
At Mich. 1682	019	10	00
	065	10	00
Mr Jo Herne ordered him to pay me / p. 90 /	007	04	06

5 Oct. 1682. I accounted with Mr Windham and I doe owe him for rent ending Mich last past nineteen pounds ten shillings. Witness my hand: *Samuell Smyth John Talbott*

072	14	06

93. Henry Smith's Credit (15)

16 May 1674	Payd Salman in full ending Mich. 1671	005	00	00
20 Feb. 1674	Payd Salman	006	10	00
	And then allowed him	004	04	10
		015	14	10
20 Feb. 1674	Rest due	022	05	02
		038	00	00
30 Nov. 1675	Payd Salman	008	00	00
30 Oct. 1676	Salman receiv'd	006	10	00
		014	10	00
	Rest due by Salman's account	029	15	02
		044	05	02
29 Nov. 1677	Salman chargeth himselfe with	025	02	09
	And respit him	015	12	05
		040	15	02
10 Dec. 1678	Salman chargeth himselfe with	020	12	04
	Allow'd in taxes	000	09	02
31 Oct. 1679	Salman account for	004	12	06
		025	14	00
	Rest to ballance *vide* p. 15	000	18	05
		026	12	05

Talbot's (281)

1 Oct. 1680	Salman account for	003	02	00
	Disbursed for me	000	18	00
10 Oct. 1681	Salman account for	002	18	00
	Smith account for	007	00	00
5 Oct. 1682	Salman account for	003	00	00
	Payd me	001	13	06
	Allow'd for 4 score and 16 comb of oats	030	06	00
	4 last payments of the tax	000	16	00
	Amonition	000	00	04

Abated out of his first years rent by reason he did not hire it till after Christmas

001	00	00

Allow'd for dreyni*n*g the meadow	001	00	00
The last 3 months of the 12 months tax for land in hand in Metton	000	13	7½
Constables disbursments for 2 years ending Mich. 1681 for land in hand	000	17	0½
	053	04	06
5 Oct. 1682 Rest due	019	10	00
	072	14	06

94. Parson Taylor's Debt (540, 530, 548)

14 Oct. 1673	For eight years rent ending Mich. 1673	012	00	00
	A years rent ending Mich. 1674	001	10	00
	At Mich. 1675	001	10	00
	At Mich. 1676	001	10	00
30 Oct. 1676	In arrear as aforesaid at Mich. 1676	016	10	00
	At Mich. 1677	001	10	00
	At Mich. 1678	001	10	00
	At Mich. 1679	001	10	00
	At Mich. 1680 / *vide p. 530* /	001	10	00
	At Mich. 1681	001	10	00
	At Mich. 1682	001	10	00
	At Mich. 1683	001	10	00
		027	00	00
A years farme rent of the ground mentioned p. 548 due at Mich. 1684		001	10	00
	At Mich. 1685	001	10	00
	At Mich. 1686	001	10	00
	At Mich. 1687	001	10	00

95. Parson Taylor's Credit (94)

30 Oct. 1676 Parson Taylor is an old humoursome man, and to this day I could never get him to account				
Mich. 1678	I owe him as much for tythe and herbage	019	10	00
1 Oct. 1680	Salman account for	001	08	10½
	Tax	000	01	01½
21 Oct. 1683 Parson Taylor and I have not yet accounted but because I owe him as much for tythe and herbage, I doe hereby give him credit for		006	00	00
From this time I'll keep Parson Taylor's account of this ground p. 94		027	00	00

96. Miles Miller's Debt (558)

14 Oct. 1673	In arrear at Mich. 1673	003	09	00
	A years rent ending Mich. 1674	002	06	00
		005	15	00
30 Nov. 1675	In arrear at Mich. 1674	002	06	00
➤ From Mich. 1674 in hand. At Mich 1677 let to Sam Smith as afore				

Smith's Debt (559, 92, 86)

	Halfe a years rent ending at Lday 1678	001	03	00
	At Mich. 1678	001	03	00
	At Mich. 1679	002	06	00
And for 8 acres late in Henry Smith's use / p. 92 /		004	00	00
	A years rent at Mich. 1680	006	06	00
From Mich 1680 the land late in Miller's use is let to Mr Doughtye p. 559 / p. 86 /		014	18	00
10 Oct. 1681	Rest in arrear at Mich. 1680	002	16	00
	A years rent at Mich. 1681	004	00	00
	At Mich. 1682	004	00	00
	At Mich. 1683	004	00	00
	At Mich. 1684	004	00	00
		018	16	00
	At Mich. 1685	004	00	00
	At Mich. 1685	004	00	00

I shall owe my land lord at Mich next eight pounds two shillings for rent. Witness my hand 23 Sep. 1686

Signed before *Jo. Salman* Samuell Smith's Mark X		026	16	00
29 Sep. 1686	Smith owe me	008	02	00
29 Sep. 1687	A years rent	004	00	00

Samuel Smith wasted what he had quarrelling with his neighbours, and ran away about Mich		012	02	00

Henry Well's Debt (479)

97. Miles Miller's Credit

16 May 1674	Payd John Salman	003	03	00
	And in tax in full ending Mich. 1673	000	06	00
		003	09	00
30 Nov. 1675	Rest due to me	002	06	00
		005	15	00
30 Oct. 1676	Payd Salman	001	00	00
29 Nov. 1677	Payd Salman	001	06	00
		002	06	00

Smith's Credit (15)

10 Dec. 1678	Salman account for	002	04	00
	In taxes 1678	000	02	00
1 Oct. 1680	Salman account for	003	10	00
	Allow'd for oats	002	06	00
10 Oct. 1681	Salman account for	004	00	00
		012	02	00
10 Oct. 1681	Rest at Mich 1680	002	10	00
		014	18	00
11 Dec. 1682	Payd Smith my man	003	00	00
21 Oct. 1683	Elden account for	001	10	00
25 Oct. 1684	Elden account for	004	00	00
17 Oct. 1685	Elden account for	002	00	00
23 Sep. 1686	Allow'd Smith for 10 comb of wheat	007	05	00
	A load of straw	000	08	00
	And for the last Land Tax	000	06	00
	Abated in the years rent 1679	000	05	00
		018	14	00
	Rest	008	02	00
		026	16	00

Oct. 1687	Received from Sam Smith's house						
	2 combs 1 bushel 2 perches meslyn at 8s:	19s					
	7 combs barly at 6s:		2s	2d			
	2 combs wheat at 14s:		1s	8d			
	3 combs 3 bushels buck at 5s 6d:	£1	0s	7d ½			
	2 loads of straw at 1 at 8s and 1 at 3s:		11s		006	00	7½
	Rest to ballance p. 15				006	01	4½
					012	02	00

98. Robert Foster's Debt (558, 92)

14 Oct. 1673	In arrear at Mich. 1673	006	00	00
	A years rent at Mich. 1674	006	00	00
		012	00	00
	A years rent at Mich. 1675	006	00	00
	Halfe a years rent at Lday 1676	003	00	00
	At Mich. 1676	003	00	00
	At Lday 1677	003	00	00
	At Mich. 1677	003	00	00
		018	00	00
29 Nov. 1677	In arrear at Mich. 1677	006	00	00
	At our Lday 1678	003	00	00
	At Mich. 1678	003	00	00

		012	00	00
10 Dec. 1678	In arrear	003	18	04
	At Mich. 1679	006	00	00
Foster left the ground for Mr. Talbot's convenience p. 92		009	18	04

99. Robt Foster's Credit

16 May 1674	Salman receiv'd	005	07	06
	And in tax in full ending Mich. 1679	111	12	06
20 Feb. 1674	Salman receiv'd	005	14	00
	And in tax in full ending Mich. 1674	000	06	00
		012	00	00
30 Oct. 1676	Payd Salman Mich. 1675	006	00	00
29 Nov. 1677	Payd Salman Mich. 1676	006	00	00
	And Salman respit him	006	00	00
		018	00	00
10 Dec. 1678	Salman account for	003	00	05
	12 months tax 6s, amonition 3d	000	06	03
	10 comb of buck at 5s 4d, 10 comb at 4s 2d	004	15	00
		008	01	08
	Rest due	003	18	04
		012	00	00
21 Dec. 1678	Payd me	003	14	04
	5 last months of the 1 months tax	000	02	06
	The 1st 3 months of the 18 months tax	000	01	06
1 Oct. 1680	Salman chargeth himselfe with £4 12s 5d; buck 5 comb at £1 5s 10d	005	18	03
2nd payment of the 18 months tax 1s 6d; amonition 3d		000	01	09
		009	18	04

100. John Woodrowe's Debt (538, 334)

14 Oct. 1673	In arrear at Mich 1673	008	05	09
	At Mich. 1674	016	11	06
	A years rent ending at Mich. 1675	016	11	06
	Half a years rent at Lday 1676	008	05	09
	At Mich. 1676	008	05	09
		058	00	03
30 Oct. 1676	In arrear at Mich. 1676	008	05	09
	At Lday 1677	008	05	09
	At Mich. 1677	008	05	09
		024	17	03
29 Nov. 1677	In arrear at Mich. 1677	009	00	09
	At < Mich.> Lday 1678	008	05	09

	At Mich. 1678	008	05	09
	At Mich. 1679	016	11	06
		042	03	09
31 Oct. 1679	Owe	008	05	09
	At Mich. 1680	016	11	06
	At Mich. 1681	016	11	06
		041	08	09
31 Oct. 1684	The barne blowne downe (p. 538)			
10 Oct. 1681	Owe	008	05	09
	At Mich. 1682	016	11	06
	At Mich. 1683	016	11	06
	At Mich. 1684	016	11	06
	At Mich. 1685	016	11	06
	At Mich 1686	016	11	06

18 Feb. 1687 Mr Windham made these allowances wit [ness] Stephen
Legge to me *Thomas Woodrowe*. *Vide* p. 334   091   03   03

101. John Woodrowe's Credit (334)

16 May 1674	Salman receiv'd	006	18	00
	And in tax	000	12	00
	And by abatement in full Mich. 1673	000	15	00
20 Feb. 1674	Payd Salman	013	13	04
	And in tax	001	08	02
	And by abatement in full Mich 1674	001	10	00
30 Nov. 1675	Payd Salman in full Mich. 1675	016	11	06
£15 1s 6d in money; by abatement £1 10s od				
30 Oct. 1676	Payd Salman £7 10s 9d, abated 15s	008	05	09
		049	14	06
30 Oct. 1676	Rest due	008	05	09
		058	00	03
29 Nov. 1677	Salman chargeth himselfe with	000	01	06
	And abated him	000	15	00
	Respit	009	00	09
		024	17	03
20 Jan. 1677	In thatching 6s 8d			
10 Dec. 1678	Salman account for	016	13	08
	12 months of tax of Ships Tax	000	12	10
31 Oct. 1679	Salman chargeth himselfe with	015	19	10
	5 last months of the ship tax	000	05	03
	6 months of the 18 months for the army	000	06	05
		033	18	00
	Rest	008	05	09

		£	s	d
		042	03	09
1 Sep. 1680	Payd Smith £7 19s 4d, 6 months of the 18 months tax 6s 5d	008	05	09
1 Oct.	Salman account for £7 19s 4d, tax 6s 5d	008	05	09
10 Oct. 1681	Salman account for	008	05	09
And Smith account for £7 19s 4d, 6 mths tax 6s 5d		008	05	09
		033	03	00
	Rest	008	05	09
		041	05	09
1 Oct. 1682	Salman account for	016	11	06
21 Oct. 1683	Salman account for	016	11	06
25 Oct. 1684	Salman account for	008	05	09
17 Oct. 1685	Elden account for	012	08	06
5 July 1687	Fairchilde account for	018	11	6
10 Feb	Thomas Woodrow payd me	015	00	00
	Allow'd for 9 comb of seed barly 1684	003	03	00
	Payd me to ballance this account	000	11	06
	Vide p. 334	091	03	03

102. Peter Abbs his Debt (42, 505)

14 Oct. 1673	In arrear at Mich. 1673	004	01	00
	A years rent at Mich. 1674	004	01	00
	A years rent at Mich. 1675	004	01	00
	Half a years rent at Lday 1676	002	00	06
	At Mich. 1676	002	00	06
		016	04	00
	At Lday 1677	002	00	06
	At Mich. 1677	002	00	06
		004	01	00
	At Lday 1678	002	00	06
	At Mich. 1678	002	00	06
	At Mich. 1679	004	01	00
	At Mich. 1680	004	01	00
	At Mich. 1681	004	01	00
		016	04	00
Mich 1682	For a years rent of this ground £4 1s ⎫			
	And for the ground late R. Abbs 9 1s ⎬ /42/	013	02	00
	A years rent at Mich. 1683 / 505 /	013	02	00
	At Mich. 1684	013	02	00
	At Mich. 1685	013	02	00
	At Mich. 1686	013	02	00
	A years rent at Mich. 1687	013	02	00

15 Dec. 1687 I accounted with Mr Wyndham and this is a true account
of my rent and payments. Witness my hand. *Peter Abbs*   078   12   00

103. Peter Abb's his Credit

16 May 1674	Payd Salman	003	19	00
	And in tax in full Mich. 1673	000	02	00
20 Feb. 1674	Payd Salman	003	16	00
	And in tax in full Mich. 1674	000	05	00
30 Nov. 1675	Payd Salman in full Mich. 1675	004	01	00
30 Oct. 1676	Payd Salman Mich. 1676	004	01	00
		016	04	00
29 Nov. 1677	Salman chargeth himselfe with	004	00	00
	6 months tax	000	01	00
		004	01	00
10 Dec. 1678	Salman account for	003	19	01
	11 months tax 1s 10d, amonition 1d	000	01	11
31 Oct. 1679	Salman account for	003	19	00
	12 months of the Army Tax 1679	000	02	00
10 Oct. 1681	Smith account for 1680	004	01	00
21 Dec	Payd Salman 1681	004	01	00
		016	04	00
1 Oct. 1682	Salman account for	004	10	06
21 Oct. 1683	Salman account for 1682	008	11	06
25 Oct. 1684	Elden account for 1683	013	02	00
17 Oct. 1685	Elden account for 1684	013	02	00
12 Dec.	Elden account for 1685	013	02	00
5 July 1687	Fairchilde account for 10 comb of mault at			
	6s 8d, and 30 comb at 7s	013	16	08
2 Aug. 1687	Mr Abbs by account of mault	000	12	00
15 Dec.	Mr Abbs payd me	011	15	04
		078	12	00

104. Widdow Feiser's Debt (540)

14 Oct. 1673	In arrear at Mich. 1673	001	10	00
	A years rent at Mich. 1674	003	00	00
	A years rent at Mich. 1675	003	00	00
	Halfe a years rent at our Lday 1676	001	00	00
	At Mich. 1676	001	00	00
		010	10	00
	At Lday 1677	001	10	00
	At Mich. 1677	001	10	00
		003	00	00

At Lday 1678	001	10	00
At Mich. 1678	001	10	00
At Mich. 1679	003	00	00
At Mich. 1680	003	00	00
At Mich. 1681	003	00	00
At Mich. 1682	003	00	00
At Mich. 1683	003	00	00
	018	00	00
A years rent at Mich. 1684	003	00	00
At Mich. 1685	003	00	00
At Mich. 1686	003	00	00
At Mich. 1687	003	00	00
	012	00	00

105. Widdow Feiser's Credit (104)

16 May 1674	Payd Salman	001	07	10
	And in tax in full at Mich. 1673	000	02	02
20 Feb 1674	Payd Salman	002	15	08
	And in tax in full at Mich. 1674	000	04	04
30 Nov. 1675	Payd Salman in full Mich. 1675	003	00	00
30 Oct. 1676	Payd Salman Mich. 1676	003	00	00
		010	10	00
29 Nov. 1677	Salman chargeth himselfe with	002	18	10
	6 months tax 1677	000	01	02
		003	00	00
10 Dec. 1678	Salman account for	002	17	10
	11 moneths tax 1678	000	02	02
31 Oct. 1679	Salman account for 1679	002	17	08
	12 months of the 18 months tax for the army	000	02	04
10 Oct. 1681	Smith account for	002	17	08
	12 months tax 1680	000	02	04
1 Oct. 1682	Salman account for 1681	003	00	00
14 Oct.	Payd Smith 1682	003	00	00
21 Oct. 1683	Salman account for 1683	003	00	00
		018	00	00
20 Oct. 1684	Robert Feaser payd me 1684	003	00	00
4 Nov. 1685	He payd me £2 19s 10d½, amonition 1d½	003	00	00
23 Nov. 1686	Payd me	003	00	00
13 Oct. 1687	Payd me in full at Mich. 1687	003	00	00
Hereafter I'll keep an account of this farm on the other side p. 104		012	00	00

106. Dawson's Account (545)

16 May and	*Memorandum:* his rent is 8s *per annum*			
20 Feb. 1674	Payd Salman in full Mich. 1674	000	16	00
30 Nov. 1675	Payd Salman in full Mich. 1675	000	08	00
29 Nov. 1677	Payd Salman Mich. 1676	000	08	00
10 Dec. 1678	Salman account for his rent Mich. 1677	000	08	00
31 Oct. 1679	Salman account for hs rent at Mich. 78	000	08	00
1 Oct. 1680	Salman account for 1679	000	08	00
21 Oct. 1682	Salman account for 1680 and 1681	000	16	00
21 Oct. 1683	Salman account for 1682	000	08	00
25 Oct. 1684	Salman account for 1683	000	08	00
Dec 1686	William Dawson payd in salt fish 3 years rent ending Mich. 1686	001	04	00

107. Nicholas Dawson's Account (545)

	His rent is 7s 6d			
16 May 1674	Payd Salman in full Mich. 1674	000	15	00
30 Nov. 1675	Payd Salman in full at Mich. 1675	000	07	06
29 Nov. 77	Payd Salman Mich. 1676	000	07	06
10 Dec. 1678	Salman account for rent ending Mich. 1677	000	07	06
31 Oct. 1679	Salman account for his rent at Mich. 1678	000	07	06
1 Oct. 1680	Salman account for 1679	000	07	06
10 Oct. 1681	Salman account for 1680	000	07	06
1 Oct. 1682	Salman account for 1681	000	07	06
21 Oct. 1683	Salman account for 1682	000	07	06
25 Oct. 1684	Salman account for 1683	000	07	06
12 Dec. 1685	Elden account for 1685	000	15	00

108. John Barker's Account. (558)

16 May and	From 14 October 1673 12s *per annum*			
20 Feb. 1674	Payd Salman in full Mich. 1674	001	04	00
30 Nov. 1675	Payd Salman in full Mich. 1675	000	12	00
29 Nov. 1677	Payd Salman Mich. 1676	000	12	00
10 Dec. 1678	Salman account in full Mich. 1678	001	04	00
1Oct. 1680	Salman account for 1679	000	12	00
1 Oct. 1682	Smith account for 1680 and 1681	001	04	00
25 Oct. 1684	Salman account for 1682	000	12	00
28 Mar. 1685	David Trasye who married Barker's widdow	006	00	00
payd me by bill of carpenter's worke, two years rent at Mich. 1684		001	04	00

Mem: Trasy gave me a note dated 7 Feb. 1687 to pay me five shillings a fortnight until the six and thirty shilling which is doe to me bee payd. And then Rook hired the same.

109. Flint's and Smith's Account (481)

Memorandum:	20 Feb 1674: Rest in arreass				
	30 Nov. 1675: more	1s			
	30 Oct. 1676: more due	1s			
	At Mich. 1677: more due	1s			
	At Mich. 1678: more due	1s			
10 Dec. 1678	Salman account for the said	7s	000	07	00
1 Oct. 1680	Salman account for		000	01	00
21 Oct. 1683	Salman account for		000	01	00

18 Feb 1687 Thomas Woodrowe payd me by the order of Nat Smyth of
Runton seven shilling for 7 years rent ending Mich. eighty seven. Witness
his hand *Thomas Woodrow*   000   07   00

110. Johnson and Elis's Account (481)

16 May and	From 14 October 1673 4d *per annum*			
20 Feb. 1674	Payd Salman in full Mich. 1674	000	00	08
30 Nov. 1675	Payd Salman in full Mich. 1675	000	00	04
30 Oct. 1676	Payd Salman Mich. 1676	000	00	04
29 Nov. 1677	Payd Salman Mich. 1677	000	00	04
10 Dec. 1678	Payd Salman Mich. 1678	000	00	04
31 Oct. 1679	Payd Salman Mich. 1679	000	00	04
10 Oct. 1681	Smith account for Mich 1680	000	00	04
1 Oct. 1682	Salman account for 1681	000	00	04
4 Oct.	Elis payd Smith Lday 1682	000	00	04
21 Oct. 1683	Salman account for Lday 1683	000	00	04
25 Oct. 1684	Elden account for Lday 1684	000	00	04
21 Dec. 1686	Stephen Legg received at Runton Court	000	00	04

111. Richard Kilbye's Account (481)

16 May and	From 14 October 1673 3s *per annum*			
20 Feb 1674	Payd Salman in full Mich. 1674	000	06	00
30 Oct. 1676	Payd Salman at Mich. 1676	000	06	00

Harvy is tenant to the said 3s *per annum*. Elvin of Norwich   000   12   00
is Harvy's executor

31 Oct. 1679	Salman account for Mich. 1677 and 1678	000	06	00
10 Oct. 1681	Salman account for Mich. 1679 and 1680	000	06	00
21 Oct. 1683	Salman account for 3 years 1681, 1682, 1683.	000	09	00

Mem: He receiv'd the said 9s of Mr Elvin

112. Frost and Lowne's Debt (544, 534/5, 228)

Memorandum: Frost and Lowne entered at Mich 1673
Crome paid for this farme £47 3s 8d *per annum* and 2 capons.

	A years rent at Mich. 1674	037	00	00
	A years rent at Mich. 1675	037	00	00
	Halfe a years rent at our Lday 1676	018	10	00
	At Mich. 1676	018	10	00
		111	00	00
30 Oct. 1676	Rest in arrear at Mich. 1676	018	10	00
	At Lday 1677	018	10	00
	At Mich. 1677	018	10	00
		055	10	00
29 Nov. 1677	Owe at Mich. 1677	018	10	00
	At Lday 1678	018	10	00
	At Mich. 1678	018	10	00
	At Mich. 1679	018	10	00
	At Mich. 1680	018	10	00
From Mich 1680 Lillye hire this farm /534/5/		129	10	00

Memorandum: 20 Feb. 1681. Frost and Lowne payd me £5 for not leaving the houses and fences in repayre.

	A years rent at Mich. 1681	037	00	00
	At Mich. 1682	037	00	00

113. Frost and Lowne's Credit (288)

20 Feb. 1674	Payd Salman	010	15	10
	And by bills	008	14	02
30 Nov. 1675	Payd Salman in full Mich. 1674	008	10	00
	More payd	016	11	09
	And then allowed < for ditching worke > *stet*	001	18	03
3 Jan. 1675	Payd my selfe	016	00	00
	And by bill of repaires full Mich. 1675	002	10	00
30 Oct. 1676	Payd Salman	018	10	00
		092	10	00
	Rest to ballance	018	10	00
		111	00	00
29 Nov. 1677	Salman chargeth himselfe with	036	10	00
Allow'd him for knight service to the manour of Sextens, and bringing deales		000	10	00
		037	00	00
	Respit him	018	10	00
		055	10	00
10 Dec. 1678	Salman account for	017	10	06

		£	s	d
	6 months tax 1677	000	19	06
31 Oct. 1679	Salman account for	034	17	02
	The last 11 months of the Ship Tax	001	16	00
	Tax for the manour	000	01	1½
	Amonition	000	01	8½
	For serving at the Sherifs turne 1678	000	04	00
3 July 1680	Payd me	010	03	06
12 months of the 18 months tax for disbanding the army		001	18	08
	Repayrs	000	13	10
	Two services at the Sherifs turne 1679	000	04	00
1 Oct.	Salman account for 1679	024	00	00
10 Oct. 1681	Smith account for	006	00	00
15 Dec. and Feb. 1 Frost payd me		028	14	10

		£	s	d
12 months tax	£1 18s 8d			
Amonition	2s 6d			
Sherifs turne	4d	002	05	02
		129	10	00

		£	s	d
10 Oct 1681	Smith account for	010	00	00
1 Oct. 1682	Salman account for	033	10	00
	Allow'd for repayring the houses	£2 4s 0d		
	Fences *silicet* wet £3 9s 2d,			
	Dry £1 12s:	£5 1s 2d	007	05	02
	Sherifs turne 1681	000	05	00
		051	00	02
	Rest	022	19	10
		074	00	00

114. Henry Grime's Debt (544)

		£	s	d
14 Oct. 1673	By bond dated 7 Nov. 1672:			
	payable 25 March 1673	022	12	04
	And halfe a years rent ending Mich. 1673	008	10	00
	A years rent Mich. 1674	017	00	00
	A years rent Mich. 1675	017	00	00
	Half a years rent at our Lday 1676	008	10	00
	At Mich. 1676	008	10	00
		082	02	04
30 Oct. 1676	In arrear at Mich. 1676	036	07	04
	At Lday 1677	009	00	00
	At Mich. 1677	009	00	00
	For forbearance of the £22 12s 4d	005	10	00
		059	18	02

William Ives's Debt (544, 115, 324)

		£	s	d
	Halfe a years rent at Lday 1678	008	10	00
	At Mich. 1678	008	10	00
	At Mich. 1679	017	00	00
	At Mich. 1680	017	00	00
	At Mich. 1681	017	00	00
	At Mich. 1682	017	00	00
	At Mich. 1683	017	00	00
		102	00	00
21 Oct. 1683	Owe me by p. 115	049	04	4½
	A years rent at Mich. 1684	018	00	00
		067	04	4½
	At Mich. 1685	018	00	00
		085	04	4½
	At Mich. 1686	018	00	00
I charge him £2 more, because I enter'd his rent in 1682		103	04	4½
and 1683 but £17 *per annum* when by the Articles		002	00	00
11 Oct 1667 it should have been £18		105	04	4½

115. Henry Grime's Credit

		£	s	d
16 May 1674	Payd Salman	007	12	04
	And in tax in full Mich 1673	000	17	08
20 Feb . 674	Payd Salman	012	00	00
30 Nov. 1675	Payd Salman	002	17	02
	And in repayres	002	02	10
	In money in full Mich. 1674	005	00	00
30 Oct. 1676	Payd Salman	015	05	00
		045	15	00
➤ 30 Oct. 1676: In arrear by Salman's account		013	15	00
	And by bond mentioned on the other side	022	12	04
		082	02	04
29 Nov. 1677	Salman chargeth himselfe with	018	10	00
	Allow'd a bill of repayres	004	08	02
20 Aug. 1677: I tooke Capon's and Bells's bond payable Christmas and				
Lady 1678 in full satisfaction of Grim's debt.		037	00	00
6 Apr. 1678	Payd Salman in full	059	18	02

Ives's Credit (135, 325)

		£	s	d
10 Dec 1678	Salman account for	003	00	00
31 Oct. 1679	Salman charge himselfe with	005	00	00
1 Oct. 1680	Salman account for	010	00	00

	Allow'd taxes for this farme and the mannour of Tuttington ending 24 Nov. 1679	002	08	11½
	Repayring houses and fences	004	04	08
10 Oct. 1681	Smith account for	008	00	00
1 Oct. 1682	Salman account for	009	12	00
26 Dec.	Payd Smith	005	03	06
	Repayrs	000	06	06
21 Oct. 1683	Salman account for	11~~j~~	~~00~~	~~00~~
		052	15	7½
	Repayrs £1 17s 6d. Rest due to me	049	04	4½
		102	00	00
25 Oct. 1684	Salman account for	019	02	08
	Salman allow'd a bill about repayres in 1683 Note 8s of it at Lyllye's	002	17	04
17 Oct. 1685	Elden account for	006	00	00
20 Mar. 1685	Elden account for	005	00	00
15 Sep. 1686	Ives payd me	000	00	10
	Allow'd him about the houses and fences	016	03	07
		049	04	05
15 Sep 1686	Ives gave me bond for	056	00	00
This is a true account *William Ives vide* p. 135		105	04	05

116. Searle's Debt (538, 288)

14 Oct. 1673	In arrear at Mich. 1673	002	00	00
	A years rent ending Mich. 1674	001	00	00
	A years rent ending Mich. 1675	001	00	00
	At Mich. 1676	001	00	00
Memorandum: Salman say Frost and Lowne did promise to		005	00	00
pay this £5 for Searle did not cut any of the alders during his time.				
	At Mich. 1677	001	00	00
	At Mich. 1678	001	00	00
	At Mich. 1679	001	00	00
	At Mich. 1680	001	00	00
	Lillye hired the Severals at Mich 1680	009	00	00
	A years rent at Mich. 1681	001	00	00
	At Mich. 1682	001	00	00

117. Searle's Credit (288)

10 Dec. 1678	Salman account for 1677	006	00	00
1 Feb. 1681	William Frost of Gresham payd me	003	00	00
		009	00	00
Observe. I doe here give Lilly credit for £2 because I charge him with the		002	00	00

118. William Parke's Debt (542,119, 268)

14 Oct. 1673	In arrear at Mich. 1672		011	10	00
	And a years rent at Mich. 1673		085	00	00
	A years rent at Mich. 1674		085	00	00
	A years rent at Mich. 1675		085	00	00
	Halfe a years rent at our Lday 1676		045	00	00
	At Mich. 1676		045	00	00
			356	10	00
30 Oct. 1676	In arrear at Mich. 1676		048	00	00
	At Lday 1677		045	00	00
	At Mich. 1677		045	00	00
1677 Parke is rated to the 17 months for building ships:			138	00	00
siciliet in	Albye	£0 18 6d			
	Colbye	2s 9d quarterly			
	Erpingham	7d			
(*Vide* the lease 542)		£1 1s 10d			
29 Nov. 1677	Owe at Mich. 1677		046	00	00
	At Lday 1678		040	00	00
	At Mich. 1678		040	00	00
			126	00	00
	Halfe a years rent at Lday 1679		045	00	00
	At Mich. 1679		045	00	00
	At Mich. 1680		090	00	00
Receiv'd and allow'd since 9 July 1679 /*p. 119*/		£135	180	00	00
Rest due to me at Mich. 1680		£045			
1679, 1680 I disbursed for repayrs £6 1s 6d		£180			

119. William Parke's Credit

16 May 1674	Payd Salman	008	0	11
	And in tax in full ending Mich. 1672	003	03	01
	And in money	046	00	00
20 Feb. 1674	Payd Salman in full ending Mich 1673	039	00	00
	And	061	16	03
	And in tax and bills in full ending Mich. 1674	023	03	09
30 Nov. 1675	Payd Salman	075	10	00
30 Oct. 1676	Payd Salman	050	11	04
	And in repayres	000	18	08
		308	10	00
	Rest due	048	00	00
		356	10	00
29 Nov. 1677	Salman chargeth himselfe with	085	10	00

	Allow'd a bill of thatching	£5 16s		
	14 Jan. 1676 and in ditching	14s	006	10	00

➤ Noat: *anno* 1677: I payd £4 6s more for repayring this

farme	Respit	092	00	00
		046	00	00
		138	00	00
9 Jan. 1677	Payd me	028	00	00
27 May 1678	Payd me	020	00	00
6 Aug. 1678	I received of Parke	015	00	00
	And then allow'd for repayres	010	00	00

And the 5 first quarterly payments of the 17 months tax for

building ships		005	09	02
	For several things sent to Felbrigg	003	01	00
28 Nov. 1678	Payd me	017	00	00
22 Feb. 1678	Payd me	026	11	04
	The last 2 months of the said 17 months tax	000	14	08
	Amonition rate	000	03	10
	Anno 1678 I disbursed £2 11s in repayres	126	00	00
10 July 1679	Parke payd me	013	14	4½

And then allow'd the 3 first quarterly payments of the 18

months tax for disbanding the army and other uses		003	05	7½
31 Oct. 1679	Salman charge himselfe with	028	00	00
7 Nov. 1679	Parke payd me	016	00	00
20 Jan. 1679	Payd me	022	00	00
1 Oct. 1680	Salman account for	020	00	00
	Payd me	020	11	09

3 last payments of the said 18 months tax.

And 6 months supply £5 9s 4d. Amonition 4s 3d		005	13	07
	Repayrs	005	11	08

120. John Richman's Debt (538, 314)

14 Oct. 1673	In arrear a years rent ending at Mich. 1673	005	00	00
	A years rent ending Mich. 1674	005	00	00
	A years rent ending Mich. 1675	005	00	00
	Halfe a years rent at our Lday 1676	002	10	00
	At Mich. 1676	002	10	00
		020	00	00
30 Oct. 1676	In arrear at Mich. 1676	002	10	00
	At Lday 1677	002	10	00
	At Mich. 1677	002	10	00
		007	10	00
29 Nov. 1677	Owe at Mich. 1677	002	10	00

	At Lday 1678	002	10	00
	At Mich. 1678	002	10	00
	At Mich. 1679	005	00	00
		012	10	00
31 Oct. 1679	Owe	007	08	1½
	At Mich. 1680	005	00	00
		012	08	1½
1 Oct. 1680	Owe	005	00	00
	At Lady 1681 / 538l	003	10	00
	At Mich. 1681	003	10	00
	At Mich. 1682	007	00	00
	At Mich. 1683	007	00	00
		026	00	00
5 Mar. 1683	Richman acknowledg'd to owe clear	002	10	00
	A years rent at Mich. 1684	007	00	00
	At Mich. 1685	007	00	00
	At Lady 1686	003	10	00
	Vide p. 314	020	00	00

121. John Richman's Credit (*quarto book* 45, 315)

16 May 1674	Payd John Salman	002	10	00
	And in tax	000	07	04
20 Nov. 1675	Payd Salman in full ending Mich. 1675	002	02	08
	And	001	10	04
	And in tax	000	03	08
30 Oct. 1676	Payd Salman	009	16	00
	And repayres	001	00	00
		017	10	00
	Respit	002	10	00
		020	00	00
29 Nov. 1677	Salman chargeth himselfe with	005	00	00
	Respit him	002	10	00
		007	10	00
29 June 1678	Payd me 1677	002	10	00
And then allow'd the 2 years first payments of the Ship				
Money ending Mich. 1677		000	01	10
7 Jan. 1678	Payd me	002	06	06
	4 last payments of the Ship Tax	000	03	6½
		005	01	10½
	Rest	007	08	1½
8 June 1680	Payd me	002	06	5½
	18 months tax for disbanding the army	000	05	06

	Amonition rate	000	00	02
1 Oct.	Salman account for	004	16	00
	1680 repayrs £4 12s 9d,	007	08	1½
	1681 more 2s. Rest	005	00	00
		012	08	1½

Oct. 1682	I had 3 cows of Richman at	006	00	00
21 Oct. 1683	Salman account for	003	00	00
5 Mar. 1683	Richman payd me	116	10	00

And then I allow'd him £5 for soe much payd Sheppard
about Mich 1682 /quarto p. 45/   005   00   00
And for 58 rods of ditching at Shepherd's in Albye.   001   09   00
                    Repayring the houses £1 1s 11d,
                    and glasing his own farme 7s   001   08   11
Amonition and the 6 months supply to disband the army   000   02   01
                                                         023   10   00
                    Rest   002   10   00
                                                         026   00   00

24 June 1684	Payd me	003	10	00
2 Feb	Payd me	003	10	00
7 Oct. 1685	Elden account for	003	10	00
2 Mar. 1685	Elden account for	003	10	00
	Vide p. 315	013	10	00

122. John Allison's Debt (535, 509)

14 Oct. 1673	In arrear for rent due at Mich. 1673	005	15	00
	A years rent ending Mich. 1674	011	10	00
		017	05	00
	A years rent at Mich. 1675	011	10	00
	Halfe a years rent at Lday 1676	005	15	00
	And at Mich. 1676	005	15	00
	At Lday 1677	005	15	00
	At Mich. 1677	005	15	00
		034	10	00
29 Nov. 1677	Owe at Mich. 1677	005	15	00
	At Lday 1678	005	15	00
	At Mich. 1678	005	15	00
	At Mich. 1679	011	10	00
		028	10	00
31 Oct. 1679	Owe	006	10	00
	At Mich. 1680	011	10	00
	At Mich. 1681	011	10	00
Richard Harding is tennant at Mich 1681 /p. 509/		029	10	00

A years rent ending Mich. 1682		011	10	00
At Mich. 1683		011	10	00
A years rent at Mich. 1684		011	10	00
At Mich. 1685		011	10	00
Half a years rent Lady 1686		005	15	00
At Mich 1686		005	15	00

30 Sep 1686. I owe Mr Windham for rent twenty nine pounds fiveteen shillings ten pence. Witness my hand.   057 10 00
X Harding's mark. Signed before *Stephen Legge*

30 Sep. 1686	Harding owe	029	15	10
29 Sep. 1687	A years rent	011	10	00

123. John Allison's Credit

16 May 1674	Payd Salman	005	02	06
	And in tax in full at Mich. 1673	000	12	06
20 Feb. 1674	Payd Salman	010	11	03
	And in tax in full ending Mich. 1674	000	18	09
		017	05	00
30 Nov. 1675	Payd Salman	005	15	00
30 Oct. 1676	Payd Salman	011	10	00
29 Nov. 1677	Payd Salman	011	10	00
	Allow'd for repayres	000	05	00
		029	00	00
	Respit	005	10	00
		034	10	00
10 Dec. 1678	Salman account for	010	16	11½
12 months tax to Aylesham 12s 6d. Amonition 6 d½		000	13	0½
31 Oct. 1679	Salman account for	009	18	07
	The five last months of the Ship Tax	000	05	03
	6 first months of the Armye Tax	000	06	03
		022	00	00
	Rest	006	10	00
		028	10	00
5 July 1680	Payd	005	08	1½
	6 months tax	000	06	03
	Amonition	000	00	7½
1 Oct.	Salman account for	005	08	8½
	Tax	000	06	3½
10 Oct. 1681	Salman account for £6 10s ⎫			
	Smith account for £5 15s ⎭	012	05	00
1 Oct. 1682	Salman account for	005	15	00
		029	10	00

1 Oct. 1682	Salman account for	004	00	00
March 1682	Elden receiv'd of Harding and payd the same to Smith	005	12	06
	Allow'd 7s 6d for gates	000	07	06
21 Oct. 1683	Elden account for	003	00	00
25 Oct. 1684	Elden acount for	002	15	00
17 Oct. 1685	Elden account for	010	00	00
30 Sep. 1686	Allow'd Harding for fences	000	08	00
	Amonition 2 years	000	01	02
	Abated the first year	001	10	00
		027	14	02
	Rest	029	15	10
		057	10	00
8 Nov. 1686	Payd me	010	00	00
July 1687	Fairchilde account for	003	05	00

124. John Black's Debt (542, 262)

14 Oct. 1673	In arrear at Mich. 1673	021	07	00
	A years rent at Mich. 1674	037	07	00
	Halfe a years rent ending Lday 1675	018	13	06
	And halfe a year ending Mich. 1675	018	13	06
	Halfe a years rent at our Lday 1676	018	13	06
	At Mich. 1676	018	13	06
		133	08	00
30 Oct. 1676	In arrear at Mich. 1676	018	13	06
	At Lday 1677	018	13	06
	At Mich. 1677	018	13	06
		056	00	06
29 Nov. 1677	Owe at Mich. 1677	019	07	00
	At Lday 1678	018	13	06
	At Mich. 1678	018	13	06
Noat: This farme is rated to the ship tax: *silicet* in		056	14	00

Colby		6s	4d
Erpingham		4d	10s 7d quarterly
Ingworth		3s	3d
Aylesham		8d	

10 Dec. 1678	In arrear	018	12	10
	At Mich. 1679	037	07	00
		055	19	10

125. John Black's Credit (124, 263)

20 Feb. 1674	Payd Salman	014	18	00
	And in tax in full ending Mich. 1673	006	09	00

	And in money	034	00	00
	And in tax in full ending Mich. 1674	003	07	00
28 Apr. 1675	Payd to my selfe in full Lday 1675	018	13	06
30 Oct. 1676	Payd Salman	037	00	10
	And then allowed him	000	06	02
		114	14	06
30 Oct. 1676	Rest	018	13	06
		133	08	00
29 No: 1677	Salman chargeth himselfe with	036	13	06
	I respit him	019	07	00
		056	00	06
10 Dec. 1678	Salman account for	035	05	2½
	12 months tax at 10s 7d quarterly p. 124	002	02	04
	Amonition	000	01	11½
	Allow'd him for keeping a stray heifer	000	07	02
And serving 3 times at the sherife's turne. Noat the last time in Oct. 1677		000	04	06
		038	01	02
	Rest	018	12	10
		056	14	00
29 July 1679	Accounted with Black and then he did bring an acquittance signed by Salman 27 Feb. 1678 for	017	14	05
And for the 5 last months of the 17 months tax for building 30 ships		000	16	11
	And for serving at the Sherifs turne	000	01	06
	Payd me this day	017	03	00
And for the 2 first quarterly payments of the 18 moneths tax for disbanding the army		001	01	00
	For serving at the Sherif's turne Mich. 1678	000	01	06
	Allow'd him towards two gates	000	08	00
28 Oct. 1679	Payd me	017	10	06
Allow'd 3rd and 4th quarterly of the 18 months tax for disbanding the army		001	01	00
	Serving at the Sherifs turne, and Leet Fee	000	02	00
		055	19	10

126. Sexton's Debt (548, 510, 286)

14 Oct. 1673	In arrear for rent ending Mich. 1673	015	00	00
	A years rent ending Mich. 1674	030	00	00
		045	00	00
	A years rent ending Mich. 1675	030	00	00
	Halfe a years rent at our Lday 76	015	00	00
	At Mich. 1676	015	00	00

		060	00	00
30 Oct. 1676	In arrear at Mich. 1676	015	00	00
	At Lday 1677	015	00	00
	At Mich. 1677	015	00	00
➤ Noat: Greenacre enter'd at our Lady 1677 at £34 *per annum* / *548* / soe		002	00	00
		047	00	00
29 Nov. 1677	Owe at Mich. 1677	017	00	00
	At Lday 1677	017	00	00
	At Mich. 1677	017	00	00

Noat: the mill is rated to the Ship Tax: *scilicet* in: 051   00   00

Ingworth	7s 3d ½
Aylesham	6d quarterly
Blicklyn	6d
	8s 3d ½

At Mich. 1679		034	00	00
For the ballance of the account 10 Dec. 1678		023	00	00
At Mich. 1680		034	00	00
At Mich. 1681		034	00	00

13 Feb. 1681. Wee accounted with Mr Windham, and there rest clear due
to him at Mich last £30 15s

William X Greenacre William X Greenacre		125	00	00
	Owe	030	15	00
	At Mich 1682	034	00	00
	Greenacre left the Mill / *510* /	064	15	00

127. Sextan's Credit (210, 286)

16 May 1674	Payd Salman	012	13	04
	And in tax in full ending Mich. 1673	002	06	08
20 Feb. 1674	Payd Salman	027	10	00
	And in tax in full ending Mich. 1674	002	09	03
		045	00	00
30 Nov. 1675	Payd John Salman	028	02	08
	Allowed in repayres in full Mich. 1675	001	17	04
30 Oct. 1676	Payd Salman	008	05	06
	And then allowed	006	14	06
		045	00	00
30 Oct. 1676	In arrear	015	00	00
		060	00	00
29 Nov. 1677	Salman chargeth himselfe with	020	10	01
	Allow'd him	000	09	11
		030	00	00
	Respit him	017	00	00

		£	s	d
		047	00	00
10 Dec. 1678	Salman chargeth himselfe with	024	12	2½
Allow'd 17 months Ship Tax 7s 9d ½ – 3 months		002	04	02
	Amonition	000	01	08
	In repayres	000	15	07
	17 months tax of my Rents of Assise	000	06	4½
➤ It cost me £2 3s 6d this sumer to repayre the wharf		028	00	00
against the pool./ 210 / . Rest		023	00	00
		051	00	00
31 Oct. 1679	Salman account for	038	04	04
	12 months of the 18 months tax for the army	001	11	02
	The same for my rents of assise	000	04	06
1 Oct	Salman account for	015	15	2½
	6 months tax for the manour	000	17	10
	Amonition	000	01	9½
	Repayres 1679	000	05	02
10 Oct. 1681	Salman account for	022	02	02
	6 months tax	000	17	10
13 Feb	Payd Salman since 10 Oct.	014	05	00
		094	05	00
	Rest at Mich 1681	030	15	00
		125	00	00
1 Oct. 1682	Salman account for	007	13	01
	And I had a cow of him at	002	05	00
	Repayrs	000	01	11
16 Oct. 1682	A bill of sale of several goods and chattels,			
	which Johnson and Barnes bought	014	16	10
	A milstone which Sexton bought	004	00	00

128. Thomas Mack's Debt (535, 558, 276)

14 Oct. 1673	In arrear for rent ending Mich. 1672		023	05	00
	And at Mich. 1673		033	05	00
	A years rent at Mich. 1674		033	05	00
	A years rent *and a ½ * at Lday 1676		049	17	06
	Halfe a years rent atMich 1676		016	12	06

➤ Noat: at Mich 1675, Mack hired the ground, which Thomas Smith
then left (and was formerly in Springall's use) at £1 5s od *per annum* ... 156 05 00

30 Oct. 1676	In arrear for his old farme	£59 15s			
	And for Springall's	1 15s	061	10	00
	At Lday 1677		017	10	00
	At Mich. 1677		017	10	00
	/ Lease 558 /		096	10	00

29 Nov. 1677	Owe at Mich. 1677	056	16	05
	At Lday 1678	017	10	00
	At Mich. 1678	017	10	00
		091	16	05
10 Dec. 1678	In arrear	050	13	02
	At Mich. 1679	035	00	00
	At Mich. 1680	035	00	00
		120	13	02
1 Oct. 1680	Owe	054	07	08
	At Mich. 1681	035	00	00
Mack died about Christmas 1680.		089	07	08

129. Thomas Mack's Credit (277, *quarto book* p. 20)

16 May 1674	Payd John Salman	020	00	00
20 Feb 1674	Payd Salman in full Mich. 1672	003	05	00
	And	011	15	00
	And in tax and bills	010	05	00
30 Nov. 1675	Payd Salman in full ending Mich. 1673	011	04	10
	And more	011	00	00
30 Oct. 1676	Payd Salman	029	00	00
		096	10	00
30 Oct. 1676	Rest due	059	15	00
		156	05	00
29 Nov. 1677	Salman chargeth himselfe with	039	13	07
	And respit him	056	16	05
1675 and 1676.	It cost me in repayres £4 4s 4d	096	10	00
1 July 1678	I allow'd Mack £3 3s 8d in full of all			
	disbursments to this day (except taxes)	003	03	08
28 Oct.	Receiv'd of Mack	010	00	00
And then allow'd the 5 quarterly, and 2 moneths payments				
for building ships		002	01	6½
	And the amonition rates	000	01	7½
10 Dec. 1678	Salman account for	025	16	05
		041	03	03
	Rest	050	13	02
		091	16	05
3 March 1678	Payd me	014	00	00
11 June 1679	Payd me	008	00	00
31 Oct. 1679	Salman account for	011	00	00
4 June 1680	Mack paid me	006	00	00
	18 months tax for disbanding the army	002	04	00
	Amonition rate	000	01	06

	Repayrs	001	00	00
1 Oct	Salman account for	024	00	00
	1679 Repayres £1 15s 6d	066	05	06
	Rest	054	07	08
		120	13	02
24 June	Salman account for	034	00	00
	Allow'd by me for 3 months tax	000	06	08
30 June 1681	Mack's son and administrators made me a			
	bill of sale of goods etc for	036	11	00
/ 227, vide quarto p. 20 /		070	17	08

130. John Winter's Debt (556, 560, 300)

14 Oct. 1673	In arrear for rent ending Mich. 1672	025	00	00
	And a years rent ending Mich. 1673	032	00	00
	A years rent ending Mich. 1674	032	00	00
	A years rent ending Mich. 1675	032	00	00
	Halfe a years rent at Lday 1676	016	00	00
	At Mich 1676	016	00	00
		153	00	00
30 Oct. 1676	In arrear at Mich. 1676	052	00	00
	At Lday 1677	016	00	00
	At Mich. 1677	016	00	00
		084	00	00
29 Nov. 1677	In arrear at Mich. 1677	056	00	00
	At Lday 1678	016	00	00
	At Mich. 1678	016	00	00
		088	00	00

Winter woud not seal a lease, therefore I turn'd him out
Plummer hire this farme from Mich 1678 / 560 /

10 Dec. 1678	Winter owe	010	00	00
	Plummer at Mich. 1679	030	00	00
	At Mich. 1680	030	00	00
		070	00	00
1 Oct. 1680	Owe	035	00	00
	At Mich. 1681	032	00	00
	At Mich. 1682	032	00	00
	At Mich. 1683	032	00	00
	Vide p. 300	131	00	00

131. John Winter's Credit (301)

16 May 1674	Payd John Salman	010	00	00
20 Feb. 1674	Payd Salman in full ending Mich. 1672	015	00	00
	And	005	17	08

	And in tax	006	02	04
30 Nov. 1675	Payd Jo. Salman	016	00	00
30 Oct. 1676	Payd Salman	038	08	07
	And then allowed in repayres	003	11	05
➤ At Mich 1673: I promised to abate 40s yearly till times mended: soe paid		006	00	00
		101	00	00
30 Oct. 1676	Rest due	052	00	00
		153	00	00
29 Nov. 1677	Salman chargeth himselfe with	026	00	00
	Abated the last year	002	00	00
	Respit by Salman's account	056	00	00
		084	00	00
28 May 1678	Receiv'd of Winter at Felbrigg	010	00	00
28 June	Receiv'd	020	00	00
10 Dec. 1678	Salman account for	043	03	06
12 months tax at 6s 3d in Dilham, 6d Worstead		001	07	00
	Thatching £1 18s 2d, mason worke 11s 4d	002	09	06
	Abated	002	00	00
		078	00	00
	Rest	010	00	00
		088	00	00
31 Oct. 1679	Salman receiv'd of Winter	009	15	04
Allow'd him the two last months of the Ship Tax		000	04	06
	Of Plummer	003	05	06
17 Dec. 1679	Payd me	007	06	05
	12 months of the 18 months armye tax	001	07	00
	Repayrs	003	01	01
1 Oct. 1680	Salman account for	010	00	00
1679	Repayres £3 5s 8d	035	00	00
	Rest	035	00	00
		070	00	00
10 Oct. 1681	Salman account for	017	16	00
	A bull sould August last for	001	02	06
1 Oct. 1682	Salman account for	006	00	00
26 Dec.	Payd Smith	008	00	00
21 Oct. 83	Elden account for	007	00	00
Anno 1681	Disbursed by two bills *scilicet:*	005	19	00
The 1st bill:for 12 months tax £1 7s 0d; amonition 1s 4d; repayrs £4 10s 8d. The 2nd bill p. 301		045	17	06
	Rest	085	02	06
		131	00	00

132. Thomas Smith's Debt (555, 292)

In arrear 14 Oct. 1673 for rent ending Mich. 1672		031	00	00
And 5 years for a farme late Springall's Mich. 1673		008	15	00
	A years rent of both farmes Mich. 1674	013	15	00
	A years rent of both farmes Mich. 1675	013	15	00
	Halfe a years rent at our Lday 1676	006	17	06
	At Mich. 1676	006	17	06
		081	00	00
30 Oct. 1676	In arrear at Mich. 1676	044	05	00
	At Lday 1677	006	00	00
	At Mich. 1677	006	00	00
		056	05	00
29 Nov. 1677				
31 Oct. 1679	Owe	055	08	08
	At Mich. 1680	012	00	00
	At Mich. 1681	012	00	00
	At Mich. 1682	012	00	00
		091	08	08

133. Thomas Smith's Credit (292)

16 May 1674	Payd Salman in full Mich 1671	007	00	00
	And	003	00	00
30 Nov. 1675	Payd Salman	015	00	00
30 Oct. 1676	Payd Salman	010	00	00
		035	00	00
	Respit by Salman's account upon Smith but for he respit	044	05	00
Thomas Mack a years rent of Springall's ending Mich 1676				
(as appears by page 128 of the booke)		001	15	00
		081	00	00
14 June 1679	Smith did bring a receipt under Salman's hand dated 6 March 1676	003	10	00
Paid the subsidye by 4 quarterly payments ending 23 Feb. 1671		000	07	00
Paid the tax by 6 quarterly payments ending 3 Sep. 1674		001	08	00
For 42 pound of clover seed deliver'd 18 March 1672		001	11	06
		006	16	06
	Rest	049	08	06
		056	05	00
By Smith's and Bush's bond 8 Nov. 1677 for £39 18s 6d payable at several days				
25 March	Smith payd me	005	15	00

1678	2 first payments of the Ship Mony	000	04	08
27 Sep. 1678	Payd me	005	15	06
	3rd and 4th payments of the Ship Monye	000	04	08
31 Oct. 1679	Salman account for	005	16	00
	the five last months of the Ship Tax	000	04	00
		017	19	10
	Rest	055	08	08
	1680	073	08	06
1 Oct. 1688	Salman account for	031	10	08
	12 months of the 18 months army tax	000	09	04
10 Oct. 1681	Salman account for	005	00	00
	15 Nov. 1681 Bush payd me	010	00	00
1 Oct. 1682	Salman account for	012	00	00
30 Nov.	Bush payd me	005	00	00
1 Dec.	Smith's widow payd Salman	005	00	00
About 10 Dec. she came to know what woud satisfie me		069	00	00

before she woud administer, I tould her £10 *Vide* 292

134. Hugh and John Windham's account of their payments (543)

9 Dec. 1669. Then payd H. Windham £45 in monye. And then he allow'd me £3 for 3 years rent of the moyety of the manour of Dilham, ending Mich 1669, and £12 for the Royall aide in full of a rent charge of £20 per annum for 3 years ending at Mich. 1669	060	00	00
19 Dec. 1671. Then paid H. W. £38, and the he allow'd me £2 for 2 years rent as aforesaid ending Mich. 1671	040	00	00
13 Feb. 1672. Then payd H. W. £18 which with £2 allowed me *scilicet* £1*for one years rent and £1 for the late subsidye is in full of the rent charge ending Mich. 1672	020	00	00
18 Feb. 1674. Payd H. W. £32 which with £6 allowed me for the 18 months tax and £2 for 2 years rent of the moyety of Dilham was in full of 2 years rent (issuing out of divers lands) due Mich. 1674	040	00	00
29 No 1675. Paid H. W £18 which (with £1 allowed me as aforesaid) is in full of his rent ending Mich 1675	020	00	00
➤ Noat: I payd to the use of John Windham eldest sonn of Wadham £152 with £28 allowed me for rent and taxes as is mentioned in H. Windham's acquittances, is in full of 9 years rent ending Mich. 1675 as by several acquittances under the hand of Mr John Lowe	180	00	00
Hereafter *vide* acquittances			

135. (115)

	Ives gave me his bond for /p. 115/	056	00	00
5 July 1687	Fairchilde account for £5 and for 20 comb of oats £4	009	00	00

136. Edmond Bale's Debt (545, 184)

		£	s	d
14 Oct. 1673	In arrear for rent ending Mich. 1672	008	03	04
	And a years rent ending Mich. 1673	036	11	00
	A years rent ending Mich. 1674	036	11	00
	A years rent ending Mich. 1675	036	11	00
	Halfe a years rent at Lday 1676	018	05	06
18 June 1676	For £5 10s which was twice allowed	005	10	00

➤ 18 June 1676: my account was examined, and all my disbursements allowed, soe rest clear due for rent ending at

		£	s	d
Lday last £31 4s 7d Witness my hand: *Edmund Bale*		141	11	10
	Due as above at Lday 1676	031	04	07
	Halfe a years rent at Mich. 1676	018	05	06
Receiv'd out of the profits of the Widdow Scipper's farme		008	12	10

14 Feb. 1676: my account was examined all my disbursements

		£	s	d
and demands allow'd to the day aboves'd. *Edmund Bale*		058	02	11
	Halfe a years rent at < Mich. > Lday 1677	018	05	06
	At Mich. 1677	018	05	06
		036	11	00

21 Dec. 1677: my account was examined and all my disbursments allow'd to this day, soe rest clear due to Mr Windham at Mich. 1677. Witness

		£	s	d
my hand *Edmund Bale*		012	15	10

➤ turne to p. 184

137. Edmond Bale's Credit (172, 192, 184)

		£	s	d
16 May 1674	Payd Salman in full Mich. 1672	008	03	04
	and	001	16	08
20 Feb. 1674	Payd Salman	017	00	00
30 Nov. 1675	Payd Salman	010	00	00
	And allowed in part of a bill in full Mich. 1673	007	14	04
	more in money	006	00	00
	And allowed by bill	017	18	01
1676	Payd Salman	017	10	00

18 June 1676 Bale was at Felbrigg and I did then allow as *per* bill £18 13s 5d for repayring the mill; £1 4s 5d fencing the woods; £1 15s 2 years Quit Rents end Mich. 1675; £2 his sallary; £9 5s 6d butter and cheese; £1 4s peas;

		£	s	d
2s 6d hollyberries		024	04	10
		110	07	03
	Rest to ballance	031	04	07
		141	11	10

14 Feb. 1676 Bale was with me at Cosen Talbot's, and I did then allow
as by bill £18 17s 10d for repayring the mill; 7s 9d fencing the woods; 12s
5d to the King's Manour and to Hingham end Mich. 1676; £2 his
sallary; £7 10s for cheese £1 16s 6d acorns / *p. 172* /   031   04   06

	Bale disburs'd since Mich. upon the account		
	of the Widdow Scipper's farme / *p. 192* /	026	18	05
		058	02	11
29 Nov. 1677	Salman chargeth himselfe with	005	00	00
11 Dec. 1677	Bale was at Felbrigg, and did then allow by			
	bill of repayres about the mill, and woods	001	11	03

1677 For two years rent to the manour of Hemnall Mich.

		10	2	
For one year to the King's		2	8	
For one year to Hingham		9	9	
		1	2	7	001 02 07

£	s	d					
23	15	2	For the 1st quarterly payments of the tax for Hoods and				
			the Dry Close	5	10		
12	15	10	For rents of Assize and the woods	3	2½		
36	11	00	Deepham Pitle 2d ½;				
			Grounsel Wood 1 8d	1	10½		
			For the 2nd quarterly payment	10	11	001	01	10
			For cheese			009	17	06
			Butter			005	02	00
			Respit £12 15s 10d			023	15	02

138. Martin Norton's Debt (545)

14 Oct. 1673	In arrear for rent ending Mich. 1673	013	06	08
	A years rent ending Mich. 1674	026	13	04
	A years rent ending Mich. 1675	026	13	04
➤ *Memorandum*: Norton *anno* 1677 payd me £2 in		066	13	04

satisfaction of wood formerly fell'd without order, and £2 towards
repayres he ought to have done by covenants. Salman's account: 29 Nov.
1677

John Jake's Debt (545, 137, 302)

	Halfe a years rent at Lday 1676	013	06	08
	At Mich. 1676	013	06	08
➤ *Anno* 1677 I layd out repayring this farme £27 11s 03d / 137 /		026	13	04
	At Lday 1677	013	06	08
	At Mich. 1677	013	06	08
		026	13	04
29 Nov. 1677	Owe at Mich. 1677	008	13	04

	At Lday 1678	013	06	08
	At Mich. 1678	013	06	08
	At Mich. 1679	026	13	04
		062	00	00
31 Oct. 1679	Owe	006	13	04
	At Mich. 1680	026	13	04
	At Mich. 1681	026	13	04
	At Mich 1682	026	13	04
	At Mich 1683	026	13	04
	Vide p. 302	113	06	08

139. Martin Norton's Credit (303)

16 May 1674	Payd Salman	012	07	06
	and in tax in full Mich. 1673	000	19	02
20 Feb 1674	Payd Salman	023	10	00
30 Nov 1675	Payd Salman in full Mich. 1674	003	03	04
	more payd him	006	16	08
30 Oct. 76	Payd Salman	016	00	00
Nov. 1676	Payd Gould of Wiklewood to my use	001	14	06
	And then allowed him in taxes etc 1675	002	02	02
➤	Gould payd Salman the £1 14s 6d: *vide* Salman's			
	account: 29 Nov. 1677	066	13	04
30 Oct. 1676	Payd Salman	008	00	00
13 Feb 1676	Payd Salman Mich. 1676	018	13	04
		026	13	04
29 Nov. 1677	Salman chargeth himselfe with the £18 13s 4d			
	stet receiv'd 13 Feb. 1676	018	00	00
	And Salman respit Jakes	008	13	04
		026	13	04

Noat: 12s 0d of the 1 11 3 which I allow'd Bale 21 Dec.
1677 (p. 137) was for this mill. And 1 2 0 of the 43 16 3
(p. 195), 14s I paid towards scouring a ditch.

10 Dec. 1678	Salman account for	020	05	3½
17 months for building 30 ships of war 1 7 2. Amonition 10½		001	08	0½
15 Jan. 1678	paid Marke my grome	012	00	00
31 Oct. 1679	Salman account for	020	13	09
	17 months of the 18 months tax for the armye	000	09	07
	Thatching the cart-house	000	10	00
		055	06	08
	Rest	006	13	04
		062	00	00
1 Oct. 1680	Salman account for	005	02	09

	Allow'd for a ferkin of butter 1679	001	01	00
	6 months tax 1679	000	09	07
10 Oct. 1681	Smith account for	014	00	00
1 Oct. 1682	Smith account for	022	06	07
	1 ferkin of butter sent 1680	001	00	00
	12 moneths tax 19s 2d. Amonition 11d	001	00	01
	Repayres	000	06	08
	Payd Mr Harris	026	13	04
21 Oct. 1683	Elden account for	013	12	05
	Amonition *anno* 1682	000	00	11
		085	13	04
	Ballance is	027	13	04
		113	06	08

140. Francis Marshall's Account (482)

	From 14 Oct. 1673 3s 4d *per annum*			
20 Feb. 1674	Salman receiv'd in full ending Mich. 1673	000	03	04
30 Nov. 1675	Salman receiv'd in full ending Mich. 1674	000	03	04
31 Oct. 1679	Salman account for Mich. 1677	000	10	00
10 Oct. 1681	Smith account for 1678 and 1679	000	06	08
1 Oct. 1682	Smith account for 1681 and1682	000	06	08

141. Kett's Account (510)

	4d *per annum*			
	Owe for 16 years ending at Mich. 1681	000	05	04
	more at Mich. 1682	000	00	04
	At Mich. 1683	000	00	04
	At Mich. 1684	000	00	04
	At Mich. 1685	000	00	04

➤ 17 Oct. 1685. Elden account twelve shillings four pence
receiv'd of Mr Neave by the Widdow Kett's order for 37
years of the ground mentioned p. 510 ending Mich. 1684   000 12 04
Note: when I charg'd 16 years arrear at Mich. 1681 I supposed
it payd in my brother's time

A years rent Mich. 1685	4d	
Two years more Mich. 1687	8d	

142. Francis Gould's Debt (547, 551, 242)

14 Oct. 1673	In arrear at Mich. 1673	030	00	00
	A years rent at Mich. 1674	060	00	00

➤ *Memorandum:* In Oct. 1673: Gould did promise before Watts and Salman in Felbrigg kitching to hold his farme 3 years from Mich. 1674 (being allowed £10 out of his old rent the 1st yeare)

A years rent according to this agreement due at Mich. 1675	050	00	00
Halfe a years rent at Lday 1676	030	00	00
And at Mich. 1676	030	00	00
	110	00	00
At Lday 1677	030	00	00
At Mich. 1677	030	00	00
Lease 55l	060	00	00
At Lday 1678	030	00	00
At Mich. 1678	030	00	00
	060	00	00
At Lday 1679. *Vide* p. 242	030	00	00

143. Francis Gould's Credit

16 May 1674	Payd Salman	027	14	00
	And in tax in full ending Mich. 1673	002	06	00
20 Feb 1674	Payd Salman	049	07	09
	And in tax	004	12	02
	And in repaires in full Mich. 1674	006	00	01
		090	00	00
30 Nov. 1675	Payd John Salman	020	00	00
25 Oct. 1676	Payd me Mich. 1675	030	00	00
30 Oct.	Payd Salman Mich. 1676	060	00	00

➤Noat: £4 3s 8d of the last £60 was allow'd in repayres.

	Vide Salman's account: 30 Oct. 1676	110	00	00
	Gould payd Bale p. 192	025	00	00
29 Nov. 1677	Salman chargeth himselfe with	031	12	04

Allow'd the charge of building a new butterye   2   13s   8d

	A court diner 14s	003	07	08
1678		060	00	00
18 June	Gould payd Marke my grome	012	00	00
2 Aug. 1678	Payd me at Norwich	009	14	10

And then allow'd the first quarterly payments of the Ship Money ending

25 March 1678 at 11s 6d a quarter	002	06	00

For 20 rod of new paling £2 6s 8d, and 12 rod of old paling

16s, and 32 pound of nayles 12s, 4 pair of hooks and eyes 2s 6d.	003	17	02
For 2 loads of straw carryed to Crownethorp this summer	001	04	00

	A court diner	000	18	00
10 Dec. 1678	Salman account for	021	11	08
	5 months tax for building ships	000	19	02
	Paid for straw and thatching at Crownethorp	001	07	08

	Mich. court diner	000	10	00
1st payment of the tax for disbanding the army		000	11	06
	Abated by agreement p. 551	005	00	00
		060	00	00
7 May 1679	Sent me to Chapple feild	020	00	00
7 Aug. 1679	Payd me	008	06	00
	Allow'd the 2nd and 3rd quarter payments of the tax for dishanding the army	001	03	00
	Paid for thatching at Crownethorp	000	11	00
		003	00	00

144. Osborne's Account

	From 14 Oct. 1673			
16 May 1674	Salman receiv'd < in full > Mich. 1673	000	18	02
	And in tax in full	000	01	10
20 Feb. 1674	Salman receiv'd	000	18	04
	And in tax in full Mich. 1674	000	01	10
30 Nov. 1675	Payd Salman in full Mich. 1675	001	00	00
29 Nov. 1677	Payd Salman in full Mich. 1677	002	00	00
10 Dec. 1678	Payd Salman 19s 5½; taxes, 8 months 6½ [d] in full Mich. 1678	001	00	00
		006	00	00
31 Oct. 1679	Salman account for 0 19 2 and 12 months tax 10[d] 1679	001	00	00
10 Oct. 1681	Smith account for 19 4; tax 8d 1680	001	00	00
1 Oct. 1682	Smith account for 19 4	001	00	00
27 [Oct.]	Payd Mr Harris 1682	001	00	00
25 Oct. 1684	Elden account for 1683	001	00	00
23 Nov. 1685	Osborne payd me at Gould's 1684 and 1685	001	00	00
16 Nov. 1686	Osborne payd Watts who brought it 22 Dec.	001	00	00
1 Nov. 1687	Payd Mr Watts	001	00	00

146. Widdow Skipper's Debt (538)

Memorandum: 9 October 1673: Skipper did bring me two bills £53 6s 5d of which I may justly except against £26 18s 5d by the covenants in her lease, but if it is bee all allowed, she does owe in clear money

14 Oct. 1673	For rent ending Mich. 1673	240	01	01
	A years rent ending Mich. 1674	127	06	08
	Halfe a years rent ending Lday 1675	063	13	04
		431	01	01
25 March	In arrear for rent ending Lday 1675	331	01	01
1675	½ a years rent ending at Mich. 1675	063	13	04
	Halfe a years rent at Lday 1676	063	13	04
	And halfe a years rent at Mich. 1676	063	13	04

	522	01	01

> Noat: in the bill of sale there were eight Scotch steers valued to me at £24 which she had sould to Peter Austen of Windham before, and receiv'd the monye for them, soe by law they were his, and I delivered them, for which I debtor her this

	024	00	00

Crownethorp Farme Loss (194, 195, 147)

The particulars in the bill of sale. *Imprimus*: the neat beasts valued at to me £93 15s of which 8 steers valued at £24 were sould before, as is expressed at the foot of the

1.	Widow Scipper's account soe came to me but	069	15	00
2.	Horse beasts	020	00	00
3.	Sheep £15 4s, swine £6 10s	021	14	00
4.	Winter corne £66, barly £40	106	00	00
5.	Oates £6 15s, peas and fetches £6 10s	013	10	00
6.	Hay £30, turnops £10, somerlyes £10 4s	050	04	00
7.	Cheeses	008	14	00
8.	Utensells of husbandry £8, household goods £29 14s 1d: Pewter £2 10s in all £40 1 4	040	01	04

Noat: I don't give my farme credit (p. 195) for soe much as the beasts improved no. 1, p. 147, because the farme (p. 194) is not charged with soe much as I left by the sale of the goods (p. 147) no. 8, which were used upon the farme till Mich. 1677

	330	01	01

147. Widdow Skipper's Credit (194)

16 May 1674	Payd Salman	035	00	00
20 Feb. 1674	Payd Salman	055	00	00
	And in tax	010	00	00
		100	00	00
25 March 1675	Rest due to me	331	01	01
25 Nov. 1675	Payd Salman	090	00	00
30 Oct. 1676	Payd Salman by his account	058	00	00
	And by the said account	020	00	00

> Skipper by bill of sale dated 29 Sep. 1676 did sell and deliver to Salman for my use as many goods and chattels mentioned in an inventory as was valued at

	354	01	01
From Mich. 1676 to 1677 (p. 194)	522	01	01

Crownethorp Farme Profit (192)

An account how the inventorye was disposed on by Bale's account 21 Dec. 1677. The neat beasts remayn'd on the

1.	premises to stock the farme, and sould *anno* 1677	075	04	06
2.	The horse beasts sould for	019	15	00
3.	Sheep £17 13s, swine £6 10s	024	03	00

4.	Winter corne 61 7 6, barly 39 9 6	100	17	00
5.	Oats £7, peas and fetches spent 6 15 0	013	15	00
6.	Hay and turnops spent upon the farme The somerlyes used *anno* 1677	050	04	00
7.	The cheeses	008	14	00
8.	The goods were used *anno* 1677 upon the farme, and sould for 31 7 9, besides more goods at Crownethorp 3	034	07	09
		327	00	03
	Lost by this account	003	00	10
➤ Page (192) see how this £327 00 3d was satisfied me		330	01	01

148. Tenants in Suffolke Debt (149, 150, Suffolke Leases 547, 549)

20 Jan. 1680	By Henry Houseman's account they were in arrears for rent ending at Mich. 1670	060	15	11
	A years rent ending Mich. 1671	215	00	00
	and for Rents of Assize	015	05	10
	A years rent ending Mich. 1672	215	00	00
	and for Rents of Assize	015	05	10
	A years rent ending Mich. 1673	215	00	00
	And for Rents of Assize	015	05	10
	A years rent ending Mich. 1674	215	00	00
	And for Rents of Assize	015	05	10
	Sum is	981	19	03
22 March 1674	Rest by Henry Houseman's account for farme rents and Rents of Assize ending Mich. 1674	170	13	03
	And upon John Nobbes who is run away	004	10	00

Memorandum: Salman is to account for two years rent of 1 acre late
Widdow Nimon's seised Mich. 1672 and let to

William Peppar for 10s *per annum*. / *149* /		001	00	00
	Farme rents and Rents of Assize for halfe year ending Lday 1675	115	07	11
	For halfe a year at Mich. 1675	115	07	11
	And at Lday 1676	115	07	11

More from William Peppar because he is to pay for Nicholl's

his farme £17 *per annum* from Mich 1675		001	00	00
	At Mich. 1676	116	07	11
		639	14	11
	Anno 1675, abated *scilicet*.			
	Houseman [£]10 in £83			

Keeble Rob	8 in £48 *per annum*
Auldred	2 in £30
	20

30 Oct. 1676:	they owe at Mich. 1676	356	18	09
	Brought to account page (150)			

149. Suffolke Credit (148)

	£	s	d
From 20 Jan. 1670 to 22 March 1674			
I have receiv'd out of the farme rents and Rents of Assize	581	00	00
And allowed for taxes	038	05	11
And in repaires	095	12	07
And in Lords rent	006	12	00
And for a fine to the manour of Bramfeld	001	06	08
And the charge of Thomas Copey	000	12	00
And for 5 court diners	005	00	00
And for 4 years sallarye to H. Howseman	012	00	00
And I have abated Robert Keeble these 4 last years £8 *per annum*	032	00	00
And H. Auldred these two last years	004	00	00
And Henry Howseman *in* these three years	030	00	00
allowed Houseman for charging himselfe more then he did really owe me	000	06	10
	806	06	00
22 March 1674 Rest to ballance	175	03	03
	981	19	03
30 Nov. 1675 Salman charge himselfe to hav receiv'd of Houseman upon account at thrice	100	00	00
12 Apr. 1676 Receiv'd of J. Mault for the upper mill	004	00	00
Of William Peppar	003	00	00
Payd my selfe upon account	029	00	00
30 Oct. 1676 Salman charge himselfe with	087	00	00
Allowed the several tenants in repayres as by Howseman's account dated 8 Oct. 1676	032	02	02
And in Lords rent	001	13	00
for 2 court diners	002	00	00
By way of abatement as *per* p. 148	020	00	00
The Muster Master	000	01	00
And one years sallarye ending Mich 1675	003	00	00
And of Salman for the rent of the one acer mentioned on t'other side	001	00	00
	282	16	02
30 Oct. 1676 Rest to ballance	350	18	09

Noat: £5 16s 8d of the said £32 2s 2d was towards rebuilding the bridge. And 13 7 0 of it for the lower mill and 7 5 0 for the upper mill. The rest layd out upon the other farmes

	639	14	11

150. Suffolke Debt (149, 224)

30 Oct. 1676	(Page 149) in arrear at Mich. 1676		356	18	09

Noat: Salman bring the £17 which he received 8 Nov. 1676 to account 30 Nov. 1677

Anno 1676 abated *scilicet:* £

Houseman	[£]10 in 83	
Keeble Rob	8 in 48	*per annum*
Auldred	2 in 30	
	20	

20 Feb. 1676	Rest upon the tenants at Mich. 1676		203	18	10
And farme rents	and Rents of Assize Lday 1677		116	07	11
	At Mich. 1677		116	07	11
			436	14	08
29 Nov. 1677	Owe at Mich. 1677		337	14	08

A particular of the rents: *Anno* 1678

Houseman	[£]80
Keeble Rob	48
Keeble Thomas	18
Auldred	30	*per annum*
Arterson	21
Peppar	17
½ acre seised	00 10
Quit rents	15 5 10
	229 15 10

5 March 1677.	Rest by Salman's account		217	07	08
	➣ turne to 224				

151. Suffolke Credit (225)

	Payd Salman *per* receipt 8 Nov. 1676		017	00	00
	20 Feb. 1676 payd to me in mony		087	00	00
	And by 6 ferkins of butter		006	00	00
	Allowed in repayres		015	14	11
	In Lords rent issuing out of my estate		001	13	00
	To the militia		001	12	00
	Sallarye and 1 court diner		004	00	00
	By abatements to all the tenants		020	00	00
20 Feb. 1676	Receiv'd and allowed		152	19	11
	Rest upon Nobb's by Houseman's account ending at Mich 1676 }	4 10 0	203	18	10
	An upon the severall tenants *per* his account		356	18	09
	end Mich. 1676	198 8 10			

	An more upon Peppar for 2 years rent of the 1 acre late seised		1 0 0	
			203 18 10	
15 July 1677	I receiv'd of Mr Houseman	039	00	00
12 Nov. 1677	Sent me a bill charg'd on Mr Stephen Stillinghurst in London for	060	00	00
		099	00	00
	The ballance	337	14	08
		436	14	8
5 March 1677	Houseman was at Felbrigg and paid	082	00	00
Repayring the two mills 10 9 0, and Houseman's farme 1 1 0		011	10	00
Lords rent issuing out of my estate Mich. 1677		001	13	00
The first four quarterly payments of the tax for building 30 ships of war		010	00	06
Abated Rob Keeble 8 in £48 and H. Houseman 3 in £83		011	00	00
	A court diner £1, sallarye £3 Mich. 1677	004	00	00
	7 years coppyhold rent of land seised	000	03	06
		120	07	00

5 March 1677	Rest due from the farmes	£198 13 0	217	07	08
	From copphyhold tenants	12 14 8	337	14	08
	And upon Peppar for 3 years of land seised by me	1 10 0			
	Upon Nobbs as by Houseman's account for 1672	4 10 0			
		217 7 8			

➤ turne to 225

152. Robert Kingsberry's Debt (546, 161, 154)

	Four years rent ending Mich. 1674	720	00	00
The 18 months tax come to £3 5s 9d every 3 months				
16 April 1675	In arrear at Mich. 1674	090	00	00
	And at Lday 1675	090	00	00
	A years rent at Lday 1676	180	00	00
	For the corne Reynols sould me by bill of sale *vide* page 161	007	00	00
		367	00	00
15 April 1676	In arrear at Lday 1676	100	00	00
	At Mich. 1676	090	00	00
	At Lday 1677	090	00	00
	At Mich. 1677	090	00	00
		370	00	00
29 Nov. 1677	Owe at Mich. 1677. *Vide* p. 154	211	00	00

153. Robert Kingsberry's Credit (155)

From 16 Feb. 1671 to 30 Dec. 1674 payd in money	423	04	02
And in taxes	023	08	00
And in repairs	116	14	06
And to Mr Nicolls for serving the cure of the church of Brunden five years ending Mich. 1674	066	13	04
Receiv'd and allowed	630	11	00
16 April 1675 Rest to ballance	090	00	00
	720	00	00
14 April 1676 I was at Brunden and did then take a receipt dated 21 May 1675 of	100	00	00
And 21 Feb. 1675 – both paid Mr Fowle	060	00	00
And for the Militia Tax	000	07	00
To Mr Nicols for serving the cure Mich. 1675	013	06	08
Paid Jo Harwold in part of the worke he did at Brunden Mill 8 March 1675	019	00	00
And in repayres about Brunden farme house. And by a bill of worke about the repayring of the mill *anno* 1675	000	16	00
	015	04	00
Payd Jo Harwold more in part of the worke he did to Brunden Mill	007	00	00
15 April 1676 Payd to me	051	06	08
	267	00	00
Rest in arrear at Lday 1676	100	00	00
	367	00	00
16 Apr. 1676 Payd John Harwold carpenter in part of a bill of worke about the mill for which £33 paid by John Kingsberry he have given me a receipt for £66	033	00	00
Allowed Jo Harwold for worke about this farme 35 14 1			
17 Nov. 1676 Payd Fowle by Mr Parish	050	00	00
9 June 1677 Payd Fowle by Mr Parish	076	00	00
	159	00	00
29 Nov. 1677 Rest	211	00	00
	370	00	00
12 Dec. 1677 Payd Fowle by Mr Golden	080	00	00
22 Feb. 1677 Robert Kingsberry was at Felbrigg 25 March 1677 and did then bring a receipt under Thomas Wotton's hand for £80 payd Mr Fowle	080	00	00
Vide p. 155	160	00	00

154. Robert Kingsberry's Debtor (546, 215, 278)

29 Nov. 1677	Page 152 at Mich. 1677	211	00	00

5 March 1677: my account was examined and there doe rest clear due
to my land lord at Mich. 1677 £12

Witness my hand *Robart Kingsberry*

5 March 1677	Owe as above under his hand	012	00	00
	At Lday 1678	090	00	00
	At Mich. 1678	090	00	00
	At Mich. 1679	180	00	00
	At Mich. 1680	180	00	00
	At Lday 1681	090	00	00
		642	00	00
	Since 21 May 1678 the miller payd him	059	00	00
	/ 215 /	681	00	00

30 April 1681: my account was examined and all payments and
disbursments allow'd soe rest due at Lday £108 9 0 *Robart Kingsberry*

	Rest as above	108	09	00
	At Mich. 1681	090	00	00
	At Mich. 1682	180	00	00
		378	09	00

155. Robert Kingsberry's Creditor (153, 279)

	Brought from p. 153	160	00	00

5 March 1677 Allowed Kingsberry which he paid Mr Nicols

for serving the Cure of Brunden two years ending Mich. 1677		026	13	04
	For the two first payments of the tax for			
	building ships ending Mich. 1677	003	07	00

Payd Harold carpenter for building the carthouse *anno* 1676 2 15, nayles				
about the carthouse 7 6, potts to the old carthouse 2		005	02	06
	Allow'd for bricks used at Brunden	002	05	10
	Carriage to the mill; *anno* 1676	000	16	00
5 March 1677	Payd them	199	00	00
	Rest due	012	00	00
		211	00	00

21 May 1678	I was at Brunden and Rob Kingsberry paid			
and then I allow'd the 3rd and 4th quarterly payments of the Ship Money		008	12	04

Memorandum: I promised Mrs Kingsberry 1000 bricks for to pave the wash-

house. He had 3 trees worth about £2 set out for his use about the farme		001	04	00
13 Dec. 1678	Parish payd Fowle	110	00	00
28 Oct. 1679	Turner payd Briggs	090	00	00

Memo: 30 April 1681. I came to Brunden and tooke in these

		£			
receipts *scilicet*:					
15 May 1679		55			
30 Apr. 1680 Payd Fowle		88			
4 Feb.		100			
15 Apr.		60	303	00	00
Parson Nicol's 3 years ending Mich. 1680			040	00	00
5 last months of 17 months Ship Tax			001	10	04
10 months tax to disband the army			010	03	00
6 months supply to disband the army			003	07	08
			572	11	00

30 April 1681	Rest due	108	09	00
		681	00	00

3 Sep. 1681	Payd Fowle £80. Noat he had the £20 the miller's wife payd me May 1681	060	00	00
15 Dec.	Payd Fowle £60	060	00	00
3 Mar.	Payd Fowle £70 of which the miller payd Robert Kingsberry £29	041	00	00
		161	00	00

156. John Kingsberry's Debt (546, 158)

1 Oct. 1670	In arrear for rent ending Mich 1669	014	18	10
30 Dec. 1674	Five years rent ending Mich. 1674	922	00	00

Memorandum: the 6 last years I did abate £10 *per annum* of

		936	18	10

the rent in the lease: / *vide 546* /

The 18 months tax comes to £4 12s in 3 months.

30 Dec. 1674	In arrear for rent ending Mich. 1674	055	02	02
	A years rent ending Mich. 1675	184	08	00
30 Dec. 1674	Rest to ballance his account of the crop of Brunden farme	039	10	11
	Halfe a years rent at Lday 1676	097	04	00

16 A[pril]. 1676 Noat: J. K say he have paid Fowle £50 in money to my use, for which he have noe receipt; therefore I did not give him credit

for it 16 A[pril] 1676	376	05	01

➤ 10 Oct. 1676. I did credit J. K. for the aforesaid £50

16. A[pril].	In arrear at Lday 1676	163	12	00
1676	Halfe a years rent at Mich 1676	097	04	00

Memorandum: 10 October 1676 I promised John Kings £10 upon condition

he would lay out £20 more in building houses for making of bricks.	260	16	00

10. Oct. 1676	In arrear at Mich. 1676	194	08	00
	At Lday 1677	097	04	00
	At Mich 1677	097	04	00
	Vide p. 158	388	16	00

157. John Kingsberry's Credit (159)

From 1 Oct. 1670 to 30 Dec. 1674 payd in money to my use	781	05	10
In taxes	035	06	08
And in repaires	057	04	02

Memorandum: I allow'd him for the service his brother
William Kingsberry did me in looking after the crop of Brunden farme

anno 1670	008	00	00
Receiv'd and allowed	881	16	00
30 Dec. 1674 Rest to ballance	055	02	02
	936	18	10

16 April 1676 I was at Brunden and did then allow of £94 paid Mr Fowle 21 M[*arch*] 1675	094	00	00
And more paid Mr Fowle 21 F[*eb*]. 1675	065	00	00

16. A[*pril*] 1676 And this *day* payd to me

more for by his discharge under my hand dated 29 or 30 Dec	020	00	00

1674 it was express'd but £94 due to me, when I did debtor

him [£]94 13 1 in this account soe	000	13	01

Payd Jo Harwold carpenter for which with £33 paid by R.

Kingsberry (p. 153) he have given me a generall release	033	00	00
(*vide* page 530)	212	13	01
16 Apr. 1676 allowed Harwold for worke about this farme 29 4 10	163	12	00
	376	05	01

10 Oct. 1676 Jo Kingsberry was at Felbrigg and payd me in money	014	00	00

And I did then allow £50 paid Mr Fowle as *per* noat under his

man's hand dated 4 April 1676	050	00	00
And for 3 years allowance to Mr Jo Elden ending Lday 1676 for mustering	002	00	00
And then I forgave him	000	08	00
	066	08	00
10 Oct. 1676 Rest ballance	194	16	00
	260	16	00

In a letter dated 12 Dec. 1676 Kingsberry write he paid Fowle
£50, 3 Nov. last, and have returned 50 more to him payable
11 of this month. Noat: ➤ The £100 was paid as apear (p. 159)

158. John Kingsberry's Debt (546, 156, 496, 272)

	Page 156, owe at Mich. 1677	388	16	00
29 Nov. 1677	Owe at Mich. 1677	288	16	00

Noat: The 17 months tax for building ships comes to

2: 5: 6 quarterly *scilicet.*	⎫	
2 0 9 in Midleton	⎬	
0 3 1 in Bulmore		Parish
0 1 3 in Heanʏ	⎬	
0 0 5 in Wickham		
2: 5: 6 *Vide* p. 496	⎭	

25 March 1677: my account was examined and there doe rest due to my land
lord Mr Windham for rent ending Mich. 1677 ten pounds: *John Kingsbury*

5 March 1677	Owe at Mich. 1677	010	00	00
	At Lday 1678	097	04	00
	At Mich. 1678	097	04	00
	At Mich. 1679	194	08	00
	At Mich. 1680	194	08	00
	At Lday 1681	097	04	00

2 May 1681: my land lord accounted with me and there doe rest due to
him for rent ending Lday 1681 one hundred thirty three pounds twelve
shillings eight pence.

	690	8	00
John Kingsbury owe	133	12	8

159. Kingsberry's Credit

16 Oct. 1677	By Fowle's account dated 16 Oct. 1677 he receiv'd of Parish by order of Jo Kingsberry			
	3 Nov. 1676: £50			
	And 22 Dec. 1676 50	100	00	00
	29 Nov. 1677 Rest	288	16	00
		388	16	00
1 Dec 1677	Payd Fowle by Parish	050	00	00
21	Payd as aforesaid	100	00	00
5 March 1677 Kingsberry was at Felbrigg and then payd me		007	04	09
By money payd Mr Fowle as by two receipts: 15 Feb. 1677				
£60; 1 Mar. 1677 £50		110	00	00
3 first payments of the tax for building 30 ships end Christmas 1677		006	16	06
	2 years mustring end Lday 1678	001	06	08
	A new buffe coat *anno* 1676 2 4 2			
	fur*ni*ture for a sadle 16 5			
	The weekes tax for trophyes 7 2	003	07	09
	Noat he ought to have paid me more	000	00	04
		278	16	00

5 March 1677	Rest due	010	00	00

288	16	00

Memorandum: 21 May 1678 I was at Midleton and was satisfied with the house mentioned p. 156, but I did not then allow the £10 because he had been too long in the wheelwright's companye before he came to me

		010	00	00
13 Dec. 1678	Parish payd Fowle	100	00	00
22 March 1678	Payd Fowle	080	00	00
28 Oct. 1679	Turner payd Briggs	100	00	00

Memo: 2 May 1681 I came to Midleton and tooke in these

	£	s	d			
receipts						
2 Apr. 1680	80	0	0			
27 Jan. 1680 Payd Fowle	100	0	0			
15 Ar. 1681	60	0	0	240	00	00
8 last months of the 17 months Ship Tax				006	01	04
18 months tax to disband the army				013	13	00
6 months supply				004	11	00
3 years mustring end Lday 1681				002	00	00
Cabeck by my order for keeping courts				000	10	00
				556	15	04

160. Francis Reynolls Debtor (548)

14 Nov. 1674	For rent ending Mich. 1674	335	00	00
15 March 1674	In arrear for rent ending Mich. 1674	188	19	05
	Halfe a years rent ending Lday 1675	027	10	00

Memorandum: I have two bonds of his for part of the money *scilicet:* £ 216 09 05

1st dated 12 Oct. 1669 payable 13 Nov. 1669 for	045
2nd 26 Sep. 1670 payable 1st Nov. 1670 for 115	160

21 May 1678   I was in Essex where I heard Reynolls receiv'd collection of the parish

Thomas Ellenford enter'd at Lday 1675 Debtor (548, 214)

A years rent at our Lday 1676		038	00	00
For some of the goods sould in Reynoll's bill				
of sale made 15 March 1674		004	05	00
Anno 1676		042	05	00
Halfe a years rent at Mich. 1676		019	00	00
Anno 1677				
At Lday 1677		019	00	00
At Mich. 1677		019	00	00
		038	00	00
29 Nov. 1677 Owe at Mich. 1677		020	00	00

By this account one may see how little mills are worth. Turne to p. 214

161. Reynolls Credit

From 8 Dec. 1670 to 15 March 1674

	Payd in money and searges	092	09	00
	By bill of sale	011	19	00
	And in taxes	006	13	09
	And in repaires	034	18	10
	Receiv'd and allowed	146	00	07
15 March 1674	Rest to balance	188	19	05
16 Apr. 1676	Allowed Jo Harwold for work about the mill in Reynoll's time £24 5s 10d Sum	335	00	00

Ellenford's Credit (153, 155, 215)

14 April 1676	Allow'd Ellenford a bill of repayres	041	10	09
	Payd to me in mony	000	14	03

And then I paid Jo Harwold carpenter for timber used about the mill *anno* 1675 as *per* bill 2nd March 1674: 66 13 9.

another bill 2nd Oct. 1675 34 01 0.38 trees out of Colledge wood *anno* 1675 used about the mill value 38 00 0.		042	05	00

Allowed R. Kingsberry for fetching of timber, straw etc about repayring of the mill (as page 153)   15 04 0.

<Repayres>   153 18 9 and 41 10 9

10 Oct. 1676	Thomas Ellenfoard was at Felbrigg and payd me in money	016	00	00
	And then allowed a bill of repayres	003	00	00
		019	00	0
1 June 1677	Payd Mr Fowle as *per* account dated 16 Oct.	018	00	00
	1677. Rest	020	00	00
		038	00	00

Ellingford died 10 Jan. 1677: made wife executrix

5 March 1677	Allow'd a bill under A. Chamber's hand of £18 payd Fowle 25 Jan. 1677	018	00	00
	R. Kingsberry payd me by her order	001	06	06
	2 first payments of the tax end Mich. 1677	000	13	04
Allow'd R. Kingsberry for carriage, forgive upon the account of this mill (p. 155) £2 5s 10d, turne to (p. 215)		000	00	02
		020	00	00

162. Wilson for the Deirey Farme: Debt (552, 190, 557)

14 Oct. 1673	In arrear for the profit of 16 cows ending Mich. 1673	031	00	00
	Item for a yeare ending Mich. 1674	036	00	00
	For the profit of 14 cows at Mich. 1675	031	00	00
	For the profit of 18 cows at Mich. 1676	040	00	00

➤ Noat: I may keep other cattle upon the Deyrey grounds, provided the
cows bee well kept   139   00   00

30 Oct. 1676	In arrear at Mich. 1676	020	05	00
	The profit of 17 cows at Mich. 1677	038	05	00
		058	10	00
29 Nov. 1677	In arrear at Mich. 1677	015	05	00

Noat: 15 March 1677 part let to Waterson p. 190 / 557 /

	The profit of 13 cows at Mich. 1678	029	05	00
	For keeping his calfes	000	09	00
		044	19	00

Ulph's (478, 163)

| | A years rent at Mich. 1687 | 006 | 00 | 00 |

24 Jan. 1687 Mr Windham made the allowances mentioned page 163 to
me. *Robert Ulfe*

163. Wilson's Credit

16 May 1674	Payd Salman	025	00	00
20 Feb. 1674	Payd him in full ending Mich. 1673	006	00	00
ditto		029	00	00
30 Nov. 1675	Payd Salman in full ending Mich. 1674	007	00	00
ditto	Payd Salman	019	15	00
30 Oct. 1676	Payd Salman	032	00	00
		118	15	00
	Respit	020	05	00
		139	00	00
29 Nov. 1677	Salman chargeth himselfe with	043	05	00
	Respit him	015	05	00
		058	10	00

7 Oct. 1678 I promised Wilson's wife to abate £5 for the profit of the
cows from that day when 9 cows came home and 4 went to Repham   005   00   00

10 Dec. 1678	Salman account for	033	19	00
31 Oct. 1679	Salman account for	006	00	00
		044	19	00

Ulfe's

5 July 1687	Fairchild account for which he receiv'd 28 Apr. 1687	001	13	06
	And then Ulph payd him more	000	06	00
	He allow'd for thatching	000	18	06
	And for glasing	000	02	00
24 Jan	I allow'd for shop goods	003	00	00
		006	00	00

164. Repham Farme Loss (552)

Noat: Mr Forby left it at Mich 1673 in Salman's account

14 Oct. 1673	he charge me for 2 comb of seed meslin	001	00	00
	And for 30 weathers	009	10	00
22 April 1674	Salman charge me wth £1 10s 0d paid Forby			
	For grass he left upon the ground	001	10	00
	And for charges incident to husbandry	008	04	04
	And for corne to sow	000	19	03
	20 weathers	007	10	00
	For halfe a years rent ending Lday 1674	026	00	00
20 Feb. 1674	Salman chargeth me for parish rates	003	01	07
	and for all other charges	034	00	05
	Halfe a years rent at Mich. 1674	026	00	00
30 Nov. 1675	Salman charge me for parish rates, and other			
	charges of husbandry	033	09	09
	A years rent ending at Mich. 1675	052	00	00
4 calfes bought of Wilson (as *per* account: 14 Oct. 1673				
page 8) of Salman		003	08	00
3 calfes bought of Wilson (as per account: 30 Nov. 1675				
p. 4) of Salman		002	10	00
		217	03	04
	A years rent ending at Mich. 1676	052	00	00
30 Oct. 1676	Salman charge me for parish rates and other			
	charges incident to husbandry	039	08	02
	And for 20 bullocks at St Fayes Fayer	035	00	00
	And for 20 bullocks at Hempton Fayer	036	10	00
24 Dec. 1676	The tythe of the farme *anno* 1676	003	11	00
	A years rent ending at Mich. 1677	052	00	00
29 Nov. 1677	For charges incident to husbandrye	028	05	02
Sexton's wages and disbursments to Mich. 1677		008	08	05
	Herbage and tythes to Hacfoard	001	15	00
26 Jan. 1678	I order'd Sexton to pay Willimot a black			
	smith for worke done before Mich.	000	16	00
15 Oct. 1678	Paid for dusting and carriage of corne	000	13	00
	Carridge of the corne growing	001	15	00

10 Aug 1681. Payd Robotham and Breese £4 10s in full of small tythes
and herbage ending Lammas last 1681. *Scilicet* 5 years to Robotham. 4
years to Breese, who hire the tythes of Hackford   260   01   07

165. Repham Farme Profit (166)

	Receiv'd at severall times for neat beasts	087	02	06
	For sheep and their wooll in 1674 and 1675	035	00	00
	Furs and brakes in 1674 and 1675	002	11	00
	Corne sould *anno* 1674	025	02	06
	The crop of corne *anno* 1675 which is now in			
17 March 1675	the barne Salman value at	040	00	00
Suppose the corne bee worth £40 I have lost in these 2 years		189	16	00
beside the interest of my stock		027	07	04
And noat: the corne was worth near £40		217	3	4
1676, 1677	The profit of sheep	006	05	06
	For 20 Scotch steers	060	00	00
	For corne in 1676	051	01	04
	more corne in 1676	001	00	00
	For 20 Scotch steers sould for	065	00	00
	The profit of other neat beasts	004	16	00
	For 30 sheep which improved	002	05	00
	The wool of the said 30 sheep sould	000	19	00
	A colt bred at Repham and sould for	002	17	00
	Corne growing *anno* 1677 wo[r]th	053	00	00
	Hay worth	003	02	06
	Peas and fetches	002	10	00
	Grass left upon the ground	001	10	00
		254	06	04
Soe lost in these two years, besides interest on my stock		005	15	03
The trouble in looking after this farme made me let it to halfes		260	01	07

166. Repham is Debtor (552)

An account how much more or less I make of this farme then the rent of £52 *per annum*, which to this day being 29 Sep. 1677 noe bodye have offer'd to hire

26 June 1678	Allowed the poor rates ending at Lday last	005	00	00
	Chimney money then due	000	09	00
	Repayring the fences and making racks	001	05	06
Clover seed which Sexton bought 1 5 0 sent from Felbrigg 5 4		001	10	04
15 Oct. 1678	Allow'd about husbandrye for mowing and			
	making the hay for the cows	000	07	08
	Poor rate to Repham ending Mich. 1678	000	12	08
➤	Utensils for the dairye cost 1 6 6			
1 March 1678	Chimney mony Mich. 1678	000	09	00
	Hackford's Cunstable's charges	000	01	09
	A years rent ending at Mich. 1678	052	06	05

		058	06	04
	A years rent at Mich. 1679	052	00	00
31 May 1680	Chimny monye	000	18	00
	Parish rates this year	002	13	00
	Charges about husbandrye	002	08	00

Noat: I reckon the cattle I breed and feed upon the farme comes to as

much as the interest and decay of my ows soe …		057	19	00
	A years rent at Mich. 1680	052	00	00
	Chimny monye	000	18	00

Parish rates *scilicet*: church, poor and constable's		004	05	10
	Charges of husbandry	002	12	10
		059	15	10
	Small tythes and herbage	001	00	00

10 Aug. 1681 Robotham and Breese agreed to take £2 5s a peice yearly in lieu of all tythes and herbage for this farme as long as I please, beginning Mich. 1681

		060	15	10

167. Repham is Creditor (166, 167, *quarto book*)

15 Oct. 1679	Then receiv'd of Sextan in part of the rent of the *10* cows and 1 heiffer	004	18	00
	And by bill of disbursments	005	17	05
1 March 1678	Payd me as by my receipt	008	05	09
21 July 1679	Payd me	004	00	00
	Then accounted for halfe the corne in 1678	022	01	03
	2 calfes bred up	002	00	00
	£	047	02	05
Lost for want of a tennant 11 4 0 Lost		011	04	00
40 16 0 Receiv'd		058	06	05

52 0 0

6   6   5 disbursed as by p. 166

47 2   5 receiv'd as by p. 167

40 16 0 rest for rent of Repham *anno* 1678

31 May 1680	Accounted with Sextan who have payd me at			
several times for the profit of 13 cows ending at Mich. 1679		029	05	00
	Corne growing *anno* 1679 at 13s for wheat,			
	8s 6d rye, 7s 6d barlye, comes to	027	04	09
		056	09	09
	Lost this year for want of a tennant	001	09	03
19 June 1682	Accounted with Sexton who have payd at			
several times a years profit of 14 cows 31 10 and for a heffer 1		032	10	00
	Furs sould for	001	04	00
	Corne growing 1680	014	08	09
		048	02	09

1680   Lost this year   012   13   01

Hereafter I'll enter the accounts of Repham and other farmes in hand in *quarto book.*

168. John Perry's Debt (14, 234)

John Perry is my bailiff to collect the rents of Assize of Toft-Overhall and Nether-hall Manour and Thurlton Banyards Manour, and by his account dated 15 May 1671 there did

then rest in arrear for both mannours ending Mich. 1670   014   05   02

The rents of Toffts Manour at £21 10s 2d yearly for 3 years

Mich 1673   064   10   06

The rents of Thurlton Manour at £3 8s 0½d yearly for 3 years

Mich. 1673   010   04   1½

                                                                  088   19   9½

26 Oct. 1674	Arrears of both manours Mich 1673				023	17	8½
	A years rent of both manors Mich. 1674				024	18	2½
	A years rent of both manors Mich. 1675				024	18	2½
	A years rent of both manors Mich. 1676				024	18	2½
	Vide t'other side	£	s	d	098	12	4
		35	15	6			
		1	8	6½			
		24	18	2½			
		62	2	3			

23 Oct. 1676	Rest due to me at Mich. 1676	062	02	03
	At Lday 1677	012	09	1¼
	At Mich. 1677	012	09	1¼
		087	00	5½

29 Nov. 1677	Rest due to me at Mich. 1677	044	17	9½
	At Lday 1678	012	09	1¼
	At Mich. 1678	012	09	1¼
	Carryed to p. 234	069	16	00

169. John Perry's Credit

From 15 May 1671 to 26 Oct. 1674

                Payd Salman in money   053   02   01

And to Mr Robert London 3 years rent 1 13 04 yearly ending

Mich. 1673   005   00   00

And for three years sallarey at 2 6 8 yearly ending Mich 1673   007   00   00

                                                                  065   02   01

	Rest to ballance	£	s	d	023	17	8½
		88	19	9½			

20 Feb. 1674	Payd Salman	011	00	00

		£	s	d
30 Nov. 1675	Payd Salman	015	05	02
	And by his account for one yeare ending			
	Mich. 1674 in wilde fowle	000	11	09
And to the Manour of Toft Monks Mich. 1674		001	13	04
	His years sallary then ending	002	06	08

➤ Noat £11 of the aforesd £15 5s 2d is in Perry's account dated 23 Oct.
1676 for one yeare ending Mich. 1675.

		£	s	d
	And to Toft Monks at Mich. 1675	001	13	04
	And his years sallary	002	06	08
	And in wilde fowle	001	13	00
	Receiv'd and allowed by me	036	09	11
At Mich. 1675 respited upon the severall tenants		035	15	06
23 Oct. 1676	Rest in Perry's hands Mich. 1675	001	08	6½
	A years rent uncollected at Mich. 1676	024	18	2½
		098	12	04
29 Nov. 1677	Payd Salman	001	08	06
Salman also chargeth himselfe with £10 which Perry in his				
account dated 22 Oct. 1677 say was paid to Mr Cooke		010	00	00
	And with the ballance of the said account	016	14	1½
And with £10 more then is included in the said account				
ending Mich. 1676		010	00	00
Allowed Perry the rent due to Toft Monks at Mich 1676		001	13	04
	And his sallary then ending	002	06	08
	Receiv'd and allow'd as aforesaid	042	02	08
29 Nov. 1677	Rest to ballance	044	17	9½
		087	00	5½

170. Edmond Bale's Debt (14, 238)

The said Bale doe collect the Rents of Assize of the Manours of
Wicklewood and Crownethorp, and 4 Oct. 1672 he did super [sic]

		£	s	d
4 Oct. 1672	Mich. 1671	004	03	04
	The rent of Wicklewood at Mich. 1672	015	05	09
	The rent of Crownethorp at Mich. 72	008	16	01
	The rent of both Manours at Mich. 1673	024	02	04
	And at Mich. 1674	024	02	04
	And at Mich. 1675	024	02	04
		100	12	08
18 July 1676	Due as on t'other side at Mich. 1675	029	12	08
	A years rent at Mich. 1676	024	02	04
	At Lday 1677	012	01	02
	At Mich. 1677	012	01	02
		077	17	04
21 Dec 1677	Owe at Mich. 1677	062	17	04

At Lday 1678	012	01	02
At Mich. 1678	012	01	02

For the ballance of the account of the profits of Crownethorp from Mich
1676 to 1677, p. 192 — 034 17 07

18 March 1678: my account was examined and all my disbursments and
demands allow'd, soe rest due to Mr Windham as by this account
appeare thirty four pounds sixteen shillings sixpence. — 121 17 3

Witness my hand *Edmund Bale* — 034 16 06

Vide p. 238

171. Bale's Credit (238)

25 Oct. 1672	Payd Salman	017	00	00
27 1673	Payd Salman	020	00	00
14 1674	Payd Salman	014	00	00
28 1675	Payd Salman	020	00	00

18 June 1676: this account was examined and there rest due — 071 00 00

to Mr Windham at Mich 1675 — 029 12 08

Witness my hand *Edmund Bale* — 100 12 08

29 Nov. 1677   Salman chargeth himself with £15 receiv'd
of Cooke by Bale's order — 015 00 00

21 Dec. 1677: this account was examined and all payments and demands
allow'd, soe rest due to Mr Windham for Rents of Assise belonging to
these manours sixty two pounds seventeen shillings fourpence. — 062 17 04

Witness my hand *Edmund Bale* — 077 17 04

5 April 1678   Payd me — 030 00 00

And then allow'd him £2 for his years sallarye ending
Mich. 1677 for collecting the Rents of Assise belonging to these manors — 002 00 00

And for his trouble in looking after my farme at Crownethorp
anno 1677 *Edmund Bale / 194 /* — 004 10 09

10 Dec. 1678	Salman chargeth himselfe with	015	00	00
	18 March 1678 payd me	010	00	00
	Allow'd as *per* bill for butter and cheese	011	06	00
	Riving and bring home 89 bunches of larth	002	15	01
	Crownethorp repayres	002	10	09
	Wicklewood Mill the houses	003	06	07
	About the woods	001	06	00

The last 3 quarterly and 2 months payments of the tax for
building 30 ships — 002 06 03

Amonition rate for Bale's and the woods and manors — 000 01 10

	Quit rents ending Mich. 1678	000	17	06
	Bale's sallarye Mich. 1678	002	00	00
		087	00	09

Rest due to me p. 238

034	16	06
121	17	03

172

Anno 1673. Noat: The Parke pay to the parsons of Felbrigg and Aylemeton 12s a peece in lieu of all tythes and herbage by prescription as appears by antient acquittances

And there 1673 are 14 chimneys in the house.

The Meadowe (betwene the Bush Close and Hill Close) about 12 acres formerly called Fulpiers Carr. The Church Close conteyne another about 37 acres not let in the memorye of man.

Memorandum: anno 1676: I paled the Nurseryre (which I hope will be carefully preserved soe long as it please God to continue it in the familye) and did then sow there 6 comb of acorns; 1 comb of ashe keys; 1 comb of haws; 2 bushells of holly berryes; 1500 chesnuts; 1 bushell of maple and sycamore keys; and a very few beech mast. I did then plant 4000 oakes: 800 ashes; 600 birches; 70 beeches; and 50 crabs which were all small.

/ *Sir H. Bedingfield gave me the oaks, Sir John Potts the ashe and birche. The beech came from Edgefeld* /.

1678   I planted the trees on the west side of the Flower Garden which Mr. Earle gave me out of Cawston Nurserye.

1681   I inclosed the corner of the Park by Aylemerton Gate to make a cops for my deer and planted it with trees out of my Nursery

1682   I inclosed a peice of ground upon the hill behind the Deer-House, and planted it with trees out of the Nurserye Feb 1682

1679   I took about 3 acres from Tompson's farme p. 28 and planted it with ashes out of the Nursery.

1687   I inlarged the Wood from the 3rd cross Walk to the wall, and planted it with trees of my sowing and setting *anno* 1676, and 1000 birches which Sir John Hobart gave me 6 Dec. 1687.

7 Dec. 1687 *Will Windham*

173

Anno 1673   The Parke (all but 30 acres behinde my house, which were sowne with severall sorts of corne) was kept for deere and to feed sheep for my house, my own sadle horses and strangers horses, and 3 or 4 cows:

Noat: I doe generally kill about 7 brace of bucks; and 6 brace of does in a yeare

The meadowe was kept for hay

The Church Close fed with my cart-horses

Annis 1674, 1675 and 1676 about 17 acres of the Church Close were sowne, the rest of the Close, and the Parke, and the meadow imployed as *Anno* 1673.

Anno 1677   About 24 acres of the upper Parke in Aylemerton broken up, some sowne with buck, some somerlyed.

1678   there was extreordinary good wheat and meslyn upon the aforesaid 24 acres 1679 sowne with barly.

1679   The rest of the Upper Parke broken up about 24 acres

1680   The first 24 acres sowne with oats and nonesuch. The other 24 was very good winter corne and <shall be> is layd down <next years with oats>. 1 April 1681

174

Anno 1613

Noat: The Sheepcourse upon the Heath at Felbrigg and Aylemerton, and Cromer, with such shacke within the feilds of Felbrigg and Aylemerton. As to the Sheepcourse belong (The Warrens, Lodge, with free libertie of breeding and killing of conies in and upon the premises excepted. And also except all manner of fuel) was let to Katherine Hobart for 6 years at £40 yearly by indenture 9 April 1613.

Anno 1623   John Spilman and R. Wigot hired the premises for 10 years at £35 yearly by indenture 1 Sep. 1623.

My father kept it in his hands

My brother let it at £22 and the keeping of 60 sheep value £3 *per annum*

Anno 1669   I came to it by purchase of my Lady Frances being part of her joynture for which I pay £4500 p. 526

175

18 Oct. 1673: Henry Bally is my sheepherd and have in his charge at five score to the hundred, seven and two sheepe: Bally's wages £10 and keeping forty sheepe value £2 yearly.

		Hun	s	
23 June 1676	The shepherd have in his charge at six score to the hundred / *Vide quarto book p. 56* /	005	05	14
8 July 1677	He have (*Vide quarto book* p. 56)	005	04	15
6 July 1678	He have (*Vide quarto book* p. 56)	005	04	19
17 Aug. 1679	He have (*Vide quarto book* p. 56)	005	03	02
26 Sep. 1679	I sould 6 years wool being 24 score and 11 stone at 3s 6d a stone paid			
8 July 1680	He have (*Vide quarto book* p. 57)	005	02	19
16 Sep. 1681	sold 2 years wool being 178 stone at 7s for £62 6s paid.			

➤ *quarto book* p. 56 is an account how many sheep have been bought, sold, killed or died every year from June 1676 to July 1680. And from this time I designe to keep the like account in *quarto book*.

176
Account of Flaggs and Brakes upon Felbrigg and Aylemerton Heaths (498)

				Received		
By Salman's account	22 Apr. 1674	*anno* 1673		012	00	10
By Salman's account	20 Feb. 1674	1674		010	07	06
By Salman's accountt	30 Oct. 1676	1675		010	07	06
By Salman's account	29 Nov. 1677	1676		010	02	11

		£	s	d	
Note: sould *anno* 1677 Flags for		10	19	9	5s 9

and	Brakes for	1	16	2	lost
		12	15	2	

		£	s	d
By Salman's booke 31 Oct. 1679 *anno* 1678		012	13	02

Sould 1679: Flags 9 13 0

Brakes 1 16 0

Vide p. 498 11 9 8 1679		011	09	08
By Smith's account sould *anno* 1680		010	18	02
1 Oct. 1682	Salman's account for 1681	009	13	02

21 Oct. 1683	Salman's account for 1682	£	s	d			
	And respite upon four persons	1	2	8	008	17	06
25 Oct. 1684	Salman's account for 1683				009	02	06
Observe:	the flag bill in 1683 comes to	7	11	6			
	the doles of brakes comes to	1	16	8			

He respite 3s for flaggs, and 2s 8d for brakes which 5s 8d makes the £9
2s 6d the full of the bill *scilicet* £9 8s 2d

| 12 Dec. 1685 | Elden account for 1684 | 010 | 10 | 08 |
| And in 1684 Pooly payd muck for 2000 flaggs at 10s | | 000 | 10 | 00 |

And then lost 3s by Richerson, which 13s makes 11 3 8

scilicet 9 7 0 flags, and 1 6 8 brakes

Oct. 1686	Banham account for 7 11 5			
	payd to me 17 0			
	for flages and brakes *scilicet anno* 1685	008	08	05

178. Mr Paston's Debt

Paston	My father lent Mr Clement Paston £3000 at	£	s	d
	£6 *per cent* as by indenture 8 May 1652.			
	And £1000 as *per* indenture of the same date	4000	00	00
	For interest halfe a yeare Nov. 1673	0120	00	00
	For ½ a yeare May 1674	0120	00	00
	For ½ a years interest Nov. 1674	0120	00	00
Backwell		4360	00	00
8 June 1681	In Alderman Backwells hand by bond £1200			
	of it was part of my wife's portion	1247	02	10
Cooper	By mortgage 1 Feb. 1685 at £5 *per cent* to	0500	00	00
Mite	Upon mortgage 21 Sep. 1686 at £5 *per cent*	1000	00	00
Reader	Upon coppyhold security 8 Oct. 1686 at £5 *per cent*	0300	00	00
Cooke	By mortgage 26 March 1687 at £6 *per cent*	0200	00	00
Earle	A mortgage 23 Apr. 1687 at £5 *per cent*	1150	00	00
Kittleburgh's	Mortgage 12 May 1687 at £5 *per cent*	0500	00	00
Bacon's trustees	upon mortgage 27 June 1687 at £5 *per cent*	4000	00	00
		8887	2	10
Earle	A mortgage 8 Feb. 1687 at £5 per cent	0250	00	00

| Kittleburgh | more upon the same mortgage 30 April 1688 | 0150 | 00 | 00 |
| Mite | 4 Oct 1688, gave a note to pay me interest for £50 from 21 March 1687 being then due for interest of the £1000 | | | |

179. Mr Paston's Credit

| 22 April 1674 | Tobias Scoller payd Salman | 0120 | | |
| 20 Feb 1674 | Payd Salman | 0240 | | |

➤ 19 Feb. 1674 I assign'd the £4000 over to my brother in
full satisfaction of £4000 which my father did give him

		0360	
		4000	
		4360	

| Backwell | Sir Joseph Ashe received the interest to my wife's use | 57 | 10 | |

at £6 *per cent* at Mich 1679. Writ 31 Oct. 1679 by me *Will Windham*   78   19

He payd interest due at Mich 1680. 25 Nov. 1680,
Cooper payd interest due 1 Feb 1686
Mites interest payd due 21 March 1686
Earle payd 27 10s 12 Jan 1687 soe due 1 5s 23 Oct.
Reeder payd interest due 8 Oct. 1687
Earle payd the 1 5s mentioned above
Bacon's interest payd to Sir Thomas Fowle due 27 De c. 1687
Cooke payd me for soe much lent him payd me in full of interest 16
Sep. 1688   0200   00   00
Kittleburgh payd interest till 30 April 1688
Bacon's interest payd due 27 June 1688
Kittleburgh payd to Briggs till 30 Oct. 1688
Earle payd Briggs 1 Apr. 1689 upon account of interest of £50
Bacon interest payd due 27 Dec. 1688

180. Robert Cook's Debt (182)

4 August 1676	£	s	d
The said Cooke did then charge himselfe with the Rents of Assize belonging to the manors of Felbrigg, Aylemerton Sustead, and Metton for 7 years ending Mich. 1678 at £18 8s 6¾ d	0198	16	5¼
And with the supers in Bonds time	0006	00	00
He did then alsoe stand charged with the Rents of Assize belonging to the manors of Runton, East Beckham Isaaks; and East Beckham Mariots for 7 years ending Mich 1675 at £8 1s 8¾d yearly	0056	12	1¼
And with supers in his father's time	0002	15	4¼
He did then also charge himselfe with the Rents of Assize belonging to the manors of Banningham, Tuttington Ingworth and Colbye for 6 years and ½ ending Mich 1675 at £40 6 6½ *per annum*	0260	03	6¼

And with the supper in Lubbock's time			0005 06 07	
by whom I lost 14 6 5				
4 August 1676	Then there did rest in supers Mich. 1675		0074 16 05	
29 Sep. 1676	A years rent of all the aforesaid manours:			
	by Cooke's owne account Mich 1676		076 10 04	
	At Lday 1677		038 05 02	
	At Mich. 1677		038 05 02	
			0́1̄1̄) 1̄) 0̄1̄	
ʊꞁ 𝘕ʊⱴ. 𝟷𝟼))	Ʊwe at Mich. 1677		0129 00 07	
	Carryed to p. 182			

181. Robt. Cook's Credit (503, 183)

4 August 1676

	£	s	d
The said Cook's account was then examined and he did then			
discharge himselfe by receipts payd to my use of	0386	10	03
And I then allow'd him for rents issuing out of my estate to			
my Lord Martiall (as appears page 503)	0033	08	08
And for soe much payd to the Constable of Banningham			
(*vide* page 503)	0000	18	08
And for his trouble of in collecting the rents of these manours			
for these 7 years ending Mich. 1675	0034	00	00
4 August 1676: Received and allowed	0454	17	07
And then he super'd the severall tenants of Felbrigg	0074	16	05
Aylemerton, Sustead and Metton at Mich. 1675: £36 0s 0d	0529	14	00

And upon the Runton, East Beckham Isaaks and East
Beckham Marriots   Mich. 1675:   £6 8s 8d
And upon the tenants of Banningham, Tuttington, Ingworth
and Colbye at   Mich. 1675:   £32 7s 1d

4 August 1676. Rest in supers		74 16 5		
30 Oct. 1676	Payd Salman as he chargeth himelfe with		0031	04 06
29 Nov. 1677	Salman chargeth himselfe with		0067	12 00
			0098	16 06
	Respit		0129	00 07
			0227	17 01

15 Feb. 1677 Cooke's account was examined and he did		
bring a receipt under Salman's hand dated 2 Jan. 1677	0005	00 00
I did then allow him for two years rent isssuing out of my estate to		
Hanworth Manor 8 1 10; and 2 years to		
Sheringham Manor 0 13 2 as appears p. 503	0008	15 00
For collecting the rents two years ending Mich. 1677	010	00 00
Payd to Banningham Leet for 2 years	0000	05 04
Carryed to p. 183	0024	00 04

182. Cooke's. Debt (180, 14, 183)

29 Nov. 1677	Owe as by p. 180 at Mich. 1677	129	00	07
15 Feb. 1677	I did discharge Cooke of all demands (the supers and the 2 1 9 excepted)			
15 Feb 1677	Rest due from the tenants belonging to my manours in Cooke's charge 1677	102	18	06

A years rent of all the manours in Cooke's charge (according to his owne account p. 180 which differs 15s 5¼d from thee account p. 14) ending at

Mich. 1678		076	10	04
	At Mich 1679	076	10	04
	For the monye in hand 15 Feb. 1677	002	01	09
27 Jan. 1679	This is a true account.			

Witness my hand. *Robert Cooke*

		258	00	11
27 Jan. 1679	Arrears at Mich. 1679	120	15	11
	A years rent ending at Mich. 1680	076	10	04
	At Mich. 1681	076	10	04
	At Mich. 1682	076	10	04
		350	06	11

The 21 October 1682 Mr Cooke examined his account and it in the presence of *Samuell Smyth. Vide* p. 183

183. Cooke's Credit (181, 504, 290)

15 Feb. 1677	Payd by p. 181	024	00	04
	and then he superd the tenants belong to my manours in his balywicke	012	18	06
	And then he acknowledg'd he had of mine in his hands which he promised to pay soon	002	01	09
		129	00	07
10 Dec. 1678	Salman chargeth himselfe with	046	12	00
31 Oct. 1679	Salman charge himselfe with	067	16	06
27 Jan. 1679	I examined Cooke's account and allow'd			
	him for rents issuing out of my estate. p. 504	011	11	02
	Banningham Leet for two years Mich 1679	000	05	04

For 2 years sallarye £10, and for going into Suffolke *anno*

1677 £1		011	00	00
		137	05	00
	And then he superd the tenants	120	15	11
		258	00	11
1 Oct. 1680	Salman account for	016	04	00
13 Oct. 1680	Payd Smith	033	11	00
10 Oct. 1681	Salman account for	017	04	06
1 Oct. 1682	Salman account for which Cooke payd in Oct. 1681	057	11	00

And for 43 12 payd in May and Aug. 1682		043	12	00
Oct. 1682	Payd Smith	025	00	00

21 [*Oct*] Cooke accounted with me and then I allow'd him for rents
going out of my estate as are particularly set downe in book p. 30 . . 017 15 9½

And for 3 years salary ending Mich. 1682	015	00	00

And for that Smith gave me account but of 33 11 0
received of Cooke Oct. 1680 when Cooke payd him 34 0 0 . . . . 000 09 10

And then Cooke ruperd the tenants	226	07	3½
belonging to the manours in his charge	121	06	07
The remaine in Cooke's hand	002	13	½

This is a true account; in witness whereof I the above   350   06   11
mentioned Robert Cooke have set my hand 21 Oct. 1682
Robert Cooke

184. Bale's Farme Debt (545, 136, 171)

11 Dec. 1677	Page 136, owe at Mich. 1677	012	15	10
	At Lday 1678	018	05	06
	At Mich 1678	018	05	06

18 March 1678: my account was examined and all my disbursements
allow'd (p. 171) soe rest clear due to Mr Windham for farme rent nine
pounds seven and four pence *Edmund Bale*   049   06   10

18 March 1678. Owe	009	07	04
At Mich 1679	036	11	00
At Mich 1680	036	11	00
At Mich 1681	036	11	00
At Mich 1682	036	11	00
At Mich 1683	036	11	00
	102	02	04
A years rent at Mich 1684	036	11	00

I must charge Bale here with £6 because of the £6 of the £18 he payd
Harris 27 Oct. 1682 was for hay which grew at Crownethorp 1677 . . 006 00 00

18 Feb. 1684. My land lord Windham was at my house and allow'd me
all my disbursements, soe I owe him for rent and arrears of rent ending
at Mich. 1684 seventy pounds fourteen shillings nine pence. Witness my
hand *Edmund Bale* in the presence of *Joseph Elden*   234   13   04

18 Feb. 1684	Bale owe me	070	14	00
	A years rent at Mich. 1685	036	11	00

24 Nov. 1685 I acknowledge to owe my land lord Windham
seven and twenty pounds thirteen shillings eightpence.
Signed in the presence of *Peter Watts Edmund Bale*   107   05   09

185. Bale's Credit (306)

5 April 1678	Bale was at Felbrigg and did then give me a bill of fencing the woods	001	06	00
	And repayrs about Crownethorp farme	001	05	07
	And of mony spent by my servants when Crownthorp was in hand *anno* 1677	000	06	05
	Crying the goods which were sould 1677	000	00	06
	Payd the man back which bought the cows which I sould 1677 *Edmund Bale*	000	01	00
10 Dec. 1678	Salman account for	027	00	00
15 Jan. 1678	Paid Marke my grome	010	00	00
		039	19	06
	Rest due	009	07	04
		049	06	10
31 Oct. 1679	Salman account for	015	00	00
1 Oct. 1680	Salman account for	015	00	00
1 Oct. 1682	Smith account for	020	00	00
27 [*Oct.*]	Payd Mr Haris	018	00	00
22 Feb	Payd Smith	008	00	00
21 Oct. 1683	Elden account for	012	00	00
25 Oct. 1684	Elden account for	024	10	00
1684	He sent me a weight of cheese	002	10	00

18 Feb. 1684   I was at Bale's and allow'd him £15 for 6
weigh of cheese, and £9 9s for 10½ ferkins of butter sent to

Felbrigg since 18 March 1678		024	09	00
	Mending fences about the woods	000	18	06

Repayrs about Crownthorp 1s, and the mill 7s 9d		000	08	09

Larth riving 105 bunches sent to Felbrigg 1681 and 1684 £1 19s 4d and
other incident charges about the larth 13s

		002	12	04
	Payd me	020	10	00
		163	18	07
	Due to me	070	14	09
		234	13	04
17 Oct. 1685	Elden account for	038	00	00
23 Nov. 1685	Bale payd me	040	00	00
	Amonition	000	01	05
	Repayring the fences where Lock brought the topwood in 1685	001	10	08
		079	12	01
	Bale owe me	027	13	08
		107	05	09

186. Nicholas Wilson's Attourney Debt (15, 535)

3 Jan. 1676 3 years rent of land in Metton at £4 3s *per annum* ending Mich. 1668 £42 9s, of which he paid me formerly £5 soe	037	09	00
Quit rent for lands holding of Aylemerton manour 8 years ending Mich. 1674 is d ¾	000	09	02
9 years rent for lands holding of Beckham Mariots at Mich. 1674	000	04	06
7 years rent of lands holding of Runton Hayes at Mich 1671	000	00	07
	038	03	03

Widow Marie's Debt (15, 535)

For rent of land in Metton Mich. 1671	003	10	00

Springall's Debt (15)

For rent of land in Dilham or Worstead ending at Mich. 1668	004	07	06
For my charges of sute	002	00	06
	006	08	00

Carryer's Debt (15, 188)

Anno 1671. I comenced a sute agst him for rent of land in Metton from Mich. 1665 and at the Assizes in Norwch he promised to pay the rent and my charges, soe 'twas not tryed.

13 Sep 1671 he gave me a bond for £22 being six years rent out of which I promised to allow taxes soon after he paid £11 at twice, soe debtor him	011	00	00
Walls had of me for charges of sute / *188* /	005	00	00

187. Wilson's Credit

30 Jan. 1676 Allow'd P. Wilson the said Nich Wilson's sonn a bill of charges and demands in his father's time concerning the sute with my Lady Frances	013	02	02
In which bill there £4 for a Post Fine paid for Thomas Mede Esq. for Lycence of Concord with Richard Chamberlaine Esq. of a Plea of Covenant for lands in Beckham. Which Post Fine concerned not my interest yet rather then dispute it with my mother, or he should lose it, I allow'd it him	004	00	00
Allow'd the taxes for the 3 years. And £3 9s 7d which his	004	15	06
father disbursed for my use in the said 3 years	003	09	07
29 Nov. 1677 Salman chargeth himselfe (which he receiv'd of P. Wilson) with	012	16	00
	038	03	03

[Widow Maries's Credit]

	I forgave her	000	10	00
29 Nov. 1677	Salman chargeth himselfe with	003	00	00
		003	10	00

Springall's Credit

30 Oct. 1676	Payd Salman	003	19	06
	Allow'd for taxes	000	08	00
29 Nov. 1677	Salman chargeth himselfe with	002	00	06
		006	08	00

Memorandum Carryer's Credit (554, 189)

At Easter Sessions in Norwich *anno* 1678 I askt him for the money, he then tould me he never hired any land, nor borrowed any money of me, would pay me none, soe I order'd Palmer to sue him. This day being 5 June 1678   He brought me   008 00 00

And promised to pay me £2 more by Mich. and pay Palmer's bill of charges, soe I gave him a noat to Palmer delivering up his bond, paying the charge, and giveing him a bill for the two pounds / *vide* 189 /

188. Caryer is Debt (186, 15)

Page 186	016	00	00

Forby's Debt (15)

For part of his rent of Repham Farme ending Mich. 1673	004	00	00

Knevet's (15)

For his half of the Alder Carr Mich. 1671	000	10	00
Flaxman owe rent by bond 27 Sep. 1679 / *15* /	004	14	02

189. Caryer is Credit (187)

	Page 187	008	00	00
	Allow'd taxes for the 6 years	002	03	00
If Caryer pay the £2 according his promise p. 187; I shall lose by him –		003	17	00
which is better then *a* sute unless it bee *in terrorem*				
13 July 1680	Payd me in part of the said £2	001	00	00
16 Nov. 1685	Carryer payd me	001	00	00
		016	00	00

Forby's Credit

| 20 June 1678 | Receiv'd of the Widdow Forby £4 and then I did give her a receipt in full | 004 | 00 | 00 |

Knevet's

10 Mar. 1687	Mrs Knevet payd me	000	10	00
Mem: Smith deducted at nine times for 3 Oct. 1680 to 3 July 1681		000	17	02
1 May 1684	He payd me	003	00	00
17 Oct. 1685	Elden account for	000	15	00
12 Dec.	Payd Elden	000	02	00
		004	14	02

190. Waterson's Debt (557)

At Mich 1678	008	10	00
At Mich 1682, he is to bee charged in respect part of it was plow'd but 3 years	005	02	00
The next 5 years ending Mich. 1687 at 18s *per* acre for 12 acres is	054	00	00
29 Feb. 1687 Mr Windham accounted with me and I owe him for rent at Mich. last past nine pounds twelve shillings.	067	12	00

Witness my hand Joseph Waterson's X marke
signed before *Stephen Legge*

| Owe as abovesaid | 009 | 12 | 00 |

191. Waterson's Credit

10 Dec. 1678	Salman account for	004	05	00
28 Aug 1679	Payd me	002	05	00
31 Oct. 1679	Salman account for	004	05	00
15 Dec. 1679	Payd me	002	03	00
13 Oct. 1682	Payd Smith	004	10	00
1 Oct. 1683	Payd me	004	10	00
Allow'd Waterson when he payd the £2 3s the 15 Dec. 1679 for hooks 1s 5d. And to a poor rate 7d		000	02	00
14 July 1684	Payd me	004	10	00
17 Dec.	Payd me	004	10	00
17 Oct. 1685	Elden account for	004	10	00
2 Dec	Payd me	004	10	00
5 July 1686	Payd John Barham	003	05	00
	Oats 5 comb at 5s	001	05	00
7 Dec.	Payd me	004	10	00
5 July 1687	Fairchilde account for	004	10	00
		058	00	00

6 Dec.	Payd me				009	12	00
					067	12	00

192. Bale is Debt (147, 194, 195, 170)

➤ Page 147 for the profit of Scipper's inventory and for 5 cows which
cost £21 part of the £175 9s 8d hereunder mentioned / *p. 194 n. 6* /,   327   00   03
and was sould by him for 17 10 0 / *p. 195 n. 1.2* /.
For hay *anno* 1677 1 16 0   019   06   00

		£	s	d	346	06	03
24 Oct. 1676	Payd me	9	18	3			
14 Feb. 1676	Payd me	15	16	6			

ditto: William Howard payd me for cheese and corne,
by bill of work   4   14   2   / *194 n.3* /.
And gave me a noat for 2   11   10   7   6   0
Neat beasts came to Felbrigg at   9   15   0
One horse came to Felbrigg worth   2   5   0
The swine came to Felbrigg worth   6   10   0
Goods came to Felbrigg worth   8   6   6
4. Corne sowne and spent upon the farme   15   17   9
5. Hay, turneps and somerly spent upon the
farme valued at   50   4   0
6. Bale's disbursements upon the premises 175   9   8
Bale sould Yaxley several things for which he is to
pay at Christmas 1677 as *per* noat 30 Sep. 1677 10
21 Dec. 1677   Bale gave me a noat for p. 170   34   17   7
                 Credit   346   6   3   346   06   03
Account of Crownethorp Farme from Mich. 1676 to Mich. 1677 / *p.194* /

Bale is also Debtor (137, 143, 195, 194)

For 26 18 5 which I did give him credit for 14 Feb 1676, / *p. 137* /
And is now included in thee above mentioned 175 9 8 no. 6   026   18   05
                 Of Gould my tenant / *143* /   025   00   00
                 Of Howard part of Crownethorp profit / *195* / 032   00   00
For corne being the remeynder of the inventory   000   11   07
Payd Salman which he chargeth himselfe with in his account.   084   10   00
                 29 Nov. 1677 from Mich. 1676 p. 194   084   10   00

Crownethorp Farme is Debtor (147, 192, 171, 196)

from Mich. 1676 to Mich. 1677
                 For a years rent ending Mich. 1677   127   06   08
2. For the loss in the sale of the horses / *147* /   000   05   00

3. 14 Feb. 1676, I allow'd Howard for boarding my servants
        and worke / *192* /   004 14 02
4. Corne sowne and spent upon the farme   015 17 09
5. Hay, turneps and somerlye   050 04 00
6. Disbursemts upon the premises   175 09 08
For 20 bullocks bought at St Fayes   042 00 00
Paid Howard for boarding my servant 6 weeks   001 08 11
        Allow'd Howard in wood for the deyrey   001 00 00
5 April 1678.   Allow'd Bale for his trouble in looking after
        my farme *anno* 1677 / *171* /   004 10 09
I did looke as carefully after this farme as I could well doe   423 16 00
and kept a strict account of it, that my son may see the
inconveniency of having farmes come into his hands.
                From Mich. 1677 p. 196

195. Crownethorpe Farme is Credit (147, 192, 197)

The sheep improved upon the farme / *147 n. 3* /   002 09 00
For sale of 5 cows which is included in the 175 9 8:
/ *192* / (p. 194 n. 6)   017 10 00
For one new cart being part of   175 9 8
which was brought to Felbrigg   008 00 00
For the two first paymentts of the tax being part of the said
                                175 9 8   002 13 10
For the money lay out in building according to my agreement
(p. 551), being included in the aforesaid   175 9 8   043 16 03
The 20 bullocks sould for in Salman's account.   065 00 00
Howard payd Bale for the profit of 20 cows £32
as *per* (p. 192), and he payd Salman in full   18   050 00 00
(p. 192 n. 2)   001 16 00
Sould the neat racks for   000 16 00
4 comb 1 bushel of peas being part of the crop *anno* 1677:
sould for   001 17 06
Noat: All the rest of the corne I sould to Isack Jecks 14 Jan
1677 for £80 payable by bond 1st May and 1st August 1678 / *197* /   080 00 00
< 5 Apr. 1678.   Allow'd Bale for his trouble in looking after
        my farme *anno* 1678 p. 171 >   <04 10 9>
Received of Gould for hay sould Bignet   001 08 00
A stack of hay worth   022 00 00
25 acres of somerlye   015 12 06
Carriage of the muck in 1677   006 00 00
Straw and chaife   007 00 00
Alders worth   001 10 00

For ditching and dreyning to improve the ground being part   013   00   00
of the 175 9 8 Repayres part of the 175 9 8   001   13   00
                                                                           342   02   01
        Lost from Mich. 1676 to Mich. 1677   081   13   11
                                                                           423   16   00

                 Rent   127   6   8
                 ballance   81   13   11
                 Clear but   45   12   9 for rent
                      127   6   8

196. Isaac Jeck's Debt (551, 143, 171, 185, 304)

        For halfe a years rent at Lday 1678   063   13   04
        At Mich. 1678   063   13   04
This is a true account. Witness my hand 19 March 1678 *Isaac Jecks*   127   06   08
Gould disburs'd for Crownethorp repayres   £   s   d
since Mich. 1677 p. 143   2   11   8
And Bale p. 171 and 185   3   16   4
                     6   8   0
Gould lay out more p. 143   11   0
        A years rent at Mich. 1679   127   06   08
        At Mich. 1680   127   06   08
        At Mich. 1681   127   06   08
        At Mich. 1682   127   06   08
        At Mich. 1683   127   06   08
                     636   13   04
21 Oct. 1683   The ballance is   225   00   00
        A years rent at Mich 1684   127   06   08
18 Feb 1684   I accounted with my land lord Windham and   352   06   08
acknowledge to owe him in rent ending Mich. last one
hundred seventy seven pounds. *Isaac Jeck*   177   00   00
        A years rent at Mich. 1685   127   06   08
                     304   06   08

197. Jeck's Credit (305)

20 June 1678   Brought me to Norwich   060   17   10
Allow'd the 3rd and 4th quarterly payments of the Ship   002   10   06
Monye.   And the weekes pay for Trophyes   000   05   00
10 Dec. 1678   Salman chargeth himselfe wth £40 which
Jecks was to pay 1 Aug. 1678 as by p. 195 n. 11
15 Jan. 1678   Paid Marke my grome   040   00   00
19 March 1678 Payd me   013   00   00
        Allow'd for repayres   005   13   03

	And the 5th quarterly and 2 months tax	002	02	01
	Butter two ferkins	002	08	00
	Crownethorp poor rate before Mich. 1677	000	10	00
		127	06	08
31 Oct. 1679	Salman account for	061	02	10
	6 months of the 18 mths Armye Tax	002	10	06
1 Oct . 1680	Salman account for	058	16	06
	Allow'd for two ferkins of butter	002	02	00
	Disburs'd for me	000	04	04
	6 months of the aforesaid tax 1679	002	10	06
10 Oct. 1681	Smith account for	060	17	10
	6 mths tax 2 10 6. Amonition 0 5 0	002	15	06
1 Oct. 1682	Smith account for	101	02	10
	6 moneths tax	002	10	06
27 [Oct.]	Payd Mr Harris	057	00	00
22 Feb.	Payd Smith	030	00	00
21 Oct. 1683	Elden account for	030	00	00
		411	13	04
	Rest due	225	00	00
		636	13	04
25 Oct. 1684	Elden account for	115	00	00
15 Dec.	Payd Elden	050	00	00
18 Feb.	Payd me at Bale's	000	17	11
	Then allow'd him for repairs	009	03	09
	Amonition	000	05	00
		175	06	08
	Rest due	177	00	00
		352	06	08
18 Feb. 1684	I tould Jecks I would owe him in respect of the great drought last summer	010	00	00
17 Oct. 1685	Elden account	064	00	00
		074	00	00

198. Blofield's Debt (*quarto* p. 20, 199, 275)

For rent of Bun's Wood Mich. 1670		005	00	00
For 3 years rent at £6 Mich. 1673		018	00	00
Lent him 400 brick and tyle		000	05	00
For wood sould him by Salman *anno* 1676		000	15	00
		024	00	00

Mr Blofield had part of Ransome's inventory at Mich 1681 at /*quarto p. 20*/

		010	00	00
		034	00	00
The ballance p. 199		002	16	07

Mem: 18 Nov. 1684. I order'd all the trees in the two upper closes of
Buns Wood to bee digged up which I guess worth worth £100 *scilicet* 39
oaks, 2 ashes used about my building *anno* 1685   036   16   07

        For the credit I give him p. 275   003   19   11

199. Blofield's Credit (186)

	£	s	d
Salman chargeth himselfe with	005	00	00
Payd me	005	00	00
In straw and chaife at severall times	003	12	01

Taxes *scilicet:* subsidye 3s and the 6 months 3s 8d   000   06   08

Allow'd for 2 nights expences at Norwich Assizes about Carryer / 186 / 000   10   00

For the tythes and herbage of the Beefe Closes and Church Closes and
for about 5 acres formerly in Carvil's use, with the meadows adjoyning
for 12 years ending Mich 1677 at 1 3 4 *per annum* being due by
certaintye of prescription and custome upon a prohibition tryed for the
same at Norwich Assizes about 1612   014   00   00

	£	s	d
By Wood	000	08	00
To the Royall Aide at 5 quarterly payments	000	15	10

Payd my part of the poor rate for lands in hand 4s   000   04   00

A years rent tythes and herbages at Mich. 1678   001   03   04

	£	s	d
At Mich. 1679	001	03	04
At Mich. 1680	001	03	04
At Mich. 1681	001	03	04
At Mich. 1682	001	03	04
At Mich. 1683	001	03	04
	036	16	07

		£	s	d
21 Oct. 1683	I owe Mr Blofield by this account	002	16	07
	A years rent tythe and herbage Mich. 1684	001	03	04
		003	19	11

200. An account of the stock of beasts upon grounds in hand *scilicet:* Loss

		£	s	d			
18 Oct. 1673		£	s	d			
	50 bullocks cost	68	0	0			
	7 cows 1 bull	16	2	0			
	6 heiffers 1 bull	5	0	0	089	02	00
	16 deyrey cows 1 bull for which Wilson pay me £36 yearly (*vide* page 162)						
22 April 1674	4 yearling calves	3	8	0	003	08	00
to 20 Feb.	46 bullocks cost	73	10	10			
	1 cow	3	0	0			
	1 heiffer	1	15	0	078	05	10
From Feb to	7 cows	23	08	0			
Aug. 1675	2 bulls	3	2	0			

3 yearling calves   2 10 0

8 bullocks   17 12 0   046 12 00

                                                        217 07 10

30 Nov. 1675   Salman chargeth himselfe with the aforesaid 46 12 0

              And for 20 bullocks bought at St. Fayes   038 08 10

              And for 20 bullocks bought at Hempton   036 12 02

30 Oct. 1676   For 29 bullocks and other neat beasts   1,0 10 06

4 Feb. 1676   17 bullocks and other neat beasts   047 06 00

                  96 bought since 5 Aug. 1675   181 05 06

             And <u>57</u> upon the grounds 5 Aug. 1675

                  153

201. An account how the stock have been disposed on to my use: Profit

              Received by Salman's account 22 April 1674   020 10 00

                 And by his account dated 20 Feb. 1674   073 10 00

And by a particular which he gave me of the stock dated

4 Aug. 1675   089 05 00

By the said account for 32 bullocks sould Sexton not paid for yet   110 08 00

                        1 cow, 1 heiffer; died in winter 1673:

                        3 fat beasts killed in Christmas 1674.

5 Aug. 1675   33 beasts not sould in grounds in hand

                         scilicet Repham and Dovehouse

                        18 in the Deirey grounds

                        <u>6</u> in the Parke

                        57

30 Nov. 1675   Salman charge himselfe to have receiv'd of Sexton £100

              part of the aforesaid £110 8s 0d.

By the same account sould Sexton 19 fat beasts for £57

30 Oct. 1676   Salman charge himselfe wth £10 8s being the

remeynder of the £110 8s, and with the aforesaid   057 00 00

Killed in the house Christmas 1675: 4

And betwene Christmas 1675 and Christmas . 1676: 3

              Sould *anno* 1676: 50 for   160 11 00

             2 died *anno* 1675 and 1676

             81 killed and sould since Aug. 1675 value

1 Feb. 1676   70 in the grounds *scilicet:*

             153   26 Scotch steers at Repham

                         6 calves

                        20 Scotch steers in Dovehouse

                        8 cows in Gresham grounds

                        3 cows in the Parke

                        <u>3</u> beasts at turnops

                        70

202. Account of neat beasts

70 in the grounds 4 Feb 1676 p. 201
45 bought since 5 Dec. 1677
  5 came from Crownethorp
120
  75 in the ground 5 Dec 1677 p. 203
  93 bought to 8 Jan. 1678
168
124 in the grounds 8 Jan. 1678
  2 bred at Repham
  20 brought since by Salman
146
  10 I had of Selfe 3 Oct. 1679. p. 162
  14 Houseman bought to stock Keebles
  11 Sextan my butcher bought
181
  92 in Norfolk and Suffolk 14 Jan. 1679
108 bought since
  2 bred at Repham
202

203. Account how the Beasts have been disposed on from 4 Feb 1676 to 5 Dec 1677 (*quarto book* p. 36)

40 sould to Sexton and Monye
  3 killed in the house and halfe sould
  1 spent in the house
  2 died
46
74 in the grounds 5 Dec. 1677 *scilicet*.
120   10 deyrey cows
               11 young beast at Repham
               11 fat beasts and
                3 calfes } turnops
               16 deyrey cows in Gresham
                3 cows in the Parke
               20 Scots in Dovehouse
               74
                1 stray heiffer at Repham
30 sould
  9 spent in the house
  4 given the poor at Christmas 1677 and 1678
  1 died

44
124 in the grounds 8 Jan. 1678 *scilicet:*
168   25 in Suffolke
                20 at Repham
                68 in my grounds nere home
                11 cows in the Parke
                ───
                124

73 sould by Salman
  1 spend in the house   │ 18 in Suffolke
  2 to the poor   │ 21 at Repham
  7 died: 6 in Norfolk   │   1 in Suffolk 10 at Selfe's p. 261
 ──   │ 20 in Sustead p. 80
 83   │
  6 sould by Houseman   │ 13 in Dovehouse
 ──   │ 10 in the Parke
 89   │
 92 in the gounds   │
 ──   14 Jan. 1679.   92
181
 65 sould in Norfolk
 24 sould in Suffolke
  2 died in Norfolk
111 in the grounds in Norfolk 1 Dec 1680
202 Here after *vide quarto booke* p. 36

206

Anno 1674: These land were in hand from Mich. 1673 *scilicet:* the Parke, Church Close, meadowe betwixt Hill Close and Bush-Close. The hay of the long meadowe in Sustead; sheep walke, flaggs and brakes upon the Heath; Sheep Closes by Aylemerton Park Gate; Dovehouse Grounds and the land Widdow Maries paid £7 *per annum* for. Repham farme.

At Mich. 1674 these alterations and additions: Thomas Sexton hired all Marie's grounds (except one peice which H. Smith paid 10s for) as page 74. < in hand >
John Drakes farme (except 12s) as page 24 in hand.
Miles Miller's farme, as page 96, in hand.

At Mich. 1675 these alteration and additions: Gregorye hired about 5½ acres of Maries's page 232, the rest of Marie's ground (except 10s before excepted) in hand.
At Mich. 1676. Scippers Farme: *vide* page **146:** in hand
At Mich. 1677. Scippers Farm let *vide:* **551**
And Repham Farm let [*vide*] **552 and 166**
Pall left about 5 acres belonging to his farme which is now in hand **p. 20**
Miller's let **p. 96**
Marie's land which was in hand at Mich 1675 let now to Gregorye **p. 232**
I let 18 acres of Drake's which came into hand at Mich. 1674 **p. 24**
This is an intricate way, I'll leave it *vide* p. 219

209. Timber sold out of Wicklewood and Crownethorpe March 1670

Oakes	To Hunt and Sewell carpenters of Norwich			
75	21 oakes out of Deepham Grove,			
	54 out of Hallwood for	176	00	00
Oakes	To Coleman and Starling carpenters of Norwich,			
263	61 in Walters Wood, 103 in Gimys Grove,			
	76 in Groundsell Wood, 23 in Hedge Grove for	520	00	00
	To Collins one old oake when I inlarg'd the Parlour			
	Garden at Felbrigg	004	00	00
		700	00	00

1670 and 1671 I planted the oaks in the bottome by the Deer house

210

1672	Johnson's farme dwelling house and all out houses were burnt by fire which began in the Kill house
Anno 1672	Timber felled to rebuild the said houses
Anno 1675	I felled all the timber used about my new building at Felbrigg: And 38 trees in Essex p. 161
Anno 1676	Timber felled to pale my Nurserye in the Parke p. 172
Anno 1677	Timber to build the stable for the plow horses, Felbrigg. Timber felled at Wicklewood and Crownethorpe to build a new barne at Crownethorpe p. 551/2
Anno 1678	About 50 dead trees felled at Repham, and used at Felbrigg – for several uses. Posts, pales, rayles, border boards.

21 May 1678, felled at Midleton 5 trees worth about £3 to bee imploy'd about the mill, and 3 worth £2 about Brunden Farme p. 155, / *215* /

In June felled in a peice of ground belonging to Allyson's farme, 5 trees worth about £4 to repayre the bank against Ingworth Mill Pool, and several trees in Gresham Close belonging to Richersons farme to pale the Privy Walk Felbrigg / *127* /

26 June felled by the Pond 2 dead oaks worth £4 to make my Coach Yard Gates. In Sep 1678 felled 43 old trees at Gresham, Sustead and Metton to fence young trees.

Anno 1679	Fell'd trees in the Closes next Metton Comon to pale from the N.W. corner of the old Nurserye to the top of the Hill where I designe to make a new Nursery for Copswood to shelter Deer.
1680	Fell'd 1 great pollard ofe a bank in a little meadow nere Metton-Hall to plank my stable. 4 Alders in the Great Close near Teeks Beck for sluces.

➤ 2nd July I had an ashe in Dovehouse 2 foot square split by thunder in 3 peeces, strangly shivered, several peeces as bigg as a man can carry, throwne 50 feet from the tree.

211

I have soe often occasion for timber 'tis troublesome setting downe every tree, and to noe purpose there fore I'll omit it but as often as I sell any I'll enter the number and price.

Noat: several trees have been felled for repaires in Norfolk, Suffolk and Essex besides those mentioned p. 210 since 1672

Anno 1680 Oct. sould Burrowes of Aylesam 14 ashes in Colbye Hall Close for £25: Payd 2 Feb 1680

212

1671	Out of Cromes farme in Tuttington, to Mr Smith for topwood growing in Hall Closes and the ground call'd Hegg, with one oake	034	00	00
	Out of Cooke's farme to Frost and Abbs part of the topwood in the 3 closes next Basingham	024	00	00
	Out of Ingland's farme in Basingham, to Colbye	003	19	00
	Topwood for Francis Gould of Wicklewood	005	10	00
1677	Topwood to Gould out of his farme	001	10	00
	Topwood to Jecks Miller of his farme	001	05	00
	To Clemence out of Winters farme	005	10	00
	To Cox for a Hedgerow in Repham £4 which cost me to new ditch 1 0 5 }soe	002	19	07
1678	and to Edmund Teney of Gresham the Hedgerow next the way on his side p. 534 for new ditching £3	003	00	00
24 Sep. 1679 sould Waterson some topwood in his ground p. 557 for £4		004	00	00

It being of noe use to keep an particular account of what topwood I sell, I'll noe longer enter it here   05   13   07

214. Widow Ellenfoard's Debt (548, 161, 215, 272)

	Page 161. Clear 5 March 1677			
	At Lday 1678	019	00	00
	At Mich. 1678	019	00	00
	At Mich. 1679	038	00	00
	At Mich. 1680	038	00	00
	At Lday 1681	019	00	00
		133	00	00
23 June 1681	Rest due to me	015	02	00
	At Mich. 1681	019	00	00
	At Lday 1682	019	00	00

Mem: Though the ballance of Totman's account p. 215 bee 5 2 2, he owe me 5 16 8 which he payd p. 272   053   02   00

Samuell Gibson's (511, 497, 278)

	His halfe years rent at Mich. 1682	019	00	00
	At Mich. 1683	038	00	00
	From Mich 1683 Rob. Kingsberry is to pay me the rent of the mill / *497, 278* /	057	00	00

215. Ellenfoard's Credit (511, 155, 214, 279)

21 May 1678	Payd me at Brunden	006	00	00
	And then allow'd the 3 and 4 quarterly payments of the 17 months tax for building 30 ships	000	13	04

Noat: she had then 5 trees worth about £3 set out to repaye the apron of
the flud gates and I did promise to give her £1 towards it   001   00   00

31 Oct. 1679	Salman account for	018	00	00
28 Oct. 1679	Turner payd Briggs which R. Kingsberry returned	011	00	00
Anno 1679	Salman set out 4 trees to repayr the water lanes and a fulling stock.			
30 April 1681	I accounted with the Miller's wife, and finde			
	Robert Kingsberry have payd	039	00	00
	She payd me this day	020	00	00

5 last months of the Ship Tax	11	2	
18 months Army Tax	2	0	0
6 months Supply	13	4	003 04 06

23 June 1681	Payd as *per* acquittance £19	019	00	00
Anno 1680	He had 4 or 3 trees allow'd	117	17	10
23 June 1681	Rest p. 511	015	02	02
		133	02	02
4 April 1682	Payd me	019	00	00
	And then he brought a noat from R. Kingsberry that he had payd him. / *155* /	029	00	00
		048	-	-
4 Apr. 1682	Rest paid 17 Apr. 1685	005	02	02
1681 allow'd trees, board timber £6 12s / *214, 279* /		053	02	02

Samuell Gibson's (511, 279, 272)

23 Sept 1682	I gave him a noat to deduct out of his halfe years rent: repayres	003	15	00
26 Aug 83	Robert Kingsberry account for £19 payd Fowle June. / *279/5* /	019	00	00
16 Feb 1683.	Jeremiah Prance write Gibson payd him for my use in Dec. last £19 / *272* /	019	00	00
8 Aug. 1684.	Gibson paid Prance / *272* /	015	03	11
	Amonition	000	01	01
		057	00	00

216

A particular account of what I have receiv'd and allow'd from 30 Oct. 1676 to the 29 Nov. 1677 and what is owing to me from these Tenants and Baylyes.

Tenants	page	Money			Tax			Repayres			Allowance			Owe		
		£	s	d	£	s	d	£	s	d	£	s	d	£	s	d
Johnson	19	63	10	00										27	17	05
Pall	21	12	15	06	00	03	06									
Gosse	23	43	12	00										00	17	00
Drake	25	00	12	00												
Selfe	27	07	10	00				01	00	00				59	10	00
Powle	29	29	12	9	00	07	03									
Morrice	31	01	12	00										01	12	00
Lyme Kill	33	10	00	00										05	00	00
Riseborow	35	00	16	00										03	10	00
Windham	37	09	13	08										02	17	2½
Abbs Thomas	39	10	16	05	00	03	07									
Bendish	41	35	05	02	00	07	10				00	07	00	09	00	00
Abbs Rich	43	09	01	00										04	10	06
Abbs Nick	45	12	04	00										06	04	00
Richerson	47	30	00	00										15	00	00
Bally	49	06	10	00										03	05	00
Flaxman	51	00	19	08	00	00	04									
Lowne	55	01	07	08	00	00	04									
Johnson W.	57	00	07	00												
Reave	59	04	16	00												
Johnson H.	61	05	12	00										02	16	00
Pall. E	63	00	03	04												
Cooke	65	38	00	00										22	00	00
Seckar	67	01	09	04												
Ingland	69													01	15	00
Ransome	71	25	19	02							02	02	06	60	00	06
Barnes	73	06	00	00										03	00	00
Sexton	75	54	00	00												
Colls	7	07	10	00												
Russells	79	11	10	00										32	12	01
Frost and Abbs	81	41	13	06										21	03	06
Yarmouth	82	00	02	08												
Hamond	83	00	01	04										00	01	04
Frost W.	84	02	00	00												
Woodrowe	85	00	05	00										00	05	00
Doughty	86													09	12	00
Warner	89	03	13	00										00	00	04

Name	Page	Money			Tax			Repayres			Allowance			Owe		
Herne	91	03	14	00										03	14	00
Smith H.	93	25	02	09										15	12	05
Taylour	94													18	00	00
Miller M.	97	01	06	00												
Foster	99	06	00	00										06	00	00
Woodrowe	101	15	01	06							00	15	00	09	00	09
Abbs Peter	103	04	00	00												
		544	04	08	01	04	06	03	02	06	03	02	00	344	10	11½

217. Brought over from the other side (218)

Page		Money			Tax			Repayres			Allowance			Owe		
	£	s	d	£	s	d	£	s	d	£	s	d	£	s	d	
	216	544	04	08	01	04	06	03	02	06	03	02	00	344	10	11½
Ferzer	105	02	18	00	01	01	02									
W. Dawson	106	00	08	00										00	08	00
N. Dawson	107	00	07	06										00	07	06
Barker	108	00	12	00										00	12	00
Smith Mr	109													00	06	00
Elis	110	00	00	04												
Harvy	111													00	00	03
Thorey	113	36	10	00							00	10	00	18	10	00
Grime	115	18	10	00				04	08	02				37	00	00
Thorey	116													06	00	00
Parke	119	85	10	00				06	10	00				46	00	00
Richman	121	05	00	00										02	10	00
Allison	123	11	10	00				00	05	00				05	10	00
Black	125	36	13	06										19	07	00
Greenacre	127	29	10	00				00	09	11				17	00	00
Mack	129	39	13	07										56	16	05
Winter	131	26	00	00							02	00	00	56	00	00-
Smith	133	03	10	00	01	15	00				01	11	06	49	08	06
Ball	137	05	00	00	01	01	10				17	13	04	12	15	10
Norton	139	01	14	06	00	12	00	01	02	02	00	08	00			
Jakes	139	36	13	04										08	13	04
Marshall	140													00	10	00-
Gould	143	56	12	04				02	13	08	00	14	00			
Osborne	144	02	00	00-												
Suffolke	151	203	12	00	01	12	00	15	14	11	31	13	00	337	14	08
R. Kingsbery	153	126	00	00										211	00	00
J. Kingsbery	159	100	00	00										288	16	00
Miller	161	18	00	00										20	00	00
Wilson	163	43	05	00										15	05	00-

Wilson Mr	187	12	16	00	04	15	06			20	11	09		
Maries	187	03	00	00						00	10	00		
Springall	187	02	00	06										
Bayliffs of Manours														
Perry	169	38	02	08				04	00	00	44	17	9½
Bale	171	15	00	00							62	17	04
Cooke	180	67	12	00							129	00	07
Old Debts	15										440	00	09
Finns of Manors		04	11	08	As by Salman's account dated twenty ninth Nov. 1677								
3 Cullyers		05	08	9½	By Salman's account Nov. 1677								
	1661	14	7½	11	02	00	34	06	04	82	13	07	232	00	08

➤ Noat: The profits of the grounds in hand are not included herein; but accounted for by Salman 29 Nov. 1677: account from Nov. 1677 to Dec 1678 p. 218

218. Account of what I receiv'd and allow'd my Tenants in Norfolk, Suffolk, and Essex since 29 Nov. 1677 and what they now owe me

Receiv'd cleare in mony and goods		1778	19	00
Allow'd them in taxes		0078	13	00
Repayres		0051	14	00
Rents which they payd for me *vide* 41, 65, 125, 137, 151, 181, 235		0013	16	00
Tythes of Brunden p. 155		0026	13	04
Court diners [pp] 143–151		0002	08	00
For collecting my Quit Rents 151, 171, 181, 268		0017	06	08
There is now owing to me from my tennants and baylyes of my manours		1689	15	00
And in desperate debts p. 15 £ s d		0436	00	09
Received as above	1778 19 00	4096	6	6
Allowed in all [as above]	190 11 09			
Rest due as above	2125 15 09			
	4096 06 06			

Noat: The profit of Repham and lands in hand is not included in this account

Noat: I payd mony for taxes, and repayres of some of these farmes and all lands in hands and Rents of Assize and for court diners which is not included in this account
Fines of manors are not in this account

Salman account for the Fines and Cully Rent   0023 15 00

219. 31 Oct. 1679. account of what I have receiv'd of and allow'd my tenants (except Worle) since 10 Dec. 678 and what they owe me upon this account

Received in money and goods		1607	12	11½
Allowed in taxes	45 17 11			
Repayres	16 12 07			

Lords rent p. 225, 235	03 06 04	
Sallarye p. 171, 225, 235	07 06 08	0073 03 06
Received and allowed as above		1680 06 5½
Tenants and baylyes owing upon this account 31 Oct. 1679		1797 15 11
Besides desperate debts p. 15 mark #		0436 00 09
		2233 16 08

The profit of the lands following are not included in the account above

Page			£ s
	Parke	Acres	60 00
	Church Close		16 00
174	Sheep Walke		25 00
176	Flags and Brakes		10 00
52	Aylemerton Closes	20	10 00
20	of Rich Pall's	5	01 05
24	of Drakes	12	04 16
	Pond Meadow		07 00
560/5	Hay of Long Meadow		07 00
162	Dairye ground		24 00
190	of Waterson's sowne		04 05
80	Frosts		40 00
203	Dovehouse		40 00
44	Nick Abbs		12 00
72	Buns Wood		06 00
166	Repham		52 00
	Keebles in Suffolk		48 00
	per annum		367 06

Noat: Salman receive the fines and Cully Rent *vide* his book and pay several rents issuing out of my Estate, *vide* his weekly bills:

220. Receiv'd and allow'd my Tenants and Bailifs of Manours since 31 Oct 1679

10 Oct 1681

Receiv'd as appear by this booke in money and goods		2982 02 08
Allow'd taxes	127 08 06	
Repayres	036 17 02	
Lords Rents and Services pp. 113, 183, 225	015 17 06	
pp. 227, 263, 265		
Courts Keeping 47, pp. 159, 225, 227, 243	005 15 00	
Tythes	040 00 00	
Sallary pp. 183, 225, 227, 235	019 06 08	0245 04 10
		3227 07 06

Noat: Profits of courts, and lands in hand, or sowne to halves are not
included in this account.

Norfolk tennants owe me	1288	01	1½			
Bailiff Cooke, Perry, Bale	0380	17	00			
Suffolk tenants	0540	13	08			
Bailiff	0028	15	10			
Essex tenants	0269	15	02			
Noat: The desperate debts p. 219 are not included in the [£]2508 02 9½				2508	02	9½

The value of my estate at Mich. 1681

Norfolk Farmes let for	1085	13	05			
Grounds in Hand / p. 499 /	0450	15	00			
Rents of Assize	0125	10	10½			
	1661	19	3½			
Suffolk Farmes let for	0207	10	00			
Rents of Assize	0015	05	00			
	0222	15	00			
Essex Estate let for	0412	08	00	2297	03	1½
Somerset The Manor of Worle worth about				0400	00	00
Profits of Court suppose				0050	00	00
				2747	03	1½

224. Suffolke Debt (150, 226)

5 March 1677	Rest due to me / p. 150 /	217	07	08
For halfe a years rent of farme rents and Rents of Assize				
ending at (as by the particular p. 150) Lday 1678		114	17	11
	At Mich. 1678	114	17	11
	Miscast	000	00	10
		447	04	04
20 Feb. 1678	Rest due	243	04	02
	At	229	15	10
		473	00	00
16 Jan 1679	Rest due upon sccount	288	16	03
	Repayres 3 18 02 Keeble's / p. 226 /			

225. Suffolke Credit

18 May 1678. I was in Suffolk and did then take a noat under Robert Keeble's hand for
payment of £69 which is and will bee due to me for rent at Mich next; besides £8
which I abated upon the account

Noat: George Fen did then alsoe give me a bill under his hand, that if Keeble did not
pay according to the agreement he would pay me upon demand.

Receiv'd of Rob Keeble	£15	
of Arteson	5	

		£	s	d
	Of H. Auldred 3	023	00	00
	/ Noat: the £15 which Keeble paid this day is noe part of the £69 /			
	Keeble payd Salman in part of £69	020	00	00
10 Dec. 1678	Salman account for	062	00	00
20 Feb. 1678	Houseman for Keeble	020	00	00
	And upon account	044	00	00
Repayring the two mills £2 1s, Houseman's pump 7s		002	08	00
The 5 last months of the 17 months tax for building 30 ships				
and 6 months of the 18 months tax for disbanding the army		009	12	04
Lords rent issuing out of my Suffolk estate ending Mich. 1678		001	13	00
	Abated Keeble 18 May 1678	008	00	00
	Court diner £1, sallarye £3 end Mich. 1678	004	00	00
	Disburs'd on account of Keeble's farme	009	06	10
	/ quarto p. 16 /	204	00	02

					£	s	d
Rest upon Houseman's account	236 14 02;				243	4	2
4 years rent of ye coppyhold and lately seised	2 00 00				447	4	4
Knobs owe me a per account 1672	4 10 00						
	243 04 02						

			£	s	d
31 Oct. 1679	Salman account for		026	00	00
18 Jan. 1679	Houseman account for £58 10s of which £29 was Keeble's	058	10	00
Allow'd for Keeble's being in hand / quarto p. 14 /			048	00	00
Disbursements upon account of Keeble's / quarto p. 16 /			038	07	09
	3, 4, 5 payments of the tax of all the lands		007	13	00
	Lords rent ending Mich. 1679		001	13	00
	Court diner £1, sallarye £3		004	00	00
	282 06 03 upon Houseman's account		184	03	09
	002 00 00 of lands seised	Rest	288	16	03
	004 10 00 Knob's 1672		473	00	00

226. Suffolke Debt (224, *quarto*, 48, 296)

		£	s	d
	Rest due upon Suffolke account / p. 224 /	288	16	03
	At Mich. 1680	229	15	10
24 Feb 80	Houseman charge himselfe with the profits			
	and stock of Keeble's farme	079	01	10
	£ [s] [d]	597	13	11

1681 *scilicet*	13 00 00 abated of the rents p. 150
	05 00 00 in Robert Keeble's
	08 00 00 in Auldred's farme p. 550

Auldred owe	087 19 01	
Peppar	035 00 00	
Keeble	016 10 00	
Arteshall	018 00 00	p. 227

Houseman	166 14 07
Rents of Assize	013 10 00
Butcher's in part for beasts	008 10 00-
	346 03 08

24 Feb 1680	Rest due as on t'other side	352	13	08
	A years rent ending Mich. 1681	216	15	10
	At Mich. 1682	222	15	10
		792	05	04

Noat. £5 of the £8 which I allow'd Houseman 31 March 1682 for sallary was for his trouble in looking after Keeble's farme in hand for Mich. 1678 to Mich. 1680

Mem. 31 March 1682 Houseman respit upon

Patrich at Mich 1681	019 00 0
Henry Auldred's account	012 17 03 / *quarto p. 48* /
Peppar	037 00 00
Keeble the late Miller	014 10 00
Arteshall the present Miller	020 00 00
Sagar's widow	021 00 00
Houseman himself	207 08 01
Rents of Assize	011 10 03
	335 05 07
The £6 10s mentioned p. 227	006 10 00
And the years rents Mich. 1682	222 15 10
	562 11 05

Arrears as above mentioned / *296* /		562	11	05

227. Suffolke Credit (*quarto* 14, 16, 48; 226, 265, 297)

1 Oct. 1680	Salman account for		018	00	00
24 Feb.	Houseman account for (besides the said £18)		115	10	09
	Keeble's farme in hand / *quarto. p. 14* /		048	00	00
	Disbursed about Keeble's farme / *quarto p. 16* /		044	10	06
	Last 3 months of the 18 months tax	2 11 00			
	And 6 months supply	5 02 00	007	13	00
	Lords rent ending Mich. 1680		001	13	00
	Amonition and other militia charges		001	09	00
	2 court diners and sallarye Mich. 1680		005	00	00

Repayrs about upper Mill 2 8 0, Houseman's farme 0 16 0		003	04	04
346 04 08 by Houseman's account / *226* /		245	00	03
002 00 00 for land seised	Rest	352	13	08
004 10 00 Knobs *anno* 1672		597	13	11
Repayrs a milstone for Upper Mill £10 10s / *265* /				
Repayrs for Keeble's besides timber 28 9 1d / *quarto p. 16* /				

31 March 1682	Houseman account for 176 9 3 payd several persons for my use since 24 Feb. 1680			176	09	03
	For brick in his yard			003	00	08
	A bill of disbursements upon Auldred's account who died 30 Dec. 1680 / *quarto p. 48* /			010	03	08
	Lords rent ending Mich. 1681			000	19	04
	Amonition and militia charges			000	15	07
	Court diner £1, sallary £8 / 226 /			009	00	00
	Repayrs about the Mill	17 18 7				
	A milstone for the Lower Mill	9 7 6		027	06	01
	Repayrs about the other farmes at Mich. 1681			001	19	04

Rest due to me by Houseman's account dated 31 March   229   13   11
1682 which was examined by me in Suffolke 19 Sep. 1682   333   05   07
Beside the £6 10s mentioned upon the foot of the former
account / 226 /   006   10   00

	And the years rent of the whole estate ending	569	09	06
	at Mich. 1682	222	15	10
		792	05	04

228. George Johnson's for part of Swifts Debt (553, 24)

Halfe a years rent at Lday 1678	003	12	00
At Mich 1678	003	12	00
At Mich. 1679	007	04	00
At Mich. 1680	007	04	00
At Mich. 1681	007	04	00

At Mich. 1681. I tooke the ground at the widdow's request   028   16   00

229. Johnson's Credit

27 May 1678	Salman paid for ditching 13s			
10 Dec. 1678	Salman account for	002	12	00
31 Oct. 1679	Salman account for.	003	12	00
	Salman promised to abate out of his 1st year rent	001	00	00
1 Oct 1680	Salman account for	003	00	00
21 May 1681	Payd Salman	003	00	00
30 Sep. 1681	I tooke Widdow Johnson's bond	015	12	00
	She have payd me	028	16	00

230. Heydon's Debt (553, 18)

For Johnson's farme at our Lday 1678	024	05	00
At Mich. 1678	024	05	00
At Mich. 1679	048	10	00

		097	00	00
31 Oct. 1679	Owe	066	00	04
	At Mich. 1680	048	10	00
Heydon wanted stock at first, and it is not prudent to trust him longer		114	10	04

1681, 1682, 1683 *Mem.* Repayrs 2 13 4 about the houses / *vide quarto p. 21 /*
And   4   5 3 about the fences

John Tomson's (483)

231. Heydon's Credit

28 March 1678	Payd to me	020	00	00
	the 3rd and 4th quarterly payments of the tax			
	for building 30 ships of war	000	16	04
	The weekes pay for Trophies	000	01	05
➤ I paid the carpenter 8s for making a new fat to the well.				
	Allow'd Heydon for cleaning the well	000	01	00
	and for nayles	000	00	06
5 Nov. 16 78	Payd me	003	10	00
17 Dec. 1678	Payd me	005	00	00
5 months of the Ship Tax in full of the 17 months		000	13	07
The 1st payment of the tax for disbanding the armye		000	08	02
	Allow'd for glasing the little tenement	000	02	02
	A load of straw used at Felbrigg	000	06	06
1678	Repayring the tenement 1 17 3	030	19	08
	The farme house 2 0 4 Rest	066	00	04
		097	00	00

21 Sep. 1680	Allow'd the five last paymentts of the 18 months			
	ArmyeTax 2 0 10, 6 months supply 0 16 4			
	Amonition 0 1 5½	002	18	7½
	Hay 1679	000	17	06
22 [*Sep*]	A bill of sale of goods valued at *quarto* 17	041	02	06
	And of his corne which I tooke for	069	11	08
	Vide. quarto [p]17 how much 'twas worth.	114	10	04

Tomson's

232. Gregorye's Debt (32)

	For halfe a years rent of 5½ acres of Marie's			
	land ending Lday 1676	001	10	00
	The Mich. rent charged p. 32			

Mr Eyre's Debt (493 S 5)

A years rent at Mich. 1686	OII	OO	OO
At Mich 1687	OII	OO	OO
11 Feb. 1687 Mr Windham made the allowances mention'd on t'other side to me, and I owe him eleven pounds *Thomas Eyre*	022	OO	OO
11 Feb. 1687 Due to me	OII	OO	OO

233. Gregorye's Credit

30 Oct. 1676 Salman chargeth himselfe with	OOI	IO	OO

Mr Eyre's Credit (86, 87)

Delivered oats 15 comb at 5s	3 15 0				
Peas 3 bushells	9				
Straw	7s	004	II	OO
Oats 8 combs	1 12	OOI	I2	OO
Oats 6 comb ⎤ at 4s		OOI	I6	OO
11 Feb. 1687 Allow'd him 3 years herbage for the park and 3 years for Atwoods		000	I3	06
Mending the fences in the Close		000	I2	OO
And then he payd me		000	II	06
		OII	OO	OO
Rest due		OII	OO	OO
		022	OO	OO

234. Perry's Debt (168, 235)

	Perry owe p. 168 at Mich. 1678	069	I6	OO
	A years rent at Mich. 1679	024	I8	2½
	[£ s d]	094	I4	2½
	36 14 06 Perry respit at Mich. 1678			
	03 15 2½ Perry charge himself with			
	24 18 2½ A years rent at Mich. 1679			
	65 07 11			
31 Oct 1679	Due at Mich 1679	065	07	II
	At Mich. 1680	024	I8	2½
		090	06	I½
21 Oct. 1680	Due at Mich. 1680	057	I8	2½
	At Mich. 1681	024	I8	2½
	At Mich. 1682	024	I8	2½
	At Mich. 1683	024	I8	2½
	A years rents at Mich. 1684	024	I8	2½
		157	II	0½

Perry's credit page 235 is		121	02	01

20 Nov. 1685 Arrears of Toft Manors at Mich. 1684 as is
particularly mentioned in his account dated 20 Nov.

1685 are	35 13 3			
Arrears at Thurlton	0 15 7½	036	08	10½

Observe. The ballance of the said account is [£]26 5 7, but
he payd me 26.5.6, which was 1d short, to the
which being added to the seid 157.10.11½ makes it

157	10	11½
000	00	01
157	11	0½

235. Perry's Credit

24 Oct. 1678 Perry in his account dischargeth himselfe of £10 payd
Salman 22 Oct. 1677 for which I have given Perry credit p. 169. He also

dischargeth himselfe of a years rents payd to Toft Monks at Mich. 1677		001	13	04
	And for his sallarye ending	002	06	08
10 Dec. 1678	Salman chargeth himselfe with	009	01	1½
20 Oct. 1679	Perry in his account ending Mich. 1678 dischargeth			
	himselfe of	012	05	02
	And of a years rent to Toft Monks	001	13	04
	And his sallarye	002	06	08
		029	06	3½
	Vide p. 234 the ballance	065	07	11
		094	14	2½
31 Oct. 1679	Salman chargeth himselfe wth the ballance of Perry's last			
	account	003	15	2½
20 Oct. 1680	Perry in his account for a year ending Mich.			
	1679 dischargeth himself of	011	14	00
	And his sallarye	002	06	08
21 Oct. 1680	Smith received the ballance of the said account being	014	12	0½
	Perry respit him both manors 1679 £33	032	07	11
	A years rent of the manors 1680 24 18 2½	057	18	2½
		090	06	1½

26 Oct 1681 Perry in his account ending discharge himself of		018	14	6½
And a years rents to Toft Monks end Mich 1679		001	03	04
	And his sallarye end Mich 1680	002	06	08
25 Oct. 1682	Perry discharge himself in his account end Mich 1681	020	04	3½
	And his sallarye	002	06	08
24 Oct. 1683	Perry discharge himself of	017	03	10
	Sallary end Mich 1682	002	06	08
19 Nov. 1684	Perry account for	025	07	03
	Sallary end Mich 1683	002	06	08

20 Nov. 1685 I was at Toft Overhall and Thurlton Courts
where John Perry payd me for ballance of his Account dated

this day for the year ending Mich. 1684		026	05	06
Sallary end ing Mich 84		002	06	08
turne over	121	02	01

236. Perry's Debt (234)

Perry respit in his account dated 20 Nov. 1685 at Mich. 1684	036	08	10½
Rents of assize for the year ending Mich 1685 for the			
Manor of Toft Overhall and Netherhall are	021	10	02
Mich 1687 For two years rent of both the manors	049	16	04
	111	30	06

237. Perry's Credit

17 Nov. 1686	Mr Perry sent me by Mr Watts who paid it me 22 Dec 1686	018	07	5½
	His sallary at Mich. 1685	002	06	08
31 Oct. 1687	Perry payd Mr Watts	020	06	10½

238. Bale's Debt (170, 306)

18 March 1678	Bale owe	034	16	−6
And for 100 of wood sould out of Crownethorp 1677 to				
Orson and Beal's widow. And for forty shilling twice	002	00	00
payd Bale. Witness my hand *Edmund Bale*	002	00	00
	For rent ending at Mich. 1679	024	02	04
	At Mich. 1680	024	02	04
	At Mich. 1681	024	02	04
	At Mich. 1682	024	02	04
	At Mich. 1683	024	02	04
	A years rent at Mich 1684	024	02	04

16 Feb. 1684: My land lord Windham allow'd me of my demands. And I
doe acknowledge to owe him eighty three pounds sixteen shillings seven

pence upon account of rents of Assize. Witness my hand *Edmund Bale*	183	10	06
In the presence of *Joseph Elden*			
18 Feb. 1684 Rest due	083	16	07
A years rent at Mich. 1685	024	02	04

24 Nov. 1685 Mr Windham allow'd all my disbursements ans demands,
soe I owe eighty one pounds three pence deducting the arrears of rents of
Assize. Witness my hand.

Edmund Bale Signed before *Peter Watts*	107	18	11
24 Nov. 1685 Due as abovesayd	081	00	03
29 Sep. 1687 For two years rent of both manors	048	04	08
Vide p. 306	129	04	11

239. Bale's Credit

31 Oct. 1679	Salman account for	010	00	00
10 Oct. 1681	Smith account for	010	00	00
1 Oct. 1682	Smith account for	013	00	00
27 [Oct]	Payd Mr Harris	017	00	00
9 Oct. 1684	Payd Watts for me	018	00	00
25 [Oct]	Elden account for	015	10	00

18 Feb. 1684   I was at Bale's and allow'd him for 6 years rent
payd Sir John Woodhouse of 9s 9d a year ending Mich. 1684   002 18 06
And 5 years rent at 5s 1d a year end Mich. 1683 to Hemnal Manor   001 05 05

	And 6 years sallary ending Mich. 1684	012	00	00
		099	13	11
	Bale owe	083	16	07
		183	10	06
23 Nov. 1685	Bale payd me	018	00	00
	Allow'd for fencing the woods	003	12	06
	Charges about larth	002	13	05
	Sir John Woodhouse's rent at Mich. 1685	000	09	09
	Queen's Manor in Windham	000	02	08
	Sallary	002	00	00

Mem: Bale surrendred all his coppyhold holden of my manors to me for
security of 93 12 11, 24 Nov. 1685   026 18 08

	Bale owe	081	00	03
		107	18	11
24 Nov. 1685	Receiv'd part of the arrear	001	17	08
16 Nov. 1686	Payd Watts who brought it 22 Dec.	016	00	00
1 Nov. 1687	Payd Watts	013	00	00

242. Gould's Debt (551, 142, 505)

	For halfe a years rent at Mich. 1679	030	00	00
	At Mich. 1680	060	00	00
	At Mich. 1681	060	00	00
	At Mich. 1682	060	00	00
	At Mich. 1683	060	00	00
		270	00	00
21 Oct. 1683	Owe	040	00	00
	Halfe a years rent at Lday 1684	030	00	00
	At Mich. 1684	030	00	00
	A years rent at Mich. 1685	060	00	00
		160	00	00
	A years rent at Mich. 1686	060	00	00
	At Mich. 1687	060	00	00

243. Gould's Credit

31 Oct. 1679	Salman chargeth himselfe with	028	14	06
	The 4th payment of the Armye Tax	000	11	06
	A court diner	000	14	00
1 Oct . 1680	Salman account for	028	17	00
	The two last payments of the said tax	001	03	00
10 Oct. 1681	Smith account for 6 months supply 1 3 0,	19	02½	
	amonition 0 2 2½, court diner 15s	002	00	2½
16 Dec. 1681	Alderman Briggs account for	030	00	00
1 Oct. 1682	Smith account for	028	15	00
	A court diner	001	00	00
	Thatching	000	05	00
27 [Oct]	Payd Mr Harris	057	13	10
Amonition 0 2 2½; a diner 1 2 0 ; repayrs 1 2 0		002	06	02
21 Oct. 1683	Elden account for	020	00	00
		230	00	00
	Rest	040	00	00
		270	00	00
25 Oct. 1684	Elden account for	068	01	03
	Allow'd repayrs	000	19	09
	A court diner at Mich. 1683 court	000	19	00
17 Feb. 1684	I tould Gould I woud give him in respect last			
	summer was soe dry	005	00	00
17 Oct. 1685	Elden account	059	05	03
	Repayrs	002	13	09
	Court diner at	001	01	00
24 Nov. 1685	Gould payd me	020	13	08
	Amonition	000	02	03
	Repayrs	000	02	01
	Court diner 23 Nov. 1685	001	02	00
		160	00	00
23 Nov. 1686	Sent me by Stephen Legg	020	00	00
17 Jan	Sent me by S. Legg	010	00	00
May 1687	Payd Legg	027	12	00
Allow'd repayrs 9s 6d, Amonition 2s 2d, court diner £1 2s				
Carrying Wood to Dr Pepper's 14s		002	07	08
21 Dec.	Payd Legg	058	00	00

244. Lowne's Debt (529, 326)

	Halfe a years rent at Mich. 1679	030	00	00
	At Mich. 1680	060	00	00
		090	00	00

3 Oct 1680		030	00	00
	At Mich. 1681	060	00	00
	At Mich. 1682	060	00	00
	At Mich. 1683	060	00	00
		210	00	00
21 Oct. 1683	Owe	040	00	00
	A years rent at Mich. 1684	060	00	00
	At Mich. 1685	060	00	00
	At Lady 1686	030	00	00
21 Sep. 1686	I owe my land lord for rent sixty pounds. Witness my hand	190	00	00
29 Sep. 1686	Lowne owe me	090	00	00

245. Lowne's Credit

29 Dec. 1679	Lowne payd me			028	06	04
	3 and 4 payments of the Armye Tax 1679			001	13	08
2 Oct. 1680	Payd			027	15	01
	5 and 6 payments of the said tax			001	13	08
	Amonition			000	03	03
	Repayrs in full of Lday 1680			000	08	00
	1679, 1680 repayrs 12 18 1			060	00	00
	Rest			030	00	00
				090	00	00
10 Oct 1681	Salman account for	27 13 04				
	A bill of repayrs	2 04 00				
	250 bricks for Felbrigg	0 03 00		030	00	00
	Smith account for	26 06 04				
	6 months supply	1 13 08				
	Repayrs	2 00 00		030	00	00
1 Oct. 1683	Salman account for			035	00	00
	Smith account for			013	09	09
	Thatching			001	10	03
2 Oct. 1683	Salman account for			059	13	10
	Amonition 3 3; repayrs 2 11			000	06	02
1681, 1682	Repayrs 12 14 11			170	00	00
	Rest			040	00	00
				210	00	00
25 Oct. 1684	Salman account for			028	00	00
	Elden account for			010	16	00
	2000 bricks for my stable			001	04	00
5 Dec.	Payd me			014	04	00
	Allow'd for bricks used at Felbrigg			000	16	00

27 Apr. 1685	Payd me	015	00	00
4 Dec. 1685	Payd me	021	02	06
	Seed corne 8 8 0; bricks 6; amonition 3 3	008	17	06
12 March	Oats 21 comb *vide*. Elden's account.			
1685	Oats 15 comb 3 bushels in the same	004	02	06
10 June 1686	Payd John Barham	010	00	00
	Wheat 10 combs at 14s; oats 20 combs 5s 6d	012	10	00
	Straw 2 loads	001	00	00
21 Sep	Lowne payd me	002	07	06
	Remit	000	00	03
		130	00	00
	Rest	060	00	00
		190	00	00
23 March 1686	Payd me	015	07	00
Oats 30 combs *scilicet* 15 comb at 4s, and 15 comb at 4s 3d		006	03	09
	3 cows and calfes	008	05	00
	Rate for Monyman's 4s. Remit him 3d	000	04	03

246. Howard's Debt (528, 531)

	Halfe a years rent at Mich. 1679	020	14	00
	A years rent ending Mich. 1680	032	00	00
	At Mich. 1681	032	00	00
	At Mich. 1682	032	00	00
	At Mich. 1683	032	00	00
		148	14	00
21 Oct. 1683	Howard	016	00	00
	A years rent at Mich. 1684	032	00	00
	At Mich. 1685	032	00	00
	At Lady 1686	016	00	00
		096	00	00
29 Sep. 1686	Owe	016	00	00
29 Sep. 1687	A year rent at Mich. 1687	032	00	00

28 Feb. 1687 Mr Windham gave me a receipt for my half years rent, and
did make the allowances mentioned on the other side to me   048   00   00
Signed before me *Stephen Legge Will Howard*

	A years rent Mich. 1688	032	00	00

247. Howard's Credit

1 Oct. 1680	Salman account for				019	11	00
	6 months tax ending Aug. 1679				001	03	00
21 March 1680	Payd me	19	17	0			
	12 months tax	1	16	0			

	Amonition				0	01	8			
	Repayrs				0	05	4	022	00	00
10 Oct. 1681	Smith account for							026	00	00
1 Oct. 1682	Smith account for							031	03	8½
	Repayrs							000	14	07
	Amonition							000	01	8½
27 Dec	Payd me							016	00	00
21 Oct. 1683	Elden account for			1	3	0,				

And for 48 comb of oats   11   5   8   612   08   00

Allow'd for 9 loads of straw to thatch the barne which fell downe

	Repayrs about the houses	11	10	6	003	12	00
	The fences	5	15	4	132	14	00
		17	5	10 Rest	016	00	00
					148	14	00
June 21 1684	Payd me since 21 Oct. 1683				031	04	00
	2 loads of straw used at Lowne's				000	16	00
21 Mar. 1684	Payd me				015	04	11
	Allow'd for repayrs about Beston Barne				000	15	01
28 Sep. 1685	Howard payd me				015	10	00
	Amonition 1 8 ½. Remit 3 ½				000	02	00
17 March 1685	Payd me				010	13	00
	Oats 20 comb at 5s 4d – 5.6.8; Remit 4d				005	07	00
28 Sep. 1686	Howard payd me				016	00	00
					096	00	00
4 March 1686	Payd me				010	00	00
19	Oats at 4s 3d *per* comb				003	14	4½
20 Apr. 1687	Payd me				002	05	06
	Remit				000	00	1½
27 Sep. 1687	Payd me				015	18	00
	A rate for the *farme* late Monyman's				000	02	00
28 Feb	Payd me				016	00	00
					048	00	00
7 Sep. 1688	Howard payd Stephen Legg				006	00	00
20 [Sep]	Payd me				009	17	00
	A constable's rate – Monyman's				000	02	08
	Remit				000	00	04

248. Johnson's Debt (528, 531, 556,)

Halfe a years rent at Mich. 1679	015	00	00
A years rent at Mich. 1680 / *531* /	045	00	00
A years rent for both at Mich. 1681 / *556, 531* /	051	00	00
At Mich. 1682	051	00	00

	At Mich. 1683	051	00	00
		213	00	00
21 Oct. 1683		102	00	00
	A years rent at Mich. 1684	051	00	00
	At Mich. 1685	051	00	00
	Halfe a years rent at Lady 1686	025	10	00
22 Sep. 1686	I owe my land lord for farme rent one			
hundred pounds, nine shillings, nine pence *Henry Johnson*		229	10	00
29 Sep 1686	Johnson owe me	126	19	09
	A years rent at Mich. 1687	051	00	00
9 March 1687.	I accounted with my land lord and this is a true account.	177	19	09

Witness my hand: *Henry Johnson* Signed before *Stephen Legge*

249. Johnson's Credit

15 Jan. 1679	Payd me				014	05	06
	3, 4 payments of the Armye Tax 1679				000	14	06
29 Nov and 22 March 1680 payd me		41	19	5			
	12 months tax	02	04	4			
	Amonition	00	02	2			
	Repayrs	00	14	1	045	00	00
10 Oct. 1681	Salman account for				025	10	00
1 Oct. 1682	Salman account for				025	10	00
	Repayrs about the houses 0 18 0				111	00	00
	The fences 2 13 3 Rest				102	00	00
	3 11 3				213	00	00
1684 May	Elden had 80 hog-sheep to put into my flock				027	12	06
15 March	Payd me				047	01	06
1685	Allow'd for straw in 1684				001	09	00
	And for alder stage poles 1685				000	07	00
28 June 1686	Payd John Barham				010	00	00
	Sheep 70 at 6s 8d	23	06	8			
	Wheat 10 comb at 14s 6d	07	05	0			
	Straw 6 loads at 10s	03	00	0	033	11	08
22 Sep.	Brought me 10 comb of wheat at 15s				007	10	00
	Repayrs				000	03	06
	Amonition rates				000	05	01
					128	00	03
	Rest				101	09	09
					229	10	00
31 May 1687	Payd me				014	14	06
	A cow	02	15	0			
	Wheat 4 comb	03	00	0	010	05	00

	Oats 20 comb at 4s 6d	04	10	o
June 20	Payd me	023	11	06
	And 7 comb of buck at 5s 6d	001	18	06
5 Nov. 1687	H. Johnson payd me	025	10	00
23 Dec.	Payd me	047	04	00
	Wheat 4 comb at 14s	002	16	00
	Straw to thatch at Lowne's	001	00	00
10 Feb	Payd me	025	10	00
5 March	Payd me in full at Mich. 1687	025	10	00
		177	19	06
	Remit	000	00	03
		177	19	09

250. Tower's Debt (528, 531, 328)

Halfe a years rent at Mich. 1679	016	00	00
At Lday 1680	016	00	00
At Mich. 1680	016	00	00
At Mich. 1681	032	00	00
	080	00	00
Halfe a year at Lady 1682	016	00	00
	096	00	00
Halfe a year rent at Mich. 1682	016	00	00
At Mich. 1683	032	00	00
At Mich. 1684	032	00	00
	080	00	00
A years rent at Mich. 1685 / 531 /	032	00	00
At Lady 1686	016	00	00
	048	00	00
Halfe a year at Mich. 1686	016	00	00
At Lady 1687	016	00	00
	032	00	00

251. Tower's Credit (329)

2 Dec. 1679	Henry Tower payd me	014	14	4½
	A deal for the Mill	000	01	00
	3d, 4, 5 payments of the Armye Tax 1679	001	04	7½
7 June 1680	Payd me	014	17	06
The last payment of the 18 months tax for disbanding the armye		000	08	2½
	Amonition monye	000	01	07
	Repayres	000	04	06
10 Oct. 1681	Smith account for	16 00	0	
	And Salman account for	15 18	0	

	Repayrs		00	02	0	032	00	00
7 June 1680	3 months tax allow'd by me					000	08	2½
1 Oct. 1682	Salman account for					015	17	09
	Repayrs					000	02	03
	And Smith account for					015	13	05
	Repayrs					000	06	07
	Repayrs 10 12 6					096	00	00
21 Oct. 1683	Salman account for					027	10	00
	He delivered 20 comb oats April 1683					004	10	00
ditto	Elden account for					005	00	00
25 Oct. 1684	Salman account for					010	16	03
	Amonition					000	01	03
	Repayrs					000	02	06
	And Elden account for					008	00	00
4 Mar. 1684	Tower brought me two receipts of Elden's							
	for 17 9 2 payd since 25 Oct. 1684					017	09	02
	And then I allow'd him for ditching					002	11	07
	Gates making 6s, irons 3s 4d					000	09	04
	Boards for the mill					000	03	01
Making a marle pit, diging and filling 125 loads.						003	06	10
						080	00	00
17 Oct. 1685	Elden account for					014	09	8½
And allow'd him 9s 3d ½ for repayrs and amonition								
scilicet 7 8 repayrs and 1 7 ½ amonition						000	09	3½
	Cheese 4 stone					001	01	00
12 Mar. 1685	Elden account for					013	01	02
	Allow'd amonition 4d; repayrs 2s 6d					000	02	10
Clearing the marle it, digging and filling 204 loads of marle						002	16	00
7 June 1686	Payd John Barham					016	00	00
						048	00	00
9 Mar. 1686	Payd me					013	02	03
	Allow'd for 198 loads of marle		2	9	6			
	Repayrs		0	8	3	002	17	09
27 June	Payd me					016	00	00
						02	00	00

252. Monyman's Debt (529, 493,)

	Halfe a years rent at Mich. 1679	012	00	00
	A years rent at Mich. 1680	024	00	00
	At Mich. 1681	024	00	00
	At Mich. 1682	024	00	00
	At Mich. 1683	024	00	00

At Mich. 1684 Monyman say he woud hold the ground noe longer at
£24. I offer'd to let him feed it this year for £22.   108   oo   oo

His father and grandfather payd £30

6 Nov. 1684. He tould Elden he woud give £22 to feed it this year, 'tis
plaine he thought I woud abate for he knowe not how to keep his stock
this winter *Vide*. 493

21 Oct. 1683		oi2	oo	oo
A years rent end Michaelmas 1684	024	oo	oo

Mem: Monyman gave me £2 for his fences being out of repair, 25 Oct.
1684 / *Vide p. 493*/   036   oo   oo

A years rent at Mich. 1685	022	oo	oo
Half a years rent at Lady 1686	oii	oo	oo
30 Sep. 1686	Monyman gave me £1 to make the fences good / *493* /	033	oo	oo
Half a years rent at Mich. 1686	oii	oo	oo

Jeremy Cushing's

A years rent at Mich. 1687   002   10   oo

253. Monyman's Credit

17 Jan. 1679	Payd me					oii	07	06
	3, 4 payments of the Armye Tax					000	12	06
24 July	Payd me	05	oi	3				
	Allow'd for 20 sheep	06	05	0				
	5, 6 payments of the said tax	oo	12	6				
	Amonition	oo	oi	3		000	13	09
10 Oct. 1681	Smith account for	11	07	7				
	6 months tax	oo	12	5		oi2	oo	oo
	Salman account for					oi2	oo	oo
1 Oct 82	Salman account for					023	18	10
	Amonition					000	oi	02
21 Oct 83	Salman account for	20	18	0				
	By oats 12 comb	03	02	0		024	oo	oo
						096	oo	oo
				Rest		oi2	oo	oo
						108	oo	oo
29 Sep. 1684	Payd me					oi2	oo	oo
25 Oct	Elden account for					oi4	oo	oo
	And for 30 hog-sheep deliver'd in May last at					oio	oo	oo
						036	oo	oo
17 Oct. 1685	Elden allow Monyman for 20 hog-sheep					006	10	oo
12 Dec.	Elden account for					004	08	09
	Amonition					000	oi	09

20 Mar. 1685	Elden account for		011	00	00
	Oats 21 comb		005	10	00
20 July 86	Payd John Barham		004	01	00
	*Oats 20 comb at 5[s] 6[d]	5 10 0*			
	Coals 2 chaldron 14 6 *	1 09 00	006	19	00
	I had but 21 comb of oats so deduct £5 10s		038	10	06
	And for a mistake 6d		005	10	06
			033	00	00
30 Sep. 1686	Monyman payd me		011	00	00
Aug. 1687	Cushing payd Fairchilde		001	05	00

254. Elis's Debt (528, 531)

Halfe a years rent at Mich. 1679		002	16	00
At Mich. 1679 let to Johnson p. 531				

255. Elis's Credit

6 Oct. 1680	Payd me		002	13	03
	6 months tax end Aug. 1679		000	02	09
			002	16	00

256. Lowne's Debt (528)

Halfe a years rent at Mich. 1679	001	00	00
A years rent at Mich. 1680	002	00	00
At Mich. 1681	002	00	00
At Mich. 1682	002	00	00
	007	00	00
A years rent at Mich. 1683	002	00	00
At Mich. 1684	002	00	00
At Mich. 1685	002	00	00
At Mich. 1686	002	00	00
	008	00	00

257. Lowne's Credit

11 Nov. 1680	Allow'd for corne	2 16 7			
	18 moneths tax	0 03 3			
	Amonition	0 00 2	003	00	00
1 Oct. 1682	Salman chargeth himselfe for 2 comb of seed wheat		001	12	00
21 Oct. 1683	Salman account for		002	08	00
			007	00	00
25 Oct. 1684	Salman account for £1 4s 2d		001	04	02
Oats 21 comb *vide* Elden's account 12 Mar 1685			005	00	00

Anno 1686. Lowne absented from his creditors p. 15		006	04	02
Rest to ballance		001	15	10
		008	00	00

258. Britiffe's Debt (528)

Halfe a years rent at Mich. 1679	003	00	00
A years rent at Mich. 1680	003	00	00
At Mich. 1681	003	00	00
At Mich. 1682	003	00	00
At Mich. 1683	003	00	00
At Mich. 1684	003	00	00
	016	10	00
At Mich. 1685	003	00	00
At Mich. 1686	003	00	00
At Mich. 1687	003	00	00

259. Britiffe's Credit

2 Sep. 1680	Payd upon account	001	08	00
29 Dec. 1680	Payd me	002	18	03
	15 months tax 1680	000	03	09
24 Jan. 1681	Payd me 1681	003	00	00
6 Mar. 1682	Payd me 1682	003	00	00
25 Oct. 1684	Payd me 1684	006	00	00
		016	10	00
5 July 1687	Fairchilde account for	007	10	00

260. Selfe's Debt (540, 27)

Owe at Mich 1679 / p. 27 /		107	00	00
26 March 1680	Lent him goods valued in the inventory	004	01	03
Selfe wanted stock, was a lazy fellow and an ill husband				
Vide quarto book 18		111	01	03

Harris's (509, 24)

	A years rent at Mich. 1682			036	00	00
1683	Halfe a year at Lday	18 00 0				
And for the ground late in the Widow Drake's use		6 /24/	018	06	00
			054	06	00
	Half a years rent at Mich. 1683			018	06	00
	A years rent at Mich. 1684			036	12	00
	At Mich. 1685			036	12	00
	At Lady 1686			018	06	00

27 Sep. 1686. I owe Mr Windham fivety eight pounds four pence.   109   16   00
Thomas Harris

29 Se[pt]. 1686 He owe	076	06	04

A years rent at Mich. 1687   036   12   00

Mem. 23 Nov. 1687. Harris had 2 14 8 allow'd in his general account
scilicet: for repayring his farme houses   112   18   04
1 12 8 and his fences 1 2s *vide* p. 87 *quarto*.

23 Nov. 1687   Harris owe me   034   00   11
29 Sep. 1688   For a years rent   036   12   00

4 Oct. 1688. Observe: whn Mr Harris pay the ballance of his general
account mentioned *quarto* p. 110 then I must give him credit for this
70 12 11 it being included in his general charge there.   070   12   11

261. Selfe's Credit

24 Sep. 1679   Selfe assign'd his stock to me for my securitye.
                 30 Sep. he gave possession. 3 Oct. 1679
                 payd by inventory valued at   062   06   00
31 Oct.   Salman charge himselfe with   004   00   00
                 And 22 comb 1 bushell of oats   005ᶜ 00   00
The corne growing 1679 at 14s wheat, 9s rye, 7s 6d barly,
8s buck, 9s 6d peas, 4s 6d oats comes to   035   07   00
                                                                     106   13   00
                 I don't expect the goods againe, so I lose   004   08   03
1679, 1680   Repayrs   22 18 2   111   01   03
                 Besides new ditching   2 14 10

Harris's (*quarto book* pp. 32, 46, 85, 87; 336)

30 Oct. 1682   Allow'd the mason's bill £1 1s, and the
                 glasier's bill £1 2s, thatching £1   003   03   00
                 Payd in his general account / *quarto book 32* /   032   17   00
                 Payd in his general account / *quarto book 46* /   018   06   00
1681, 1682.   Repayres houses 6 5 11, fences 13s 6d   054   06   00
13 May 1685   Harris payd me   016   02   06
27 Sep. 1686   Alow'd him repayrs about the houses 4 12 7
                 And fence 3 5 4   007   17   11
                 Amonition rate   000   04   08
Payd by disbursements in his general account p. 85 *quarto*   027   10   07
book   051   15   08
                 Rest   058   00   04
                                                                     109   16   00
4 Dec. 1686   Payd me   050   00   00
1686   By 20 comb of oats   004   10   00

May Fairchilde had 43 sheep at 6s 9d	014 10 03
23 Nov. 1687 Harris demanded £4 15 0 for the said 20	
comb of oats. And 14 13 10 for the 43 sheep, soe add	000 08 07
I must also here credit him for 9 8 7 because the farme rent	009 08 07
is included in his general account *quarto* p. 86 where the	078 17 05
ballance is but	034 00 11
Mem: 4 Oct. 1688. I allow'd Harris in his general account	
12 00 10 for repayring the houses and 2 1s for the fences of	112 18 04
this farme, (*vide* p. 87 *quarto*)	

                        Anno 1688 *vide* 336

262. Black's Account (124, 537)

A years rent at Mich. 1680	037	07	00

Mem: 11 Sep. 1680 to encourage Black to hold this ground I agreed to
lend him £30 *gratis* during the lease 537 for which he gave me a noat 21
Oct. 1680

Halfe a years rent Lady 1681	017	13	00
At Mich. 1681	017	13	00
At Mich. 1682	035	07	00
At Mich. 1683	035	07	00
	106	01	00
21 Oct. 1683 Owe	035	07	00
A years rent at Mich. 1684	035	07	00
3 March 1684 I owe my land lord Mr Windham halfe a			
years rent clear. *John Blacks*	070	14	00
Rest due	017	13	06
A years rent at Mich. 1685	035	07	00
At Lady 1686	017	13	06
A year and a half ending Mich. 1687	053	00	06

8 March 1687 This is a true account and I owe thirty five pounds, seven
shillings besides the thirty pounds I borrowed *Anno* 1680. Signed before
me *Stephen Legge John Blacks*   123   14   06

263. Black's Credit (125)

5 July 1680 Payd me	017	09	00
6 last mths of the 18 months tax	001	01	00
Amonition rate	000	02	00
Sherifs Turne 1679	000	01	06
20 Oct. 1680 Payd me	017	10	00
The 6 months supply to disband the armye	001	01	2
Sherifs turne	000	01	06
	037	07	00

10 Oct. 1681	Smith account for 17 11 6,			
	Sherifs turne 1s 6d, Leet fee 6d	017	13	06
1 Oct. 1682	Salman account for	032	00	00

Allowd him for serving twice at the Sherifs turne: *scilicet* in May and

Nov 1681		000	03	00
	Leet fee	000	00	06
	Amonition	000	01	09
	Rayling at Ingworth Hall 40 rods £2			
	Ditching there at Kilbye's ground 0 15 10	002	15	10
21 Oct. 1683	Salman account for	017	17	05
	Sherifs turne 1s 6d. Leet fee 6d	000	02	00
		070	14	00
	Rest	035	07	00
		106	01	00
25 Oct. 1684	Elden account for	017	13	06
1 Dec.	Payd me	017	00	00
3 March	Payd me	018	01	1½

Allow'd for serving twice at the Sherifs turne 3s, and two

years Leet fee 1s		000	04	00

For two poor and one church rate ending at Mich. 1684 for

the part of Albye farm which lye in Colbye.		000	01	10½
		053	00	06
3 March 1684	Rest due	017	13	06
		070	14	00
17 Dec. 1685	Black payd me	020	00	00
17 July 1686	He payd John Barham	020	00	00
18 March	Payd me	030	11	11
	Amonition 1s 7d, Leet fee 6d, *anno* 1685	000	02	01
19 Sep. 1687	Payd my wife	017	00	00
8 March	Allow'd a Leet fee 6d and the Sherifs turne	000	02	00
	Payd me	000	11	06
		088	07	06
	Rest	035	07	00
		123	14	06

264. Bendish's Debt (511, 493)

31 Oct. 1679	Page 40, owe	018	00	00
	A years rent at Mich. 1680	036	00	00
Anno 1680	Used 13 bunches of my owne larth	054	00	00
	Mich. 1681	036	00	00
	Mich. 1682	036	00	00
	Mich. 1683	036	00	00

		108	00	00
16 Nov. 1683	Owe	046	00	00
	A years rent at Mich 1684	036	00	00
	Halfe a years rent ending Lady 1685	018	00	00

The 25 Feb 1684 Bendish writ me word she heard I was selling my house and begg'd she might quietly enjoy it according to my promise, p. 511, for she had let the ground and tenements, upon which I sent for her and tould her if she brought me a purchaser I would give her £20 which is the reason that [*sic*] / *493* /   054   00   00

265. Bendish's Credit(264)

9 Aug. 1680	Payd to Smith	009	00	00
1 Oct.	Salman account for	006	08	00
	Disbursed for a mill stone for Suffolke	010	10	00
	2 years City rent at Mich. 1679	000	02	00
	6 months at	000	13	00
	Amonition, Muster Master and Souldier	000	05	00
	Repayrs	000	02	00
29 Nov.	Payd Smith	010	00	00
	6 months tax 13s, amonition 4s	000	17	00

5000 tyles £4 tyler, tilepins and sand 2 11 3, mason 1s 8d
lyme 7s, nails £1, carpenter for stuf and worke 1 15 6   009   15   05
9 Feb. 1680 Paid Smith   004   12   08
Mason for stuf and worke 18s 10d, carpenter 16s   001   14   11

		054	00	00
10 Oct. 1681	Smith account for	018	00	00
1 Oct. 1682	Smith account for	025	12	03
	Amonition and other Militia charges	000	05	10
	Repayrs	008	01	11
16 Nov. 1682	Payd Mr Briggs	010	00	00
	Repayrs 2 6 6.	062	00	00
	Rest	046	00	00
		108	00	00

16 Feb 1683. She sent me a note signed by Augustine Briggs Junior
for the said £20 was payd 7 June 1683   020   00   00
Allow'd her several bills of repayrs done 1682 and 1683
as by acquittances   007   00   10
4 years City rent ending Mich. 1683 as *per* receipt signed by Tovey   000   04   00
Amonition and other Militia charges   000   05   09
4 Mar. 1683 Payd Briggs   016   09   05
Note the parish have lately been at an extreordinary charge   044   00   00

about the church in respect whereof I remit		002	00	00
		046	00	00
14 June 1684	Payd Briggs	015	16	3½
9 Oct.	Payd me	000	02	03
	Allow'd Militia Charges	000	07	05
	Repayrs	001	14	0½
31 March 1685	Mrs Bendish accounted with me for £14 payd	014	00	00
	Briggs 8 Nov. last			
	And by bill of repayrs in Feb. and Mar. last	003	10	09
	Militia charges	000	02	06
	And I did freely discharge her of / 264 /	018	06	09
		054	00	00

266. Frost's Debt (533, 64, 232)

1 Oct. 1680.	Owe /64/	020	00	00
	At Mich. 1681	040	00	00
	At Mich. 1682	040	00	00
	At Mich. 1683	040	00	00
➤ 17 Dec. 1683 Frost payd Salman three pounds for me		140	00	00
for timber which he tooke out of my ground without my knowledge				
	Owe my by p. 267	040	00	00
	A years rent at Mich. 1684	040	00	00
Observe: when Haddon died, Teney took his part.				
At Mich. 1684 Teney let Haddon's part and his owne part to Walker at £29		080	00	00
	A years rent at Mich 1685	040	00	00
From Mich. 1685: Mr Eyre hire £11 of this £40 / 232 /				

Walker's Debt (493)

	A years rent at Mich. 1686	029	00	00
	A years rent at Mich. 1687	029	00	00

267. Frost's Credit

10 Oct. 1681	Smith account for				020	00	00
	Salman account for				005	10	00
1 Oct. 1682	Salman account for				034	07	06
	Amonition				000	02	06
21 Oct. 1683	Salman account for				033	06	10½
	Allow'd Frost for 15 combs of oats	4	10	0			
	And for spars and straw delivered	2	00	0			
	Disburs'd to a rate for me	0	3	1½	006	13	1½
					100	00	00

	Rest	040	00	00
		140	00	00
21 Oct. 1683	Elden charge himself with	050	10	00
11 Oct. 1684	Teney payd me	030	00	00
14 [*Oct.*]	He payd me	000	09	10
	Disbursed for me to a Rate	000	03	00
25 [*Oct.*]	Salman account for	002	07	02
	\<then\> Elden account for	018	00	00

28 Feb Teney accounted with me for 7 comb 2 bushels of seed wheat at 16s *per* comb, and 1 comb 2 bushels of rye at

10s, and 2 comb of fetches at 22s	008	19	00
And for a close of turneps	005	10	00
Carriage of eleven loads of timber £ 1. 3s and a load of Blicklyn hay	001	08	00
He payd me	002	03	00
Frost payd me	005	10	00
	080	00	00

22 June 1685	Rich Walker by Tene's order	014	10	00
9 Dec. 1685	Frost payd me	014	10	00
	Then Richard Walker payd me	014	10	00
		048	00	00

Walker's Credit

July 1686	Walker payd me	014	10	00
6 Jan.	Payd me	014	10	00
11 July 1687	Payd my wife	014	10	00
10 Jan	Payd me	014	10	00

268. Parke's Debt (118, 508/4, 509/4, 505, 310, 508)

	Parke owe at Mich. 1680 / 118 /	045	00	00

Noat: He died 14 Dec. 1680 and left his brother executor

	At Mich. 1681	090	00	00
	At Mich. 1682	090	00	00
	Vide 508/4 and 509/4	180	00	00

➤ 2 June 1683. Parke agreed to allow me £8 in consideration that the
farme was not left in repayre according   008   00   00
to the covenants in the lease. From Mich. 1682 to Mich.

1684 Shepherd sow'd part of this farme to halfs p. 509.   188   00   00

At Mich 1684 Downing hired the same part at £60. *vide.* 505 and 310

21 Oct. 1683   Owe me   005   19   04

A years rent of part of Parke's farme due from Robert Barber (508)
at Mich. 1683   029   00   00

	At Mich. 1684	029	00	00
	At Mich. 1685	029	00	00
	At Lady 1686	014	10	00
21 Sep. 1686.	I owe my land lord for rent sixty seven pounds	101	10	00

fiveteen shillins one penny. Witness my hand
Signed in the presence of *Edward Hagerchild*
Rob X Barber his mark

29 Sep. 1686	Barber owe me	082	05	01
	more at Lady 1687	014	10	00

5 July 1687. I owe Mr Windham sixty seven pounds one penny at Lday
last made before *Edward Hagerchild*. Robert X Barber mark   096   15   01

269. Parke Credit (331)

10 Oct. 1681	Smith account for	045	00	00
12 Oct. 1681	Payd me	038	19	02
	Allow'd for repayrs	005	08	04
	Charges which Bunn put him to	000	12	06
March	Payd my wife	044	17	05
	Amonition	000	02	07
5 Aug. 1682	Payd me	020	00	00
1 Oct. 1682	Salman charge himself with £5 received of Robert Barber	005	00	00

In May 1683 Parke came to Felbrigg, when I allow'd him as followeth
scilicet:

	Payd Smith in Jan. last	015	00	00
	Barber payd Elden in March *stet*	007	00	00
	Parke payd me in April	010	00	00
	Oats 29 combs 1 bushel at 5s	007	00	00
	Filling and spreading muck	001	00	00
	Thrashing the corne, for the straw etc. / *quarto* 44 /			
	Charges at several times about Bunn	001	19	00
1 June	Barber payd Salman	007	00	00
2 [*June*]	Parke payd Salman	006	00	00
	Barber disburs'd about repayring the houses			
	2 7 8, and fences 6s 3d	002	13	11
	Shephard had of Parke in hay	001	10	00
	Repayrs 8 9 7 houses ⎱	182	00	08
	And 7 9 4 fences ⎰ 1681, 1682, 1683 Rest	005	19	04
		188	00	00
3 Feb. 1683	Parke payd Wortlee by my order	005	19	04
25 Oct. 1684	Elden account for £12 15s 00d	012	15	00
14 May 1685	Barber payd me	010	14	00
	Amonition	000	01	02

	He disburs'd in 1684 to a constable's rate			
	for Shephard's part of Park's farme / *509* /	000	04	09
23 Dec. 1685	Barber payd me	009	00	00
21 Sep. 1686	Barber payd me	001	00	00
		033	14	11
	Rest	067	15	01
		101	10	00
5 July 1687	Robert Barber payd me	000	00	00
	And he have payd Fayrchild for my use at			
	3 payments since 21 Sept. 1686	012	14	00
	And 10 comb of wheat at 16s	008	00	00
		029	15	00

270. Gosse's Debt (544, 530, 22, 271)

	Page 22, owe 1 Oct. 1680 / *530* /	028	00	00
From 7 July 1679 to 17 Dec 1680 Gosse have deliver'd 481 rabits				
	At Mich. 1681	022	00	00
12 July 1682.	Accounted for 370 rabits			
	At Mich. 1682	022	00	00
	Halfe a years rent 2 Feb 1682	011	00	00
29 Nov. 1682	Accounted for 155 rabits	073	00	00

7 Feb. 1682.   Accounted for 113 rabits and payd me £5 in lieu of 181
rabits which were not delivered but due at or before the 2 Feb. 1682 / *271* /

Goss grew rich, married, and woud noe longer endure the hardship of a warrener's life.

3 Feb. 1682 Wegg agreed to pay me for 300 conies which
Goss left upon the warren above the stock of 1300 / **511** /

Observe. **492 s 5** mentioned in the lease p. 511		009	00	00
	A years rent ending 2 Feb 1683	022	00	00
	And for 300 rent conies then due	009	00	00
	A years rent the 2 Feb. 1684	022	00	00
	And 300 conies	009	00	00
	A years rent 2 Feb. 1685	022	00	00
	And 300 conies	009	00	00
16 Aug 1686 I owe Mr Windham £21 10s in money and 66		102	00	00

covenant conies £1 13s due 2 Feb. last. Witness my hand
in the presence of *Stephen Legge Thomas Wegg*

16 Aug. 1686	Owe as above	023	03	00
	Half a years rent at Mich. 1686	011	00	00
2 Feb. 1686	Half a years rent	011	00	00
	And 300 conies	009	00	00
2 Feb. 1687	A years rent and conies	031	00	00

085	03	00

9 Nov. 1687. I accounted with Mr Windham and acknowledge there will
bee due to him 2 Feb next 33 10 0 in monye, and five score and six conies
at 2 13 0 – in all thirty six pounds three shillings. Witness my hand
Signed before *Stephen Legge Thomas Wegg*

036	03	00

271. Gosse's Credit

31 Jan. 1681	Payd me	020	00	00
1 Oct. 1682	Salman account for	010	00	00
	Smith account then for	005	00	00
27 Nov. 1682	Payd Smith	015	00	00
7 Feb. payd me £16. Noat: £5 of the said £16 was in lieu of				
ten score and one rent conies soe received for rent		011	00	00
Then allow'd Goss for 300 conies which were adjug'd to				
bee upon the Warren 2 Feb 1682 above the stock of 1300				
at six score to 100		009	00	00
28 May 1684	Payd Mr Bamfeild for me	003	00	00
		073	00	00
7 Dec. 1683	Wegg payd me	005	10	00
22 Feb. 1683	Wegg payd me	005	00	00
Then wee accounted for 200 conies wanting 6 at £3 *per* 100 is		005	17	00
7 Nov. 1684	Wegg payd me	013	00	00
17 Jan	Payd me	010	00	00
15 Dec. 1685	Payd me	015	00	00
28 June 1686	Wegg payd John Barham	005	00	00
18 Aug. Wegg brought me tallies that he delivered into the				
house *anno* 1684 – 360 conies, and *anno* 1685 – 300 conies		019	10	00
		078	17	00
	Rest due	023	03	00
		102	00	00
29 Nov. 1686	Payd me	006	00	00
3 Dec.	He payd me	014	00	00
	And by tallies 200 and 40 conies	007	00	00
6 Jan.	Payd me	005	00	00
25 Feb.	Payd me	004	00	00
9 Nov. 1687	And by tallies 300 and 40 conies	019	00	00
	And in monye	003	00	00
		049	00	00
	Rest	036	03	00
		085	03	00
3 Dec. 1687	Payd me	007	00	00
3 Jan.	Payd me	006	00	00

| 20 Feb. | Payd me | 002 | 00 | 00 |
| | And by tally of conies 5 score and six | 002 | 13 | 00 |

272. John Kingsberry's Debt (546, 158)

2 May 1681	Page 158, due at Lday 1681	133	12	08
	At Mich. 1681	097	04	00
	At Mich. 1682	101	08	10

11 April 1683, Mr Windham accounted with me and made me the
allowances mentioned on the other side; which fully satisfie me upon all
account Witness my hand

| In the presence of *Jo Gatman John Kingsbury* | 425 | 04 | 08 |

Prance's Debt (497)

	His halfe years rent at Lady 1683	097	04	00
	At Mich. 1683	097	04	00
16 Feb 1683	Prance writ me that he received of Gibson the miller for my use p. 215	019	00	00
	A years rent ending Mich. 1684	194	08	00
	Half a year at Lady 1685	097	04	00
17 Apr. 1685	Prance charg'd himself to have receiv'd of Gibson the miller	015	03	11
8 Aug. 1684	And of Abraham Totman the former miller p. 215	005	16	08
	He receiv'd for a pair of old pistolls	000	05	00

17 April 1685 my land lord Mr Windham accounted with me, and
allow'd all my demands so rest clear due to him two hundred thirty
pounds seven shilling four pence. Witness my

hand. In the presence of *Mark Hayton Jeremiah Prance*	526	05	07
	Ballance of the account is	231	07	04
	Half a years rent at Mich. 1685	097	04	00
	At Lady 1686	097	04	00
14 May 1686	Prance borrowed upon his bond	050	00	00
	At Mich. 1686	097	04	00

5 Nov. 1686. I owe my land lord Windham four hundred seventeen
pounds seventeen shillings eleven pence for rent.

| | 572 | 19 | 04 |

Witness *Stephen Legge Francis Robinson Jeremiah Prance*

273. John Kingsberry's Credit (497, 279)

14 June 1681	Payd Briggs for my use	130	00	00
23	Payd me at Felbrigg	003	12	08
3 Nov.	Payd me at Felbrigg	097	04	00
4 Apr. 1682	Payd me	097	04	00

11 April 1683	John Kingsberry was at Felbrig and brought			
	two receipts under Mr Briggs hand for £80.			
	Scilicet: 30 Jan. 1682, £70 and 6 Feb. £10	080	00	00
	For a years sallarye for mustring	000	13	04
	He payd me this day	006	10	00
	I freely give him upon several accounts / *497* /	010	00	08
1681	Plowboot and cartboot / *279* /	425	04	08

Prance's Credit (332)

16 Oct. 1683	Payd Fowle	050	00	00
16 Feb. 1683	Prance write he have this week return'd £70			
	to Fowle which was payd 7 March 1683	070	00	00
! Aug. 1684	Payd Fowle	050	00	00
6 Dec.	Payd Fowle	057	00	00
23 [Dec.]	Ditto	013	00	00
21 March	Ditto	050	00	00
17 April 1685	Allow'd Prance for 2/3 of a pair of pistolls			
	and houlsters, sadle etc.	001	19	02
	Mustring 2 years ending Mich. 1684	002	00	00
	Amonition for the said 2 years	000	19	01
		294	18	03
	Rest	213	07	04
		526	05	07
1 Oct. 1685	Payd Mr Fowle	050	00	00
5 March	Payd Fowle	050	00	00
3 Nov. 1686	Allow'd for mustring in the year of Monmouth's Rebellion	004	02	04
	Amonition for 2 years	000	19	01
5 [Nov.]	Payd me	050	00	00
		155	01	05
	Rest	417	17	11
		572	19	04

274. Ransome's Debt (555, 70, 15)

	Owe at Mich. 1681 / *70* /	082	16	03

Ransome is soe old and his son soe lame they can't order the ground as it should bee therefore I advised him to leave farming and tould him I would forgive him £10 of the arrears

29 Sep. 1681	Owe	059	08	05
31 Oct. 1684	Barne blowne downe			
1686	Built upon a new foundation			

Thomas Blofield's Debt (531, 494, 320; *quarto* 104; 275)

A years rent at Mich 1682	020	00	00
At Mich 1683	020	00	00
A years rent at Mich 1684	020	00	00

Dec 1684 Mr Blofield left his owne house for fear of being arrested, his   060   00   00
nephew Leo Blofield to whom he made over his estate, agreed pay the
years rent ending Mich. 1685

	020	00	00
	080	00	00

At Mich 1685. Thomas Ransome enter'd this farme. *Vide* pp. 494 and 320

For ballance of the account / *vide quarto 104* /	011	19	3¾

275. Ransome's Credit

22 Sep 1681	Accounted with Ransome and finde he have			
	paid Salman since 1 Oct. 1680	009	00	00
	And to Smith	005	17	06
	6 months tax	000	13	00
	Butter and cheese	003	01	00
	Carriages for me	003	04	06
	Church rate for land in my hand	001	12	03
		023	08	03
	Rest at Mich. 1681	059	08	05
		082	16	08
29 Sep. 1681	Payd by sale of goods and chattels	033	15	00
	I forgive Ransome *gratis*	010	00	00
21 July 1682	Alow'd for corne, hay, straw and chaife as			
	in quarto book p. 28	015	11	04
	Disburs'd for me to a parish rate	000	02	01
		059	08	05

Blofield's Credit (15)

3 May 1683 I tould Mr Blofield I woud allow him out of his
rent for the service he had done me about my Rents of Assize   005   00   00

Allow'd him a bill of repayrs beginning 3 Oct 1681 and ending 29 Dec
1682 *scilicet*

About the houses £6 12s, fences 8s 8d   007   00   08

Salman disburs'd 1681 and 1682 about Blofield's fences
7 6 6, and about the house 7s.

2 Nov. 1685	Leo Blofield according to his promise p. 274 Payd me	020	00	00
	Blofield's credit p. 199 is	003	19	11
	I allow Tom Blofield for collecting my rents			
	of assize a year and a half ending Mich. 1684	007	10	00

And for going to Norwich about my sutes with Bunn and Mr Herne			000	10	00

Nov. 1684. He disburs'd to pay my Cosen Francis Wyndham
and Yarmouth their rents. / *quarto* 105 /   002   19   3¼

Payd my man Smith *anno* 1682   010   01   00

Allow'd him for making a new ditch in the feild   3 8 4

Disburs'd about the houses and fences   8 9   003   17   01

For 21 combs of oats   004   10   00

Church rate for lands in hands *anno* 1684   002   13   09

                                                                      060   00   8¼

Vide page 15 the ballance of this account is   011   19   3¾

                                                                      080   00   00

276. Mack's Debt (535, 128, 509, 530)

Page. 128, owe at Mich. 1681   018   10   00

Mack's son is not fit to manage the farme, therefore I release him. And
have agreed with John Appelbye to sow the ground to halfs. / *509* /
Appelbye hired the said farme / *530* /

Disburs'd about repayrs by Salman's bills in
1681, 1682, 1683,   £6   1s   od
1681   Appelbye layd out   £2   03   7 in repayrs
1682, 1683   Appelbye layd out   £7   11   2 repayrs

Apleby's Debt (530)

A years rent at Mich. 1684   030   00   00
At Mich. 1685   030   00   00
At Lady 1686   015   00   00
At Mich. 1686   015   00   00
A years rent at Mich. 1687   035   00   00

                                                          125   00   00

Mack's Credit (*quarto* pp. 54, 55)

Clover seed   001   00   00
3 months tax   000   06   08
27 June 1682   Payd by corne   013   04   04
Allow'd for repayrs   0 14 8,
Carrying muck   2 10 0
Turnup seed   0 01 0   003   05   08
Mistaken when the account was made   000   13   04
From Mich. 1681 to 1683 *Vide quarto* 54 and 55.   018   10   00

Apleby's Credit

22 June 1685	Allow'd a bill *scilicet*: repairing the house			
	7 2 10, well 6 6, fences 1 8 6, amonition 1 6	008	19	04
17 Oct. 1685	Elden account for	021	00	08
5 Jul. 1687	Fairchild account for	015	00	00
	And more	002	00	00

278. R. Kingsberry's Credit (516, 154, 49), 300)

	Page 154, owe at Mich. 1682	378	09	00

23 Sep. 1682 my account was examined and all my payments and disbursements to this day allow'd, soe there will bee just a years rent due to my land lord at Mich. next.
Witness *Samuell Smith Robart Kingsberry*

29 Sep. 1682		180	00	00
	At Lady 1683	090	00	00
26 Aug 1683	All my payments and demands were allow'd.	270	00	00
	And I owe seventy four pounds ten pence			

Witness *Stephen Legge Robart Kingsberry*

26 Aug. 1683	Kingsberry owe me	074	00	10
	At Mich. 1683	090	00	00
	At Mich. 1684	180	00	00
	At Lady 1685	090	00	00
	For a years rent and a half of Brunden Mill			
	ending Lday 1685 / *497* /	057	00	00

18 April 1685 My land lord Windham allow'd all my payments and demands soe rest due from me to him one hundred seventy nine pounds nine shillings seven pence. Witness my hand *Robart Kingsberry*
Signed in the presence of *Mark Hayton*

		491	00	10
	Owe as above	170	09	07
	Half a years rent at Mich. 1686	090	00	00
	Vide p. 308	260	09	07

279. R. Kingsberry's Credit (155, 215, 509)

	Page 155, payd	161	00	00
23 Sep. 1682	Payd me at Brunden Mill	011	12	04
	Allow'd the Parson's sallary Mich. 1681	013	06	08
	For pavements and bricks	000	18	00
	Plowboot and cartboot for the use of John Kingsberry			
	anno 1681	005	00	00
	400 x 12 foot of thick board & and other			
	timber for to repayre the mill 1682	006	12	00

23 Sep. 1682.	R. K. owe me £90	198	09	00
29 [*Sep*]	He will owe £90 more	180	00	00
		378	09	00
26 Aug. 1683	Allow'd Robert Kingsberry £100 which he			
	payd Mr Briggs at three payments	100	00	00
	And to Mr Fowle 20 April last	080	00	00
	And £1 of £20 payd Fowle 5 June the other			
	£19 being the Millers / 215 /	001	00	00
	The Parson's sallary Mich. 1682	013	06	08
	Militia Tax	000	05	06
	Given him 1000 bricks to pave the Bakehouse	001	04	00
	Disburs'd about the miller's fences	000	03	00
		195	19	02
	Ballance is	074	00	10
		270	00	00
21 Sep. 1683	Payd Fowle	060	00	00
19 Oct.	Payd Fowle	014	00	00
14 Apr. 1684	Robert Kingsberry write he payd to Mr Fowle £160	160	00	00
17 Feb.	Payd Briggs	050	00	00
18 Apr. 1685	Allow'd the Parson's sallary 2 years ending Mich. 1684	026	13	04
	Amonition for the farme and mill	000	06	07
	A load of brick and 200 tyles	000	11	04
		311	11	03
	Ballance is	179	09	07
	Vide p. 509	491	00	10

280. Talbott's Debt (92, 93, 479, 481)

	Page 93, owe 5 Oct. 1682	019	10	00
	Mich. 1683	019	10	00
	A years rent at Mich. 1684	019	10	00
		058	10	00
	At Mich. 1685	019	10	00
	Half a years rent at Lady 1686	009	15	00
24 Sep. 1686.	I owe Mr Windham for farme rent ending at	087	15	00
Lady last forty pounds nine shillings five pence. *John Talbott*				
29 Sep. 1686	He owe me	050	04	05
	A years rent at Mich. 1687	019	10	00
At Mich. 1687	I tooke the land and let part to H. Well p. 479	069	14	05
and some to Howse p. 481				
29 Sep 87	Mr Talbott owe me	024	15	05

John Howse (481)

281. Talbott's Credit (15)

26 Mar. 1684	By Elden's account Mr Talbott deliver'd 42			
	combs of oats at 4s *per* comb	008	00	00
7 Oct. 1685	Elden account for	007	10	00
	Allow'd for 42 comb of oats	019	00	00
	And 2 load of straw	002	00	00
July 1686	Mr Talbott deliver'd oats 33 comb 5s 6d	009	01	06
24 Sep	Allow'd Mr Talbott to a church rate end			
	Mich 1684 for lands in hand in Metton	001	14	01
		047	05	07
	Rest	040	09	05
		087	15	05
Feb. 1686	Mr Talbott by 5 neat beasts	010	00	00
July 1687	For two cows	005	00	00
	20 sheep at 6s, and 4 at 3s a peice	006	12	00
	4 load of hay	003	10	00
	5 comb of barly at 7s *per* comb	001	15	00
	3 acres of wheat judged 10 comb at 12s	006	00	00
	7 acres of barly judged 3 comb *per* acre and 7s	007	00	00
	8 acres of oats at 3 comb *per* acre 4s *per* comb	004	16	00
		044	19	00
	The ballance is	024	15	05
		069	14	05
	I tould Talbott I woud remit him *gratis*	010	00	00
	Page 15 the ballance is	014	15	05
		024	15	05

John Howse

282. Lymeburner's Debt (540, 33)

	Page 33, rest 1 Oct 1682	003	06	10
	At Mich. 1683	007	00	00
	At Mich. 1684	007	00	00
Gregorye the Lymeburner died about Mich 1684, and Evered hired it		017	06	10
	A years rent at Mich. 1685	007	00	00
	At Mich. 1686	007	00	00
Mich. 1686, and two years rent of a peice of ground belonging to Cosen's				
farme which he have for a way to the Kill		000	05	00
And for 2 roods which Gregorye hired of Cosen's ground 1683		000	03	06
		031	15	04
27 Nov. 1686	Ballance is	000	05	06
	A years rent at Mich. 1687	007	00	00

And for the way aforesaid	000	02	06
	007	08	00
Ballance is	000	01	00
	000	07	09

283. Lymeburner's Credit

21 Oct. 1683	Salman account for	007	00	00
25 Oct. 1684	Salman account for	003	10	00
	And Elden account for	003	10	00
17 Oct. 1685	Elden account for	007	00	00
12 May 1685	Elden account for	003	10	00
27 Nov. 1686	Allow'd him for lyme 1686	006	19	10

Observe: besides this 6 19 10, allow'd Sexton 4 5 0 for lyme *Vide* pages 39, 51

	031	09	10

Note: Sexton and Edmund Evered are partners in the Kill since Greorye died.

Rest due	000	05	06
	031	15	04

27 Nov. 1686	Allow'd for the use of 2 barrows	000	02	00
6 Feb. 1687	Allow'd for 24 ½ c[hauldron] of lyme at 6s *per* chauldron	007	07	00

Mr Windham made us these allowances in full of all demands

	007	09	00

Signed before *John Francis* Edward X Evered
William X Sexton

Credit exceed debt	000	01	00

284. Yaxely's Executors Debt (542, 46)

Page 46, owe at Mich. 1682	075	00	00

Maris clear'd the bond 6 June 1683 *WW*

Masters (510)

A years rent ending at Mich. 1683	040	00	00
At Mich. 1684	040	00	00
At Mich. 1685	040	00	00
Half a years rent Lady 1686	020	00	00

21 Sep. 1686. I owe my land lord eighty three pounds	140	00	00

sixteen shilling three pence. Witness my hand
Signed in the presence of *Edward Hagerchilde John Masters*
4 Dec 1686   Masters made me a bill of sale of all his goods
and chattels for [£]103.16.3

29 Sep. 1686 Masters owe me	103	16	03

29 Sep. 1687	A years rent more	040	00	00

14 Feb 1687 I owe Mr Windham for rent due at Mich. last one hundred
and twelve pounds eleven shillings ten pence   143   16   03
Witness my hand. *John Masters*

14 Feb. 1687	Owe me	112	11	10

285. Yaxly's Executors Credit (47)

	Page 47, payd and allow'd	010	00	00
	Due upon Mr Maries bond	064	19	09

Masters

1683	Salman disbursd about the houses £6 14s 4d			
20 June 1684	Payd me	010	00	00
25 Oct. 1684	Salman account for	008	00	00
	And Elden account for	004	00	00
17 Oct. 1685	Elden account for	010	00	00
	Carting brick a day and ½	000	06	09
12 Mar. 1685	Elden account for	006	00	00
	Wheat 10 combs 2 bushels £8			
	Oats 10 combs 2 bushels £2 15s	010	15	00
	A load of straw	000	09	00
26 Apr. 1686	Masters payd John Barham	006	00	00
	Oats 10 comb at 5s 6d, a load of straw 10s	003	05	00
21 Sep.	Allow'd him for lyme	000	03	00
	Master's deliver'd but 10 comb 2 bushels of	058	18	09
	oats, therefore I deduct	002	15	00
		056	03	00
	Rest	083	16	03
		140	00	00
27 Dec. 1686	Masters payd me	006	00	00
5 July 1687	Fairchilde account for	012	00	00
14 Feb.	Allow'd for 7 comb of rye	002	12	06
	And 25 comb of barly	008	06	03
	Carriage of coals 15s 8d, of deals 10s	001	05	08
	Straw 2 load	001	00	00
		031	04	05
	Rest	112	11	10
		143	16	03

286. Ingworth Miller Debt (510, 126,15, 478)

	Page 126 Greenacre at Mich. 1682	064	15	00
31 Oct. 1683	Greenacre owe me for rent due Mich. 1682			
	vide page 15	035	18	02

Sextan's Debt (510)

A years rent at Mich. 1683	030	00	00
Half a years rent at Lady 1684	015	00	00
At Mich. 1684	015	00	00
	060	00	00

Bloome's Debt (510)

	A years rent at Mich. 1685	030	00	00
	At Mich. 1686	030	00	00
March 1685 Bloome died and the widdow left the mill at		060	00	00
Lady 1686 so deduct		015	00	00
		045	00	00
	Samuell Curril at Mich. 1686 / 478 /	007	10	00
	Richard Bygrave Mich. 1687 / 478 /	015	00	00

287. Ingworth Miller Credit (127)

	Payd page 127	028	16	10
21 Oct. 1683	Remaine clear due to me from Greenacre	035	18	02
		064	15	00

Sextan's Credit

21 Oct. 1683	Salman account for	Repayrs 1682	1	2	6	011	04	06
2 Apr. 1684	Payd me					015	00	00
30 Sep.	Payd me					014	15	06
25 Oct.	Elden account for					015	00	00
	Repayrs					003	15	01
	Frivolous pretences					000	04	11
						060	00	00

Bloome's Credit

7 Oct. 1685	Elden account for	015	00	00
12 Dec.	Elden account for	008	00	00
Apr. 1687	Widdow Bloome payd Salman	010	10	00
	Allow'd for repayrs in Bloome's time	001	00	00
	And for the milstones valued (when R.			

	Bygrave enter'd) more then Bloome had	010	10	00
Observe: Bygrave promise to pay me the £10 10s		045	00	00
Dec. 1686	Curril run away			

288. Lillye's Debt (534, 113, 117)

	Page 113, owe 1 Oct. 1682	022	19	10
	Page 117, for 2 years rent of the Alder Carrr	002	00	00
Mich. 1682	A years rent of the farme and Alder Carr	038	00	00
		062	19	10
21 Oct. 1683	Lilly owe at Mich. 1683	025	10	10
	A years rent at Mich. 1684	038	00	00
	At Mich. 1685	038	00	00
	At Mich. 1686	038	00	00
	A years rent at Mich. 1687	038	00	00
		177	10	10

289. Lillye's Credit

29 Nov. 1682	Lilly payd Smith £14			
5 March	He payd him 4 19 0	018	19	00
21 Oct 83	Salman account for	018	10	00
	Repayrs 1 12 6	037	09	00
	Remaine due	062	19	10
25 Oct. 1684	Salman account for	015	16	04
	And Elden account for	018	10	00
	Repayrs in 1683	002	08	08
	Serving the Sherif's turn	000	05	00
10 Mar. 1684	Payd me	013	05	06
	Repayrs	004	15	00
	Serving at the Sherif's turn twice	000	05	00
20 Mar. 1685	Elden account for	012	00	00
26 July 1686	Lilly payd me	012	00	00
5 July 1687	Fairchilde account for	023	00	00
8 [July]	Payd Fairchilde	002	00	00
24 [July]	Payd Fairchilde	002	00	00
25 [July]	Payd him more	009	00	00
	And more	001	00	00

290. Cooke the Bailiff's Charge (183)

21 Oct. 1682 rest due to me from tenants holding of my manours in

Mr Cooke's charge for arrears of rent ending Mich. 1682 / *183* /	121	06	07
Mr Cooke owe me for the ballance of his account made up 21 Oct. 1682	002	13	04

Mem. 29 Jan. 1682 I order'd Mr Cooke to receive noe more rents for me, for hereafter my menial servant shall collect them.

291. Cooke's Discharge

29 Jan. 1682	Payd Smith	003	10	00

292. Smith's Debt (555, 132)

	Page 132, at Mich. 1682	091	08	08

Steward's (537)

	A years rent at Mich. 1683	011	00	00
	A years rent at Mich. 1684	011	00	00
	At Mich. 1685	012	00	00
	Half a years rent Lady 1686	006	00	00
	A year and a half at Mich 1687	018	00	00
		058	00	00
	Note the 12 5 0½ ought to bee 12 0 5½	000	04	07
	/293/	058	04	07
12 Feb. 1687		022	00	00

293. Smith's Credit (133)

	Page 133, payd	069	00	00
13 Dec. 1682	She payd Salman	010	00	00
	I forgive the remeyning *gratis*	012	08	08
		091	08	08

Steward's

21 Oct. 1683	Salman account for	005	00	00
25 Oct. 1684	Salman account for	001	19	10
	Amonition	000	00	4½
	House repayrs £1 2s 0d; fences 17s 4d	001	19	04
17 Oct. 1685	Elden account for	012	15	0½
1687	Fairchilde account for	005	00	00
5 Feb.	Steward payd me	010	00	00
I owe Mr Windham twenty two pounds 15 Feb. 1687		036	04	07
Witness my hand *William Steward*	Rest due	022	00	00
Signed in the presence of *Stephen Legge*		058	04	07

294. Thomas Sextan's Debt (497, 492 s. 1)

Rich Benslee (478)

A years rent at Mich. 1685	050	00	00
Half a years rent at Lady 1686	025	00	00
A year and a half ending Mich. 1687	075	00	00

➤ Observe: He owe me £42 as *per* p. 478 besides the ballance of this
account 31 Jan, 1687 — 150 00 00

31 Jan. 1687   Owe me   .   057 09 04

295. Thomas Sextan's Credit (492)

Richard Benslee

5 July 1687	Fairchilde account for	016	00	00
	And 45 comb of oats at 4s 3d	009	05	03
10 Dec.	Benslee payd me	025	00	00
31 Jan	I allow'd him for £19 payd me 18 Dec. 1685 and £17 Oct. 5 1686	036	00	00

	Repayrs about the houses and fences as *per* bill Dec. 1685	5	8	8		
	Amonition 2s 3d					
	Carriage of corne 14s 6d, both	16	9	006	05	05
				092	10	08
	Rest due			057	09	04
				150	00	00

296. Suffolke in Houseman's account Debt (226)

Page 226, arrears at Mich. 1682	562	05	11

And because the 562 5 11 should bee 562 11 5   000 05 06

£ s d	Houseman alsoe stand charg'd in the foot of his last account dated 31 Mar. 1682 which I			
14 12 6	examined 19 Sep. 1682 for goods and chattels			
01 10 9	belonging to me sold for	014	02	06
04 00 0	And with 1 10 9 twice allow'd him	001	10	01
20 03 3	And for part of Knight's £7 fine	004	00	00

Mem: Houseman by bill of sale 20 Sep. 1682 made over all he had to me
in consideration of 241 10 4 then due to me for rent of his farme and for
mony wch he had receiv'd of the tenants and other persons as my
bayliffe in Suffolk. And in consideration of his half years rent (being £40)
ending at Mich. next without giving him any account of the same, for
and in respect that he well knewe that it woud not near satisfie the said
281 10 4. These are the words of the said bill of sale.   582 14 08

Noat: Houseman was loath to leave the farm and I to take it into my hands

At Mich. 1682 I made Mr Francis Robinson of Walpole bailiff of my Suffolke estate.

Noat:Though the ballance of the last account is 544 13 8 as is mentioned p. 297. I will keep an account in this book only of the mony due from the present tenants and for the Rents of Assize being 239 6 1 /492 /. And I will keep account of

					239	06	01

Houseman's	281	10	4	/quarto 52/
And of Keeble's	014	10	0	
And of Auldred's	002	17	3	/quarto book 51
And of the sayd	006	10	0	
	544	13	8	

297. Suffolke Credit

20 Sep. 1682 Houseman account for £32, payd Harris in July	032	00	00
Repayrs about the mill 2 8 0, Patrich's barne 3s	002	11	00
Sallary ending next Mich.	003	00	00
Militia charges	000	10	00
	038	01	00

20 Sep. 1682

Houseman owe besides the 20 03 3.	221	07	01				
Charged on the other side p. 296	020	03	03				
Sagar owe	042	10	00				
Arteshall owe	027	10	00				
Patrich owe	033	00	00				
Arrears of Rents of Assize ending at Mich 1681	011	10	03				
Rest upon Thomas Keeble's account	014	10	00				
And upon Auldred's account	002	17	03				
	419	2	10				
Halfe a years rent of five farmes at Mich. 1682	103	15	00				
A years rent of assize	015	05	10				
And the 6 10 00 mentioned upon the foot of the last account p. 227	006	10	00	544	13	08
Vide page 296	544	13	8	582	14	08

Mr Robinson's Account

298. Russell's Debt (560, 78,)

Page 78, Russell's debt at Mich. 1682 is	075	09	05
When he made the bill of sale mentioned p. 79			
I allow'd him as is set downe p. 299			

	A years rent at Mich. 1683	011	13	00
		087	02	05
21 Oct. 1683	Russell's owe me	039	19	01
	Two years rent ending Mich. 1685	023	16	00
	Half a years rent at Lady 1686	005	16	06
	A year and a half ending Mich. 1687	017	09	06
9 March 1687	Mr Windham examined my bills, and I owe	086	11	01

him forty pounds nineteen shillings eleven pence. Witness

Signed before me *Stephen Legge* my hand *Robert Russell*

	Owe as abovesaid	040	19	11

299. Russell's Credit

	Page 79, he have credit for				028	02	08
	Allow'd him Nov. 1682 for taxes formerly						
	payd by him to disband the army.				000	17	06
	Repayrs 1679, 1680, 1681				002	12	6
	For 15 comb of wheat delivered into the						
	house at several times 1680 and 1681				010	08	06
	For a cow 1680				002	00	00
Since Nov. 1682 to 21 Oct. 1683.							
He have deliver'd 1 comb 2 bushel of wheat at		0	18	0			
5 comb oats 1 5 6, peas 12s 1 comb 1 bushel		1	17	6			
fetches 1 comb 6 8					003	02	02
	Repayrs 7s				047	03	04
	The arrear is				039	19	01
					087	02	05
6 Oct. 1684	Payd me				004	00	00
25 [*Oct.*]	Salman account for				002	00	00
	But Elden's account Russels brought me in						
	Jan. and Feb. 1683 6 comb of wheat				003	06	00
	Worke in 1683 at his owne farm				000	19	03
1683	At Felbrigg Hall		0	10	0,		
	At Shepherd's at Albye		0	08	6½	000	18	06
5 July 1687	Fairchilde account for				004	00	00
	And 5 comb of barly				001	10	00
Dec.	3 comb of wheat £1 16s.						
	And 5 comb of barly £1 6s				003	02	00
9 March 1687	I accounted with Russells and allow'd for mason's work						
	done at several times in and						
	about my owne house		19	17	1.			
	And about several farmes		3	06	0.			
	Repayrs about his own farm		2	12	4	025	15	05

			045	11	02
Rest			040	19	11
			086	11	01

300. Plummer's Debt (560, 131)

21 Oct. 1683	Page 131, his debt exceed his credit	085	02	06
	Two years rent at Mich. 1685	064	00	00

Plummer was in debt when he came had losses and the times
so bad, I could not get another tennant

		149	02	06

Thomas Copland's Debt (491)

	A years rent at Mich. 1686	028	00	00

Copland died Oct. 1686, the widdow not able to hold the farme

23 Dec. 1686 she payd me for good and chattels her husband bought of
me 4 Sep. 1685 £14 which I had of Plummer Aug. 1685

301. Plummer's Credit

Anno 1682	Allow'd a bill of repayrs	002	14	11
	1681, 1682 Salman disbursd 2 15 0 repairs			
24 Mar. 1683	Sent me by Mr Harris	005	00	00
25 Oct. 1684	Salman account for	004	00	00
	And Elden account for	004	00	00
17 Oct. 1685	Elden account	005	00	00

By bill of sale 27 Aug. 1685 of all his cattel, corne, hay
utensils of husbandry, turnups, and the feed of the ground

	076	06	00
	097	00	11
Soe lose by Plummer	052	01	07
	149	02	06

Copland's Credit

23 Dec. 1686	I accounted with Widdow Copland who			
	payd Fayrchild at several times	018	14	00
	Payd me	001	00	00
	2 comb 1 bushell of wheat at	001	17	00
	Allow'd for plowing and carrying muck	000	08	09

She craved to bee allow'd 3 2 4 for ditching, and 2 6 0
for repayrs, which I did more out of charity than reason.

	005	08	04
Remit above all pretences	000	11	11
	028	00	00

302. Jecks's Debt (545.493, 139)

21 Oct. 1683	Page 139 Jeks owe	027	13	04
	A years rent at Mich. 1684	026	13	04
18 Feb. 1684.	I gave Jecks a hedge row of ashe worth about £1 10s besides ditching.	054	06	08
	A years rent at Mich. 1685 / 493 /	026	13	04
	At Mich. 1686	026	13	04
He died 21 Dec. 1686 A years rent at Mich. 1687		026	13	04
		080	00	00

303. Jecks's Credit

18 Feb. 1684	Allow'd for a ferkin of butter sent 1681.	001	00	00
15 Dec 1684	John Jeck's accounted for £13 payd Joseph Elden for me	013	00	00

➤ And payd me £14 13s 4d when in truth he did owe but 13 13 4 as he and his wife affirm'd, but could not make it apeare having forgot the said butter

		014	13	04
Elden charge himself in his account dated 25 Oct. 1684 with		026	13	04
		055	06	08

18 Feb 1684   I did tell Jecks I woud owe him £3 out of his half years rent in respect the last summer was soe very dry

		003	00	00
	He payd me £1 too much as aboves'd	001	00	00
24 Nov. 1685	Payd me at the mill	013	13	04
	Allow'd him for worke about the dam	001	19	09
23 Nov. 1686	Sent me by Stephen Legge	018	00	00
3 May 1687	Payd Legg	014	00	00
	Repayring the tyles 2 13 6½	002	13	6½
26 Dec.	Payd Step. Legg	013	00	00

304. Jecks's Debt (494, 196)

	Page 196 at Mich. 1685	304	06	08
	Half a years rent at Lady 1686	063	13	04
	At Mich. 1686 63 13 4			
	At Mich. 1687 127 06 8	191	00	00
	A years rent ending at Mich. 1688	127	06	08
		686	06	08

305. Jecks's Credit

	Page 197	074	00	00
24 Nov. 1685	Jecks payd me at Crownthorp	040	00	00
23 Nov. 1686	Sent me by Stephen Legg	067	00	00
3 May 1687	Payd Legg	030	00	00

19 Dec.	Payd Legg	030	00	00

306. Bale's Farme Debt (545, 184)

24 Nov. 1685	Page 184, owe me	027	13	08
	A years rent at Mich. 1686	036	11	00
	At Mich 1687	036	11	00
		100	15	08

307. Bale's Credit

24 Nov. 1685	Bale payd me	001	00	00
24 Nov. 1686	Bale payd me	012	00	00
May 1687	Payd Legg	006	00	00
20 Dec	Payd Legg	016	00	00

309. Robert Kingsberry's Debt (497, 278)

	Page 278	269	09	07
29 Sep. 1685	Half a years rent of my mill	019	00	00
	A years rent of Brunden Farme and Brunden Mill ending Mich. 1686	218	00	00
4 Nov. 1686.	I owe Mr Windham for rent two hundred and	506	09	07

eleven pounds nineteen shillings seven pence.
Witness my hand *Robart Kingsberry*
Signed in the presence of *Stephen Legge Francis Robinson*

	Owe as above	211	19	07
	A years rent at Mich. 1687	218	00	00
		429	19	07
	A years rent at Mich. 1688	218	00	00
	At Lday 1689	109	00	00

309. Robert Kingsberry's Credit

1 July 1685	Briggs charge himself with	080	00	00
3 Jan. 1685	Kingsberry sent me	100	00	00
8 June 1686	He sent to Felbrigg which John Barham account for	100	00	00
4 Nov. 1686	Allow'd the Parson's sallary at Mich. 1685	013	06	08
	Amonition 2 years	000	13	02
	Bricks and tyles	000	10	02

Mem. April 1687. I gave K. ten trees in full of my promise   294   10   00
p. 497 for 2 years past and 8 to come, as *per* note

	Rest due	211	19	07
		506	9	7
29 April 1687	Payd Stephen Legg my man	050	00	00

22 Aug. 1688	Sir Thomas Fowle account for £100 receiv'd of Parish order of Robert Kingsberry 11 March 1686	100	00	00
	And of *ditto* order of *ditto* 17 May 1688	100	00	00
12 Sep.	Payd Sir Thomas Fowle	050	00	00
24 [Sep.]	Mr Briggs account for £50 receiv'd of Robert Kingsberry 21 Feb. 1687	050	00	00
1 March 1688	Payd Sir Thomas Fowle	100	00	00

310. Downing's Debt (505)

	A years rent at Mich. 1685	060	00	00
	Half a years rent Lady 1686	030	00	00
		090	00	00

27 Sep. 1686. I owe my land lord thirty three pounds four and nine pence for rent due Lady last. James X Downing
Signed before *John Salman*

29 Sep. 1686	James Downing debt is	063	04	09
	And at Lady 1687	030	00	00
		093	04	09
	At Mich. 1687	060	00	00

311. Downing's Credit

12 Mar. 1685	Elden account for	002	05	00
2 June 1686	Downing payd John Barham	020	00	00
	Buck 8 comb at 6s 2 8 0			
	Wheat 20 comb at 15s 15 0 0	017	08	00
27 Sep.	Allow'd him for repayring houses	010	15	01
	And the fences	006	07	02
		056	15	03
	Rest	033	04	09
		090	00	00
5 July 1687	Downing payd me	007	12	09
	And Fairchilde for my use at 3 payments since 27 Sep. 1686	015	00	00
	And 40 comb of wheat at 16s £32,			
	And 20 comb of oats at 6s £6			
	Repayring houses 11 [s], fences 2 1 0	040	12	00
		063	04	09

Windham allow'd me all my disbursements (but amonition) and I owe him thirty pounds Downings mark X
signed be fore *Edward Haverchild*

030	00	00
093	04	09

312. Green's Debt (491)

A years rent at Mich. 1686	006	oo	oo
At Mich. 1687	006	oo	oo

313. Green's Credit

3 Jan. 1686	Payd me	006	oo	oo
2 Dec. 1687	Payd me	006	oo	oo

314. Richman's Debt (538, 121)

Observe: page 121 want to ballance p. 120 at Lady 1686	006	10	oo
A years rent at Lday 1687	007	oo	oo
At Mich. 1687	003	10	oo
	017	oo	oo
15 Feb 1687	Richman owe me	004	10	oo

315. Richman's Credit

5 July 1687	Fairchilde account for	006	10	oo
	And of him	001	oo	oo
15 Feb.	John Richman payd me	005	oo	oo
		012	10	oo
	Rest due to Mr Windham	004	10	oo
signed before me *Stephen Legge* John X. Richman marke	017	oo	oo

316. Bale's Debt (545, 185)

< Ballance of p. 185 at Mich 1685	037	13	08
A years rent at Mich. 1686	036	oo	o>

➤ By oversight I writ the 2 lines above, and the 1st line p. 317 after the 1st line p. 306 and 307 therefore X

317. Bale's Credit

24 Nov. 1685	Bale <payd me>	<01	oo	o>
	Vide page 316 why the line above is X

318. Martin Thompson's Debt (537, 28)

Page 28, owe at Mich. 1686	031	10	oo
A years rent at Mich. 1687	015	oo	oo
9 March 1687	This is a true account and I owe Mr Windham	047	10	oo
	fiveteen pounds *Martin Thompson*

319. Tompson's Credit

8 Nov. 1686	Payd me	005	04	00
	6 comb of wheat in Oct. last at 16s	004	16	00
18 March	Payd me	012	10	00
Oct. 1687	6 comb of wheat at 14s	004	04	00
	A load of straw	000	09	00
9 Mar.	Payd me	005	07	00
		032	10	00
	Rest	015	00	00
		047	10	00

320. Thomas Ransome Debt (494, 274)

	A years rent *vide* p. 274 Mich. 1686	020	00	00
	At Mich. 1687	020	00	00

321. Thomas Ransome Credit

	Agreed to allow for want of barne and stable	001	10	00
9 Oct. 1686	Payd me	007	04	07
	Repayrs houses [£]1 1 7, fences 3s 10d	001	05	05
5 July 1687	Fairchilde account for	004	00	00
28 Jan	Ransome payd me	005	14	00
	3 bushells of peas	000	06	00
28 Jan 1687	Mr Windham made these allowance to me			
	Thomas Ransome			

322. Prance's Debt (496, 272)

5 Nov. 1686	Page 272, owe	417	17	11
	A years rent at Mich. 1687	194	08	09
10 Feb. 1687	I acknowlege to owe Mr Windham for rent	612	05	11

due last Mich. (Thomas Voyce dues pay the last £50
according to his note) three hundred sixty two pounds five
shillings elevenpence. Witness my hand *Jeremiah Prance*

10 Feb. 1687	Owe me	362	05	11
	At Mich. 1688	194	08	00
	At Lday 1689	097	04	00

323. Prance's Credit

16 Feb. 1686	Payd Sir Thomas Fowle	050	00	00
20 June 1687	Payd him more	050	00	00
16 Sep.	Payd him more	050	00	00

21 Dec.	Payd him	050	00	00
8 Feb	Prance payd John Voyce Mr Parish partner			
	to pay Sir Thomas Fowle for me.	050	00	00
This £50 was to pay to Fowle by Parish 17 May 1688		250	00	00
	Rest due	362	05	11
		612	05	11
12 Sep. 1688	Payd Sir Thomas Fowle	060	00	00
10 Oct.	Payd me at Midleton	008	10	00
Dec.	Payd by Mr Parish to my man	031	10	00
17 April 1689	Payd Sir Thomas Fowle	050	00	00

324. Ward's Debt (478, 114)

	A years rent at *vide* p. 114 Mich. 1687	017	00	00

325. Ward's Credit

326. Lowne's Debt (529, 244)

15 March 1686	Page 244, owe a years rent	060	00	00
29 Sep. 1687	A years rent	060	00	00
		120	00	00

327. Lowne's Credit (252)

27 Dec 1687	John Lowne payd me	023	19	00
	Allow'd 5 comb of wheat	003	10	00
	1 comb of peas	000	10	00
	2 load of straw for thatch	000	18	00
	Poor and church rates for Monyman's / 252 /	000	06	08
	2 load of straw more for thatch	000	16	00

328. Tower's Debt (531, 250)

	From page 250 at Mich 87	016	00	00

William Tower signed this book before me *Stephen Legge*

329. Tower's Credit (251)

18 Jan. 1687	From page 251 payd me	014	00	00
	Allow'd for 6 loads of marle	001	11	09
	Making the pit	000	05	03
	4 deals for shrouds	000	03	00
18 Jan. 1687	Mr Windham made these allowances to me	016	00	00
	William Tower			

330. Barber's Debt (508, 268)

5 July 1687	Page 268, owe me	067	00	00
	At Mich. 1687	014	10	00
		081	10	00

331. Barber's Credit

17 Feb 1687	Accounted with Barber for 12 combs of wheat brought to Felbrigg	007	04	00
And 8 combs of barly carryed to Cromer to mault for me		002	12	00
	Then payd John Barham for me	018	00	00
	Payd Barham	001	00	00

332. Sexton's Debt (560, 74)

16 Jan 1687	Page 74 for ballance	017	06	00

333. Sexton's Credit

6 March 1687	For butcher's meat	014	18	09

334. Thomas Woodrow's Debt (538, 100)

	From page 100, a years rent at Mich. 1687	016	11	06

336. Harris's Debt (509, 260)

	From page 260.	070	12	11

337. Harris's Credit

Leases

(294) 5 July 1684, Richard Benslee hired Repham farme for 7 years ending Mich. 1691 at rent and covenants in Sextan's agreement (p. 497), and I lend him £40 *gratis*. Memo: he had £42 of me in stock as *per* note 30 Sep. 1684, which is £2 more than I promised.

(538) James Scepper by indenture 20 Dec. 1655, to keep the houses in repayr for dawbing, thatching, ground selling and glasing, and all the fences, being allow'd 400 of one bond wood.

(48, 534) 24 Sep. 1686, Henry Bally agree to hold the ground he now hath in use of Mr Windham for 7 years ending Mich. 1693, and to leave it as it ought to have been left, if this agreement had not been made.
Witness his hand *Henry Bally* Signed before *Edward Hagerchild* my balyle

(324, 544) 26 July 1686, John Ward of Aylsham hired Ives's farme for 7 years ending 1693 at £17 the first 4 years, and £18 the last 3 years.
He is to have the same covenants Ives had.

(286) 28 May 1686, Samuell Curril hired the Ingworth Mill paying £7 10s at Mich. 1686, and £30 a year the 3 next years and £34 the next 4 years, upon Willis's covenants (p. 548). 4 Dec. he carryed away his goods in the night.

(286) 27 Jan. 1686, Richard Bygrave of Felmingham hired the said mill paying £15 at Mich, and £30 the next 3 years, and £32 the last 4 years, 60 eles and 2 pullets every year. I am to repayre the houses, he the banks and mill being allow'd rough timber; other usual covenants.
Observe: corne is so low and millers doe so scramble for grist by fetching and carrying (which was not formerly done) 'tis hard to get a tennant.

(162) *Anno* 1686, Ulph agreed to give me £6 a year to let him live in the redhouse and to have 2 cows goe in the ground all year, and a horse running from 1 Nov. to 1 May. John Barham was by.

(246, 531) 7 Nov. 1687, William Howard of East Beckham agreed to take a new lease of the houses and land which he now have of Mrs Windham for 9 years beginning at Mich. next at the rent and covenants in the lease made by Mr and Mrs Chamberlaine 16 May 1670. And the said William Howard and William Windham agree to seal a lease accordingly when either of them shall desire it. Witness their hands 7 Nov. 1687.

Signed before *Jon Francis* my butler *Will Windham Will Howard*

(96, 553) 9 Nov. 1687, Henry Wells of Metton agreed to hire the ground which Sam Smith had till Mich. 1694, and also the Hallyard and meadow adjoyning late in Mr Talbotts use at £6 a year for 6 years and £6 10s the last year upon reasonable covenants. Signed before *John Leverington*, Norwich, joyner. Witness our hands *Will Windham Henry Wells*

➤Noat: the Hallyard and meadow is reputed 4 acres, and Well payd Talbott £2 10s a year for it.

480

(528, 556) 31 Dec. 1687, John Lowne hired of Mr Windham Beestons House with the Portal Barne in East Beckham and 90 acres and half a rood of land now in H. Johnson's use particularly mentioned in his lease of the same farme 23 Sep. 1670, and 19 acres more in his use at Aylmerton, the said Lowne paying for the same £36 a year for 13 years ending Mich. 1701, he using and leaving the ground as H. Johnson ought to doe by his lease of 23 Sep. 1670. And by his articles 26 Feb. 1677, and performing such covenants, and will seal a lease according to this agreement when tendred to him.

Witness our hands 31 Dec 1687. *Will Windham John Lound*
Signed before us *Step Legge Will Howard*

(246, 531, 528) 1 Feb 1687, William Howard hired Mr Windham's fouldcourse in East Beckham now in Harry Johnson's use, and before his time William and John Howards and John Ellis use, for 9 years, beginning at Mich. next paying £15 a year at Lady day and Mich. Mr Windham reserve for himself and his heirs all timber, wood and thornes and libertie to take and carry away what he please except necessary thorns which the said William may take in season for fencing the ground. Mr Windham reserve the royaltie for game, and Mr Windham and Howard covenant and agree to seal a lease according to this their agreement when either of them desire it. Witness our hand this 1 Feb 1687.

Signed in the presence of *Jon Francis* my butler *Will Windham Will Howard*

(108, 481) Barker married Chris Rooke's widdow, she hired of me 28 Feb. 1665 one acre and a half in Runton for a year ending 1 Oct. 1666 at 12s as *per* book of attournement.

Observe: Margaret Rooke widdow 1609 hired 2 acres and a half of farmland at 5s a year which was sometime in her use by coppy and seised by the lord because 'twas demeans of the manor of Runton. *Anno* 1630 Christopher Rooke held it at the same the rent. Anno 1635 held it at 12s a year, 1 days work and 1 hen. In a booke of the farmland of John Windham made by Thomas Blofield 1660 Christopher Rooke is charged 12s for 2 acres in 2 peeces in the East Feild of Runton and payd it 18 Oct. 1660. The audit bookes examined by me 6 Feb.

481

(109, 480) Mr Smith for 1 rood of farme ground in Runton feild.
Observe: 1609 Robert Mariner hired it at 1s a year 'twas once granted by coppy, and seised as Rooke's was (*vide* p. 480)
1630 Thomas Smyth hired it at the same rent
1653 John Smyth hired it at 12d *per annum*. 1655 John Smyth, clark held it.
Note the rent payd all along, *ex* the audit books 6 Feb 1687. W. W.
Nathaniel Smith tenant to the 1 rood at this time.

(108) Christopher Rooke, Tracy's wife's son hired of me the land, late in Tracey's use for a year ending Mich. 1688 at 12s, 1 days work and 1 hen as *per* agreement 7 Feb. 1687.

(280) John Howse of Metton hired of me 26 acres 1 rood of land in Metton (part of the ground which Talbott hired, and left at Mich. last) for 7 years ending at Mich. 1694 at £13 2s 6d a year as by articles 6 Feb. 1687.

(266, 493) Richard Walker hired the grounds now in his use and Mr Eyres, and which were late in Frosts, Haddon and Tene's use (p. 533), to hold them 3 years from Mich. 1688 at £40 a year, and upon the covenants in their agreement (p. 533), and may keep his fat cattel there till Christmas after the 3 years paying but £5 for that quarter as *per* agreement 9 Feb 1687.

(322) 11 Feb. 1687, Prance agreed to hold Midleton Hall farme 14 years from Mich. 1689 at the rent and covenants in his lease (p. 497). I fear he will not bee able.

(110) 14 Feb. 1687, I finde in the audit bookes the 4d a year have gone on all along in the names of Johnson and Ellis *scilicet* Johnson for 1 rood in East Beckham 2d, and Elis for a rood there 2d under the charge of farme lands.

(111, 482/4) Blofield who came to bee my brothers steward anno 1654, charged John Kilbye for 2 roods in a close of his betwene Tuttington and Banningham 3s a year, and received the rent all along, as particular of the estate made *anno* 1661 and by the audit books. But in the audit booke dated 16 June 1645, John Kilbye charg'd 3s for 1 ½ rood late in the farme of Ann Doughty widow, deceased.

482

(140) Marshall pay the 3s 4d for 2 roods in 2 peces nere Hoods, which 2 roods was anno 1662 in the use of Thomas Woodcock; and in 1654 in Thomas Cotterills use, and before several others as *per* audit bookes examined by me 15 Feb 1687.

(83, 482/3) From *16*58 [sic] to 1617 Thomas Rugg *Esq. * payd 1s 4d a year for 5 roods of land in 2 peeces. Anno 1612 William Rugg Esq. for a farm of 5 roods in 2 peeces in Rowton 1s 4d ditto per ditto before as by audit bookes.

(62, 482/2) Edmond Pall charged until 1659 before that time the widow Pall charged the like 3s 4d anno 1657. She is charged 3s 4d for 1 rood of farme ground ditto 1655, and payd all along which is all I find of it in the audit book, but in a quarto made 1 Apr. 1654 ditto charged ditto.
➤Observe: in a particular of my brother's estate made by Thomas Blofield his steward anno 1661, he charge Edmund Pall for two roods lying in two peeces in Aylemerton feild 3s 4d, which I suppose he was informed of, for before 1661 he calls it but 1 rood and after 1661 he does not say for what 'tis payd.
Note in the same particular, he charge the landholders of Thomas Rugg Esq. for 2 roods in 2 peeces in Felbrigg feild 1s 4d (vide p. 482 s. 2).
I rather thinke 'tis in Rowton, when I am better informed I'll set it downe in this booke.

(481/8) In the same book 31 May 1644 the same Ann is charged 3s for the said 1½ roods.
1 Jan. 1637 the said Ann is charg'd ditto per ditto late in the farme of James Allen.
1620 John Crome the like for 1½ rood.
1618 William Doughty the like for 1½ rood late in the farme of Richard Allen being part of 1 acre and ½ rood in 2 peeces in the north feild of Tuttington 6s.
1610 James Allen payd 6s for the rent of 1 acre ½ rood of land some time in his possession by coppy and now seised by the lord because 'twas part of his demeasne.
/ Examined the audit books 17 Feb 1687. W. Windham /

(56) I searched the audit books for the land in Johnson's use (p. 538), where 1609 John Deane for the farme of Hall green 4d and for 3 roods in Aylmerton 7½d, and 1 rood inclosed 2d.
1624 Michael Goodrowe ditto per ditto. 1620 Mary Deane ditto per ditto,
1632 Michael Goodrowe for Hall green and 1 acre in 2 peeces 1s 2d,
1639 M. Goodrowe per ditto 10s a year, 1642 ditto per ditto for 8s,
1655 M. Goodrowe for 1 acre 8s, 1659 William Johnson 8s,
1660 in quarto book which Blofield collected the rents by, he received of William Johnson 8s for 1 acre nere the house of the said William Johnson.

483

(230) 7 March 1687, John Tomson of Gresham hired the farme late in Heydon's use in Felbrigg for 7 years ending Mich. 1695 at £33 a year, and 3 days thatching with all materials yearly. He is to keep the glass, locks, and keys, fences, gates and etc in repayre being allow'd rough timber with good covenants to use and leave the farme. Note: Curdle Close and the 10 acres on this side both in Heydon's use are not included in the aforesaid agreement with Thomson. And whereas I have let ofe 8

acres 1 rood of the land late in Heydon's, Tomson is to have said 8 acres 2 roods late in Pall's use in lieu of the said 8 acres 1 rood as by our articles signed and sealed 7 March 1687.

(258) 20 Sep. 1688 Thomas Bothell of Sheringham hired 16 acres of Mr Britiffe's use (p. 528) from Mich. next to Mich 1690 at £3 a year.

491

(507) When yours came, I was from home whence I have been long absent. As to the land I am at your dispose. The 4 years rent at Mich. next I acknowledge and will pay, as soon as soe much rent comes in and as to the charges I hope you will bee merciful to your humble servant, Clement Herne, 24 Aug. 1685. I writ his letter obleiged me to bee his servant.

12 Dec. 1685, Mr Clement Herne payd me thirty pounds for four years rent ending Mich. last for nine acres one rood of farme ground in Metton, which wee had a tryal for at Norwich assise, 1684, and in satisfaction of charges of sute in the presence of Joseph Elden my servant who tould the money, and see me give him an acquittance aforesaid: 14 16 for rent

15   4 charge

Will Windham   £30 00

(300, 560) 4 Sep. 1685, Thomas Copland of Tunstead hired the farm late Plummer's for 7 years ending Mich. 1692 paying £28 the first year, £30 a year the next five years, and £32 the last year. I am to repayr the houses by Feb. and the fences by Mich. Copland is to doe 3 days work of a thatcher and 3 days dawbing finding materials yearly, and to keep and leave the fences in repayr, being allow'd rough timber. He is to lay all the muck upon the premises, and to leave the straw and chaif of the last crop. He is to have the use of the barne till May day 1693. With other covenants how the ground shall bee used and left as *per* articles signed and sealed.

(312) 11 Nov. 1685, Antony Green hired 13 acres 2 roods in Felbrigg feild. And 16 Dec. 1685, he hired 1 acre 2 roods more there for 9 years end Mich. 1694, paying £6 a year for the said 15 acres as *per* articles signed and sealed. / *Observe* /

492

(294, 478) Sextan of Repham died Dec. 1683. Next lease p. 478

(296) The particulars of the £239 6s 1d mentioned (p. 296)

42	10	00	Sagar
45	15	00	Peppar ⎱ Owe for rent ending
27	10	00	Arteshall ⎰ at Our Ladyday 1682
33	00	00	Patrich

21	10	00	Sagar
08	15	00	Peppar ⎤ Their half years rent
19	10	00	Arteshall ⎰ ending Mich. 1682
14	00	00	Patrich
11	10	03	Rents of assize due Mich. 1681
15	05	10	A years rents of assize Mich. 1682
239	06	01	

(497) *Memo*: Prance in a letter dated 10 Apr. 1684, say Robert Kingsberry and the miller are agreed, he gave him £20 to take the mill.

Note: the said £20 is in consideration that the mill is not in repayr.

26 Apr. 1684, Rob. Kingsberry write, the miller and I are agreed.

(505) To avoid a sute, I agreed to let him have 4 milch cows *gratis* leaving 4 of the same sort and ages at the end of the determination of his terme as *per* note under his mark made in the presence of John Talbott.

30 Sep. 1684, I did also promise him before Talbott and Salman to release him at 3 years end if grounds and fences were then in as good a condition as now. He is also to have £2 worth of hay, peas and fetches and to leave so much.

(270) 10 Nov. 1684. I tould Thomas Pall of Felbrigg, Wegg had a warrant to serve upon him for killing conies upon the warren, when he mow'd his doles, Pall said 'twas noe great crime to kill a few once a year ofe his owne ground. At last he gave Wegg £1 for satisfaction, and promised before Bansted and others nere to do the like: Ashe was by.

493

(76, 538) 24 Nov 1684, Black of Thurgarton said he hired the ground late in Colls use from Mich. 1682 at £5 yearly. And that there was 9 acres *scilicet* three 2 acre peeces, two 1 acre peeces, one 3 rood peece and a single rood and all but the rood inclosed.

(252, 493/7) 4 Dec. 1684, L. Monyman agreed to pay me £22 a year for 2 years ending Mich. 1686 to feed the grounds mentioned (p. 529). And by reason I had £2 of him in lieu of fences being in *out of * repair, he may leave them to the value of £2 out of repair. Elden present.

(264) 26 Feb 1684, Robert Adams of Carrow in Norwich, mercer gave me 3 ginneys in hand, and agreed before Mrs Bendish and Robert Osborne to pay me £650 more for my house in Norwich.

31 Mar 1685, I seal'd the writings, and he gave me Briggs note for £250, and morgaged the house to me for payment of £400 with interest at four half year payments ending Lady 1687.

Memo: the house was bought in my uncle Mede's name in trust for me before I came of age of Sir Nicholas Bacon of Gillingham in Suffolk, it cost £650.

(266, 481) 22 June 1685, Richard Walker of Gresham hired the grounds (mentioned in the 2nd section of p. 534 to bee in the use of Tene and Haddon) at £29 for 3 years ending at Mich. 1688 to feed only, as *per* articles.

(266, 481) 26 June 1685, Mr Eyre, Minister of Aylemerton came to desire he might have the grounds in Frosts use mentioned in 2nd section p. 534 for 3 years ending Mich. 1688 at £11 *per annum* which I agreed to.

18 Feb. 1684, John Jecks agreed to hold the mill 11 years ending Mich. 1696 at the rent and covenants in Norton's lease (p. 545), allowing him 2 loads of fire wood yearly as *per* articles.

(21, 529) Jeremy Cushing hire the land in Aylmerton feild late in Monyman's use at £2 10s a year

494

(242) 17 Feb. 1684, Francis Gould agreed to hold the farme he now lives in 7 years ending 1692, at the rent and covenants in his lease (p. 547 section 2nd). If Gould dye, his wife may leave the farme at Mich. upon 9 months notice as by articles.

(304, 197) 18 Feb. 1684, Isaac Jecks agreed to hold Crownethorpe farme 8 years ending Mich. 1693 at the rent and covenants in his lease (p. 551), with this condition that he may feed the fatting pasture with cows the last year, as by articles. I did then agree to make a new plank thrashing floor, and repayr the barne floor, and lay boards over the calf-house, and send twenty deals for shelves for the cheese chamber, and to ditch in the mowing meadow. And did give him £10.

Note: at Mich. 1684, Robinson my Suffolk balye enter'd upon Patrich's farme (p. 550). And 23 Feb. 1684 I let the land on the southside of the way from Walpole to Southhold late in Patrich's use and before that in Henry Aldred's use (p. 547) to the widdow Sagar for 3 years ending 1687 at £14 a year with covenants to leave the ground well and the fences in repayr. I am to allow her 2 loads of one bond wood as *per* articles.

24 Feb. 1684, Patrich earnestly desired to hold the house and homestall belonging to the farme late in his use (p. 550) at £12 a year beginning Mich. 1684 which I agreed to during my pleasure before Robinson and Elden. He is to have one load of wood yearly.

(320, 531) 2 March 1684, Thomas Ransome of Thurgarton hired the farme late in William Ransome's use (p. 555) and now in Blofield's (p. 531) for 7 years ending Mich. 1692 at £20 a year the 3 first, and £22 for the 4 last years. He is to agree to doe 2 days thatching yearly, finding all materialls, and keep all fences in repayre, being allow'd rough timber, and doe all the dawbing. He is to spend all the stover upon the premises the first 6 years and to leave me £2 8s 4d worth of straw and chaife at the end of the lease. He is to leave the dreyns in good repayre with other usual covenants as *per* articles.

Memo: Mr L. Blofield payd me £2 8s 4d mentioned (p. 531).

495

From Mich. 1682, Houseman's farme in hand to 23 Feb. 1684, and then John Boone of Chelton agreed to pay me £96 at Christmas for the feed of the ground and hay of the meadows belong to said farme till Mich. 1685, and for 32 beasts bought at Hoxen Fayre which cost me £56.

Observe: I made so little of this farme the last 2 years that I chose rather to take £40 profit then use the ground till Mich. At which time Boone is to enter the said farme and Pepper's farme mentioned (p. 549) for 7 years ending Mich. 1692 at £80 a year payable Midsomer and Christmas except the last half year which it is to bee paid 28 Sep. He is not to break up meadow or mowing ground nor plow above 40 acres in any year, nor sow oats 2 years togeather upon one peice. He must spend the hay and other stover upon the premises the 6 first years, and keep the houses in as good repayre ➤ as they shall bee at this entry or at any time within 6 months after (being allow'd rough timber), and the fences and drayns. I reserve the royalties, timber, woods, bushes and trees to fell and carry away. I may enter upon any 20 acres of the ploughlands in Feb. 1691 and use them as I please. Boone covenant to keep all cattle out of Mells Wood and Stubb Wood by mending gapps. I am once in 2 or 3 years to new tap the fences about the said woods, and allow 8 loads of one bond wood yearly. He is to leave the last years muck cast up in the yards with other usual covenants as *per* indenture dated 23 Feb. 1684. He gave bond to perform these covenants, and to pay the said £96.

(560, 300) 27 Aug. 1685, Francis Plummer made a bill of sale to me of 4 horses, 7 neat beasts, 2 swine, hay, corne in houses and feild, turnups and of his husbandry things in satisfaction of £76 6s of the arrear of rent and delivered the possession of the farme to Elden.

I don't expect to make nere the mony they are valued at because I tould Elden he need not insist upon a reasonable valuation, because he had nothing else but poor household stuff which I bid him leave for his wife and children.

496

Memorandum: 2 May 1681 John Kingsberry said the 3 months tax came to

£	s	d		
02	02	10½	in Midleton	
00	03	01	Bulmore	Parish
00	00	08	Heany	
00	00	05	Wickham	
02	07	00½		

I did then allow but £2 5s 6d because he could give me no reason why Midleton rate was altered.

(**158**) Noat: He produced an acquittance dated 20 Apr. 1678 that Heany was but 8d. I believe he was mistaken when he tould me 1677 'twas 1s 3d.

Noat in a lease made 1657 to Robert Kingsberry for 10 years, there is a schedule of the lands conteyning 437 acres 38 perches £170 *per annum.*
Noat 1658: he hired the woods for 9 years particularly there expressed conteyning 117 acres 1 rood at £24 8s.
Whole 554 acres 1 rood 38 perches at £194 8s *per annnum*

	a.	r.	p
1. High Wood Crofts	12	1	0
2. High Woods }Bulmore togeather	34	0	0
3. Wigging Wood }			
4. Colledge Wood Midleton	46	0	0
5. Brick Hill Wood in Bulmore	18	0	0
6. Colledge Wood in Wickham		7	0
	117 a.	1r	0

(**497**) 26 Aug. 1681, I agreed to make Jeremiah Prance of Pentlowe in Essex a lease of Midleton farme for 7 years ending Mich. 1689 at the same rent and upon the same covenants as John Kingsberry's lease (p. 546), with this alteration only, that he is to have noe plow or cart boot as *per* noat under our hands (*vide* p. 497).
I beleive John Kingsberry will repent he did not agree with me, for he thrive and have not used the ground as if he had a minde to leave it. He insisted upon plowboote and cartboot, and some abatement of rent. I was resolved to run the hazard of getting a new tennant, than doe either for 'tis an extreordinary good farme, and cartboot is a means to destroy young timber.
I am glad John Kingsberry goes out, for I have found inconvenience in having brothers my tennants.
/And I am sure noe tennant will take less care of the timber and young stands than John Kingsberry have done/.

497

(**272, 481**)23 Sep. 1682, Prance sealed the counterpart of the lease according to the agreement 26 Aug. 1681. (p. 496), and gave me a bond to performe his covenants.

(**273**) 11 April 1683, John Kingsberry pleaded he had layd out about for the brick office above £100 though he was not obleiged to lay out above £30 as by (p. 156), and that he had noe timber assign'd for plow or cartboot in 1677, 1678, 1679, 1680 which was near £20 loss to him. In consideration of which, I allow'd him the £10 and would have allow'd him more. But that at his going away he sould the brick boards and other utensils and in the aforesaid 4 years did take downe many trees without assigment, which I am credibly informed he converted to his own use. As for certaine his father did very many.

(278, 492) 27 Aug. 1683, Robert Kingsberry agreed with me to hold Brunden farme 11 years ending 1696 upon the terms in his lease (p. 546). And that he would from Mich. next take upon himself to pay the rent and performe the covenants in the miller's lease (p. 511). And at the expiration or determination of Gibson's lease, he would take a lease of the mill upon the terms Gibson now have it, until Mich 1696.

Noat: Robert Kingsberry is to deal with Gibson as he see cause. And I did promise Robert Kingsberrry a tree yearly towards repayr of the mill from Mich. 1683.

The poverty and knavery of millers made me earnest to bring Robert Kingsberry to the aforesaid agreement.

(294, 492) 2 July 1683, Thomas Sextan hired Repham of me for 7 years ending Mich. 1690 at £50 yearly and 3 days thatching, and all the dawbing (except the dwelling house). He is to keep the windows and all the fences in repayr and leave all hay, straw and chaife with covenants how to use and leave the grounds. Noat: I let him £40 *gratis* upon securitye

498

Flags cut by Pye	1679	s	d	Flags cut by Fox	1679	s	d
For Philip Pall	1500 x	7	6	Mr Smith	2000 x	10	0
Mary Smith	1500 x	7	6	Robert Brese	1000 x	5	0
Nick Abbs	1500 x	7	6	Robert Brese elder	1000 x	5	0
John Yaxlye	2000 x	10	0	Brese junior	500 x	2	6
Thomas Abbs	2000 x	10	0	Clim Wodrowe	1000 x	5	0
Sexton	1000 x	5	0	Nick Dauson	1000 x	5	0
Ann Cosens	1000 x	5	0	Robert Fox	800 x	4	0
Parson Taylor	1000 x	5	0	Widow Williams	700 x	3	6
Thomas Locksmith	1000 x	5	0	Widow Miles	700 x	3	6
John Cason	1000 x	5	0	Mary Morslye	600 x	3	0
Thomas Cosens	1000 x	5	0	John Wodrowe	500 x	2	6
Edmund Pall	1000 x	5	0	William Dauson	500 x	2	6
Martin Thomson	1000 x	5	0	Clem Wodrowe	400 x	2	0
Richard Abbs	1000 x	5	0	John Leaslye	400 x	2	0
Denis Flaxman	800 x	4	0	Widow Moy	200 x	1	0
Martin Pye	600 x	3	0	John Marriner	200 x	1	0
John Richerson	600 x	3	0	All paid	2	17	6
Thomas Hilton	600 x	3	0	Doles of Brakes	1679		
Widow Flogden	600 x	3	0			s	d
Mayham	600 x	3	0	Thomas Smith		5	0
Thomas Morris	600 x	3	0	Widow Johnson		5	0
Flaxman	700 x	3	6	Nick Whalls		3	6
Robert Flaxman	500 x	2	6	John Barker		2	8

Edward Wilton	500 x	2	6	Thomas Wodrowe		2	8
John Bond	500 x	2	6	Nick Evered		2	6
William Woodhouse	500 x	2	6	Widow Leaslye		2	0
Nick Dauson	2 0						
Buxton	500 x	2	6	John Bessesson		2	0
John Abbs	500 x	2	6	Sam Beales		1	10
John Cason	400 x	2	0	Edward Pall		1	8
Nick Abbs	500 x	2	6	John Bret		1	6
Widow Pye	300 x	1	6	Robert Brese		1	0
Gregory Morris	300 x	1	6	Henry Bally		1	0
	6	15	6	Greene	1	0	
	2	17	6	Gregory Morris	0		10
Flags	9	13	0	John Bond	0		6
Brakes	1	16	8	All payd £1	16		8
	£11	9	8				

Flags are cut when any bodye speake to the gravers for some.
Brakes a certaine yearly rent.

499

Page				
220	Lands not let at Mich. 1681			
	Parke	070	00	00
	Church Close	016	00	00
	Pond Meadow	007	00	00
38	Hill and Bush close	011	00	00
24	Swifts	012	00	00
20	16 acres of Pall's	015	00	00
230	Heydons	048	00	00
174	Sheep walke	025	00	00
176	Flags and brakes	010	00	00
44	300 rabits	009	00	00
52	Aylemerton Closes	008	00	00
	Dovehouse grounds	036	00	00
541	Closes in Nick Abb's use	012	00	00
80	Sustead Close	040	00	00
72	Buns Wood	005	00	00
162	Dairy grounds	024	00	00
190	Rush Close	010	00	00
560	Long Meadow hay	007	00	00
276	Macks farme	035	00	00
543	Out of Dilham manour	002	00	00
34	Cromer house	002	00	00

509	Roughton Dovehouse		002	00	00
166	Repham		052	00	00
537	Ashe's Nursery		001	10	00
			450	15	00

Wicklewood Woods ⎫
Suffolk Wood   ⎬ not let

500

Rents payable to several manours out of my free and coppyhold land and tenements:

/ *Hanworth Manour ffyne 6d per annum* / I finde my father payd Henry Dix Bayliffe (to the Earl of Arundell) of the Manour as *per* receipt 19 March 1617 out of the manours following *scilicet:*

	s	d			s	d *per annum*
Aylemerton	10	0		Metton	1	0
Sustead ...	5	0		Runton	16	0
Banningham	3	0		Colby	12	0
And for lands in Suffield					1	4

25 Oct. 1630: my father paid Edmund Harmer bayliffe to the
afores'd manour 5s for Beckham Hall which he had then
newly purchased of Tuke, and for a tenement and lands in
Sustead late Abb's 5s 1d
3 Oct. 1639: my father paid the said Harmer 11d more
(which I have heard was for lands late Russell's)

			£	s	d
4 Dec. 1654: Robert Thompson paid Edmund Lubbock more for Carr's land £1 1s 3d and Downing's land 4d			004	00	11

/ *Cully Rent* / Felbrigg manour hold of the manour of Hanworth by
socage tenure paying at

	St. Andrew	17s 10d	Lday	2s 8d			
	Midsumer	17s 10d	Mich	17s 10d	002	16	02

501

Manour *per annum*

Toft Monks	for free-rent		001	13	04
Gunners	coppyhold for a house in Cromer		000	10	11
Suffield	free rent		000	02	02
Somerton Hall	free and coppyhold lands late Carr's		000	03	06
Gunton	free rent for land late Carr's		000	01	00
Sexten's	out of Banningham manour	2s 8d			
	out of Tuttington manour	1s 2d			
	and for Hear's land	1s 4d			
	out of Ingworth manour	12s 7½	000	17	09½

Kidlams	free land late Russell's			000	00	10½
Beeston Regis	and for Deane's and Feiser's lands	1s 6d				
Beeston Priory		11s 11d	000	13	05
Bromehold	in Worstead free		000	01	00
Roughton	2½d of coppyhold lands late Webster's		000	00	02½
Thurgarton	paid in 1601 to the bishop of Norwich		000	02	00
Sheringham	free rent for lands in Beckham		000	06	07
Carbrooke	Sir John Windham paid it 26 May 1630 for the use of Sir Thomas Southwell		000	02	00
Smalborowe	Debney's lands	7s 0d			
	and for Scrivener's	3s 0d			
	for 3 geese	3s 0d			
	for 10 bushells of barly *stet* < uncertaine >				
		12s 6d	001	05	06
Worstead			000	02	09
Hempnall	out of the manour of Wicklewood		000	05	01
Hingham	for suit of fines out of Wicklewood and Crownethorpe and payable to the bayliffe of Forehowe		000	09	09
Dominus Regni:	out of the said manours		000	02	08
Leete Fee:	due to the King's leete in Banningham paid to the bayliffe of South Erpingham hundred		000	02	08
Leet Fee:	payable to the constable of Gresham		000	00	06
	rent issuing out of Felbrigg manor every 30 weekes to the King		000	00	10½

502

Worstead	for Scrivener's lands 3s			
St. Andrew	for Debney's lands (p. 504) 4s 11d	000	07	11
Hacford Hall	for Repham	000	07	06

503

25 Sep. 1675
Receiv'd of Mr Windham in full for Sextens rent due to the
manour of Sextens for one yeare ending Mich. 1674 as followeth:
out of the Manour of Banningham 2s 8d, out of Tuttington 1s 2d,
more of lands late Hear's 1s 4d, out of Ingworth 12s 7d ½
for me *Tho. Empling* balyfe of the said mannor   000   17 09½
4 Aug. 1676
Receiev'd of Mr Windham of Felbrigg twenty eight
pounds six shillings five pence for seven years rent due to
the manour of Hanworth at Mich. last past   028   06   05

And two pounds six shillings one pennye
due to Sheringham manour for seven years then ending.   002 06 01
And two pounds sixteen shillings two pence for cully rent
due to the manour of Hanworth at Mich. 1673   002 16 02
per me Robert Cooke Bayliffe for the said manour
4 Aug. 1676
Mr Windham allowed me 18s 8d for years leet fee ending
Mich last which I payd to the constable of Banningham
at 2s 8d yearly *per me Robert Cooke*
15 Feb 1677. Receiv'd of Mr Windham £8 1s 10d for
two years rent due to Hanworth manour (and 13s 2d for
2 years then due) at Mich. 1677 to Sheringham manour
Robert Cooke   008 15 00

504

7 December 1678
Received then of Col. William Wyndham Esq. for eight years
Thurgarton free rent due at St Michall last (the sume of sixteen
shillings received by me) to the manner of Thurgarton.   000 16 00
Roger Wiggett [*this entry in Wigget's hand*]
Worstead 14 Jan. 1679: Briggs paid Rolph for 14 years quit
rent due to the deane and chapter of Norwich   005 10 09
Hanworth 27 Jan 1679: Receiv'd of Mr Windham eight pounds
one shilling ten pence for two years rents issuing out of the
some of his lands to the manour of Hanworth, and thirteen
shillings two pence.
Sheringham / *Cully rent* / for two years to Sheringham manour,
and two pounds sixteen shillings two pence for one years
Cully rent due to Hanworth manour at Mich 1679 (p 183).
Robert Cooke bailiff of the said manor.   011 11 02

505

(84) 1683, I was informed William Frost of Gresham had plow'd up a meer which lay betwene the ground he hire from me (p. 84), and his owne, upon view I sent for Frost, who pretended 'twas carelesly done and promised to lay it downe as formerly. 13 Feb 1683, Salman see meer stones set downe. Frost have [*blank*] acres in [*blank*] peeces [*blank*] or the £2 rent.

(42, 102) 12 Feb 83, Salman and Laurence Moneyman of Aylmerton made me a particular of the lands late in Richard Abb's use, which Peter Abbs now hire of me at £9 1s. He have 10 peeces conteining 30 acres ½ rood *scilicet*: two 5 acre closes and a 4 acre close, the other 7 peeces are in Aylmerton feild. If upon further examination, I find any mistake in the said particular, I'll set it downe in this book and refer to it by a figure.

(242, 494/1) 16 Aug. 1684, Francis Gould agreed to hold his farm one year ending Mich. 1685 at the rent and covenants in his lease mentioned (p. 547) as by note under his hand, signed in the presence of Edmund Bale.

(302, 493/6) 15 Aug. 1684, Jakes the miller agreed to hold the mill and etc one year end Mich. 1685 at the rents and covenants in Norton's lease (p. 545) as *per* note under his mark made in the presence of Edmund Bale.

(268, 310, 492/4) 22 Sep. 1684, James Downing of Metton hired the farme now in Shepherd's use in Alby for 7 years ending Mich. 1691 at £60 a year, 3 days thatching and 3 days dawbing with all materials (being allow'd £5 out of his first years rent to bye muck with). He is to keep and leave the fences in repayr, and performe other good covenants as *per* articles signed by us in the presence of John Salman, John Spurrell (*vide* below).
➤ Mem: Shepherd being loath to leave the farme used such means to discourage Downing from coming into the farme, that he was resolved not to go in, upon which I sent for him and found him such a sullen fellow that ... (*vide* p. 492 s. 4)

506

(559, 31, 507) 28 Jan 1681, I writ Doughty word 'twas unreasonable to desire such a lease. That I was willing to seal a lease with usual covenants according to our agreement anno 1679. He came to Hanworth and sent to me about setting out ground for a new house. I spoke to him of the lease and made him sensible that the covenants were extreordinary. He sayd they proceeded from his earnest desire to take away all possibilitye of a dispute with me for he said he had rather have a sute with the king, than me. When wee parted, he said he would order some things to be left out, and hoped I would yield to his humour a little. Which I intend to doe, rather than have a sute with him for a way.
Note: Doughty have several times sent me word by Salman and Blofield he would waite upon me and pay me. And this sumer he tould Mr Blofield, after Mich. he would pay the 4 years rent togeather.
I fancy he have a minde to see what success I shall have with Herne, and will act accordingly, though the cases are nothing alike. *This will be *1 July 1684
29 Oct. 1684, Mr Blofield went to Mr. Doughty for £9 4s od being 4 years rent due at Mich. last. Blofield brought me word, he own'd there was £9 4s due to me, which he would pay when lease was sealed. And if for time to come, I would agree to take £2 *per annum* free of all namer of deductions, he should think himself beholden to me, if not, he would take a lease for 99 years with usual covenants at £2 6s.
23 Oct. 1684, I writ to him to hasten the lease, and that the way to keep us friends, was to offer nothing unusual to me.

30 [*Oct.*] He tould me he had given his counsel order in it, and I writ to Mr Bacon to dispatch it.

10 Dec. Mr Doughty brought a lease of 95 years, which I sealed rather than have it longer unsetled, though it is partially drawne.

507

(532) 7 Nov 1682, I gave Mr Palmer order to prefer a Bill against Herne for the land.

13 April 1683, Mr Herne sent Green the atturny to tender me 9s 3d, for a years rent of the 9 acres 1 rood mentioned (p. 532) as coppyhold, which I refused.

4 Oct. 1683, wee examined witnesses at Norwich.

6 Feb. 1683, the case was heard before Lord Keeper North, who order'd a tryal next summer assizes.

17 July 1684, the cause was tried before Lord Chief Baron Mountague, and I had a verdit for the sayd nine acres one rood. Mr Herne and I were present.

31 Oct. 1684, Bretton and Palmer our attorneys met here by Herne's appointment in order to set me out the said 9 acres 1 rood. But the weather was so extreordinary bad, Herne did not come. I order'd Palmer to let Herne knowe if I had not satisfaction he must proceed.

13 Nov. Herne dined here and wee view'd the ground. He said he was willing to set me out 9 acre 1 rood to give what our atterneys thought reasonable for charges. He promised to come agayne in a fortnight. 14 Nov. I writ to Palmer to stay 29th, Herne have been here these two days, and exprest an earnest desire to accommodate the difference friendly, which I took so kindly, I offer'd to take £30 in satisfaction of rent and charges. He said he was satisfied, he ought to pay the 3 years rent at £3.14s *per annum,* and must pay my comon law charges but he said, he was informed £10 or £12 was as much as I could expect at comon law, and that Chancerye would give me more in fine, he desired time to give his positive answere, he seemed pleased with my carriage.

21 Aug. 1685, I writ to Mr Herne to send his resolution concering rent and charges and to let him know, if he comply'd, he might hire or leave the ground. He was not at home 24 Aug 1685 he writ as is mentioned (p. 491).

508

16 Jan 1679, it is agreed between Thomas Arteson of Mells Hamblet in Suffolk and W. Windham of Felbrigg, that Arteson shall have a lease of the mill now in his use, and of the mill now in Thomas Keeble's use at £39 yearly for 7 years from Mich. next upon the covenants in their several leases (p. 547 n. 1.3). Witness our hands *Samuell Smyth Will Windham Thomas Arteston*
In the presence of *John Salman*
Memorandum: Thomas Keeble 14 Jan. 1679 desired to leave the mill at Mich. next because Arteshall had got many of his customers.

(20) 17 Oct. 1670, Richard Pall hired 12 acres and 5 acres nere Cony Hill in Felbrigg field for 12 years ending Mich. 1682 at £5 19s. He is to leave 5 acres 3 years olland. Noat: He hire 2 acres more at £7, *scilicet*: 16 acres in the field and 5 acres bordering on the heath.

(80) 4 May 1681, Thomas Harris of Roughton hired the grounds lately in Abbs and Frost's use (p. 541) until 26 Dec next at £40 payable 25 June and 26 Dec. I am to have the hay in the Hallyard. He is to leave the ground fairly fed after his fattening cattle as *per* articles.

(509/4) *Memorandum:* June 1681, I promised Parke to take the farme at Mich. 1682, if he would leave the ground according to my minde, before Mr Butler of Holt.
23 July, I agreed to let Robert Barbour of a lease of the little farm and of ground now in Park's use for 7 years beginning Mich. 1682 at £29 yearly. 2 days thatching and all the dawbing with good covenants as *per* articles.

509

(122) 15 Aug. 1681, Richard Harding hired the ground in Allison's use (p. 535) for 7 years ending Mich. 1688 at £11 10s and 2 fat capons yearly. He is to keep and leave the gates all the fences in repayr, being allow'd rough timber. He is to leave 4 acres of winter corne stubble, 4 acres of olland buck stubble, 6 acres olland of 2 years lying, not to sow oats two years togeather as *per* note under his hand.

(276, 530/8) 27 Sep. 1681, John Applebye of Tunstead agreed to sow Mack's farme to halfs for one year ending Mich. 1682 according to articles signed and sealed by us. I could not let it without a great abatement.
6 July 1682, agreed with him for one year more

(260) 11 Oct. 1681, Mr Harris of Roughton hired the farme late in Selfe's use (the Dovehouse only excepted) for 3 years ending Mich. 1684 at £36, 4 days thatching and 4 days dawbing yearly. He is to have the straw, chaife and colder of the corne in the barne, and soe leave it with covenants how to use and leave the ground. as *per* articles at large appear. 10 March 1683, he promised me to hold it another year.

(508/4, 505/5) 20 June 1682, for feare I should not git a tenant for the rest of Parke's farme I agree with Dan Sheppard to let him live in the house rent free. He is to pay but 40s a cow. He is to plow and sow when, where and what I please, and to bee at all charges belonging to husbandrye, and to give me half the corne, as 'tis dress'd up. He is to have the chaif and coulder, and my cows the straw. He is to have 4 acres for peas and fetches and grounde to tye his horses upon. I am to pay parish rates. He is to keep the windows and fences in repayr and to leave soe much somerlye soe plow'd *12 acres 2 roods in the 4th earth* and well muck'd for winter corne, as he shall finde it at Mich. This agreement is to continue soe long as I will, giving him 3 months notice as *per* articles.

510

(141) 11 Jan 1647, Thomas Windham granted Thomas Kett, his heires and assigns for ever, a peice of ground forty yards long and one twenty foot broad adjoyning upon the east of his capital messuage in Wicklewood to inclose paying 4d yearly at Mich.

Noat: before this deed was made, Kett's ground extended full four foot from the house towards the comon, and is not part of the afores'd ground.

Memo: I knewe nothing of this till about two years ago I found the counterpart, since I have carelesly omitted to speak or send to him about it. *W. Windham.* 11 May 1681

(40, 511) 1 Feb 1667, John Norris Esq. hired the houses and grounds in the parish of St Michael of the Thurne in Norwich (purchased of Sir Nicholas Bacon) for 4 years ending Lady 1672 at £36 yearly. He is to leave the windows and locks in repayre. He is to keep the fruit trees in order, and not digg any of the grounds, which have not been broken up within a year, as *per* indenture.

(284) 9 Aug. 1682, John Masters hired the farme late in Yaxley's use (p. 542) and the sheep closes (p. 52) for 7 years ending Mich. 1689 at £40 rent, and 2 days work of a thatcher yearly with covenants to keep and leave the windows and gates and fences in repayre, and how the ground is to bee used and left as *per* [*articles*].

(126) 28 Sep. 1682, William Greenacre brought me word his son was run away, and begg'd that I would release him.

(286) 30 Sep. 1682, I let the mill to Robert Sextan (the late miller) for one year at £30 upon the covenant in Greenacre's lease (p. 548).

Summer 1683, Sextan agreed for another year at £30.

1683, I sent to knowe whether Sextan woud take a lease of my mill. He insisted upon an abatement and alteration of the former covenants.

21 Feb. 1683, Francis Bloome of Alborow miller hired the said mill for 7 years ending Mich. 1691 at £30 the 3 first, and £34 the 4 last years upon the covenants in Willis his lease, and eles, fish and capons yearly as *per* articles (p. 478). Noat: this Bloome was bred in Ingworth.

/ When Blome hired it, Sextan tould me was sorry he did not agree with me. This is not the first time he have been disappointed /.

511

Memorandum: 23 June 1681, I offerd Abraham Toftman (who married Ellenfoard's widdow) £15 to take a new lease of the mill at same rent and covenants for 7 years (rough timber excepted) which he agreed to. But when this agreement was writ, he would not sign it unless he might have £15 for 5 years. Soe I parted with him in anger. I beleive I shall repent it for if I finde timber I am sure I will devour much more.

(214) 16 Aug. 1681, Sam Gibson of Great Cornard in Suffolk hired the mill for 7 years ending Lady day 1689 at £38 yearly upon the covenants in Ellenford's lease, except rough timber, which Gibson is to finde. The said mill   repairs   premises being first put into good repaire.

(215, 497) 23 Sep 1682, AbrahamTotman and I gave Gibson £3 15s a peice to take the repairs upon himself and Gibson released me of the obligation of puting the mill into repaire, and sealed the counterpart of the lease which is dated 25 Jan. 1681

(82) 12 Jan. 1682, I found a loos leaf of an account booke in 1637. Wherein amoung other farm rents was written with his *my father's* hand as followeth: William Paston Esq. for the ff. [farm]of Whitings Ollands, lying as I take it in the Great Furr Closes at Aylmerton o 2s 8d. Noat: my father did generally make a 'ff' for farme.

(270) 5 Jan 1682, Thomas Wegg of Barningham hired the warren (now in Goss his use) for 7 years from 2 Feb next at £22 and 300 conies yearly at Mich. and Candlemas. He is to leave 1300 conies at sixscore to the 100 or pay £4 a 100 in lieu thereof as *per* indenture.

(264, 493) 16 Feb. 1683, Mrs Bendish writ me she was inform'd I was selling my house and gave me notice, she would leave it at Mich. unless she might be certaine to have it 3 years from Mich. next at the rent of £36. I writ her I would make her *a* lease at £36 for 3 years upon reasonable Norwich covenants.

512. Dr Peppar's Credit (515)

Imprimus: due to him for ballance of his last account ending Lday 1671	046	02	06
Paid Mr. Chamberlaine	075	00	00
To my Ladye Bacon	026	11	03
To George Dale	000	10	00
Sir Cap Luckins	001	10	06
Payd me Sep. 1671	000	15	00
Charges at Hadscoe Sep. 1671	001	10	00
A post fine to Lambert Oct. 1671	008	05	00
	160	04	03

For procuring £450 which Dr Peppar say he borrowed upon my account when he acted in my concernes, though he did not acquaint me with it, till 6 months after he had left my business which was above 2 years after the mony borrowed   000   10   00

For interst of the same	020	05	00
For a bible	000	18	00
26 Nov. 1677, payd Alderman Briggs to my use / *p. 515* /	050	00	00
➤ For attending upon me two years after I came from Cambridge, I forgave him the remeynder, being	055	08	11
19 Jan 1677	127	01	11

513. Dr Peppar's Debt (209)

Receiv'd of Hunt and Sewell for timber 1 May and 1 Nov. 1671 / *p. 209* /	176	00	00
Of Salman	050	00	00
Farme rents	044	08	03
Quit rents	001	16	11
Fines	008	01	00
Of Mr Chamberlaine	007	00	00
	287	06	02
Credit	160	04	03
1 May 1677, rest due to me by this account	127	01	11

514. Alderman Brigg's Credit (525)

8 Oct. 1678	Payd Collinges's (p. 527)	039	12	02
5 Nov. 1678	Payd Mrs Chamberlaine	030	00	00
14 Nov. 1678	Maidstone had a noat to receive	005	18	05
10 Dec. 1678	Salman chargeth himselfe with £30 receiv'd of Briggs 9 Oct. 1678		030	00
13 Dec. 1678	Maidstone had my noat to receive	010	00	00
16 Dec. 1678	Payd me by a bill of goods value	020	18	06
6 May 1679	Payd William Blyth of Lyn	030	08	08
	Then payd Peast of Lyn	008	11	06
8 May 1679	Payd Brewster Hobart's servant	040	19	10
16 July 1679	Payd Richard Carter by my order according to an order of sessions	050	00	00
31 July	Payd Mr Mede for cloth	003	05	00
15 Aug.	Payd Mr Tennant which I lent him	020	00	00
25 Aug.	Payd Mr Carter towards the entertainment of Sir John Hobart's and Sir Peter Gleane's freeholders at their election	040	00	00
1 Sep.	Payd Sir John Hobart upon account and *ditto*	040	00	00
13	Payd Mr Bokenham of Norwich	017	04	00
		396	18	01
	Debt exceed credit	045	01	11
		442	00	00

25 Nov. 1679	Payd Fowle to pay Chamberlaine (p. 517)	250	00	00
14 Jan. 1679	Payd Mr. Rolph	005	10	9
2 Feb. 1679	Order'd Briggs to pay the treasurer for the prisoners in the castle £50	050	00	00
14 July 1680	Payd Sir Frances Bicklye one of the treasurers for the maymed soldiers	135	15	08
22 [July]	Payd Mr Barham	022	10	00
16 Aug.	Payd Mr Burton of Cley	013	15	05
21 [Aug.]	Payd Mr Pennyng	010	00	00
15 Oct.	By a bill of goods	012	03	05
30 Nov.	Payd Bacon for my Lord Townshend who is to pay me in London	500	00	00
Noat: 31 July 1679 Briggs paid Mede £3 10s		000	05	00
6 Dec.	Returned to Mr Fowle and *Sir Joseph Ashe* £1 15s 9d	400	00	00
	Brigg's debt exceed his credit	1399	19	03

515. Brigg's Debt (525)

26 Nov. 1677	Dr Peppar paid him as (p. 512)	050	00	00
14 May 1678	Isack paid (p. 195 n. 11)	040	00	00
22 May 1678	I sent him by my grome	040	00	00
20 June	I sent him by my grome	050	00	00
15 Jan. 1678	I sent him by my grome	062	00	00
16 July 1679	Mr Negus one of the treasurers for the maymed soldiers payd him	200	00	00
		442	00	00
	Brigg's payd (p. 514)	396	18	01
	Brigg's owe me	045	01	11
		442	00	00
1679	The ballance of the last account	045	01	11
17 Oct.	Salman payd him	075	00	00
25 [Oct.]	Salman payd him	125	00	00
4 Nov. 1679 Brigg's write Houseman payd him £28 18s the 31 May last and Turner payd him £201 the 28 Oct: noat £201 came out of Essex		229	18	00
14 Jan. 1679	Brigg's tould Smith Mr Browne payd	043	00	00
2 Feb 1679	Payd Briggs	200	00	00
25 [Feb]	Payd Briggs by Salman	120	00	00
13 July 1680	Payd by Carter	035	15	08
7 Oct.	Payd by Houseman	060	00	00
16	Payd by Smith £28 ⎤			
26	Payd by Smith £180 ⎦	208	00	00
30 Nov.	Payd by Smith	260	00	00
		1401	15	09

516. Mr Chamberlaine's Credit

< 23 or 24 > Feb. 1669 I borrowed £2000 of him (to pay off debts contracted in my minoritye upon my account as my mother pretended) for which I morgaged my estate in Wicklewood and Crownethorpe to him.   2000 22 00

11 July 1671 I did enter'd into a bond of £2000 to pay my mother £150 *per annum* during her life according to a decre in chancerye made 5 July 1654

Mrs Chamberlaine's £2000: I borrowed of Mr Chamberlaine belong to my mother during her life credit

Memorandum: 29 Sep. 1676 I morgaged Gould's farme to my mother for £500 and 1 Nov. 1676 I paid James Herriott gould smith in London * 500* £1500 by my mother's order to the use of Sir Charles Harbord; upon which my Mother released the 1st morgage of £2000 as is mentioned on other side

20 Nov. 1679, my sister Chamberlaine (my mother's executrix) sealed a release upon the back of the £500 mortgage.

517. Mr Chamberlaine's Debt

24 Feb. 1674   The interest of the £2000 have been duely payd as by
                 receipts under Mr Chamberlaine's hand to the 24 Feb.
                 1674

24 Jun 1675   The annuitye have been also paid as by receipts under
                 their hand to the 24 June 1675

Noat: in Aug. 1675 Mr Chamberlaine died

28 Sep. 1676   mother and trustees released the mortgage made 24
                 Feb. 1669   2000 00 00

Mrs Chamberlaine's Debt

1 April 1678   Payd my mother by bill to Mr Fowle in part of the £500 166 13 01

Noat: the interest of the £500 and her annuitye have been duely payd to our loan 1678

5 Nov. 1678   I accounted with my mother for her interest
and annuitye, and halfe paid her part of the £500   083 06 08

And then she did acknowledge under her hand, that I did owe her but £250

20 Apr. 1679   Paid her in full of interest and annuitye ending 25
                 March 1679

8 July 1679   Paid her anuitye ending Midsummer 1679

29 July 1679   My mother died of a painfull cancer in her breast, aged 55

31 Oct. 1679   I payd my sister Chamberlaine £8 15s in full
of interest to this day for £250

29 Nov. 1679   Fowle payd my sister Martha Chamberlaine my mother's
                 executrix the   250 00 00
                                                             500 00 00

518. John Windham's Credit (179)

23 Nov. 1675 my brother had a decre in chancerye against me of £1000 upon these word in my father's will *scilicet:* and unto every other sonn which I shall henceforth have £1000 a peice, though he was borne five months before the date of the said will, where my father give him £4000 for his portion / *p. 179* / upon my mother's single testimonye that my father did tell two or three days before he died, his sonn John should have £5000, £1000 out of his personall estate, and £4000 out of the manour of Worle.

Noat: my mother was not examined till 1675, which is 22 years after my father's death.

		£	s	d
1 Dec. 1675 I did give him my bond for the		1000		
For interest to the 1 May 1676		0025		
		1025		
13 May 1676	Payd me by Mr Bealing	0010		
		1035		
	Debt exceed credit	10		
Noat: the bond is cancelled *scilicet:*		1035	10	00

29 Charles II: the next session of parliament 'twas enacted, that noe will in writing concerning goods or chattels, or personal estate, shall be repealed, nor shall any clause, devise or bequest therein, be altered or changed by any words, or will by word of mouth only, except the same bee in the life of the testator comitted to writing, and after the writing thereof read unto the testator, and allowed by him and proved to bee done, by three witnesses at the least.

519. John Windham's Debt (521)

12 Jan 1675	Payd him upon account	0020		
23 Feb. 1675	Payd Fowle to his use	0500		
27 Mar. 1676	Payd himselfe	0010		
1 May 1676.	Payd Fowle for his use	0500		
	Fowle payd for interest of the 1st £500	0005	10	
	Sum	1035	10	00
May 1676	Due to me upon ballancing the account	0000	10	00

Memorandum: My brother died 2 June 1676 out of whose estate I had £1000 (vide p. 521)

520. Lady Maidstone's Credit

	£	s	d
14 July 1676: for her portion in my father's will	1500	00	00
Interest from 1667 to Midsummer 1676 at £6 *per cent*	0787	10	00
Allow'd her above interest of the £1500 as is express'd on the other side	0625	00	00
Sum	2912	10	00
Payd as on the other side	1689	16	00
14 July 1676, rest due to my sister	1222	14	00

➤ By agreement, I am to pay ¼ of my brother's debts: expences in his sickness, funerall charges and cost of adminstration, which come to by this account.

	£	s	d
	0086	10	3¼
	1309	04	3¼

26 Aug. 1677 for the ¼ of the money which Maidstone have and is to lay out as per (p. 523)

	£	s	d
	0048	04	09

➤ Noat: my sister Maidstone was not willing to allow me the interest of the £45 which I lent my Lord *anno* 1670, soe I here give her credit for it, it being included in the £21 13s on t'other side

	£	s	d
	0015	12	0¾
Maidstone's debt (p. 522) is £63 16s 9 ¾ d	0063	16	9¾

Memorandum: 26 Aug. 1677, wee gave one another general releases.

521. Lady Maidstone's Debt

	£	s	d
From Mich 1667 to Mich 1672 I payd for my sister's use £70 every ½ yeare	0700	00	00
From Mich. 1672 to Midsummerr 1676 I paid to her use £50 every quarter day	0750	00	00
	1450	00	00
Besides the said £1450, I lent Lord Maidstone *anno* 1670	0045	00	00
And to my Lady Maidstone June 1674	0010	00	00
More in January 1675	0160	00	00
For interest of the 3 last sums from the respective payments	0021	13	00

For interest of £37 10s which she receiv'd of me, to make the £100 a year which I allowed her, and the interest of her portion: £200 *per annum*

	£	s	d
	0003	03	00
	1689	16	00

Noat: I allow'd my sister as an addition to her present maintenance from Mich. 1667 to Mich. 1672: £50 *per annum*. And from Mich. 1672 to Midsummer 1676 £100 *per annum*, which comes to £625 for which I credit her on t'other side

➤ 15 July 1676, I did release all my right by my brother's estate (out of which I was to have £1000 by agreement upon a nuncupative will) to my sister Maidstone, who then gave me a receipt for her portion, upon my

bond to pay what should bee justly due upon account soe payd	1000	00	00
2 Sep. Salman payd her	0010		

25 [*Sep.*] Fowle payd Mrs Metwold for soe much disburs'd in my
brother's sickness, and his funerall charges with £20

allowed her for his falling sick in her house	0108	03	07
And to White the herald, the remeynder of £13 19s in full	0005	04	00
And to Wiseman the proctour in full	0004	01	06
And to Richardson, apothecarye in full	0008	00	00
And to Whitehead for a hearse and etc. in full	0006	00	00
	1141	09	01

522. Lady Maidstone's Debt

Brought from the foot of the last side	1141	09	01
5 Oct. 1676, Fowle paid my uncle Mede due upon my brother's bond	0112	00	00
And to my cosen Margaret Corbet	0001	01	06
And to himselfe for mourning rings	0039	16	00

Fowle alsoe paid in his account dated 30 Oct. 1676 to my uncle Mede,
(which my mother accepted in part of £40 which Maidstone promised by

sisters for their mourning)	0030	00	00

Noat: These sums following I payd myselfe:

Dr Hue's advice	0002	03	00
Mr Burleigh's advice, and to his clerke	0001	15	00
Proctours: to Borage £2, Swallow £1, Pinfold £1,	0004	00	00
Parson Taylour £1, Harmer £1	0002	00	00
Poor of Felbrigg £1, parish duties	0000	07	06

To my Uncle Mede for soe much paid Wines of Elmdon, by my brother's order	0009	00	00
To Collup my brother's man for his wages, board, wages and disbursements	0011	09	00
Disburs'd from 14 July to 14 Oct. 1676	1356	01	01
Receiv'd (as by page 520)	1309	04	3¼
14 Oct. 1676, rest due	0046	16	9¾
26 Aug. 1677, I payd Maidstone	0017	00	00
Maidstone's credit (p. 520) is £63 16s 9d ¾	0063	16	9¾
14 Nov. 1678 gave Maidstone a noat (p. 514) for	0005	18	05
23 July 1678 for ¾ parts of £7 12s, payd Walker for cloth for my brother	0005	14	00

523.

26 Aug 1677, account of what money my sister Maidstone payd,
of which I must allow a fourth part (p. 520)

To my aunt Talbot for mourning	010	00	00

To my mother	020	00	00
Mrs Osborne for gloves	026	15	00
Given my brother's man Robin	005	00	00
Gibbs the proctour	000	10	00
A monument	021	10	00
	083	15	00

26 Aug 1677: Maidstone gave me a noat under her hand to pay these debts following *scilicet:*

To Mr Corbet	60	00	00
To aunt Talbot	10	00	00
My brother's boy Ned	10	00	00
To my mother	09	00	00
To Wiseman the proctour	05	00	00
To Hobart a milliner	14	04	00
	109	04	00

£83 15s 0d

£109 4s 0d

£192 19 0d

£ 48 4s 9d is the 4th part and she have credit for it (p. 520)

Maidstone is to pay Buxton £23 13s 8d of which I must pay her the 4th part	005	18	05
19 Jan. 1679, Maidstone payd me	005	14	04

524. Brigg's Credit

25 Jan 1680	Payd me	001	15	09
16 Feb.	Return'd to Fowle by Thomas Newton payable by W. Wilkinson 2 March	150	00	00
30 July 1681	A bill of goods	024	04	08
12 Oct.	Payd Lady Maidstone for soe much paid by her order to Sir Joseph Ashe for me	300	00	00
16 Dec 1681	Order'd Briggs to pay Mr Fowle £500	500	00	00
27 July 1682	Payd Fowle	150	00	00
12 Aug.	Payd Smith for us	010	00	00
27 Dec.	I writ to him to give Clere Talbot	002	00	00
20 Jan.	Order'd Briggs to place to my sister Maidstone's account for £600 lent me about Christmas 1681	630	00	00
25 [*Jan*]	He writ, there wanted £5 6s 9d in mony I sent him by John Barham 13 Nov. 1682 of £300	005	06	09
24 Apr. 1682	Payd Melcher the braisier of Norwich	003	18	00
	Briggs payd	1777	05	02
	Briggs received as *per* (p. 525)	1669	15	09
By the account above Briggs have payd more than receiv'd		107	09	05

20 July 1683	Payd Fowle	150	00	00
27 [July]	Payd Fowle	060	00	00
4 Jan. 1683	I sent Alderman Bucknam a note to receive of Briggs	010	00	00
	And Alderman Wenman a note	020	00	00
	And sister Kate Chamberlaine	004	00	00
25 [Jan.]	A note to Palmer to receive	060	00	00
7 Mar. 1683	Payd Briggs to ballance the account for shop	020	15	11
	wares	432	05	04
Briggs have his hand as per his owne account 7 March 1683		141	14	01
		573	19	5

525. Brigg's Debt (514, *quarto* book p. 66)

	Rest upon account	001	15	00
16 Jan. 1680	Payd his son	100	00	00
14 Feb	Payd Mr Briggs	050	00	00
23 Apr. 1681	Smith payd Briggs	018	00	00
14 June	John Kingsberry payd Briggs	130	00	00
	Abraham Totman	005	00	00
28 July	Henry Houseman £50 and 15 April last £25	075	00	00
3 Oct.	In 3 bags by content	200	00	00
29 [Oct.]	Smith payd him	125	00	00
8 Nov.	Smith payd him	125	00	00
16 Dec.	Smith payd him	150	00	00
Briggs charg'd himself with £30 receiv'd of Gould 29 July 1681		030	00	00
3 July 1682	Sent by Salter	150	00	00
13 Nov.	Sent by John Barham	300	00	00
30 Dec.	Mr. Harris payd him	100	00	00
24 Jan.	Briggs charge himselfe wth £10 receiv'd of Mrs. Bendish 16 Nov. 1682	010	00	00
	And with £100 of Robert Kingsberry	100	00	00
	scilicet: £22 ... 27 Nov.	1669	15	09
	And £40 ... 5 Dec. 1682			
	And £38 ... 19 Dec.			
30 Jan 1682	John Kingsberry payd him £70			
	And 6 Feb £10	080	00	00
24 March	Smith sent by the poste	030	00	00
6 June 1683	Elden payd him	075	10	00
15 [June]	Elden payd him	120	00	00
8 Dec. 1683	Elden payd him	182	00	00
	Mrs Bendish payd him 1683 (p. 265)	020	00	00
2 March.	Sir Robert Kemp tould me, he payd Brigs this weeke by Robinson's order	050	00	00

4 [*March*] Mrs Bendish payd him	016	09	05
	573	19	05

➤ From this day being 8 March 1683 see quarto book (p. 66) where debtor Briggs the said 141 14s 1d

526. Mr Thomson's Credit

7 July 1669 Maurice Thomson did undertake that John Thomson and the Lady Frances his wife (for £4500) shall convey to me all the right the said Lady Frances ever had to any reall estate of my brother John Windham's her former husband. Noat: my Lady Frances was to have all his personal estate.

31 July 1669, in pursuance of the said agreement which was confirmed by chanceyre, all persons concerned did seal deeds, and at the same time I payd the £4500.

➤ Noat: Thomson was to receive the profits of my Lady's joynture ending Mich. 1669 and to pay me in lieu thereof £125: (p. 527)

6 Aug. 1669 Mr Thomson sould me the corne which Pall and Foster valued in the feild at	053	05	00
And the hay in the barne at	019	00	00
The fallow in Bush close	006	06	00
Herbage of soe much of the parke as the deer fed, *anno* 1669	005	11	01
7 Aug. 1669 The goods in Felbrigg were valued and I bought soe many as came to	087	13	08
	171	15	09

Sir John Thomson's Credit

19 Aug. 1678 This day Dr Collings's son brought me an order from Sir John Thomson to deliver the rest of his goods to him, who had power to dispose of them, and then brought so many as came to	027	13	00
7 Sep. 1678 Dr Collinges's son sent Parker's waggon for the goods, and then I bought soe many as came to	011	19	02
	039	12	02

527. Thomson's Debt

9 Sep. 1669. For halfe a years rent of my Lady Frances joynture due to me	125	00	00
25 April 1676, Mr Thomson and I settled our accounts in Hatton Garden before Sir Joseph Ashe and Sir John Thomson, and then he allow'd me for my father's books, which were decreed to me and carryed away by his son	010	00	00
And for several rates due before Michaelmas 1669 which I payd	002	09	01
For 4100 bricks used at Felbrigg in my lady's time	002	17	04

28 April 1676 Powle payd Monteth for the use of Thomson in full of all
account

031	09	04
171	15	09

Sir John Thomson's Debt

8 Oct. 1678, payd Collinges by noat to Alderman Briggs of Norwich
(p. 514)   039   12   02

Then Dr Collinges discharged me by Sir John Thomson's order of all the
goods.

528

(246, 531) William and John Howard hired by indenture 16 May 1670 of R. and
E. Chamberlayne Copshall, Bestons Barne, and the jaile 84 acres 3 roods of land
particularly mention'd in the said lease for 9 years ending Mich. 1679 at £32 *per
annum*. Tenants are to doe 4 days thatching yearly, and keep and leave the windows
and fences in repayre and the ground in a husbandlye manner.
Observe: the lease before was for 7 years at £36 to Henry and Thomas Howard as
per indenture 1 Oct. 1663

(246/2) The same William and John by articles 12 Feb. 1671 hired of R. and
E. Chamberlayne part of Beckham fouldcourse for 9 years ending Mich. 1680 at
£9 8s *per annum* lands are particularly expressed in the articles.

(248/3, 529 n. 3, 480) Henry Johnson of Gresham hired by indenture 23 Sep. 1670,
of R. and E. Chamberlayne Beston's house with a Portall Barne and 90 acres and
½ rood of land particularly mentioned for 9 years end Mich. 1679 at £30 yearly
and 3 days thatching. He is to keep and leave the windows and fences in good
repayre and the ground in a husbandlye manner.

(254/4, 531) John Ellis by indenture 29 Sep. 1671. hired of Mr and Mrs Cham-
berelaine the Sheppards house and part of the fouldcourse for 9 years ending Mich.
1680 at £5 12s *per annum*. He is to keep and leave the house and fences in repayre.

(250/5, 531) James *and Henry* Tower of West Beckham by indenture 1 Sep. 1668
hired of Mr and Mrs Chamberlayne the windmill with the house and yards late
in Robert Dix's use, and 64 acres in E. and W. Beckham and Sheringham for 7
years ending Mich. 1675 at £32. They are to keep the mill and house and fences
in repayre (being allow'd rough timber), and leave the goods belonging to the mill
particularly expressed in an inventory of the same value, if of a greater value, they
are to be allow'd for them, with covenants how to use the farme.

(256/6) Richared Lownes for Kistrells Close about 6 acres £2

(258/7, 483) Mr Britiffe of Baconsthorpe for the 3 mill closes conteyning 16 acres
£3 *per annum*.

529

(244) John Lound of Aylemerton hired by indenture 26 July 1677 of Mrs Chamberlaine Beckham Hall house and gardens with 113 acres of land particularly mention'd for 12 years ending Mich. 1689 at £60 yearly and 3 days thatching, he is to keep the windows and fences in repayre being allow'd rough timber and fencing stuf. He is not to lease or let out any of the premises without leave, he may use the brick kill, there are large covenants how to use and leave the same.

(252, 493) Lawrence Monyman of Aylemerton hired by indenture 29 Sep. 1672 of R. Chamberlaine, Lucas Close and 2 pightles adjoyning conteyning 48 acres 1 rood, and 30 acres divided into 4 closes call'd Holtman's in East Beckham and Beeston, and 6 acres in peeces in Aylemerton field, and 2 doles conteyning 20 acres upwards lying in E. Beckham heath. One abutt upon Beeston pasture north, 'tother on Holtmans south for 10 years ending Mich. 1682 at £24, 2 days harvest worke, 4 capons and 20 rod of new ditching yearly, he is to keep and leave the fences in good repayre. He is to leave half of the said 48 acres 1 rood four years lying and half of the 36 acres two years lying.

(531 n. 1,2) Memorandum: 4 Sep. 1679 William Howard refused a new lease of Copshall (p. 528. n. 1) unless I would abate £2 a year, and resolv'd not to hold his part of the fouldcourse (n. 2) longer than Mich. 1680 but offer'd me £62 for Copshall and Johnson's (n. 3) which I refused, and agreed with Johnson for all the houses and lands (p. 528 n. 1, 2, 3, 4) for 7 years at £77 upon the covenants in their several leases. I promised to repayre the house and fences, and allow £2 a year for two years towards marling the ground as *per* noat under our hand the day abovesaid. 12 Sep. this agreement was made void.

530

15 April 1676. *Memorandum:* that I John Harwold of Sudberry in the county of Suffolke carpenter for and in consideration of sixty six pounds to me in hand paid by William Windham of Felbrigg in Norfolk doe fully discharge the said William Windham and all his servants and workmen of all suits bills and demands for worke or timber to the abovesaid.
Witness my hand *John Harwold* Witness *Jo Salman*

(22, 511) 7 Feb. 1677, Gorse agreed to hold the Warren 5 years longer from 2 of this month at the same rent and covenants in his last lease (p. 544), and gave bond to performe this agreement.

(94, 548) *Anno* 1679, I sent Salman to Parson Taylour to demand the arrears of rent, and tell him if he woud not come to account with me, and promise to pay the rent for the future, I woud take the land from him at Mich. Salman was not admitted to the Parson (under pretence of his being sick). But his son John promised to tell his father, and that the rent would be payd hereafter.

(276, 509) 19 May 1683, John Applebye hired the farme late Macks (p. 558) for 7 years ending Mich. 1690 at £30 the first 3 years, and £35 the last 4 years, 3 days thatching and all the dawbing. He is to keep and leave the windows and fences in repayre being alow'd rough timber, as by articles signed by Salman and Applebye. 4 July 1683. Noat the farme is to bee left at Mich. 1690 as by articles dated 21 Sep. 1681, he ought to have left it at Mich. 1682.

531

(480) 12 Sep. 1679, Mr Windham doth demise and to farm let unto H. Johnson and to Henry his son the houses and lands which H. Johnson hired of Mr and Mrs Chamberlayne by indenture 23 Sep. 1670 (p. 528 n. 3). and the fouldcourse which Howard and Elis have now in use, (n. 2 and 4) for 9 years ending Mich. 1688 at £45 *per annum* upon the covenants in their leases. Mr Windham is to put the houses and fences in repayre. Witness our hands. *Will Windham* Henry Johnsons marke H *Henry Johnson* in the presence of *Sam Smyth*

(246, 479, 480) 12 Sep. 1679, Mr Windham demise and to farm let unto William Howard the houses and lands which the said William and John Howard hired of Mr and Mrs Chamberlaine by (p. 528 n. 1) indenture May 1670 for 9 years ending Mich. 1688 at the rent and covenants of the said lease. Mr Windham is to put the houses and fences in repayre. Howard is to keep and leave them soe. Witness our hands *Will Windham Will Howard*
In the presence of *Samuell Smyth*

(274,494) 22 Sep 1681, Mr Blofield hired Ransome's farme of me for £20 a year upon the covenants in the lease (p. 555), with this addition that he is to leave so much straw and chaif as Ransome's shall bee valued at, which William Frost and Robert Foster valued at 1s 8d *per* comb, which come to £2 8s 4d. Note signed by them and writ by Blofield 8 Dec 1682.

(250, 328) 29 Aug. 1683, William Tower hired the farme and mill and house thereunto belonging late in his fathers use at the rent and covenants in his lease (p. 528) for 7 years ending Mich. 1690, with this addition that the said William shall lay on 200 loads of marle yearly the first 6 years, I diging and filling the same. He is to lay 12 loads of muck up on every acre he sow with winter corne.

532

(90) *Memorandum:* 21 Sep. 1672, Sir R. Baldocke and I met Sir Robert Yallop and Mr Clement Herne at Norwich to discourse about a farme rent for 9 acres 1 rood in Metton which have been duely payd, as appear by audit books from 1609 to 1665. First, William Hobard payd £1 7s *per annum* for rent of the said 9 acres 1 rood. Afterwards F. Symonds (who married his widow) paid the same rent. In the year 1640 the rent was raised at £3 13s 4d and paid by him. In two or three years

after 'twas paid by Thomas Herne, who married her daughter < After his death by his son Thomas > since his death by his widow, and in her time by Clement, who then refused to pay the said rent to me, at which time I gave Sir Robert Baldock order to draw a bill in Chanceyre against his mother and him.

Memorandum: 4 June 1673, John Herne a younger son of Mrs Herne desired me to stay the sute, and by her order gave me his bond of payment of £28 10s the 15 October following of which £23 13s was in full (taxes deducted) ᵼ ꝓ ᵼᵣᵥᵅᵤ ᵼᶜᵢᵼ ending Mich. 1672 – 'ᵼᵣᵼᵣᵣ ᵼᶠ ᵼᵥᵣᵤᵤᵤ ᵼᵤᵧ ᶜᵼᵼᵅᵣᵍᵉˢ ᵒᵼ sute. He did alsoe promise ᵼᵼᶜ ᵼᵼᵼᵼᵼᵼᵣ should pay me £3 14s yearly soe long as she continued the land. She died in winter 1681. *Will Windham*

(507) 10 Jan. 1681, I writ to Clement Herne to send me word whether he woud pay me the £3 14s *per annum*, he was then baylye. He could not write, but sent word he would waite upon me about it when he came from London. Wee are now soe good friends, that I will waite to know his mind.

1682, in the beginning of April, he came to Felbrigg and desired me to give him some time to look over his writings.

26 July 1682 I met him at Sir John Hobart's and asked him whether he would pay the rent. He proposed a reference which I refused and tould him I would advise how to recover it.

533

(64, 493 s. 4, 5) *Memorandum* 4 Nov. 1678: William Frost, William Haddon, and Edmond Teney, the younger, all of Gresham hired of Mr Windham of Felbrigg all his inclosures at Gresham (late in Mr Cookes use) for seven years ending Mich. 1685, paying to Mr Windham, his heires, and assignes, forty pounds yearly, at Lady day and St Michael, by equal portions, and 3 fat fowles every year at Christmas. The tennants may break up the close conteyning 5 or 6 acres on the left hand on the gate called Hel Gate the first 4 years of their terme, which they are to muck well and take but 3 crops, and the last 3 years to let it lye olland in payne of forty shillings an acre yearly above the rent. They are not to break up any more of the premises during their term in pain of forty shillings an acre above the rent. They are not to put any cattel the last three months of their term in any of the ground but the same cattel which are fed there all the summer, and at the end of their term they are to leave all the grass growing which their cattel shall leave. They are to keep and leave the dreynes fences and gates very well being allow'd rough timber and necessary fencing stuff at seasonable times in the year. Mr Windham reserveth himself timber, and all the wood with libertie to cut and carry away the same at his pleasure. And lastly the said William Frost, William Haddon, and Edmund Teney for themselves, their executors and assigns, are hereby covenant with the said Mr Windham his heires and assignes to performe this their agreement. Mr Windham covenant that then they shall quietly enjoy the lands without any disturbance from him his heires, or assignes. Turne over.

534

In witness of the agreement mention on the other side of this leaf the said parties above set their hands and seals this 19 November 1678
In the presence of *John Salman Will Windham* William Frost's marke X
Stephen Legge Edmond Tene William Haddon's marke W

£11 Frost tell me he have the ground on the left hand of the high-way at £11.
£16 Tene on the right hand, to the Hel Gate at £16, and Haddon have all the
£13 grounds on the left hand of the of the green-way at Hel-Gate at £13 *per*
£40 *annum* going from Gresham to Hel Gate.

(48) Henry Bally hire the Hal Close 5 acres lying nere and south of Johnson's house, and 5 Closes together adjoyning upon the heath reputed 16 acres at £6 10s yearly *scilicet:* The Hall close at 10s; Heath Ground at 5s.

(48, 478) 30 October 1679, Mr Windham doe let Henry Bally the ground now in his use for 7 years ending Mich. 1686 at £6 10s. The Hal Close to bee left one years olland or to bee sowne with clover, Mr Windham finding seed. Halfe the heath grounde left 3 years olland. Bally is to keep and leave the fences in good repayre. Witness our hands. *Will Windham Henry Bally*
Witness *Samuell Smyth* Murget's Close is not included 1s *per annum*

(112) 13 April 1680 Richard Lilley of Tuttington hired the farme now in Frost's and Lowne's use for 7 years ending Mich. 1687 at the rent and covenants in their articles (p. 544 n. 3) as by noat under his hand indorsed upon the back of the said articles.
25 July 1687 Lilly agreed to hold it as above 7 years ending 1694 as *per* agreement under his hand.

535

(186/1) 1 March 1665 Mr Wilson hired the land late in Crosby's his use conteyning 28 acres 1 rood in Metton and Rowton at £14 3s.

(74/2, 540, 554) Anno 1668 Robert Maris hired 14 acres 1 rood of the land late in Wilsons use (p. 535) at £7. Noat: Smith hired the rest (p. 554) and *anno* 1670 he hired 2 peeces of Maris's conteyning one large acre at 10s which is part of his £4.

(122, 509) 22 Feb. 1665 John Allison of Banningham hired about 27 acres 3 roods in Aylesham late in Jo Neve's use for 2 years ending Mich. 1667 at £11 10s yearly, and 2 capons upon covenants in his lease dated 4 October 1652

(128, 558/5) Thomas Mack hired the farme purchased of Scrivener (except 2 acres in Worstead in Springall's use) until Mich. next at £35 and 2 capons, 26 Feb. 1665.

(66) Eliz Seckar of Thurgarton, widow, and Joseph Seckar and Elizabeth his wife hired a tenement wherein the said Eliz the widow now dwelleth with 1r thereunto

belonging, and 1 acre of meadow nere adjoyning call'd the Car lying in Thurgarton and Sustead, for 99 years, if any of them live soe long at £1 10s and 1 days harvest worke and doing suit of court at Sustead-dams, they are to keep the premises well repair'd by indenture 11 Aug. 10 Charles 1 [*1634*]

(541/4) Thomas Love and Richard Johnsons hired the two closes in Sustead, one now sowne with wheat, 'tother with oats, alsoe the Wood Pightle, and Pull's Pightle < both > now with oats (reputed together 60 acres) for 12 years at £48. They are not to sow any of the premises in payne of £5 an acre. They are to keep and leave the ditches and fences well scoured and repayr'd. They may enjoy the premises till Christmas after the end of their terme paying £12. They are not to assigne over premises as by indenture, 9 August 1658.

536

(509) 17 October 1679, articles of agreement between Mr Windham and John Fincham concerning Selfe's farme, until Mr Windham shall otherwise dispose of it.

1. Mr Windham is to lay on soe many cows as Mr Britiffe of Baconsthorpe thinke the farme will maintaine, for the profit of which cows Fincham is yearly to pay Mr Windham five and forty shillings a peice at our Lady and Michaelmas. This yeare Mr Windham is to abate soe much as Mr Britiffe shall thinke fit.

2. Fincham is to take great care of the cows.

3. Fincham is every year to plow soe much ground as Mr Windham shall appoint, and sowe therein such graine as he shall order and to bee at all charges incident to husbandrye, and to carry all the corne into the barnes belonging to the farme, and to deliver Mr Windham half the corne as 'tis drest by the taskers.

4. Mr Windham is to bee at halfe the charge of thrashing, and to allow Fincham four acres of pasture to tye his horses upon, and to pay the parish rates.

5. Mr Windham is to have all the straw, Fincham the chaife and colder, which is to bee spent upon the premises.

6. The peas and fetches are to bee devided in the feilds, and Fincham is to carry Mr Windham's part into the barn, and spend his owne upon the premises.

7. And because there is now nine acres of buck stuble upon olland of 3 years lying, muck'd and fit for winter corne, Fincham is to leave nine acres of buck stubble so muck'd.

8. And because Windham have lent Fincham two horses valued at eight pounds Fincham to deliver Mr Windham (when he shall dispose of the farme) 2 horses worth in the opinion of two men indifferently chosen or pay Mr. Windham eight pounds.

9. And because Fincham have had of Mr Windham £4 5s worth of peas and fetches, Fincham is to leave soe many as shall be indifferently valued at four pounds 5s.

10. Fincham is to have chaife and colder of the corne in the barnes and in lieu leave all the chaife and colder of the last crop.

537

(537/4) And the said John Fincham doe hereby binde himself, his executors, administrators and assignes to performe these articles with Mr Windham, his heires and assignes and Mr Windham promise to performe his part. Witness our hands and seals the day above said. In the presence of *Samuell Smyth Will Windham John Fincham*

(541, 28, 20) October 1679, I inclosed abut 3 acres belonging to the farme late in Grand's use, and planted it with ashes for which I abate Thomson £1 10s. Anno 1680, from Mich. 1680, he have 5 acres upon the heath late Pall's in lieu of the 3 acres inclosed.

(542, 538, 262) 11 Sep. 1680, Black agreed to take a new lease of all the lands in his lease Sep. 1671 (except Cullender's Close 5 acres and 1 acre in a close nere Colbye Comon) for 10 years ending Mich. 1690 at £35 7s yearly upon the same covenants in his present lease as appear under upon the back of the said lease.
Noat: 6 Sep. 1680, Richard Snelling of Colby offer'd me £21 for this land (except the said 6 acres and Ingworth Hall Close) reputed 37 acres and a half.

(537/1, 509 n. 3) Fincham was too poor to continue; so I let it to Harris

(38) 29 Dec. 1682, William Sexton of Aylemerton hired the Bush Close and the little pightle by Sustead Lane Gate for 7 years ending Christmas 1689 at £7 10s yearly, payable at Midsumer and Christmas. He must not break up any of the grounds as *per* articles.

(292) 16 Jan. 1682, William Steward of Worstead hired the farme late in Smiths use for 7 years ending Mich. 1689 at £11 *per annum* for the 2 first years, then £12 *per annum* and 2 pullets. He is to find materialls for 2 days thatching, and keep the walls well dawbed, and leave the fences in repayre, with usual covenants.

538

(146, 478, 551) James Scipper 20 December 1655 hired Crownethorpe farme for 16 years at £127 6s 8d *per annum*. The widdow held it 5 years upon the covenants in the said lease.
Richard Kett payd £130 *per annum* as appears by the counterpart of his lease ending Mich. 1640. Brooke then hired 70 acres of the ground (which the said Kett had plowed twenty years togeather) at £44 *per annum* for years as by indenture, and Roger Scipper then paid for the other part of Crownethorpe farme £93 6s 8d
137 6s 8d

29 Mar. 1677. I let it. (vide p. 551)

(56, 482) William Johnson hired about halfe an acre in Aylemerton from Mich. 1665 to 1 Oct. 1666 at 8s, 28 Feb. 1665

(60, 556) John Elis hired 19 acres in Aylemerton til 1 Oct. 1666 at £6, 28 Feb 1665.

(76, 493) John Colls hired 8 acres 1 rood in several peeces in Thurgarton till 1 Oct next, at £5, 28 Feb 1665.

(560 n. 3) Robert Maris by indenture 23 Sep. 1655 hired of Mr John Windham all his houses and lands now or late in the use of Thomas Russells for 12 years ending 1667 at £11 13s. He is to keep and leave the houses and fences in repayre, and leave the muck and the 2 closes call'd the Rythe in Suotead, olland.

(100) John Woodrowe hired a barne and about 26 acres of land in Runton til 1 Oct. 1666 at £16 11s 6d, 28 Feb 1665.

(116) Searle for the alders (as Knivet and Carter had p 539 n. 6) £1

(120) John Richman hired a cottage and 3 peeces of land in Colbye about 6 acres til Mich. Next at £5, 27 Feb. 1665.
From Mich. 1680 he is to have 6 acres of Blacks land (p. 537) at £2 *per annum*.

539

27 Feb. 1665, Thomas Casen hired the house in Cromer from the death of Mr. John Windham till 1 Oct. 1666 at £2 10s, formerly let for £5 yearly.
1670 Pye had Cromer house at £2.
27 Feb 1665, Thome Catherin hire two closes in Metton nere Dovehouse at 5 acres and 4 acres in the feild at £3 10s from Mr Windham's death to 1 October 1666 as by agreement under his hand.
1 October 1666, Henry Betson hired the house and grounds late in Peter Abbs and William Frost's use till Mich. next at £36. Noat: Abbs paid £38 yearly and was not to break up any of the inclosed grounds in Gresham.

(558 n. 3) Dybol had the 1 acre in Antingham afterwards let to Wodrowe.
22 Feb. 1665, Thomas Knivet and Humphrey Carter both of Banningham hired the sweepedge of alders growing on the severals in Tuttington till Mich. next at £1.
Dennis Flaxman hireth a house and land in Felbrigg from Mich. 1665 to 1671, at £15, two capons and 1 days harvest worke yearly upon the covenants in a lease made to him by Mr John Windham 16 Dec 1659, as by agreement under his hand, 26 Feb 1665
Doughty for a farme in Tuttington since let to Grime (p. 544)

(24, 553) John Drake hired about 32 acres in Felbrigg and Routon call'd Swifts at £12 12s from Mich. 1665 to 1666 and 2 pullets as by agreement, 28 Feb 1665

(30) Gregory Morrice hired about 4 acres in Felbrigg from Mich. 1665 to 1 Oct. 1666 at £1 12s, 28 Feb 1665

(54) Lownd hire 3 peeces of land in Aylemerton about 2 acres till 1 Oct. 1666. 28 Feb. 1665. at 14s.

540

(26) Stephen Davie by articles of agreement dated 28 April 1665 hired of my brother John Windham all his lands and tenements (late Webster's) then in the use of John Drake or his assigns, for 10 years ending Mich. 1675 paying the 1st 3 years £40 yearly, t'other 7 years £44 yearly and 2 fat capons. Davie is to doe at his owne charge 4 days work of thatching, and 2 of dawbing every yeare during the said tearme, and to leave fences, gates and etc. (being allowed rough timber) in good repayre, with covenants for leaving the ground in good heart. The said Drake pay'd £44 yearly and 2 capons for 12 years ending Mich. 1665; as by leas to which there is a schedule of the lands: 69 acres 2 roods

(26, 536) Richard Selfe by articles date 26 April 1675 hired the aforementioned farme now *in* the use of Widdow Davie for 7 years ending Mich. 1682 paying the 1st year £37, the next 5 years £38 yearly, and the last yeare £45 and 2 fat capons every yeare upon 29 Dec. and performing the aforesaid covenants in Davies articles with other good covenants to leave the ground in a husbandlye manner.

William Sextan by indenture dated 21 Sept. 1670, hired the Lyme Kill and 12 acres of land in Felbrigg feild for 6 years ending Mich. 1676. Paying £7 yearly, and furnish me lyme at 6s chalder, marle 3d a load. 10 March 1687 William Sextan and Edward Evered hired this farme for 21 years from Mich. 1687 at the same rent and covenants by lease.

(194) Robert Feazer son of Susan Feazer widdow hired 2 peices of land in Runton: 1st peice 6 acres; 2nd peice 3 acres for 21 years ending Mich. 1692. Paying £3 and 1 capon, and doeing 1 days harvest worke every yeare during the said tearme. He is to keep and leave the gates and fences in good repayre, as by indenture dated 18 Sep. 1671
5 Oct. 1682, Mr Talbot tould me the 2 peices mentioned (p. 535/3) in Smith's use, are two as good 3 roods peeces as any in the towne.

541

(18, 553) John Johnson by articles of agreement dated 11 June 1673 hired the farme late in the use of Andrew Mason, and Kirdell, and one peice (lying south of the Church Close) call'd the 10 Acres for 4 years ending Mich. 1677. Paying £48 10s 0d yearly; and doeing 3 days worke of a thatcher and his man every yeare of his tearme, *and all the dawbing worke* with very good covenants for leaving farme in very good condition.
Nicholas Abbs of Aylemerton (by indenture dated 20 Nov. 1676) hired the Clover-grass Close with the two pitles adjoyning lying east of the said close in Metton for 7 years ending Mich. 1678. Paying 1st yeare £10; the 6 years after £12 yearly; he is to leave the gates, fences and etc. in good repayre (being allowed hedgeboot and

rough timber) and not to plow any part of the premises the two last years in paine of 20s an acre above the rent. He also hires in Aylmerton at 4s *per annum.*

(28, 537) John Powle by indenture dated 10 March 1670 hired the house and grounds lately in the use of William Prest and formerly in Miles Grand's use, for 7 years ending Mich. 1677. Paying £15 yearly, he is to keep and leave the houses and fences in sufficient repayre, (being allowed rough timber) with other covenants how to leave the ground.

5 Aug 1677, Miles Grand hired the aforesaid farme for 7 years ending Mich. 1684 at the rents and covenants in Powles lease.

(80, 535/6, 199, 508) Peter Abbs and William Frost (by indenture dated 9th Nov. 1671) hired the 2 great closes and Old Hall yard in Sustead for 3 years ending Mich. 1674. Paying £41 yearly upon 1st May and 1st Nov. not to plow any part of the premises on pain of 40s an acre above the rent, and to leave the gates and fences in good repayre (being allowed rough timber). The last summer of their tearme they are not to put in any cattle, more than were fed the whole summer upon the ground. Memorandum: they pay 13s yearly above the said rent to be freed from herbage, which is certaine, (p. 199).

542

(46, 510) Thomas Richerson by indenture dated 1 April 1671, hired the house and ground (purchased of Heaslop) and also a house with 23 acres lately in Thomas Walker's use, and two closes conteyning 40 acres all which premises are in the parishes of Aylmerton etc. for 8 years ending Mich. 1679. Paying £30 yearly and doeing two days worke of a thatcher and his man at this owne charge every yeare, and shall keep and leave the glass windows, gates and fences in good repayre (being allowed rough timber) with covenants to leave the ground in a husbandlye manner. At Mich. 1679 John Yaxly came into this farme at the same rent and covenants.

(118) William Parke by indenture 1 April 1671, hired the house and grounds in Albye etc. for 7 years ending Mich. 1677, paying the first 5 years £85, the two last 2 years £90 yearly, and 2 capons every yeare, and doeing 5 days worke of thatcher and his man, 5 days worke of a dawber and his man at his owne charge every yeare of the tearme, and leaving the gates and fences in sufficient repayre (being allowed rough timber) with very good covenants to how to leave the ground, 100 of wood. 24 Jan. 1676, Parke agreed to take lease for 7 years ending Mich. 1684 at £90 yearly upon the covenants in the former lease, being allow'd £10 out of first halfe years rent. 20 Feb. 1676, lease was seal'd.

(124, 537, 546/4) John Black by indenture dated 18 Sep. 1671, hired Ingworth Hall Close conteyning 20 acres and Colbye Hall Close 11 acres, and 2 peices in the little feild of Colbye; 9 acres and 7 peices in the great feild of Colbye; 14 acres and

Cullenders Close 5 acres and 1 acre in a fur close at Colbye, and 3 ½ acres lying in Erpingham (all which said premises were last in use of Henry Empson) for 9 years ending Mich. 1680. Paying £37 7s od and 2 capons yearly, not to plow during said lease Ingworth Hall Close in paine of £5 an acre yearly, nor to plow Colbye Hall Close for the last 4 years under the said penaltye, with other covenants how to leave ground.

543

(134) By indenture dated 20 Jan. 1622, Sir John Windham granted the scite of the manor of Thurleton, houses, and all his lands there unto belonging to George Windham jun. (late Sir George of Cromer) and * Humphrey * < [?] Anthony > Windham (now Sir *Humphrey* Windham) for several lives. Paying only 40s yearly soe long as it is devided and when the whole comes to bee enjoyed by one person £10 yearly, as by indentures at large apear.

(36) Noate: Lady Windham of Cromer hires Humphreys moietye, and pays the whole rent of £2 *per annum*. She also pays 15s 9d yearly for 6 peeces of ground conteyning 7 acres 3 roods in Cromer, as are particularly mentioned in a lease made by Sir J. Windham to James Underwood dated 3 June in the 5th year of King Charles 1 [1629] expired.

(134) By indentures dated 20 Jan. 1622, Sir John Windham granted manour of Dilham, and all lands thereunto belonging to Hugh and Wadham Windham for several lives. Paying 40s yearly until the whole estate comes to bee enjoyed by one person and then £10 yearly; as by the indentures at large appear.

(134) Sir John Windham did also charge divers lands in Felbrigg, Aylemerton, Metton and etc. with the annual rent of £40 yearly and equally to bee paid to the said Hugh and Wadham or their assignes at Lday and Mich. for 99 years, after the death of Joan (my grandmother). If the said H. and W. and the said wifes of H. and W. and their eldest sonns, which should be living at the several deaths of H. and W or any of them should soe long live as by indenture dated 22nd May in the 9th yeare of King James [1611] over Ingland, at large appeare.

544

(114, 478) Henry Grime by indenture dated 14 October 1672, hired my farme in Tuttington (late in use of Robert Doughty) for 5 years ending Mich. 1677. Paying the first four years £17 yearly, and the last year £18 and doeing every yeare one days worke of a thatcher and his man, and two days of a dawber. He is to keep and leave the fences in good repayre, and the doors, locks, keys, and windows sufficiently mended, with other covenants to leave the ground.

➤11 Oct. 1677, William Ives hired the farm at the same rent and covenant in Grime's lease, for 7 years end Mich. 1684

(**22, 530, 511**) Thomas Gorse of Heaverland hired my warren for five years ending 2 Feb. 1677 at £22 yearly payable 29 Sep. and 2 Feb and 300 coneis yearly, counting 120 to 100, or to allow me at the rate of £3 – 100. And he is to leave upon the premises 1300 breeding coneis: at a 120 to a 100 in payne of £4 100 as *per* indenture dated 24 Sep. 1672.

Memorandum: Gorse pay'd me £30, 25 Mar 1673 to secure the said stock (for which he have my bond) to pay him with interest, he perfoming the covenants in the said indenture. *Anno* 1620 warren was let for 21 years at £25 and 180 conies yearly, the stock was then 20 hundred.

(**112, 534 n. 5**) William Frost and Richard Lowne hired the farme late in the use of John Crome in Tuttington for 7 years ending Mich. 1680 at £37 yearly, doeing at their owne charge two days thatching, and two days dawbing with other covenants how to leave the ground as *per* articles dated 11 Aug. 1673.

The said Crome did take a lease of the farme for 8 years ending Mich. 1668 at £47 3s 8d and 2 capons *per annum*, as by indenture 10 Sep. 1660 where lands are mentioned.

Noat: when Crome's lease expired I was loathe to take the farme into my own hands not living them in the countye. The times were hard, and he was a lazy ignorant man, and wasted his stocke, which brought an ill repute upon the farme that I could not let it to able men for more.

545

(**68**) George England by indenture 4 July 1670, hired 6 acres of ground in Basingham and Thurgarton for 13 years ending Mich. 1680 at £1 15s 0d and 4 pullets yearly, and doeing suite of court for Sustead mannor as the tenants of the said mannor ought to doe, with covenants how to leave the ground.

(**106**) William Dawson by indenture 27 Oct. 10th King Charles [1634] hired 5 roods in the east feild of Runton for 7 years at 8s one pullet, 1 days harvest worke yearly.

(**107**) Richard Dawson by indenture 27 Oct. 10th King Charles [1634] hired 1 acre and half in east feild of Runton 7 years at 7s 6d one pullet, 1 days harvest worke yearly.

(**136**) Edmond Bale by indenture 6 Dec. 1670, hired the land late in the use of Mr Kett and Matt Gould conteyning 87 acres and 2 roods in Wicklewood and Crownethorp for 11 years ending Mich. 1681 at £36 11s yearly, he is not to break up any part of the 19 acres next the comon pasture in payne of 30s an acre, he is to keep and leave the fences in good repayre (being allowed rough timber), with other covenants how to leave the ground.

(**138**) Martin Norton by indenture 20 Dec. 1663 hired of my brother John the watermill with houses and land thereunto belonging for 12 years ending Mich. 1675, doeing all necessary repayres and leaving muck in the yard the last yeare at £26 13s 4d yearly * in Wicklewood *.

(138, 505) John Jakes hired the premisses aforesd for 7 years ending Mich. 1682, at the same rent, and upon the same covenants as *per* articles 29 March 1675. From Mich. 1682 to Mich 1683 the said Jakes is tennant at will.

5 June 1683, he agreed to hold it to Mich. 1684, as by noat under his hand.

546

(156, 496/2) Robert Kingsberry by articles 9 April 1668, hired the manour of Midleton Hall in the county of Essex with appertances thereto belonging, & all the rents of Assize (profits of Courts excepted) belonging to the said manour, And also the woods conteyning 117 acres (timber excepted) for 7 years ending Mich. 1675 at £194 8s, he is to leave the houses and fences in good repayre (being allowed rough timber and 20 loads of faggot wood), he is not to break up any of the pasture grounds in payne of 40s an acre yearly, with other good covenants how to leave the ground, (*vide* number of acres p. 496/2)

(156, 496 n. 3) Alice Kingsberry (relict of the aforesaid Robert) and John Kingsberry her son hired the aforesaid manour and premises for 7 years ending Mich. 1682 at £194 8s yearly, upon the former covenants as by indenture 17 Aug. 1675.

(152, 497) Robert Kingsberry (son of R. Kingsberry of Midleton) hired Brunden farme in Essex with all houses and lands thereunto belong (except the mill and 12 acres adjoyning) conteyning togeather 456 acres 1 rood 23 perches, tythe free, for 15 years ending Mich. 1685 at £180 yearly. The said Robert is to keep and leave the houses and fences in good tenant like repayre, (being allowed rough timber and tyles) with extraordinary good covenants for leaving the grounds, as by indenture 4 Aug. 1670.

Noat I pay Mr. Nicholls £13 6s 8d yearly for serving the cure of the church of Brunden in lieu of all dues.

(542/3) 1 July 1680, I viewed Blacks farme, and find 6 acres of the 9 acres in the little feild inclosed, and 7 acres of the 14 acres in the high feild of which 7 acres, 2 acres is mowing ground. Cullenders Close divided into 4 acres and 1 acre, and 2 acres of 3½ acres in Erpingham inclosed.

547

(148, 508/1) Thomas Arteson by indenture 27 Sep. 1673 hired the Lower Water Mill with 2½ acres of meadowe at Wenhaston for 7 years ending Mich. 1680 at £21 *per* yeare. He is to repaire every thing that don't necessarily amount to above 20s single (being allowed sufficient millstones with irons to fix the same, and rough timber, one load of one bond wood). If any hurt comes to the premises through his carelesness, he is to make it good, and leave all things in as good a repayre as he found them.

(142, 551) 10 August 1655, F. Gould hired the manor house in Wicklewood with lands thereunto belonging for 20 years ending Mich. 1674 at £60 yearly, he is to doe all necessary repaires, and leave the muck in the yard, deducting £2 3s for somerlye which is to bee left the last yeare.

(148, 508/1) Thomas Keeble by indenture 27 Sep. 1673 hired the Upper Water Mill with ½ acre of meadowe in Wenhaston for 11 years ending Mich. 1684 at £18 *per annum* (being allowed sufficient millstone with irons to fix the same; timber and other necessaries to repaire the mill, and two loads of one bond wood) he is to repaire every particular thing, that don't necessarily amount to 20s single. If any hurt comes to the premises through his carelesness, he is to make it good, and leave them in good repaire.

(148, 550/3) Henry Aldred by articles 10 April 1676, hired the farmehouse and grounds (now in his use) in Wenhaston for 3 years ending Mich. 1679 at £30 yearly, and 2 days thatching of a thatcher and his man, and 20 rods of ditching, and keep the walls well dawbed with clay, and to keep the gate etc. in good repayre, being allowed rough timber and 6 load of fier wood yearly, with other covenants.

548

(160) Francis Reynolds by articles 8 April 1668, hired Brunden Mill in Essex with about 12 acres of Land for 3 years ending Mich. 1671 at £55 *per annum*, he is to keep and leave the mill and fences in good repayre (being allowed rough timber) not to break up any of the grounds (except what is in tillage) in payne of £2 an acre yearly.

(160, 511) Thomas Ellenford by indenture 17 March 1674, hired the above mill and ground for 7 years ending Lady day 1682 at £38 *per annum* upon same covenants. I am to put the mill in good repayre: one spindle and ryne, value 20s is to be left in the mill.

(126) 1673 *anno*, Sextan hire Ingworth Mill for £30 *per annum* from year to year. Bartholomew Willis had a lease of the said mill for 21 years at £34 halfe a hundred good roasting eles, and halfe of all other fish and 2 fat capons yearly, doeing all repayres to the mill and mill house, above, within and underwater (being allowed rough timber) he is also to clear the damm, to keep and leave the banks, cawseys and fences in good repayre, and not to plow any of the ground in payn of £5 an acre increase of rent, as *per* indenture dated 30 Dec. 1663.
Noat: Bartholomew Willis died and left the mill and his wife: she lost the custome and died about Mich. 1671. About our Lady 1672 Sextan came into her.

(126, 510) 19 Dec. 1676, William Greenacer of Calthorp and William his son, hired the said mill at 34 yearly, delivering the eles, fish and capons, and upon the same covenants, in the afore mentioned lease or Willis's for 7 years ending March 1684.

(94, 530) 27 Feb. 1665, James Taylour, clark hired of me 3 peeces of pasture conteyning 3 acres in Metton from Mich. last to the 1 Oct. 1666 at £1 10s as by agreement under his hand. *Vide* the booke wherein the tenants turned tennants to me after my brothers death.

549

(148) H. Howsman by indenture 4 Oct. 1654, hired the house and grounds (late in tenure of John Page or his assignes) for 7 years ending Mich. 1661 at £80 *per annum* yearly, and performing the office of bayliffe in collecting the rents and profits of the manour, and to keep houses and fences in repayre, being allow'd rough timber, thorns, other fencing stuff, and 5 loads of bond wood on request, he paying for felling, making and carriage; not to sow above 40 acres in any one year, nor convert more to tillage, nor sow oates two years togeather.
Noat: Page pay'd £100 *per annum*.

Before Houseman's lease expired, he had £3 *per annum* added to the lease, and he payd £83 till my brother's death at Mich. 1665. About that time, comodities were low, and I did allow him £3 *per annum* for collecting the Quit rents and farme rents and looking after the woods and repayres. < From > At Mich. 1672 to Mich. 1676, I abated £10 a years as *per* account (p. 149).

(495) Houseman by articles dated 24 Feb 1676, hired the farme for 3 years ending Mich. 1679 at £80 *per annum*, doeing 3 days thatching, and all the dawbing, and keeping the fences in good repayre, being allowed rough timber and other fencing stuffe, and 8 loads of one bond wood, with covenants how to plow and leave the grounds.
William Peppar by indenture 29 Sep. 1675 hired one messuage with a brick kill, and lands belonging conteyning 27 acres 1½ roods and 17 perches (mentioned in a schedule) in Mells in Suffolke for 21 years ending Mich. 1696 at £17 yearly, which £17 is all to * bee * payd the last year at our Lady-day. He is to keep and leave the houses well thatch'd and dawbed, and the fences in repayre; the glass, doors, locks and keys in order. And one 3rd arrable in winter corne, one 3rd summer stubble, 3rd olland or somerlye, muck left in yards, and other good covenants. / 1 load of wood and timber /

550

(148, 550 s. 2) *Memo:* Robert Keeble pay'd my father £42 yearly, about 1652; in 1654 my brother abated £2 yearly. Afterwards Keeble hired the Parliament ground, which was £8 *per annum*, and Pear's Close £3 *per annum* more, which in my brother's time he paid £48 for, soe 'twas when I came to the estate in 1665 and soe continued till anno 1671. Then (he being a very antient man and times hard) I abated him £8 *per annum* though I have been well informed 'tis well worth £48 yearly.

18 May 1678, I ordered Keeble to leave his farme at Mich. because for 7 years past he declined in his estate, as the infirmities of old age came upon him.

(494) 21 Feb 1679, Thomas Sagar hired the farme late Robert Keeble's use for 7 years ending Mich. 1687 at £43 the first 6 yrs, and £48 the last year. He is to keep the houses and fences in repayre (being allow'd rough timber) and 6 loads of fier wood yearly, with covenants how to use and leave the grounds as by articles under his hand.

Noat: Henry Aldred died 30 Dec. 1680

(494, s. 3, 4) 28 Jan, 1680, Robert Patrich hired Aldred's farme for 5 years ending Mich. 1685 at £22 the 1st year, £28 next two years, £30 the last 2 years; he is to do 3 days thatching, 20 rods of ditching. All the dawbing. He is also to keep the dreyns and fences in repayre (being allow'd rough timber and 5 loads of one bond wood) with covenants how to use and leave the farme as as by articles signed by us. Noat: Aldred's stock is to remaine upon ground till 1st April 1681.
Memo: butter and cheese but 11s a load.

551

(142, 505) 17 March 1679, Francis Gould doe promise to take a lease of his farme for seven years if he live soe long) at £60 *per annum* (being allowed £5 out of 1st halfe years rent). Upon the same covenants in his last lease. And if he dye before the 7 years expire, his wife to bee free the Mich. twelve month after his decease; and if he leaves noe wife his executors to bee free at the same time, and the lease to begin at Mich. next. In witness herunto wee set our hands. *Francis Gould Will Windham*

(196, 494) 29 March 1677: lease was seal'd 24 Aug. 1678. Articles of agreement made between William Windham of Felbrigg, and Isaak Jakes of Cranworth both in Norfolke. *Imprimis:* The said William Windham doth demise and to farme let unto the said Isaak, his executors and assignes the house and grounds belonging to the said William in Crownethorp (late in the use of widdow Scipper) for eight years begin at Mich. next, yielding and paying £127 6s 8d yearly, upon the covenants mentioned in the counterpart of a lease made by John Windham to James Scipper dated 20 Dec. 1655 (p. 478). And further 'tis agreed that the said Isaak shall leave all the straw and chaife which arise upon the premises the last year of his tearm, in lieu of the straw and chaife which arise upon the premises this sumer. The alders to bee left the same growth they are now, the dreynes to bee all new cut the last year, and the grounds left according to paper which wee have this day signed. A barne to bee built by the last of August to the value of £40. In witness wee have set our hands this 29 March 1677: present *John Salman Isaac Jecks Will Windham*

552

Noat from Mich. 1673 to Mich. 1677, I kept * Repham * in my hands.

(166, 497) 25 June 77, I agreed with Sexton to lay on 20 cows and let him the profit of them for £45 *per annum* for 5 years from Mich. 1677. He is to have the keeping of one horse in the said grounds, and firs for firing, diging them clean up. * 1 load of topwood * . He is to bring up 4 calves every yeare upon the premises 'till they are a yeare old, then I am to have two, and he is to dispose of the other. 'Twas also agreed, that Sexton should plow and sow soe many acres as I should appoint and carry the corne into the barne, of which I am to have halfe (finding one to thrash) with him. He is to have running for 3 horses more. He is to have all the chaife and coulder, I the straw, as *per* articles signed and sealed the abovesaid. Noat: I am to lay on what stock I please besides, for owne benifit, leaving sufficient pasture for the cows.
Noat: The first he to have but 10 cows.

(38, 537) 16 Nov. 1670, William Abbs of Aylemerton hired the Bush Close and the Hill Close for 11 years ending Mich. 1681 at £11 yearly. Tenant covenant to muck well where he sow winter corne, and not to sow oats two years together, and not to sow any part of the Bush Close the last 3 years with any graine and to leave the fences in good repayre as *per* articles appeare.

(162) 13 Jan. 1670, Micheal Wilson agreed to give me £2 5s a cow for the profit of 10 or 12 cows from May day to New years day, he is to have his dwelling at my house in Gresham and the cows are to bee kept upon the ground by the house, he may put 2 calves into the ground till 14 Sep. The money payable 1 Aug. and 1 Jan.
Noat: every year after he is to have soe many cows as we shall yearly agree on at £2 5s *per* cow.

553

5 Dec. 1676, Simon Rice of Southreps hireth the farme in the use of John Johnson for 7 years ending Mich. 1684 at the rent and covenants in Johnson's articles (p. 541).
Noat: Rice died June 1677, and I released his widdow.

(230, 483) 30 July 1677 William Heydon and Clement his son hired the farme for 10 years ending Mich. 1687 at the same rent (being £48 10s yearly) and Covenants in Johnson's articles with this covenant more, that they are to leave 4 acres sowne with clover.
Noat: I bought Johnson's muck at £6 for the use of the new tenants, and they have given me a bill under their hands and seals 11 Aug 1677 to pay me £6, 29 Sep. 1687.

(19) *Memorandum:* I have allow'd Johnson £1 for bringing the muck to the place

where it now lyethe, for which if I bye their muck they are to bring it soe far, * if * not to pay me the said £1

(228) 29 Jan. 1677 George Johnson of Roughton baker hired two closes conteyning 18 acres being part of three closes called Swifts, late in Drake's use, for 9 years ending Mich. 1686 at £7 4s *per annum*. The tenant not to take above 4 crops, of which not above one of oats, close next the feild of 3 years lying, fences in repayre, etc as by articles under our hands and seals.

(554, 540/5) *Memo*: the 3 acres in Smiths use lieth in Metton upper feild in 4 peices. The 4 acres lieth in the same feild *scilicet* 3 acres abut south on a way leading from Sustead to Routon, and 1 acre upon a close called Buffets south. The 1 acres lieth in the said feild in 2 peices.

554

(92, 535) H. Smith of Metton hired about 14 acres lying in Metton and Roughton which (were lately in Mr Nicholas Wilson's use) and are particularly mention'd in Smith's lease for 9 years ending Mich. 1678 at £7 yearly. The tenant not to cut away any turfe nor to sow oats 2 years togeather. He is to leave two acres of buck stubble * being * olland the last year and 2 acres more olland, keep and leave fences in repayre with other good covenants as *per* indenture 29 Sep. 1669.

(96, 553/3, 535 n. 2) Noat: The said Smith hireth land to the value of £4 *per annum* more in Metton at lose farme *scilicet* 3 acres formerly in his father's use, 4 acres in Kudrin's, and 1 acre in Maries's use, (*vide* abuttals p. 553).

(88, 186) 7 Oct. 1609, in the 7th of King James, Sir John Windham did demise 12 peices of land in Metton conteyning 8 acres to Robert Gobert and Helen his wife for 40 years, if either of them live soe long, at £1. The tenant to provide mans meat and horse meat for the surveyor, steward and bayly of the manour, and their servants, as often as the court shall bee kept, as *per* the said indenture, wherein the lands are particularly mentioned at large appear.

Noat: *anno* 1625, John Gobert payd £3 13s 4d *per annum* for the said land, as by p. 84 of the audit booke for that year appears.

Cicilye his wife held the land at £3 13s 4d *per annum* during my father's life who died March 1653. When I come to the estate * in 1665 * John Carrier was tennant to the said 8 acres who refused to pay the rent, upon pretence 'twas coppy hold, upon which I comenced a suit against him, and the 13 Sep. 1671, he gave me bond for payment of £22 being six years rent ending Mich. 1671, and promised to pay my charges in the suite.

(88) From Mich. 1672, Warner is tenant.

555

(132, 537) By indenture 20 Sep. 1649, James Smith of Worstead hired one tenement with outhouses and homestalls thereunto belonging and 19 acres particularly mentioned (which Thomas Windham purchased among other lands of Debney) for 21 years ending Mich. 1670 at £12 and two capons. Tenant to doe all repayres, being allow'd rough timber, all the last years muck to bee left; and 6 acres in winter corne stubble, 8 acres in sumer graine stubble, the rest olland, summerlye, or buck stubble, not to sow oats two years togeather, not let any of it without leave.

(128) Noat: Smith at Mich. 1668, hired about 2 acres 2 roods more (late in Springal's use) at £1 15s yearly. At 1675, Mack hired this ground.

(70, 531) 20 Sep. 1656, William Ransome hired one tenement with outhouses and homestalls lying in Sustead, and about 37 acres thereunto belonging for 12 years ending Mich. 1668 at £22 and 2 fat capons yearly. He is to doe 3 days thatching and 3 days dawbing finding all the materialls, and keep the fences in repayre (being allow'd rough timber, and necessary fencing stufe) The first 11 years he is to spend all the stother and lay the muck upon the premises, the last years muck to bee left in the yard, and alsoe leave 4 acres wintercorne stubble, which was somerlye and muckt the year before, 4 acres in peas or fetch stubble. He is to be reasonably satisfied for the muck and the 4 acres of somerlye, not soe oats 2 years togeather, nor let any of it without leave as *per* the said indenture to which there is a schedule.

556

(58) Reave for land formerly in Besseson's use. Noat: John Besseson by indenture 19 Feb. 1649 hired of Thomas Windham one peice of land conteyning by estimation 1 acre 1 rood in Aylmerton for 1 year, and soe long after us both shall please, at 8s and 1 fat hen yearly and 1 days worke in harvest.

(60, 480) H. Johnson of Gresham and Henry his sonn hired one peice of land in Aylemerton conteyning 19 acres late in John Elis his use for 13 years ending Mich. 1690 at £6 yearly. The tenants are to muck where they sow winter corne, and when any part of the premises that have layne olland bee broken up 'tis to be sommerleyed, or sowne with buck, and wintercorne next, not to sow oats two years togeather, they are to leave 9 acres and a halfe of 3 years lying, as by articles dated 26 Feb. 1677.

(130, 560) John Winter by indenture made 20 May 1653, hired a messuage with outhouses and homestalls belonging conteyning 2 acres lying in Dilham and 46 acres and ½ more (all which were then in use of Christopher Amis) for 12 years ending Mich. 1665 at £32 and 2 capons yearly. The tenant covenant to keep and leave the houses and walls well thatched and dawbed, and the fences in good repayre (being allow'd rough timber and fencing stuffe) and to leave the windows well glased, and locks and keys. Tenant to lay all the muck upon the premises the first 11 years, and the last year shall leave it in the yards. Tenant shall leave one 3rd part of the premises in winter corne stubble; one 3rd in summer grayne stubble, the other 3rd olland, somerlye, or buck stubble.

Tenant not to let any of it without leave, as by the said indenture at large appeare, wherein the lands are particularly mentioned.

(50, 537/8) Flaxman hireth the little close on the right hand of the gate going from my house to Sustead lane.

557

(190, 162) 15 March 1677: It is agreed betwene Mr Windham of Felbrigg and Theophilus Waterson of Gresham that the said Waterson shall have the use of the Rush Close lying in Gresham from this day to 29 September 1690 upon the conditions following. That is to say Waterson is to pay £8 10s 00d for the feed of the close till Mich. 1678. And in the space of 7 years after, Waterson is to break it all up, and keep it all in tillage 4 years, and noe part of it above 4 years. And for soe many acres as are not plow'd Waterson is yearly to pay after the rate of eighteen shillings an acre, and all parish charges. And as for the ground soe broken up, Waterson is to levell and dreyne and plow and lay on soe much muck upon every part thereof as Mr Windham shall appoint and sow, weed, reap and doe all things incident to good husbandry at his owne cost and charge. And the corne arriving upon the premises is to be yearly equally divided in the field by a person who Mr Windham shall appoint. And Waterson is yearly at his charge to bring Mr Windham's halfe into his barne at Felbrigg when Mr Windham shall appoint. For soe much as in tillage Mr Windham is to pay parish rates. Noat: every part of the ground as it shall bee brought in tillage is to be sowne with buck or somertilled the 1st year, and the next year sowne with wheat, the next year with barlye, and the year after with oats. The five last years of the terme, Waterson is to let it all lye olland. And pay unto Mr Windham or his assignes at the rate of eighteen shillings *per* acre * 12 acres * yearly at our Lady day and Michaelmas day. It is also agreed that Waterson shall yearly doe 10 rods of ditching by appointment, and keep and leave the gates and fences in good repayre (being allow'd rough timber and fencing stuf). Which said agreement the said Theophilus Waterson doe hereby covenant for himselfe his executors and assigns in witness where of wee have hereunto set our hands and seals the day abovesaid.

In the presence of *Jo. Salman, Richard Edwards* Waterson's marke X
Will Windham

558

(96) Robert Miller of Hanworth hired the horse close conteyning 5 acres lying on the south part of Metton Comon and 1½ acres arrable land lying betwene the land of the said Robert, towards the east; and lands late Thomas Doughtye's towards

the west; for 21 years ending Mich. 1674 at £2 6s and 1 hen yearly. The horss close not to be plow'd at all, nor the other close the three last years. The fences kept and left in good repayre. The tenant not to let any part of it, as by indenture made 22 Oct. 1653.

(98) Robert Foster of Roughton hireth of me at lose farme 12 acres 1½ roods lying in 10 peices: 9 of them in Metton, 1 in Felbrigg at £6 yearly.

(85) Woodrow hireth at loose farme 1 peice of ground in Antingham (reputed 1 acre) at Barrow Hill at 5s and 1 capon yearly upon the covenants in a lease made thereof to Robert Harmer for 21 years ending Mich. 1677, who was not to break up nor let the same as by indenture 16 Oct. 1656.

(108, 480) John Barker hireth by loose farme 1 close in W. Runton conteyning 2 acres at 12s and 1 pullet. Noat: Peter Abbs of Runton had a lease of the said close for 21 years ending Mich. 1679 at 12s, 1 hen, 1 days harvest worke, not to break it up the last 2 years as by indenture 20 Aug. 1658 and did turne tennant to me 20 Feb. 1665. Will Windham 1 Feb 1687/8.
/I was mistaken when I writ this for J.B. never had this close, P. Abbs kept it, and have it/.

(128, 509) Thomas Mack hired the house and lands now in his use in Dilham for 5 years ending Mich. 1682 at £35 yearly. He is to keep and leave clay walls, and all the fences in repayre, and the windows well glased, and the locks in good order, he is to 4 days thatching at this owne charge by my appointment and leave all the muck in the last year in the yard for my use. And ⅓ part of arrable ground belonging to the farme in winter corne stubble; ⅓ part sumer corne stubble, ⅓ olland, summerlye and buck stubble. Noat he is to have the use of great barne and of the neats parr till May day after end of his terme as by article 19 April 1678.

559

(96, 558) Smith hired the land late in M. Millers use for 1 year ending Mich. 1678 at the rent in Miller's lease, (*vide* p. 558)
Memorandum: in March 1677, Smith complayn'd that Mr Doughty had forbid him going through his ground, upon which, I writ Doughty word, if he did not lay open the same way, which was to it before my father seised it, or another as convenient, I would take my remedy at law, and would waite upon at the sessions to know his minde, accordingly. I did goe to him at Alderman Payne's 10 April 1678 and then he promis'd before Payne, that Smith should have a way. And that at Mich. he would hire it of me at the rent and covenants in Miller's lease, and woud make a memorandum upon the lease, which was the way to it.
Noat: The dispute came thus: The land did belong to Thomas Doughty by coppy of court roll, who for divers years neglected to pay the rent, he died, and because

for 6 years noe body came to take up the same, my father seised it (as at large appeare in the audit booke for the year 1651 and 1652 p. 11) and let it to Miller (as by p. 558) who went through his owne grounds to it and in that time Doughty of Hanworth made up the former way, which before that lease ended, was soe growne, the old way was scarce discernable.

17 Sep. 1678, Doughtye came to Felbrigg and tould me he woud not hire the ground, for he had a right to it, soe I bid him take course, and I would take mine.

(86, 596) 14 Jan, 1673, Doughty and I met with councel to discuss this matter, and then I agreed to make him a lease of the land for 99 years from Mich. next at £2 6s yearly.

17 Jan. 1681, having occasion to send to Sir Robert Baldock I order'd my servant to call upon Mr Doughty for the lease, upon which Sir Robert writ these words: it is drawn so much awry as you may perceive by notes and crosses through it, as really I doe not remember that I ever saw any thing so crooked.

560

(130, 556, 495, 491) 4 June 1678: Bee it knowne that 'tis this day agreed between Mr Windham of Felbrigg and Francis Plummer of Waborne in Norfolk, that the said Francis Plummer shall have a lease of Winter's farme in Dilham for 11 years from Mich. next at the rent and covenants mentioned in counterpart of said Winter's lease dated 20 May 1653, with this alteration: that he should leave the 2 acres soe well somertilled as land ought to bee for to sow wheat, upon which the said agreement the said Plummer doe hereby covenant to performe and to seal a lease accordingly, when it shall be tender'd to him. Mr. Windham promise to put the houses in good repayre, and to abate him £2 yearly the first 2 years. Witness our hands and seals the abovesaid.

In the presence of *William Harmer John Salman Francis Plummer Will Windham*

(64) Mr Cooke hireth the inclosures in Gresham on both hands of the high way going from Gresham to Helgate at £40 yearly.
Noat: he payd £45 for the said grounds for several years.

(78) Robert Russells hired a tenement in Hanworth and 17 acres *scilicet:* 10 acres 1 rood in Hanworth, 6 acres in Sustead and 3 roods in Roughton at £11 13s yearly performing covenants in Maries lease (p. 538) as by agreement 30 Sep. 1667

(72) William Barnes of Sustead blacksmith hireth Bunswood grounds conteyning at £6 *per annum.*

(74) Thomas Sexton of Northreps hire Sustead Church Close and the rawing of the Long Meadow at £36. Noat: Robert Billington payd £45.

561

(564) Articles of agreement made 24 July 1678 between Mr Windham of Felbrigg and John Masters of Bodenham in Norfolke concerning hiring a dairie of cows, and plowing ground to halfes.

1. First the said Masters is to live in the Dogg house in Felbrigg Parke, rent free, and to have the profit of soe many cows as Mr Windham please to keep in or near the parke, paying after the rate of five and forty shillings a peice yearly, upon 1 Aug. and 1 Jun. And if any of the cows bee not ready for the dairie by May day Masters may deduct soe much as Mr Edmund Britiffe thinke reasonable for that time.

2. Masters may bring up two cow calfes every year and keep them one year in some of Mr Windham's ground and then Mr Windham shall choose one, and Masters shall dispose of the other.

3. Masters is to have 2 hundred of furs yearly and may keep two swine in the parke

Masters is yearly to plow what ground, and sow thereon what grayne Mr Windham or his heires shall appoint and to bee at all charges incident to husbandrye and deliver to Mr Windham or his heires half the corne, as it is drest by the taskers.

Masters is to have the use of Mr Windham's barne and new stable, and some of his corne chambers.

Masters is to have all the chaife and colder, and Mr Windham is to have all the straw.

The pease and fetches (except only four acres which Masters is wholly to have) are to bee divided in the feild and Masters is to bring Mr Windham's part into the barne, and to spend all his owne upon Mr Windham's ground.

Masters is to have all the muck is made every year to lay upon Mr Windham's plowground, except only soe much as the gardner have occasion for.

9. Mr Windham promise to let his flock tathe 4 or 5 acres yearly, or to bye soe much muck as is necessary for 5 Acres.

562

10. Masters is to have the running of soe many horsses in some of Mr Windham's ground near the parke, as are necessarily imployed about the husbandrye.

11. Mr Windham is to pay all parish rates and to satisfie the parsons of Felbrigg and Aylemerton for the tythe of the corn, which shall grow in the parke, which tythe the said Masters is to bring unto the barne and thrash it and deliver it clean drest to Mr Windham, and for soe doing Masters is to have a tenth of the tythe, and the chaife and colder.

12. Masters is to keep the windows, locks, fences in good repayre. Masters is to have all the chaife and colder and many peas and fetches as he shall have occasion for this first winter. And in lieu therof, he is to leave all the chaife and colder and as many peas and fetches to the use of Mr Windham at the end of his terme. And soe many peas and fetches as Masters bring with him he shall have libertye to carry

away at the end of the terme, provided he leave soe many as he have at his entrance of Mr Windham.

13. Masters is to carry out the muck the last year and to leave 3 acres of somerlye mucked, and plowed under.

14. Masters is to come into the house at Michaelmas next, and continue there, upon these termes for seven years ending Mich. 1685.

15. Mr Windham is to lend Masters five horses and some utensells of husbandrye for the value of about forty pounds, which are to be valued by two indifferent men the 27 or 28 of September next, for which matters doe ingage to pay Mr Windham interest. And at the end of his terme to leave stock (in the opinion of two men indifferently chosen) to the use of Mr Windham his heirs, or assignes of the same value.

16. And lastly, the said John Masters doth for himselfe, his executors, administrators and assignes, covenant, grant and agree to and with the said Mr Windham, his heires, assignes, to performe and keep this agreement. And Mr Windham doe ingage to performe his part of the said agreement.

563

It is also agreed, that Masters shall bring all Mr Windham's hay out of his meadows and lay it into his barne and stable in Felbrigg as soon as possibly he can after the hay, or any of it is ready, for which Mr Windham is to pay him twelve pence a head. In witness thereof wee have set our hands and sealed this 24 July 1678.

Signed and sealed in the presence of *Will Windham William Harmer Jon Dawson John Masters*

The great charge I finde a gentleman must be att in husbandrye more than a yeoman, made me make the afores'd agreement with Masters by which I shall have the conveniencye of a dairie near me and bee free from the trouble of plowman and I don't doubt to make more of my land, than if I had kept it in my own hands.

Memorandum. That I John Masters have this 1 Oct. 1678 bought of Mr Windham five horsses for two and twenty pounds, two carts at seven pounds, two plows one pound, three iron harrows at thirty shillings, some utensells of husbandry ten shillings, for which thirty two pounds. I am to pay interest and principal according to my agreement with Mr Windham 24 July 1678. Witness my hand this 1 October 1678.

Signed in the presence of *William Harmer John Masters*

Memorandum: Masters brought with [*him*] seven loads of peas and fetches and three loads of hay for which he may carry away [*blank*] loads of fetches, if he leave soe many as he have.

564

Memorandum: 14 Jan 1680, the agreement wee made 24 July and 1 Oct. 1678 mentioned [pp.] 561, 562, 563 of this booke was made void upon terms agreed on betweene us. Witness our hands and seals. *Will Windham*

Signed and sealed before *Sam Smith John Masters*

Masters wife died, which made him not fit for imployment.

At Mich. 1681 my wife let the cows in the park to Mark's wife for £2 5s a peice upon the first 3 articles in Masters agreement (p. 561) from year to year.

At Mich. 1687 she takes the dairy.

At Mich. 1688 Tom Cosen hired it.

Index

Places are indexed as they are specifically named in the Green Book. Many holdings are not identified as to place but they can be roughly located using Tables 1–4 on pp. 35–41 and Windham's Particular on pp. 48–51, together with his cross-references. Similarly, Windham frequently refers to persons by surname only. These have been tentatively matched with fully-named individuals but there is a possibility of error, especially where more than one family member occurs as tenant or employee.